一"顾"千金

雅思的测试精神是开放的

雅思，是一种评估型测试，任何人参加考试都可以得到对应的分数，这样的分数用来衡量实际的英语水平。

雅思，接纳每一位考生，在跟考生的动态交流中不断提升自己。

雅思，欢迎每一位英语爱好者，致力于全球化推广，将国际化概念进行到底。

雅思，是一种针对非英语国家考生的英语测试，却竭诚邀请最专业的老师提供专业的英语教育理念。

这就是雅思，引领全球人性化测试，影响并且渗透了广泛的英语测试领域。

雅思的测试形式是细腻而客观的

A&G：雅思首先用 A、G 类的观念将学术英语和生活英语分开。须知拥有不同经历、不同学习目的的人，学习习惯不同，学习内容不同，测试要求当然也有差异，这才能保证雅思成绩的实用性。

L、R、W、S：雅思听、读、写、说将语言的不同表现形式分开。书面语与口头语有所不同，所以在能力提升上，讲究听说并进，读写共举。口语常见话题与写作常见命题相差很大。即使是同一个题材的讨论，写作更为深入和严谨，口语更为生动和感人。这就要求学生具有多种语言表现能力。

SECTION、PART、TEST：即使在同一种测试形式中，也会采用不同的测试栏目，进一步细化测试环节。在听力考试中，有填空、选择等不同的题型，"消灭错别字"成为当务之急。在阅读考试中，不仅有速读的能力要求，而且有判断的准确性要求。这样细腻的安排，使得测试的成绩更为准确、全面。

0~9：每一种测试形式分为 0~9 分，每一位考生都能找到对应分数。即使某一项分数失利，其余测试也不受影响，这样的成绩依然具有参考价值。

BAND：雅思的成绩包括平均成绩和单项成绩，可以形象地描述测试对象的语言优缺点。

雅思的题材是实用的

A 类考生在参加完考试之后要面对学校的各类报告和论文。良好的图表描述能力、流程叙述能力和分类比较能力，是基本的报告要求。准确的回答、严密的逻辑、正确的语言表述和丰富的词汇量，是所有考生论文的评判基础，这也是雅思写作的阅卷要求。

G 类考生在到达国外之后的首要问题是生存，这就需要通过"信件"的形式解决工作和生活中的种种问题，所以会有"咨询""求职""感谢""投诉""介绍"等多种功能性书信。即使就某一问题发表观点，也会相对"生活化"。这一点也体现在听力、阅读和口语三项测试中。

因此不同测试目的的考生需要选择自己的侧重点。雅思，不仅是一种考试，更需要一种能力准备。

那些年，被误解的雅思

我们的雅思被反复"误解"过。特别是在"主观题"部分，往往各执一词。

有人追求过"加分词汇"和"加分句型"。殊不知词汇和句型本身并不能加分，正确地使用它们方为立足之本，任何脱离了文章本身的语言和词汇都没有意义。

有人强调过"俚语"和"俗语"，可是学术英语本身要求相对规范。此外，每个地区的方言不一定都能被其余地区的人所理解。如果你用到了考官不懂的语言或者文字，一定会影响你的思想表达，这不但不会加分，还会减分。

看，剑桥这样说：

雅思，希望准确、清晰的语法概念；

雅思，希望鲜明、严谨的观点论述；

雅思，希望丰富、规范的语言表述；

雅思，希望清晰、明了的结构形式。

这才是真实的雅思，一个能够代表先进测试理念的雅思，一个能够推进语言教育发展的雅思。

顾家北手把手教你雅思写作 5.0 版

1.0 版：原名《顾家北手把手教你雅思写作》，奠定最初的"手把手"概念。强调细致的写作批改，开创新的雅思培训风格，影响到听说读写各个领域。

2.0 版：原名《顾家北手把手教你雅思写作（剑 9 版）》，雅思写作图书单科销量排行第一，提出词伙理念和词伙教学，强调扎实的学术风格，对雅思培训，乃至更多的语言培训产生影响。

3.0 版：原名《顾家北手把手教你雅思写作（剑 10 版）》，问鼎雅思图书销冠，开创立体化写作教学，通过点评和对比，梳理写作思路，传授综合写作观念。

4.0 版：书名《顾家北手把手教你雅思写作（4.0 版）》，把标准书面语教学形成科学体系，词伙概念单独开山成派，《顾家北手把手教你雅思词伙》付诸出版。

5.0 版：强调学习的计划性（新增 34 天学习计划）；紧扣评分标准，增加学生观点点评，并修改了大部分的范文；结合最新动态，增加了《剑 12》的 3 篇范文；形成了独特的语法理论，奠定了《顾家北手把手教你雅思语法》的基础。

雅思征途，一"顾"千金

顾家北老师常年生活在新西兰，他热爱写作，热爱考试。

顾家北老师是一位一年写 50 万字文章的人，对文字的理解和自信超乎寻常。

顾家北老师是一位强调学习体系的人，在他看来，良好的学习方法和持续的学习积累是真正让人无往而不胜的武器。

他不是大师，只想做老师，强调真诚、扎实的培训，在海外留学生中享有美誉。那些屡败屡战的"烤鸭"遇到顾老师之后，可以在短期内结束屡战屡败的"焙烤"生涯。

一"顾"千金，真正的价值是品质和责任心。

求学之路，再"顾"倾"诚"

千万不要觉得获得了"可接受的"雅思成绩就万事大吉，其实这只是征途的开始。在整个留学环节中，"写"是不可忽略的元素。

当你在异国他乡的夜晚，忽然感到下笔无物的时候，你会忍不住想起那个让你"认真"去写的顾老师。

真诚永远是感人的。

吕蕾公众微信号：lvlei 1973

吕蕾微博地址：http://weibo.com/lvlei1973

吕蕾博客地址：http://blog.sina.com.cn/wonderfullei

一直播：76304044

群号：572129683

IELTS

writing...

剑12

顾家北

顾家北◎编著

手把手教你

雅思写作 5.0版

包括最新雅思教学成果，紧随剑桥最新考试动态

中国人民大学出版社
·北京·

序　言

我从事作文培训很多年（包括雅思、托福、SAT 和 GMAT），但是真正大量接触中国大陆地区考生还是四年前，当我开始搞网络教育的时候。

那时候，一些国内的老师对我说，大陆考区考生压分，大陆考区考生很难获得 7 分，即便老师也考不到 7 分，中国考生作文成绩全球倒数第二（5.26 分），主要是因为外国人不希望中国人出国等，诸如此类。

为此，我在中国深圳考了 3 次雅思，作文都是 8.5 分。2013 年我的培训基本上每个月出一个 8 分学员。步入 2014 年、2015 年和 2016 年后，雅思考题变难，8 分减少，但是 7 分和 7.5 分在我的微博上是常见的分数。

可能中国大陆考区作文确实不容易，但是其难度被高估了。在和国内一些同行交流的过程中，还有看过网络上一些所谓的高分范文，我深深觉得：其实不是雅思作文难，而是很多人对雅思作文的评分标准和外国人眼里高质量的作文是怎样的不了解。我们很多学生和老师还是用国内考试（如大学英语四、六级写作）的眼光去看书面语。

这就是为什么我基本上重新写了《顾家北手把手教你雅思写作（5.0 版）》，将以前的版本全部放弃。与其给读者一大堆范文、单词、句子去背，还不如先告诉他们方向是什么，要写什么样的文章才可以得到雅思考官的认可。

新版书的重心在于讲解雅思作文的评分标准，并且细致地讲解了学生应该怎么去做，才能符合雅思写作的要求。

三年前，我认识了一个澳大利亚学生，名叫 Victor，他考了 20 多次雅思，考了两年，将澳大利亚和中国的培训机构的课上了个遍，都没有获得 7 分。我看了他的文章，问题有两个：（1）不注意拓展，内容重复；（2）文中竟然出现了 idioms。后来，他在我这里学习了一个月，写作获得 7 分，移民成功。

另外一个澳大利亚学生，叫孟超，他在上我的课前，考了 7 次雅思，作文写了两大本，100 多篇文章，都没有考过。我第一次看完他的文章，整整训斥了他一个小时，因为他的文章充满了中国学生的常见错误：模版、套句、使用不恰当的替换词，同时语法错误也很多。我叫他先从语法开始学起，后来，他作文考了 8 分。

本书完稿前不久，北京的一个小伙子，考了 3 次雅思 5.5 分，在我这里学习，我叫他多注意思路的衔接，不要跳跃，他将我上课的范文翻译成中文，一句话一句话地看思路，最后一节课，我看了他的文章，我说，你现在有拿 7 分的可能了。结果，他最后考了 7.5 分。

这样的例子数不胜数，以至于有些旁观的学生甚至怀疑我们的提分不是真实的。

其实雅思不难，至少没有传说中的那么难，如果你们真的知道雅思考什么的话。

在大家不了解不清楚不知道的时候，只能以讹传讹，半信半疑，但是等大家按照本书的要求一步步提高自己的写作能力，然后获得理想的分数，当然会深信不疑。

我的学生很多已经去海外学习，但他们还不时地在网络上留信息，说我教的东西和他们老师教的东西一模一样。也有人说他们大学作业现在写起来很轻松，还有同学说自己毕业后没上课去考作文，竟然一下就考到了移民的成绩。

其实，英文书面语的标准一直就是那么一些，雅思作文只是一个窗口，让我们知道他们书面表达的价值观，仅此而已。

希望大家通过此书，改变自己对英文作文的理解和观念，为留学、工作和移民准备。

很多同学总是希望尽快通过考试，总想几天通过，结果考了几次都没考过，要么出不了国，要么只能多交不少钱去读语言。

中国人所谓的捷径在雅思考试中走不通，而本书会告诉你考好雅思的正道应该怎么走。

走正确的路，才是最快的路。

本书在编写过程中，陈业基、黄玉珠、黄忠武、黄玉英、黄欣、张靖娴、吕依儒、陈志爽、贾红梅、杨志、李伟、袁伟、贾玉梅、凌美媛、廖竹房、廖勤也参与了资料的搜集和部分整理工作，在此一并表示感谢。

顾家北

2017年8月

剑 12 版 (5.0 版) 的修改及思考

主要修改	原因
设计了 34 天的学习进度，方便读者知道每天要完成的学习任务。	本书内容不断增加，很多同学会觉得不知道从哪里学起。有了学习进度表，读者会知道 finishing this book is doable。
调整了顺序，改错和翻译练习放到书的最前面，让学生知道基础的重要。	相关的词伙会放在我的公共微信（搜索：gu_writing）上，方便学生学习。
22 篇全文翻译增加一项内容：学生观点点评。	很多学生审题和思考观点都有很大问题，本书提醒大家注意这两个问题。也方便自学的同学对照自己的观点是否恰当。
22 篇全文翻译更改部分句子，修改了最后的范文。	确保范文更有逻辑，更加扣题，质量更高，更加符合雅思的评分标准。
22 篇全文翻译增加了读者自学步骤的说明。	读者会更加清楚每一步要做什么。
全文翻译错误的句子和正确的句子改变颜色，方便学生查阅。	以前版本有学生反映说容易看混，橙色不好阅读。
增加了全文翻译和句子翻译的使用说明。	很多学生机械翻译，效果不佳。新版加入了两篇关于翻译的说明，提升学习效果。
加入了 3 篇范文（包括 1 篇大作文，1 篇流程图，1 篇地图），题目来自《剑 12》。	《剑 12》没有官方范文，我的范文可以方便学生更好地学习《剑 12》。
增加了一个 9 分学生的反馈。	这个学生不仅是读者，还上了网课，获得了作文 9 分，充分说明我们的方法是正确的。
公共微信中设计了一个栏目，专门用于《手把手教你雅思写作》。	读者在上面提问，也可以获得相关音频，还有句子翻译和全文翻译的词伙提示。

目　录

第1章

雅思写作简介及主要学习方法

1.1 雅思作文考试简介

雅思考试考查学生听、说、读、写的能力。考试一般是从听力开始，然后是阅读，接下来是写作，最后是口语。

写作考试的时间是 1 个小时。考试的时候，监考员首先会发试卷和答题卡，考生先在答题卡上填写名字和其他信息，但是不能翻看试卷，不能提前看考题。如果提前看，监考员会给出警告。时间到了不能再动笔写，否则也会受到警告，如果受到警告后继续写，那么就会被取消成绩。

雅思考试分成学术类和普通类两种。这两个考试主要区别是 Task 1。

学术类的考生一般是希望到英语国家留学的学生: 考试第一部分(Task 1)是图表作文(要写 150 字)，需要 20 分钟完成；第二部分 (Task 2) 要写一篇 250 字的议论文，需要 40 分钟完成。

普通类的考生一般是希望移民到其他国家的学生: 考试第一部分(Task 1)是信件(要写 150 字)，需要 20 分钟完成；第二部分 (Task 2) 要写一篇 250 字的议论文，需要 40 分钟完成。

在平时备考的过程中，我建议大家多关注 Task 2，因为议论文的题材广泛，变化比较多，在过去的几年考试中有变难的趋势。另外一个原因，就是 Task 2 占作文三分之二的分数，而 Task 1 只占作文三分之一的分数。

这也就是为什么本书很大篇幅和 Task 2 有关系，而且我会先讲 Task 2 大作文，然后才去讲 Task 1。

根据剑桥雅思官方公布的数据，雅思作文是中国考生表现最差的部分，平均分只有 5.26 分。根据我从事作文教育十多年的经验，主要原因是中国考生对作文有很多错误的观念(如喜欢用大词，盲目换词，使用套句，死记硬背等)。这些错误的观念要么形成于过去备考国内考试，如大学英语四、六级的时候，要么就是在一些培训机构上课的时候被灌输了错误的思想。

除了翻阅本书外，大家可以平时关注我的新浪微博（搜索 "gu_writing"），那里会不断更新有关雅思作文的信息。

1.2 34天学习计划

日期	学习内容	页数	完成请打 ✓
Day 1	阅读第 1 章的内容，包括 1.1，1.2，1.3。 完成 2.1.1 句子翻译。 阅读 2.2.1 冠词和名词单复数的相关错误。		
Day 2	完成 2.1.2，2.1.3 和 2.1.4 句子翻译。 阅读 2.2.2 谓语错误。		

Day 3	完成 2.1.5 和 2.1.6 句子翻译。阅读 2.2.3 和 2.2.4，词性的错误和句子结构的错误。		
Day 4	完成 2.1.7，2.1.8 和 2.1.9 句子翻译。阅读 3.1。		
Day 5	阅读 3.2，3.3，3.4，3.5。		
Day 6	翻译 3.6.1 全文，阅读相关内容。		
Day 7	翻译 3.6.2 全文，阅读相关内容。		
Day 8	翻译 3.6.3 全文，阅读相关内容。		
Day 9	翻译 3.6.4 全文，阅读相关内容。		
Day 10	翻译 3.6.5 全文，阅读相关内容。		
Day 11	翻译 3.6.6 全文，阅读相关内容。		
Day 12	翻译 3.6.7 全文，阅读相关内容。		
Day 13	翻译 3.6.8 全文，阅读相关内容。		
Day 14	翻译 3.6.9 全文，阅读相关内容。		
Day 15	翻译 3.6.10 全文，阅读相关内容。		
Day 16	翻译 3.6.11 全文，阅读相关内容。		
Day 17	翻译 3.7.1 全文，阅读相关内容。		
Day 18	翻译 3.7.2 全文，阅读相关内容。		
Day 19	翻译 3.7.3 全文，阅读相关内容。		
Day 20	翻译 3.7.4 全文，阅读相关内容。		
Day 21	翻译 3.8.1 全文，阅读相关内容。		
Day 22	翻译 3.8.2 全文，阅读相关内容。		
Day 23	翻译 3.9.1 全文，阅读相关内容。		
Day 24	翻译 3.9.2 全文，阅读相关内容。		
Day 25	翻译 3.9.3 全文，阅读相关内容。		
Day 26	翻译 3.9.4 全文，阅读相关内容。		
Day 27	翻译 3.9.5 全文，阅读相关内容。		
Day 28	阅读 3.10，3.11，4.1，4.2，4.3 全部内容。		
Day 29	写 4.4.1，4.4.2 和 4.4.3 图表作文，对照范文学习。		
Day 30	写 4.4.4，4.4.5 和 4.4.6 图表作文，对照范文学习。		
Day 31	写 4.4.7，4.4.8 和 4.4.9 图表作文，对照范文学习。		
Day 32	写 4.4.10 和 4.4.11 图表作文，对照范文学习，并且阅读 4.5 和 4.6。		
Day 33	阅读 4.7，学习流程图。		
Day 34	阅读 4.8，学习地图，并且阅读附录中的范文。		

注:

- 本时间表主要是针对考学术类(Academic)雅思的学生,考普通类(General)的学生在 Day 30 和 Day 34 之间学习书信相关内容,学习计划如下所示:

日期	学习内容	页数	完成请打 √
Day 30	阅读 5.1 和 5.2 的内容。		
Day 31	阅读 5.3.1 和 5.3.2 的内容。		
Day 32	阅读 5.3.3 和 5.3.4 的内容。		
Day 33	阅读 5.3.5 的内容,选择 5.4 的一个题目来练习,然后对比范例学习。		
Day 34	选择 5.4 的两个题目来练习,然后对比范例学习;阅读附录 4。		

- 如果读者知道顾家北比较晚,备考时间不多,可以主要关注大作文和图表作文的评分标准,翻译和阅读范文。

- 读者在阅读本书的时候,一定要关注重点,彻底放弃以前有关作文学习的一些错误观念,如依赖模板、套句、素材、连接词、替换词等,这样才可以考出好成绩。

本书的主要内容和功能如下表所示。

内容	功能
作文中常见语法错误	• 总结常见语法错误,帮助考生在短时间内熟悉语法和句法的基本规律,在写作中规避语法错误。
句子翻译练习	• 句子翻译练习可以让学生知道怎么写句子。很多考生总是以为雅思作文和国内的语言考试一样,可以通过背诵和预测考题通过,很多时候连一个正确的句子都不会写。这些考生几次考不过,就会开始研究句子怎么写。
雅思大作文考生常问问题和误区	• 雅思考试作为一项主流的出国考试,每年有几十万考生备考。可惜,大部分考生都有很多错误的看法和误区,本章中会有相关讲解。
雅思大作文(Task 2)的评分标准	• 知己知彼,方能百战百胜。首先你要知道雅思考官喜欢什么作文,要求你写什么作文,才能做到事半功倍。
22 篇全文翻译	• 很多考生学习雅思作文几个月,还在问一些结构、拓展、审题等问题。我觉得这些问题并不复杂,书中设计的 22 篇全文翻译可以让考生清楚地知道一篇作文要写几段,每段写几句话,以及每句话应该写什么。我相信,22 篇文章翻译完后,考生就会知道雅思作文要写什么。

细致解释如何满足雅思作文四个评分标准	• 写作是个细活，有很多要点决定考生是否符合四个大的写作标准。 • 每一篇全文翻译之后，我都会讲解雅思作文的一个要点，增加考生对不同要点的理解，而不是让考生每天像傻地背句子，背段落，背范文，都不知道背的东西好不好，对不对。
雅思 Task 1 图表作文的评分标准分析	• 和大作文一样，很多考生对图表作文也有很多误区，所以大家要先好好看一下评分标准，知道图表作文考官关注什么。
雅思 Task 1 图表作文范文	• 创新性地将范文通过表格的方式表现，非常直观地让考生知道图表作文的写作思路和次序。 • 在每一篇范文之后，我都会讲解一个写作要点。包括分段、选数字、如何写总结段、如何变换句型等。这些都是考生薄弱的地方，也是需要提高的地方。 • 和普通图表的形式类似，本书不仅讲解流程图和地图题的解题步骤，而且还通过表格的方式写出范文，让考生清楚地知道流程图和地图题的思路。
雅思 Task 1 书信概述和范例	• 本书也细致地剖析了书信写作的主要评分标准以及书信写作的步骤。 • 总结了书信的分类和常用语，方便考生学习。
附录	• 本书词伙一览表。 • 核心词汇帮助考生掌握一些常用的词汇和标准表达，增加考生独立完成作文的信心。

本书中一项革命性的创新是把 22 道雅思常考题目设计成中文表述的形式，引导考生进行全文翻译，后面辅以翻译的改错以及正确的翻译。笔者统计了 2006 年至今的所有雅思学术类和普通类题目，总结出了 22 道最常见的题目。本书适合初次接触雅思考试、希望通过自学在 2～3 个月之内获得 6～7.5 分的考生。目前市面上的大部分作文书主要是讲解和提供范文，考生自己提笔还是困难重重，本书的巨大优势在于给予考生更多的练习和体验的空间，而不是单向地输出信息。

全文翻译的练习有以下几个优点：

结构：每一篇文章一般是 14～16 句话，4～5 个段落(开头段，主体部分讨论两到三段，结尾段)。通过练习，考生可以非常直观地认识和熟悉雅思 Task 2 作文的结构。其他作文书只是对文章结构提供概括性的讲解和一些范文，考生需要花费时间了解。

论述：每个主体段的句子都清晰地注明具体的功能(中心句、解释、结果、举例、对比等)，考生通过反复练习，可以增强自己的论述能力。

素材：22 道题目包括 Task 2 作文的主要题材(如全球化、政府、教育、生活方式等)，通过练习，考生可以增加不同题材的背景知识，为写作积累素材，提高思考观点的能力，从而更加有效地应对同一题材下的其他题目。

表达：每个练习里出现大量的常用表达和关键词，体现作者强调"搭配"而不是"个体单词"的教学思路。这些词语搭配都是地道的书面语表达，解决了很多考生"中式表达"的问题。考生通过练习，容易增强记忆，比纯粹地通过词汇表记单词要有效。很多作文书只是提供一些常用词汇，却没有提供例句和练习，考生使用起来往往有差错。

语法改错：语法改错是保 6 争 7 的重点。考生可以通过练习后面的语法改错，提高自己对常见语法错误的理解，从而在写作中避免同类的错误。目前大部分作文书并不重视考生的语法能力。

1.3 如何做句子翻译练习来更好地提升写作能力

翻译句子是一种很好的提升语言能力的练习，也是被很多语言教育学家认可的方法。这在我多年的教学中，已经得到了很好的验证。

本书中有大量的句子翻译和范文翻译；然而，不是说所有的句子翻译都有效果。翻译要掌握正确的方法，才会有最好的效果。

首先，句子翻译的英文要地道，不能出现中式英文。

其次，这些英文能够常用，否则，学生做了很多翻译练习，但是在自己的书面和口语交流中却用不到，也没有意义。

最后，句子翻译的主要目的是帮助考生将中文常见表达变成英文思维，在这个过程中，词伙的使用和句子结构的掌握是关键。

很多考生练习翻译句子的时候，感觉效果不好，因为他们是将中文句子里一个个中文字逐字按照顺序翻译的，这样不仅没有学会词伙，也没有熟悉英文的句子结构。考生自己的句子不仅翻译得很中式，和例句相差甚远，而且自己在写作文的时候，也记不起来词伙和句子结构如何使用。

我建议大家按照下面的方法来进行翻译。记住，翻译练习的核心不是逐字翻译，而是用地道的词伙和英文句型来表达出中文的意思。Translate ideas, rather than words.

为了方便大家掌握和理解句子翻译的步骤，我用两个句子作为例子。

例 1：在旅游旺季交通噪声是个很大的问题。

第一步要思考词伙。

旅游旺季怎么说，交通噪声怎么说，很大的问题又怎么说。

要懂得在句子中寻找有可能使用词伙的中文，然后围绕词伙去翻译句子，而不是一个个中文字逐字去翻译。

第二步要找词伙，可以看一下答案用的是什么词伙。

如果一些词伙自己不懂，那就看一下例句，找出词伙。

"旅游旺季"是 tourist season，"交通噪声"是 traffic noise，而"很大的问题"可能很多考生自己本身就知道：a serious problem, a big problem, a severe problem 等。

第三步要问自己，用什么句子结构。

这句话出现了"是个"，用主系表结构的可能性比较大。

最后写出来：Traffic noise is a big problem during the tourist season.

第四步，如果自己的句子写错了，要看看自己错在哪里。

很多考生未必一下子就能写出和例句一样的句子，如果是表达变化，没有什么问题，无所谓，但是如果是语法错误，一定要总结。

如有些考生写 noise become，那就是主谓不一致，而且时态也不对。

如果有考生写 during tourist season，那就是 season 这个可数名词"裸奔"了，没有加冠词。

例2：欧洲的一些城市以它们丰富的历史和壮观的历史建筑而出名。

第一步要思考词伙。

丰富的历史怎么说？历史建筑怎么说？壮观的建筑怎么说？

第二步要找词伙，可以看一下答案用的是什么词伙。

如果一些词伙自己不懂，那就看一下例句，找出词伙。

"丰富的历史"是 rich history。

"历史建筑""壮观的建筑"是 historical buildings, spectacular buildings, monumental buildings, ancient monuments 等。

第三步要问自己，用什么句子结构。

这句话中的"以……而出名"一般是用主系表结构居多。

famous for, well-known for 等。

最后写出来：Some cities in Europe are famous for their rich history and spectacular monuments.

第四步，如果自己的句子写错了，要看看自己错在哪里。

如有些考生写 famous as 是不对的，famous as 的意思是"作为什么而出名"。

有些考生写 spectacularly historical buildings 也不对，因为 spectacularly 是副词，不能修饰名词。

小结：这样做句子翻译和全文翻译，才会有效果。

为了方便大家掌握词伙，避免逐字翻译，我在公众微信号里设计了一个栏目"手把手教你作文"，会提供本书翻译练习的相关词伙，读者可以通过词伙去做翻译，避免中式思维。

第2章

如何打好写作基础

2.1 句子翻译练习

语法学习在雅思写作里是很重要的。

能够写出没有错误的句子（error-free sentences）是剑桥雅思考试的明确要求。其实，即便我们中文也是如此，如果一篇文章的句子都不通顺，小错误很多，分数怎么可能会很高呢？

很多考生说到语法就很害怕，因为以前中学六年、大学四年都没搞懂的东西，如果现在要搞懂，岂不是要过 10 年才能通过雅思考试？

其实，传统的教学方法太过注意一些不重要的细节，导致语法学习过于繁重。语法学习只有两个部分：句子结构和语法错误。掌握这两个部分的内容其实只需要 2～3 天的时间。

我们首先说一下怎么学习句子结构。这主要分两步。

第一步：学习词性（如名词、动词、形容词等词性），搞清楚这些词都是作什么成分的。

第二步：学习单句和从句。

我们现在通过一些简单的句子，稍微讲解一下一些常见的词性和句子结构。

（主 + 谓 + 宾）翻译练习：汽车和飞机的尾气导致空气污染 (air pollution)。

答案：The emissions from vehicles and planes can cause air pollution.

	The emissions	from vehicles and planes	can cause	air pollution.
词性	冠词 + 名词	介宾短语	助动词 + 主动词	名词 + 名词
成分	主语	定语	谓语	定语 + 宾语

（主 + 谓 + 宾 + 宾补）翻译练习：现代科技让富人更加容易积累财富 (accumulate wealth)。

答案：Modern technology has allowed rich people to accumulate wealth more easily.

	Modern technology	has allowed	rich people	to accumulate wealth	more easily.
词性	形容词 + 名词	助动词 + 主动词	形容词 + 名词	不定式	副词
成分	定语 + 主语	谓语	定语 + 宾语	宾语补足语（补充说明宾语的成分）	状语

（主＋谓＋间宾＋直宾）翻译练习：电脑科技可以给人们相互交流的机会。

答案：Computer technology gives people opportunities to communicate with each other.

	Computer technology	gives	people	opportunities	to communicate with each other.
词性	名词词组	主动词	名词	名词	不定式
成分	主语	谓语	间接宾语	直接宾语	后置定语修饰 opportunities

（主＋被动语态）翻译练习：那些重犯 (serious offenders) 需要被送到监狱 (sent to prison) 服刑。

答案：Those serious offenders should be sent to prison.

	Those serious offenders	should be sent	to prison.
词性	限定词＋形容词＋名词	情态动词＋助动词＋过去分词	介宾短语
成分	定语＋主语	谓语	补语 (补充说明 offenders)

（主＋不及物动词）翻译练习：学费 (tuition fee) 一直在上涨。

答案：The tuition fee has been rising.

	The tuition fee	has been rising.
词性	冠词＋名词＋名词	助动词＋现在分词
成分	定语＋主语	谓语

（主＋系＋表）翻译练习：长时间工作 (work long hours) 已经成为公司里的惯例。

答案：Working long hours has become the norm in companies.

	Working long hours	has become	the norm	in companies.
词性	动名词短语	系动词的完成时态	定冠词＋名词	介宾短语
成分	主语	谓语	表语	状语

（there be 句型）翻译练习：有很多应聘者 (job applicants) 竞争有限的职位。

答案：There are many job applicants competing for limited positions.

	Many job applicants	are	competing for limited positions.
词性	限定词＋名词＋名词	系动词	现在分词＋介宾短语
成分	定语＋主语	谓语	后置定语

（it 充当形式主语或者宾语）翻译练习：创造幸福、繁荣的社会(prosperous society)将会是很难的。

答案：It would be difficult to create a happy, prosperous society.

	It	would be	difficult	to create a happy, prosperous society.
词性	代词	情态动词 + 系动词	形容词	不定式
成分	形式主语	谓语	表语	真正的主语

(状语从句) 翻译练习: 一些国家的人如果犯罪会面临长期服刑。

答案: People in some countries have to face a long prison term if they commit crimes.

	People	in some countries	have to face	a long prison term	if	they	commit	crimes.
词性	名词	介宾短语	动词	冠词 + 形容词 + 名词	连词	代词	动词	名词
成分	主语	后置定语	谓语	定语 + 宾语	连词不充当成分, 只是连接句子	从句的主语	从句的谓语	从句的宾语

(名词性从句) 翻译练习: 一些人认为严厉的惩罚可以减少犯罪 (deter crime)。

答案: Some people argue that harsh punishments can help deter crime.

	Some people	argue	that	harsh punishments	can help	deter crime.
词性	限定词 + 名词	动词	代词	形容词 + 名词	情态动词 + 主动词	省略了 to 的不定式
成分	定语 + 主语	谓语	引导宾语从句	从句的主语	从句的谓语	从句的宾语

(定语从句) 翻译: 减税对于那些生活拮据 (live on a tight budget) 的人有好处。

答案: Tax reductions are beneficial to those who live on a tight budget.

	Tax reductions	are	beneficial	to those	who	live on a tight budget.
词性	名词词组	系动词	形容词	介宾短语	代词	不及物动词 + 介宾短语
成分	主语	谓语	表语	beneficial 的宾语	引导定语从句	从句的谓语

通过分析这些简单的句子, 我们大概了解了 8 种常见的单句和 3 种常见的从句。

单句: ①主 + 谓 + 宾; ②主 + 谓 + 宾 + 宾补; ③主 + 谓 + 间宾 + 直宾; ④主 + 被动语态; ⑤主 + 不

及物动词；⑥主 + 系 + 表；⑦ there be 句型；⑧以 it 作形式主语或者宾语的句子。

从句：① 状语从句；② 名词性从句；③ 定语从句。

然后，大家也要熟悉下面 8 种句子成分和 12 种词性。搞懂了这些，你的写作基本上就入门了。否则，你写句子的时候都是糊里糊涂的。

主语或者宾语	① 名词 ② 代词 ③ 动名词 ④ 不定式 ⑩ 数词
谓语动词	⑤ 动词
表语或者补语	① 名词 ④ 不定式 ⑥ 形容词 ⑦ 现在分词 ⑧ 过去分词 ⑨ 介宾短语
定语	① 名词 ② 代词 ④ 不定式 ⑥ 形容词 ⑦ 现在分词 ⑧ 过去分词 ⑨ 介宾短语 ⑩ 数词 ⑫ 限定词
状语	② 代词 ④ 不定式 ⑦ 现在分词 ⑧ 过去分词 ⑨ 介宾短语 ⑪ 副词
同位语	① 名词 ② 代词 ③ 动名词

	主语或者宾语	谓语	表语或者补语	定语	状语	同位语
① 名词	✓		✓	✓		✓
② 代词	✓			✓	✓	✓
③ 动名词	✓					✓
④ 不定式	✓		✓	✓	✓	
⑤ 动词		✓				
⑥ 形容词			✓	✓		
⑦ 现在分词			✓	✓	✓	
⑧ 过去分词			✓	✓	✓	
⑨ 介宾短语			✓		✓	
⑩ 数词	✓			✓		
⑪ 副词					✓	
⑫ 限定词				✓		

2.1.1 简单的主谓宾结构

翻译 1：经常做运动会提高人的自信。

✕ 错误的句子：Exercise regularly can rise one's confidence.

错误 1：这里 exercise 如果是动词，应该用其动名词形式，如果是名词，不能用副词修饰。

错误 2：rise 是不及物动词。

√ 正确的句子：Regular exercise can increase one's self-confidence.

句子结构：主语 + 及物动词 + 宾语（confidence）

翻译2：教学质量对学生成绩有很大影响。

✗ 错误的句子：Teaching qualities are important to students improve academic performance.

错误1：quality 表示质量的时候是不可数名词。

错误2：to 是介词，后面不用加句子。

√ 正确的句子：The quality of teaching can make a huge difference to students' academic performance.

句子结构：主语 + 谓语 + 宾语

翻译3：家长和老师应该努力去减少小孩看电视的时间。

✗ 错误的句子：Parents and teachers should do their efforts to curb the time of watching TV on children.

错误1：make an effort to 是固定表达。

错误2：curb 一般是抑制某种行为，后面不接 time。

错误3：watching TV on children 也不通。

√ 正确的句子：Parents and teachers should make an effort to limit children's screen time.

句子结构：主语 (parents and teachers) + 及物动词 (make) + 宾语 (effort)

翻译4：经济的下滑（economic slowdown）导致失业率的上升。

✗ 错误的句子：Economic slowdown made the climbing unemployment rate.

错误1：描述事实，不要用过去时。

错误2：句子前面加定冠词好一点，如果强调的是一个目前正在发生的经济增长变慢的过程。

√ 正确的句子：The economic slowdown has led to a climbing unemployment rate.

句子结构：主语 + 及物动词 + 宾语

翻译5：经济的发展需要年轻的劳动者。

✗ 错误的句子：The economic development requires a great number of fresh working forces.

错误：没有 working forces 这个表达。

√ 正确的句子：A country's economic development relies on a supply of young workers.

句子结构：主语 + 及物动词 + 宾语

翻译6：工作量大的人没有时间去休息。

✗ 错误的句子：People do with heavy workload cannot have adequate times to rest and recharge batteries.

错误1：do 的功能不详，本句已有谓语。

错误2：time 在这里是不可数名词。

错误3：cannot 表示不可能，这里应该用 do not 表示没有。

√ 正确的句子：People with a heavy workload do not have adequate time to rest.

句子结构：主语 + 及物动词 + 宾语

翻译 7：在中国，很多学生晚上都要上自习。

✕ 错误的句子：Large number of students in China have to study at night.

错误：a large number of 是固定搭配。

√ 正确的句子：A large number of students in China have to do self-study at night.

句子结构：主语 + 及物动词 + 宾语

翻译 8：文化遗产（heritage sites）因为城市发展而受到威胁。

✕ 错误的句子：The development of cities have pose a threat on heritage sites.

错误 1：have pose 动词形式错误，而且主谓不一致。

错误 2：pose a threat to 是固定搭配。

√ 正确的句子：The development of cities has posed a threat to heritage sites.

句子结构：主语（development）+ 及物动词（pose）+ 宾语（threat）

翻译 9：我们不能忽视面对面的交流。

✕ 错误的句子：It cannot be ignored by people to have some face-to-face communication.

错误 1：it 指代不清楚。

错误 2：to have face-to-face communication 不对，不定式一般表示没有发生但有可能发生的事情。

√ 正确的句子：We should not ignore face-to-face communication.

句子结构：主语 + 及物动词 + 宾语（communication）

翻译 10：有些公共服务很难做到收支平衡。

✕ 错误的句子：Some public services have problems in break even.

错误：break 是动词，在这里 in 是介词，后面应该加动名词。

√ 正确的句子：Some public services have problems in breaking even.

句子结构：主语 + 及物动词 + 宾语（problems）

翻译 11：我们需要考虑社会和经济环境。

✕ 错误的句子：We have to consider about social and economic context.

错误：consider 是及物动词，后面不需要加介词。

√ 正确的句子：We have to consider the social and economic context.

句子结构：主语 + 及物动词 + 宾语（context）

翻译 12：密度种植对生物多样性造成了威胁。

✕ 错误的句子：Intensive farming poses a threat to stemming the lose of bio-diversity.

错误 1：pose a threat to stemming the loss of bio-diversity，翻译得太啰唆了。

错误 2：lose 是动词，而 of 前后一般要加名词。

√ **正确的句子**：Intensive farming can pose a threat to bio-diversity.
句子结构：主语 + 及物动词 + 宾语 (threat)

翻译 13：平等接受教育能帮助解决学生学习成绩不好的问题。

✕ **错误的句子**：Equal access to education can overcome educational underachievement.
错误：overcome educational underachievement 搭配不好；educational underachievement 是指"学生成绩不好"。

√ **正确的句子**：Equal access to education can help tackle educational underachievement.
句子结构：主语 + 及物动词 (help) + 宾语 (to tackle... 这里省略了 to)

翻译 14：接触不同的文化可以促进创新。

✕ **错误的句子**：Contacting with a wide variety of cultures can promote the creativity of native culture.
错误 1：Contacting with 是中国式英文。

错误 2：native culture 这个搭配别扭，不知道为什么要说本土文化。

√ **正确的句子**：Exposure to different cultures can encourage creativity.
句子结构：主语 + 及物动词 + 宾语

翻译 15：政府应该重视社会福利（welfare services），尤其是医疗服务。

✕ **错误的句子**：The government should give a priority to social welfare, especially the healthcare.
错误：give priority to 中没有 a；healthcare 是不可数名词，不要加定冠词。

√ **正确的句子**：The government should give priority to welfare services, especially healthcare.
句子结构：主语 + 及物动词 + 宾语

翻译 16：教育或许决定了人的工作机会。

✕ **错误的句子**：Education may do hold the key to one's job prospects.
错误：may 和 do 不能连用。

√ **正确的句子**：Education may hold the key to one's job prospects.
句子结构：主语 (education) + 及物动词 (hold) + 宾语 (the key)

翻译 17：使用化石燃料可能对环境造成破坏。

✕ **错误的句子**：Use fossil fuels can cause damage to the environmental problem.
错误 1：use 是动词，不能作主语。

错误 2：cause damage to 已经表示出对环境的破坏，不需要再说 problem。

√ **正确的句子**：The use of fossil fuels can cause damage to the environment.
句子结构：主语 (use) + 及物动词 (can cause) + 宾语 (damage)

翻译 18： 建造住宅楼有助于解决城市的拥挤问题。

× **错误的句子：** Building apartment blocks contribute to solve the crowed problem in cities.

错误 1： building 是动名词，主谓不一致。

错误 2： contribute to 后面要加名词，而不是动词原形。

错误 3： 没有 crowed problem 这个表达。

√ **正确的句子：** Building apartment blocks helps solve overcrowding in cities.

句子结构： 主语 + 及物动词 (helps) + 宾语 (solve overcrowding，前面省略了 to, 本来是不定式 to solve overcrowding)

翻译 19： 贫穷的人可以通过努力工作来提高社会地位。

× **错误的句子：** People at disadvantage are likely to improve their social status by working hard, studying hard.

错误 1： 没有 at disadvantage 这个表达。

错误 2： working hard 和 studying hard 间缺少连词。

√ **正确的句子：** People from disadvantaged backgrounds can improve their social status by working hard.

句子结构： 主语 (people) + 及物动词 (improve) + 宾语 (status)，from disadvantaged backgrounds 是 people 的定语

翻译 20： 因为全球化，人们需要和来自不同背景的人一起工作。

× **错误的句子：** Because of the globalisation, people should work with others who comes from different backgrounds.

错误 1： the globalisation 中的 the 比较多余。

错误 2： who comes from 没有必要用定语从句。

错误 3： should "必须" 语气过重。

√ **正确的句子：** Because of globalisation, people need to work with those from diverse backgrounds.

注： 这里的 those 就是 "其他人" 的意思，不能说 those people，这样会和主语重复。

句子结构： 主语 (people) + 及物动词 (need) + 宾语 (to work)，because of globalisation 介宾短语充当状语

翻译 21： 我们需要采取措施去解决一些棘手的问题。

× **错误的句子：** We must take measurement to tackle thorny problems.

错误： measurement 的意思是 "测量"。

√ **正确的句子：** We need to take action to solve some thorny problems.

句子结构： 主语 (we) + 及物动词 (need) + 宾语 (to take...)

翻译 22：媒体通过夸大受害者的伤痛去吸引现众。

✕ 错误的句子：Medias exaggerate the hurt of victims to attract public attentions.

错误 1：media 本身就是复数形式，不用再加 s。

错误 2：hurt 是动词，而 of 前后一般要加名词。

错误 3：attention 是不可数名词。

√ 正确的句子：The media attract public attention by sensationalising victims' suffering.

句子结构：主语 (the media) + 及物动词 (attracts) + 宾语 (attention)；"by + ..."方式状语

2.1.2 主语＋及物动词＋宾语＋宾语补足语

翻译 23：基因工程让人们培养新品种农作物。

✕ 错误的句子：Genetic engineering allows people to nurture new species crops.

错误：species crops 的语序有问题。

√ 正确的句子：Genetic engineering allows people to nurture crop varieties.

句子结构：主语 + 及物动词 + 宾语 (people) + 宾语补足语 (to nurture...)

翻译 24：经常运动使得人们保持健康的心态。

✕ 错误的句子：Doing exercises regularly helps people maintain a healthy state of mind.

错误：doing exercise 一般是不可数。

√ 正确的句子：Doing exercise regularly helps people maintain a healthy state of mind.

句子结构：主语 + 及物动词 + 宾语 (people) + 宾语补足语 (to maintain... 省略了 to)

翻译 25：不健康的生活方式让人们处于生病的危险之中。

✕ 错误的句子：Unhealthy lifestyle is likely to make people at risk of illness.

错误 1：make somebody do something 或者是 make somebody +形容词是更常见的用法。

错误 2：lifestyle 是可数名词，要加冠词，或者用复数形式。

√ 正确的句子：An unhealthy lifestyle may put people at risk of illness.

句子结构：主语 (An unhealthy lifestyle) + 及物动词 (put) + 宾语 (people) + 宾语补足语 (at risk of illness)

翻译 26：奖学金可以鼓励更多的学生去学习研究生课程。

✕ 错误的句子：Scholarship could be regarded as something to inspire more students to take postgraduate curriculum.

错误 1：scholarship 是可数名词，应该用复数形式或者前面加冠词。

错误 2：regarded as something 过于啰唆。

错误 3：curriculum 不是 course 的替换词，curriculum 的意思是"课程大纲"。

√ **正确的句子**：Government grants could encourage more students to take postgraduate courses.

句子结构：主语（government grants）+ 及物动词（encourage）+ 宾语（students）+ 宾语补足语（to take postgraduate courses）

翻译 27：社区改造为罪犯提供了获得职业技能的机会。

✕ **错误的句子**：Replacing the long sentence by working for the locals provides offenders with transferable skills.

错误：主语很别扭，两种事物没有替换性。

√ **正确的句子**：Community service provides offenders with opportunities to acquire transferable skills.

句子结构：主语 + 及物动词 + 宾语（offenders）+ 宾语补足语（with opportunities to...）

翻译 28：法律应该将醉驾定为刑事犯罪。

✕ **错误的句子**：The government should introduce a law which is drunk driving a criminal offence.

错误：定语从句还原后是"a law is drunk driving"，这显然不对。中国考生有个误区，就是觉得一定要写从句才能加分。

√ **正确的句子**：Legislation should make drink driving a criminal offence.

句子结构：主语（legislation）+ 及物动词（make）+ 宾语（drink driving）+ 宾语补足语（a criminal offence）

翻译 29：乡村地区给人们提供远离现代生活的压力和噪声的机会。

✕ **错误的句子**：Rural area provides people with opportunity to escape pressure and noises of modern life.

错误 1：rural area 是可数名词，前面缺冠词，或者用复数形式。

错误 2：opportunity 在这里用复数形式比较好。

√ **正确的句子**：Rural areas provide people with opportunities to escape pressure and noises of modern life.

句子结构：主语（rural areas）+ 及物动词（provide）+ 宾语（people）+ 宾语补足语（with opportunities to...）

翻译 30：人口老龄化促使国家提高法定退休年龄（statutory retirement age）。

✕ **错误的句子**：Compulsory retirement age will be abolished, and the reason is attributed to population aging and urban.

错误 1：age 是可数名词，前面要加冠词。

错误 2：reason is attributed to 这个搭配不恰当。

√ 正确的句子：The ageing population has prompted countries to raise the statutory retirement age.

句子结构：主语 (ageing population) + 及物动词 (prompt) + 宾语 (countries) + 宾语补足语 (to raise...)

2.1.3 主语 + 及物动词 + 间接宾语 + 直接宾语

翻译 31：政府应该给一些城市提供资金去保护历史建筑 (historic buildings)。

✗ 错误的句子：Many areas now pay attention to protect historic buildings.

错误：pay attention to 中的 to 是介词，后面不能加动词。

√ 正确的句子：Governments should offer some cities funds to preserve historic buildings.

句子结构：主语 (governments) + 及物动词 (offer) + 间接宾语 (some cities) + 直接宾语 (funds)

2.1.4 被动语态

翻译 32：学校应该允许老师强制捣蛋的小孩离开教室。

✗ 错误的句子：Schools should allow teachers to make the children with disruptive behaviours go out of classrooms.

错误：children with disruptive behaviours 略显啰唆。

√ 正确的句子：Teachers should be permitted to use force to remove disruptive children from the classroom.

主动语态：Schools should permit teachers to use force to remove disruptive children from the classroom.

句子结构：主语 (schools) + 及物动词 (permit) + 宾语 (teachers) + 宾语补足语 (to use force...)

翻译 33：农村的失业问题在某种程度上可以通过城乡转移 (rural-to-urban shift) 来解决。

✗ 错误的句子：Unemployment in rural areas can be address by rural-to-urban shift.

错误 1：被动语态中缺少过去分词。

错误 2：shift 是可数名词，前面要加冠词。

√ 正确的句子：Unemployment in rural areas can be addressed partially by the rural-to-urban shift.

句子结构：（主语 + 及物动词 + 宾语）的被动语态

翻译 34：高层建筑有时候被认为是城市里的碍眼之物 (eyesore)。

✗ 错误的句子：Occasionally, high-rise buildings are tend to be regarded as the eyesore of a city.

错误 1：occasionally 表示"偶尔地，很少地"。

错误 2："be + do"是错的。

√ 正确的句子：High-rise buildings are sometimes regarded as eyesores of the city.

注. 这句话里如果说 the eyesore 就是特指，意思是城市只有一处难看的地方，但事实上未必如此。

句子结构：somebody regards something as something 是"主语＋及物动词＋宾语＋宾语补足语"的结构，而这句话是这个结构的被动语态

翻译35： 太空科技的投资应该获得政府的支持。

✕ 错误的句子：The investment on space technology should be supported by government.

错误1：investment in 是固定搭配。

错误2：应该用 governments or the government。

✓ 正确的句子：The investment in space technology should be supported by the government.

句子结构：主语＋及物动词（support 的被动语态）＋宾语

翻译36： 历史文物因为它的历史重要性而被保存。

✕ 错误的句子：Antique heritages should be completely preserved due to its historical importance.

错误1：没有 antique heritages 这个表达。

错误2：heritage 是不可数名词。

错误3：既然主语是复数，为什么后面用代词 its？

✓ 正确的句子：Historic relics should be preserved for their historical significance.

句子结构：主语＋及物动词（preserve 的被动语态）＋宾语

翻译37： 学校活动要能让孩子体会到成就感，提升他们的幸福感。

✕ 错误的句子：The main purpose of the school activities which can give the children's a sense of accomplishment is to promote the students's well being.

错误1：主语里加了个定语从句，太长。

错误2：给学生成功感和提升学生的幸福感应该不是方式和目的。

✓ 正确的句子：Sports and other school activities can be designed to give children a sense of accomplishment and to promote their well-being.

句子结构：主语＋及物动词（design 的被动语态）＋宾语

翻译38： 一些员工被鼓励去打破陈规。

✕ 错误的句子：Employee can breakthrough the obsoleted rules.

错误1：breakthrough 是个名词，没有动词含义。

错误2：没有 obsoleted 这个词，只有 obsolete。

错误3：employee 为什么用单数形式，难道只有一个员工？

✓ 正确的句子：Some employees are encouraged to break the mould.

句子结构：主语（省略）+ 及物动词（encourage 的被动语态）+ 宾语（employees 变成了主语）
　　　　　　+ 宾语补足语（to break the mould）

翻译 *39*：因为堵车，上下班的时间变得更长了。

✕ 错误的句子：Commuter time was prolonged because of traffic congestion.

　　错误 1：commuter time 不是固定词伙。

　　错误 2：was 时态错误。

✔ 正确的句子：Commuting time has been prolonged because of traffic congestion.

　　句子结构：主语 + 及物动词（prolong 的被动语态）+ 宾语

　　中文翻译：因为堵车上下班时间变得更长。

翻译 *40*：电脑技能可以运用到学习和工作中。

✕ 错误的句子：Computering applying in their academic study as well as their career life.

　　错误 1：applying 谓语不完整。

　　错误 2：career life 这个词伙不是很恰当。

✔ 正确的句子：Computer skills can be applied in their studies as well as their working lives.

　　句子结构：主语 + 及物动词（apply 的被动语态）+ 宾语

翻译 *41*：大部分的环境破坏都可以归咎于人类的活动。

✕ 错误的句子：The most of environmental degradation is contributed to human activities.

　　错误 1：the most 后面一般加形容词，构成最高级。

　　错误 2：contribute to 一般用主动语态，而且和 attributed to 意思相反。

✔ 正确的句子：Most of environmental degradation is attributed to human activities.

　　句子结构：原句是"主语 + 及物动词 + 宾语 + 宾语补足语"（attribute something to something）
　　　　　　　这个句子是被动语态

翻译 *42*：许多孩子每天接触暴力内容。

✕ 错误的句子：Many children are expose to violent contents in every day.

　　错误 1：content 作"内容"讲时是不可数名词。

　　错误 2：expose 是及物动词，"be + do"这个结构错误。

　　错误 3：every day 本身可以充当状语，不用加介词 in。

✔ 正确的句子：Many children are exposed to violent content every day.

　　句子结构：主语 + 及物动词（expose 的被动语态）+ 宾语补足语（to violent content）

　　主动语态是：something exposes children to violent content（主语 + 及物动词 + 宾语 + 宾语
　　　　　　　补足语）

翻译 43：家庭环境被认为对小孩成长的影响最重要。

× 错误的句子：Family environment is widely thought to be the most important influence on children development.

错误：children development 没有使用所有格。

√ 正确的句子：The family environment is widely thought/believed to be the most important influence on children's development.

句子结构：主语 (family environment) + 及物动词的被动语态 (is thought) + 宾语补足语 (to be)

翻译 44：随着越来越多的年轻人参加志愿者工作，社区的凝聚力 (cohesion) 会加强。

× 错误的句子：With more young people join the volunteer works, community's cohesion will be enhanced.

错误 1：with 是介词，后面不能加句子。

错误 2：work 在这里是不可数名词，不能用复数形式。

√ 正确的句子：With an increasing number of young people participating in volunteer work, community cohesion will be enhanced.

句子结构：主语 (community cohesion) + 及物动词的被动语态 (be enhanced)，而 "with an...participating in" 是 "介词 + 名词 + 分词" 结构，充当状语

翻译 45：移民有时候被认为是对社会团结的一个威胁。

× 错误的句子：Immigrants sometimes was recognised as a threat to the social cohesion.

错误 1：句子的时态错误。

错误 2：主谓不一致。

错误 3：cohesion 是不可数名词，不需要用 the 去特指。

√ 正确的句子：Immigrants are sometimes recognised as a threat to social cohesion.

句子结构：原句可能是 "People sometimes recognise immigrants as a threat." 结构是主语 (people) + 及物动词 (recognise) + 宾语 (immigrants) + 宾语补足语 (as a threat)。这句话是被动语态。

2.1.5 主语 + 不及物动词

翻译 46：没有受过高等教育的年轻人只能找到低技术的工作。

× 错误的句子：Young people without tertiary education qualifications normally have low-skilled jobs.

错误 1：have low-skilled jobs 里的 have 语气比较弱，表示不出 "只能找到" 的意思。

√ 正确的句子：Young people without tertiary education qualifications normally end up working in low-skilled jobs.

句子结构：主语 + 不及物动词（end up）+ 状语（分词 working in…）

翻译47：一些人不支持转基因食品。

✕ 错误的句子：People hold the objection to the proliferation of genetically modified food.

错误：hold the objection to 这个表达很不恰当，而且啰嗦。

√ 正确的句子：Some people disapprove of genetically modified food.

句子结构：主语 + 不及物动词（disapprove）

翻译48：旅游景点竭力满足游客的需要和品位。

✕ 错误的句子：Tourist spots devote to fulfilling tourists' needs and tastes.

错误1：devote 是及物动词，后面要有宾语。

错误2：fulfil tastes 不是惯用词伙。

√ 正确的句子：Tourist spots endeavor to cater for tourists' needs and tastes.

句子结构：主语 + 不及物动词；to do 不定式

翻译49：在竞争激烈的社会，有工作的成年人关心职业发展。

✕ 错误的句子：In the highly competitive society, working adults are usually focusing on career advancement.

错误1：应该用 a，而不是 the，否则，别人还以为世界上只有一个激烈竞争的社会。

错误2：用进行时有点怪。

√ 正确的句子：In a highly competitive society, working adults usually focus on career advancement.

句子结构：主语 + 不及物动词（focus）；in a highly competitive society 是介宾短语充当状语

翻译50：审美观是因文化而异的。

✕ 错误的句子：Perception of beauty is differed from culture to culture.

错误：differ 是不及物动词，没有被动语态。

√ 正确的句子：Perception of beauty differs from culture to culture.

句子结构：主语 + 不及物动词；from culture to culture 是介宾短语充当状语

翻译51：因为费用的下降，航空业最近几十年发展得很快。

✕ 错误的句子：The airline has sharp development in recent decades, with the cost decline.

错误1：时间状语是 in recent decades 时，句子一般要用现在完成时。

错误2：has sharp development 表达比较别扭。

错误3：with 是介词，后面不能接句子。

√ 正确的句子：Because of low-cost carriers, the aviation industry has developed at an astounding pace over the past decades.

句子结构：主语 (the aviation industry) + 不及物动词 (developed)；because of low-cost carriers 是原因状语；over the past decades 是时间状语；at an astounding pace 是程度状语

翻译 52：动物实验有时候不能检验出药物的不良副作用。

✗ 错误的句子：Animal experiment is occasionally unable to examine drugs side effects.

错误 1：animal experiment 是可数名词，要用复数形式。

错误 2：occasionally 意思是"偶尔地，极少地"。

错误 3：drugs side effects 没有使用所有格。

√ 正确的句子：Animal experiments sometimes fail to detect the undesirable side effects of drugs.

句子结构：主语 + 不及物动词 (fail) + 状语 (to...)

翻译 53：非法捕杀导致某些动物的灭亡。

✗ 错误的句子：Hunting illegally leads to the extinct of species.

错误：extinct 是个形容词，而 lead to 后面要加名词。

√ 正确的句子：Some animals have died out because of illegal hunting.

主语 (some animals) + 不及物动词 (have died out) + 状语 (because of...)

翻译 54：电脑对人的交流技能的影响随年龄而变化。

✗ 错误的句子：The impact on people's communication skill from computer, varies between ages.

错误 1：skill 是可数名词，要用复数形式。

错误 2：varies between ages 表达不恰当。

错误 3：the impact...from computer 表达不恰当。

√ 正确的句子：The impact of computers on communication skills varies across ages.

句子结构：主语 (impact) + 不及物动词 (varies)；of computers on communication skills 都是定语

2.1.6 主系表结构

翻译 55：很多女孩都不愿意在男人居多的行业里 (male-dominated world) 找工作。

✗ 错误的句子：A number of girls are not willing to hunting jobs in the male-dominated world.

错误 1：willing to do something 是固定搭配。

错误 2：a number of 在这里感觉意思是"一些"。

错误 3：定冠词不恰当，因为世界上男人居多的行业有很多，不可能特指一个。

√ 正确的句子：Many girls are not willing to seek employment in a male-dominated world.

句子结构：主语 + 系动词 + 表语 (willing)

翻译 56：学校的主要功能是给下一代灌输知识 (impart knowledge)。

✗ 错误的句子：The main function of school is impart knowledge to the next generation.

错误 1：school 是可数名词，前面要加冠词或者使用其复数形式。

错误 2：is + do 这个结构是错的。

√ 正确的句子：The main function of schools is to impart knowledge to the next generation.

句子结构：主语 + 系动词 (is) + 表语 (to impart knowledge to the next generation)

翻译 57：艺术不属于学校的主科。

✗ 错误的句子：Arts is not regarded as a core curriculum at school.

错误 1：主谓不一致。

错误 2：curriculum 是所有课程的总称。

√ 正确的句子：The arts are not among core subject areas at school.

句子结构：主语 (the arts) + 系动词 (are) + 表语 (介词 among + 宾语，充当表语)

翻译 58：因为不够明朗的经济前景 (economic outlook)，很多公司不可能招聘新的职员。

✗ 错误的句子：Because of unclear/ambiguous economic outlook, many companies are unlikely to recruit new employments.

错误 1：ambiguous 一般不修饰 outlook。

错误 2：employments 用词不当，应该是 employees。

√ 正确的句子：Because of the uncertainty about the economic outlook, many companies are unlikely to recruit new employees.

句子结构：主语 + 系动词 + 表语；because of 是介词词组引导原因状语

翻译 59：空运可能产生很多温室气体。

✗ 错误的句子：Air freight is likely to exhaust a large number of greenhouse gases.

错误 1：exhaust 作动词时，没有"排放"的意思，这是很常见的错误。

错误 2：a large number of 很少形容 gases, goods 强调总量，而不是个数的东西。

√ 正确的句子：Air freight is likely to create enormous greenhouse gases.

注：这句话也可以使用完成时态：Air freight has produced enormous greenhouse gases. 完成时在这里最大的问题是把 air freight 变成了一个持续的完整的事物，而我们都知道空运是有次数分别的。

句子结构：主语 + 系动词 + 表语

也可以用比较状语从句扩充：

Air freight is likely to create more greenhouse gases than other modes of transport.

中文翻译：空运可能比其他运输方式产生更多的温室气体。

翻译 60：孩子很有可能有行为的问题。

✗ **错误的句子：**The children are likely to meet behaviour problems.

错误 1：meet problems 搭配不对。

错误 2：behavioural problems 是固定搭配。

√ **正确的句子：**Some children are likely to have behavioural problems.

句子结构：主语 + 系动词 + 表语 (likely)

翻译 61：人口的扩大是大量垃圾产生的原因。

✗ **错误的句子：**Population expansion constitutes the main reason of enormous garbages.

错误 1：reason for 是固定搭配。

错误 2：garbage 和 waste 都是不可数名词。

√ **正确的句子：**The rapid population expansion is the main reason for the huge accumulation of waste.

句子结构：主语 + 系动词 + 表语 (reason)

翻译 62：严厉的惩罚是减少犯罪的有效手段。

✗ **错误的句子：**Stiff sentences is an effective method to decrease crime rates.

错误 1：主谓不一致。

错误 2：decrease crime rates 表达不恰当。

√ **正确的句子：**Imposing stiff punishment is an effective method to reduce crime.

句子结构：主语 + 系动词 + 表语 + 不定式 (to reduce crime)

翻译 63：我们的环境还是很糟糕。

✗ **错误的句子：**Our environment still be in a dire state.

错误：没有谓语动词。

√ **正确的句子：**Our environment is still in a dire state.

句子结构：主语 + 系动词 + 表语 (介宾短语 in a dire state 充当)

翻译 64：因为失业率高涨，大学生感到有压力而努力学习。

✗ **错误的句子：**Undergraduates are forced to study under pressure due to severe situation of unemployment rate is ascending currently.

错误 1：due to 是介词，后面要加名词。

错误 2：ascend，"坑爹"替换词。

√ **正确的句子**：Undergraduates feel under increasing pressure to study hard, because of the soaring unemployment rate.

　句子结构：主语 (undergraduates) + 系动词 (feel) + 表语 (介宾短语 under pressure 充当)

翻译 *65*：种族歧视仍然很严重。

✗ **错误的句子**：People find it hard to overcome the racial discrimination against some social groups.

　错误：这个句子比较大的问题是 people 和后面的 social groups 是相同的，既充当句子的主语，又充当介词的宾语很奇怪。

√ **正确的句子**：Racial discrimination remains a serious problem.

　句子结构：主语 + 系动词 (remain) + 表语

翻译 *66*：死记硬背乘法表并不是提高算术能力的最好方式。

✗ **错误的句子**：Learning time tables by rote are not the best way that improves arithmetic ability.

　错误 1：动名词作主语，谓语动词应该用单数 is。

　错误 2：way that... 定语从句太烦琐。

√ **正确的句子**：Learning the times table by rote is not the best way to improve numeracy.

　句子结构：主语 (learning the times table by rote) + 系动词 (is) + 表语 (the best way)； 而 to improve numeracy 是后置定语修饰 way

翻译 *67*：贫穷国家的首要问题是满足人们的基本生存需求。

✗ **错误的句子**：Deprived countries concern how to satisfy citizens' requirements of survive.

　错误 1：concern 类似于 worry 或者 involve, 在这里不恰当。

　错误 2：requirements 语意理解错误。

　错误 3：of 后面要加名词，而 survive 是动词。

√ **正确的句子**：The top priority for deprived countries is to satisfy citizens' basic needs.

　句子的结构：主语 (priority) + 系动词 (is) + 表语 (to satisfy citizens' basic needs)

翻译 *68*：转基因食品对健康的影响仍然未知。

✗ **错误的句子**：The impact that genetic food has on our health still remains unknown.

　错误 1：在定语从句中，最好要规避这种先行词充当从句宾语的情况，读起来比较别扭。

　错误 2：remains 已经包含 still 的意思，语意重复。

　错误 3：genetic food 这个表达不是很好。

√ **正确的句子**：The health effect of GE food remains unclear/yet to be known.

　句子结构：主语 (health effect) + 系动词 (remains) + 表语 (unclear)

翻译 *69*：网络购物已经成为很多人生活中很普通的一部分。

✕ 错误的句子：It has become an important part for most people to shop online in daily life.

　错误：part of daily life 是固定的说法。

√ 正确的句子：Online shopping has become a normal part of people's everyday life.

　句子结构：主语＋系动词＋表语

翻译 70： 在一个消费社会里，人们不再满足于生活必需品（bare necessities）。

✕ 错误的句子：In a throw-away society, people are not satisfied with bare necessities any more.

　错误1：throw-away society 这个词伙不对。

　错误2：not...any more 一般是形容量的东西，而 no longer 强调动作的持续性。

√ 正确的句子：In the consumer society, bare necessities are not able to satisfy people's needs.

翻译 71： 人们不健康的生活方式是他们倾向于依赖科技的结果。

✕ 错误的句子：Unhealthy lifestyle is the result of trend to rely on science and technology.

　错误1：unhealthy lifestyle 是可数名词，需要加冠词。

　错误2：trend toward doing something 还有 tendency to do something 是常用搭配。

√ 正确的句子：People's unhealthy lifestyle is the result of their tendency to rely heavily on technology.

　句子结构：主语（unhealthy lifestyle）＋系动词（is）＋表语（the result）; of... 是定语

翻译 72： 贫穷是社区犯罪增多的原因。

✕ 错误的句子：The reason which cause increasingly number of community crimes in society is poverty.

　错误1：reason which cause，从句的主谓不一致，而且搭配不好。

　错误2：increasingly number 副词不能修饰名词。

　错误3：这个考生硬是把简单的事情啰嗦地说出来，很别扭。雅思考试考查的是语言的通顺和地道，而不是考查你的句子是否够复杂。

√ 正确的句子：Poverty is responsible for the crime wave in many communities.

　句子结构：主语（poverty）＋系动词（is）＋表语（responsible）

翻译 73： 电子汽车的发明是我们维护环境所做努力的其中一部分。

✕ 错误的句子：The invention of electric vehicles is a part of our efforts aiming at preserving the environment.

　错误1："其中一部分"一般表达是 part of。

　错误2：effort to do something 在这里更为通顺。

√ 正确的句子：The invention of electric vehicles is part of our effort to sustain the environment.

　句子结构：主语（invention of electric vehicles）＋系动词（is）＋表语（part）; of... 是定语

2.1.7 It 作形式主语或者宾语的句子

翻译 74：送贵重的礼物（lavish gifts）是中国的习惯。

✗ **错误的句子：** It is very common for Chinese to send lavish gifts to other.

错误：other 是形容词，充当定语，这里需要一个名词性的代词，充当介词 to 的宾语。

✓ **正确的句子：** It is very common for Chinese people to exchange lavish gifts.

句子结构：主语 + 系动词 + 表语；it 是形式主语，to exchange lavish gifts 不定式是真正的主语。

其他译法：Exchanging lavish gifts is a tradition in China.

句子结构：主语 + 系动词 + 表语

翻译 75：未来几十年，我们很难保护植物多样性。

✗ **错误的句子：** We will find it difficult for us to protect the biodiversity of vegetation in the coming decades.

错误 1：we...for us 重复。

错误 2：biodiversity of vegetation 略显重复。

✓ **正确的句子：** We will find it difficult to preserve biodiversity in the coming decades.

句子结构：主语 + 谓语 + 宾语（it，形式宾语）+ 宾语补足语（difficult）；不定式是真正的宾语

翻译 76：随着年龄增长，很难和朋友和家人保持联系。

✗ **错误的句子：** As the growing age, people is hard to connect with their families and friends frequently.

错误 1：没有 as the growing age 这个表达。

错误 2：people is 主谓不一致。

错误 3：人无难易之分，hard 在这里不恰当。

错误 4：connect frequently 搭配不当。

✓ **正确的句子：** With age, people find it difficult to maintain contact with family and friends.

句子结构：主语 (people) + 谓语 (find) + 宾语 (it，形式宾语) + 宾语补足语 (difficult)；不定式是真正的宾语

注：contact 作动词时是及物动词，不能加介词，如 people find it easy to contact their friends today.

翻译 77：免费上大学使得家境不好的学生有同等的上学机会。

✗ **错误的句子：** Free tuition fees makes it possible for students from less well-off background have equal access to tertiary education.

错误 1：make it possible for somebody to do something 是惯用搭配，to 不能省略。

错误 2：background 应该用复数形式。

√ 正确的句子：Free university education makes it possible for students from less well-off backgrounds to have equal access to tertiary education.

注：access 是不可数名词，access to something 是习惯搭配；access 也可以作及物动词，但是一般没有 access education 这个说法。tertiary education=university education

句子结构：主语 + 谓语 + 宾语（it，形式宾语）+ 宾语补足语（possible）；不定式（to have equal access to tertiary education）是真正的宾语

翻译 78：很多人觉得自己有必要赶时尚。

✕ 错误的句子：Many people think that they are necessary to chase after fashion.

错误：人没有 necessary 这么一说；chase 在这里用作及物动词比较好。

√ 正确的句子：Many people consider it necessary to follow fashion.

句子结构：主语（many people）+ 及物动词（consider）+ 形式宾语（it）+ 宾语补足语（necessary）；真正的宾语是 to follow fashion

翻译 79：经费削减让很多年轻人很难接受大学教育。

✕ 错误的句子：Cutting the budget of the education pose a threat to the opportunities of the young people who want to take part in the higher education.

错误 1：动名词 cutting 作主语，但是谓语动词没有用单数形式。

错误 2：pose a threat to the opportunities 搭配不当。

错误 3：后面用定语从句也是过于累赘，opportunities to do something 是习惯表达。很多中国考生的问题是习惯把表达复杂化，觉得那样才是好作文，其实 native speaker 更加注意文字的简练和清楚。

√ 正确的句子：Budget cuts make it difficult for many young people to receive a college education.

句子结构：主语（budget cuts）+ 及物动词（make）+ 宾语（it 形式宾语）+ 宾语补足语（difficult）；真正的宾语是 to receive a college education

翻译 80：有时候，很难去评估人类行为的环境代价。

✕ 错误的句子：Sometimes, it is difficult to evaluate the environmental costs of people's behaviors.

错误 1：environmental cost 在这里用单数就好，因为是在说整个影响，而不是不同的影响。

错误 2：应使用英式拼写 behaviours。

错误 3：behaviours 在这里不如 activities 好，因为 behaviours 是指人的瞬间举动，activities 一般指动作持续时间比较长。

√ **正确的句子：** Sometimes, it is difficult to evaluate the environmental cost of human activities.

句子结构：主语 (it) + 系动词 (is) + 表语 (difficult)；to evaluate the environmental cost of human activities 不定式充当形式主语。

2.1.8 There be 句型

翻译 *81*：在大城市有一些贫困的社区。

✗ **错误的句子：** In large-scale cities have some deprived communities.

错误：in large-scale cities 是介宾短语，不能充当主语。

√ **正确的句子：** There are some economically deprived communities in large cities.

句子结构：there be 句型

翻译 *82*：按照能力分班和学生的成绩没有明显的联系。

✗ **错误的句子：** There is no clear link between selection in terms of students' ability and their academic performance.

错误：in terms of 是一个被中国考生用烂的短语，有时候显得过于啰唆。

√ **正确的句子：** There is no clear link between grouping students by ability and their levels of attainment.

句子结构：there be 句型

2.1.9 并列句

翻译 *83*：体育课可以促进身体健康，增强信心。

✗ **错误的句子：** The PE class not only improves students physical conditions but also boosts their confidence.

错误 1：not only...but also... 一般连接两个并列的、联系不密切的事物，而不是有因果关系的事物。在这里，improve physical conditions 很明显会 boosts their confidence，二者具备因果关系。

错误 2：students 要用所有格 students'。

√ **正确的句子：** The PE class improves students' physical condition and boosts their confidence.

句子结构：两个并列句结构相同，都是主语 + 及物动词 + 宾语

翻译 *84*：竞争激烈，一些城市处于弱势，因为缺少资源，比如天然气和化石燃料。

✗ **错误的句子：** Countries competition are intensively and lack of resources such as the natural gas and fossil oil.

错误 1：主谓不一致。

错误 2：intensively 是副词，不能充当表语。

错误 3：第一个 and 后面没有接句子。

√ **正确的句子**：The competition is intense and some countries are at a disadvantage because of the lack of resources such as natural gas and fossil fuels.

　　句子结构：两个并列句结构相同，都是主语 + 系动词 + 表语

翻译85：在发展中国家开设新的分公司可以降低生产成本，产生巨大的利润。

✕ **错误的句子**：Opening new branches in developing countries can reduce the cost of production and earn huge profits.

　　错误：opening new branches 不可能是 earn 的主语。

√ **正确的句子**：Opening new branches in developing countries can reduce the cost of production and generate huge profits.

　　句子结构：两个并列句结构相同，都是主语 + 谓语 + 宾语

翻译86：生活方式的轻微变化也能够产生巨大的变化，并且可以减少我们日常活动对环境的影响。

✕ **错误的句子**：The slightly lifestyle changes make a huge difference and alleviate impacts caused by our daily activities on the environment.

　　错误 1：slightly 是副词，不能修饰 lifestyle。

　　错误 2：减少影响不能用 alleviate。

　　错误 3：impacts caused by 是中式英语。

√ **正确的句子**：Small lifestyle changes can make a huge difference and reduce the environmental impact of our daily activities.

　　句子结构：两个并列句结构相同，都是主语 + 谓语 + 宾语

2.2 雅思大作文常见语法错误总结

2.2.1 冠词和名词单复数的语法错误

A. 冠词的使用错误

冠词分为不定冠词（a 或者 an）和定冠词（the）。

a. 可数名词前一般要加定冠词或者不定冠词；可数名词如果使用定冠词，要么表示一类东西，要么表示特指。否则的话，要变成复数形式。另外一种可能性是使用所有格的形式。

不可数名词则无此约束。它们意思的区别见下表。

可数名词加不定冠词	例：I need to read a book about how to combat crime.
	意思：世界上有很多关于如何打击犯罪的书，我需要看其中一本，随便哪一本都可以。
可数名词加定冠词	例：I need to read the book about how to combat crime.
	意思：我手中可能有好几本书，其中一本是关于如何打击犯罪的，我需要看这本书，可能这本书以前就和别人提起过。

可数名词加复数	例：I need to read books about how to combat crime.
	意思：我需要读关于打击犯罪的书，不只一本。
可数名词的复数加定冠词	例：The books about how to combat crime are among the best sellers of the bookshop.
	意思：书店有很多书，强调其中某种类型的书。

例1：Computer is a machine for collecting, processing and presenting information.

错误：computer 是可数名词，要加冠词。

改正：The computer is a machine for collecting, processing and presenting information.

翻译：电脑是一台用来收集、处理和发布信息的机器。

例2：Government should provide students from low-income families with more support.

错误：government 一般用作可数名词，要加冠词，或者用复数 governments。

改正：The government should provide students from low-income families with more support.

翻译：正确。政府应该给低收入家庭的学生提供更多帮助。

b. 不可数名词一般不用定冠词，除非特指。可数名词复数一般也不用定冠词，除非特指。

例1：The education is important to one's job prospects.

错误：education 是不可数名词，如果出现冠词，表示特指。

改正：Education is important to one's job prospects.

翻译：教育对于一个人的工作前景是重要的。

例2：The parents tend to prefer boarding schools to day schools.

错误：因为是泛指所有的父母，所以不应该加定冠词。

改正：Parents tend to prefer boarding schools to day schools.

翻译：父母倾向于喜欢寄宿学校，而不是走读学校。

c. 有一些形容词前面常加定冠词，比如说 only, main, same, top。

例：People with same experience should be paid same.

错误：same 前要加 the。

改正：People with the same experience should be paid the same.

翻译：经验相同的人应该工资相同。

d. 序数词和形容词最高级前要加定冠词。

例1：Tourism has become the top earner of foreign currency for many countries since late twentieth century.

错误：twentieth 这个序数词前要用 the。

改正：Tourism has become the top earner of foreign currency for many countries since the late twentieth century.

翻译：目从 20 世纪后期开始，旅游业已经成为很多国家赚取外汇的首要手段。

例 2：The cigarette is most common method of smoking tobacco.

错误：most common 是形容词最高级形式，所以 most 前要加 the。

改正：The cigarette is the most common method of smoking tobacco.

翻译：纸烟是吸食烟草的最普遍方式。

e. 有一些词虽然以元音字母开头，却要用不定冠词 a。如 unique, university, union，European，而另一些词虽然以辅音字母开头，却要用不定冠词 an，如 hour, honour。

例：An university is an institution where students study for degrees.

错误：university 前不能加 an。

改正：A university is an institution where students study for degrees.

翻译：大学是学生通过学习获得学位的地方。

B. 名词的单复数问题

a. 有一些词或者短语后面一般要加可数名词的复数形式，如 a few, few, a variety of, various, other, numerous, a number of, different, one of, many, several, these。

例：Smoking cessation is one of the likely factor that contribute to the development of obesity.

错误：one of 的后面要加名词的复数形式。

改正：Smoking cessation is one of the likely factors that contribute to the development of obesity.

翻译：停止抽烟是可能导致肥胖症的一个因素。

b. 有一些词后面一般要加可数名词的单数形式，如 any other, another, each, neither, either。

例：Many teenagers begin smoking habits due to peer pressure but not for any other reasons.

错误：any other 后不可以加名词的复数形式。

改正：Many teenagers begin smoking habits due to peer pressure but not for any other reason.

翻译：很多十几岁的年轻人出于同伴的压力而开始抽烟，而不是因为其他任何原因。

c. 有一些词或者短语后面一般要加不可数名词，如 a little, little, less, much, a large amount of。

例：Little progresses have been made towards tackling poverty.

错误：little 后不能加可数名词的复数形式。

改正：Little progress has been made towards tackling poverty.

翻译：在解决贫困问题上，目前的进展甚微。

d. 不可数名词没有复数形式。如 information, knowledge, evidence, behaviour, news, research, waste, pollution。

例：There are evidences that rules can lead to children's anti-social behaviour.

错误：evidence 是不可数名词，没有复数形式。

改正：There is evidence that rules can lead to children's anti-social behaviour.

翻译：有证据表明：规则会导致小孩的反社会行为。

e. 有些可数名词的复数形式变化不规则，不是仅仅加 s 或者 es。

单数	复数	单数	复数	单数	复数
child	children	datum	data	phenomenon	phenomena
means	means	medium	media	species	species

例：The datas are a valuable asset to the company.

错误：data 本身已经是复数形式。

改正：The data are a valuable asset to the company.

翻译：数据对公司来说是一项宝贵的财产。

f. 注意代词的单复数形式，代词 he, she, it, one, anybody, everybody, somebody, nobody 都是单数形式，而代词 they 是复数形式。

例：Anybody who does not save money for their retirement will have to accept a lower standard of living in later years.

错误：anybody 是单数，而后面的代词是 their。

改正：Anybody who does not save money for his/her retirement will have to accept a lower standard of living in later years.

翻译：任何不能为退休提前存钱的人都要接受晚年比较低的生活标准。

2.2.2 谓语错误

A. 主谓不一致

a. 动名词和不定式作主语时，谓语动词一定是单数形式。

例 1：Raising standards of literacy are the government's priority.

错误：句子的主语是 raising standards，而不是 standards。

改正：Raising standards of literacy is the government's priority.

翻译：提高文化素质是政府的首要任务。

例 2：To rear a child alone are challenging to any parent.

错误：句子的主语是 to rear a child，所以谓语动词要用单数形式。

改正：To rear a child alone is challenging to any parent.

翻译：独立抚养一个小孩对于任何父母亲都是有挑战性的。

b. 不可数名词作主语时，谓语动词一定是单数形式；如果主语是 "...of..." 的词组，谓语的

数需要和 "of" 之前的名词保持一致。

例：The adequacy of financial resources are crucial to the operation of a not-for-profit organisation.

错误：adequacy 是不可数名词，谓语动词不应该用 are。

改正：The adequacy of financial resources is crucial to the operation of a not-for-profit organisation.

翻译：资金的充足对于非营利机构的运作是至关重要的。

c. 当主语后跟 with, together with, coupled with, combined with, as well as, like 时，谓语动词的数跟随主语变化。

例：Overworking, combined with a poor diet, lead to physical degeneration.

错误：主语是 overworking, 不可数名词。

改正：Overworking, combined with a poor diet, leads to physical degeneration.

翻译：工作过度，连同不良的饮食，会导致体质下降。

d. 一些代词 (anybody, anything, everybody, everything, nobody, nothing, somebody, something, each, every, none) 后面的谓语动词一定是单数形式。

例：Even if somebody fall sick, everything go on as usual.

错误：somebody 和 everything 后的动词都应该用单数形式。

改正：Even if somebody falls sick, everything goes on as usual.

翻译：即便有人病了，一切还是照常进行。

e. there be 句型中谓语动词的数跟随其后面的名词变化。

例：There is a number of countries which perform poorly in containing pollution.

错误：主语是 countries，谓语动词应该用复数形式。

改正：There are a number of countries which perform poorly in containing pollution.

翻译：有不少国家在控制污染上表现很差。

f. 由 what, whether, how, that, where 引导的主语从句中，谓语动词常用单数形式。

例：How we cope with massive technological change in the 21st century are an interesting issue.

错误：how 引导的主语从句后的谓语动词用单数形式。

改正：How we cope with massive technological change in the 21st century is an interesting issue.

翻译：我们如何处理 21 世纪的大规模技术变化是一个有趣的问题。

B. 情态动词的使用错误

a. 使用情态动词 (can, could, must, need, may, might 等) 时，需要注意它们意义上的区别。

情态动词	一般意义	表示推测的意义
can/could	有能力 (或者有可能) 去做某事	可能会

should/ought to	一定要去做某事	必定会去做
must	必须要去做某事	必定会去做
will/would	有意愿去做某事	以后会去做
may/might	可以做某事	可能做的事情

例：Children's confidence should be shaken if they are not given adequate support.

错误："小孩的信心"不是"一定"被动摇。

改正：Children's confidence can be shaken if they are not given adequate support.

翻译：小孩的信心可能被动摇，如果他们没有被给予足够的支持。

b. 情态动词后面只加动词原形。

例 1：This trend can persisted for years.

错误：情态动词后面一般只加动词原形。

改正：This trend can persist for years.

翻译：这个潮流能持续很久。

例 2：Clothes for travel should was lightweight and practical.

错误：was 的原形应该是 be。

改正：Clothes for travel should be lightweight and practical.

翻译：旅游用的衣服应该轻便和实用。

c. 如果情态动词后是被动语态，动词应该是 be done 的形式。

例：Environmental problems should be solve as soon as possible.

错误：被动语态应该是 should be solved。

改正：Environmental problems should be solved as soon as possible.

翻译：环境问题应该尽快解决。

C. 助动词的使用错误

a. 助动词使用时需要符合下表的搭配。不难发现，当 **be, been, being** 出现时，后接的动词不是原形，而是动词的现在分词或者过去分词形式。

	一般时态	进行时态	完成时态	完成进行时态
现在	speak/speaks	am/are/is speaking	has/have spoken	has/have been speaking
过去	spoke	was/were speaking	had spoken	had been speaking
将来	shall/will speak	shall/will be speaking	shall/will have spoken	shall/will have been speaking
过去将来	should/would speak	should/would be speaking	should/would have spoken	should/would have been writing

例1：A country should be balance the budget each year.

错误：be 动词后不可以加 balance 的动词原形。

改正：A country should balance the budget each year.

翻译：一个国家每一年都必须平衡开支。

例2：Teachers are always play an important role in formal education.

错误：be 动词后不可以加 play 的动词原形。

改正：Teachers always play an important role in formal education.

翻译：老师总是要在正式教育中扮演一个重要的角色。

b. 初学者需要不断参考前面的表格，确保谓语动词完整。

例：One of the many benefits of travelling overseas learning how to cope with the unexpected.

错误：这句话并没有谓语动词，learning 是现在分词，不能构成完整的谓语动词。

改正：One of the many benefits of travelling overseas is learning how to cope with the unexpected.

翻译：去外国旅行的众多好处中的一个，是学习如何处理突发事件。

c. 下面是几种常用时态的区别。在雅思大作文中，很少出现过去时，主要是现在时和将来时。

时态	说话时动作的情况	例句
现在进行时	动作正在进行，还没结束（暂时的情况），说话的时候动作正在进行	The builders are building a house.
一般现在时	重复的动作，或者所有时候的动作（永久的情况）	Builders build houses every day.
现在完成时	过去某个时间到现在所发生的动作（强调动作的结果）	She has read this book.
现在完成进行时	强调一个过去到说话的时候还在持续的动作	She has been reading this book.
一般过去时	强调过去发生的动作或行为；过去的动作和现在没联系；说话的时候动作已经结束，现在不再发生	She was a teacher ten years ago.（现在应该不是老师了）

例：This incident reflected the decline of team sports in today's universities.

错误：如果是一般过去时，就意味着和现在已经没有联系和影响。

改正：This incident has reflected the decline of team sports in today's universities.

翻译：这个事件反映了在当今大学里团体体育运动的衰落。

d. 很多充当时间状语的副词或者短语提示句子的时态。

例：During the last decade, there was much discussion and controversy over the impact of global economic integration.

错误：时间状语是 during the last decade，提示句子需要用现在完成时。

改正：During the last decade, there has been much discussion and controversy over the impact of global economic integration.

翻译：在过去十年里，有很多讨论和争论是关于国际经济一体化的影响。

e. has/have 有可能是助动词，用于完成时；也可能是实义动词，表示"有"。

例：Obesity has a problem to many Americans for decades.

错误：has 在这里是"有"的意思，"肥胖有问题"，明显不恰当。

改正：Obesity has been a problem to many Americans for decades.

翻译：几十年来，肥胖对于很多美国人来说，都是一个问题。

2.2.3 词性的错误

A. 主语一般由名词或者具备名词性质的短语、词语或者从句充当，而动词不可以充当主语

例：Give children a comfortable home environment is parents' duty.

错误：give 是一个动词，不能充当句子的主语。

改正：Parents' duty is to give children a comfortable home environment.

翻译：父母的责任是给孩子一个舒适的家庭环境。

B. 宾语一般由名词或者具备名词性质的短语、词语或者从句充当，而动词不可以充当宾语

一些动词，如 continue, start, pretend, intend, attempt, decide, learn，后面经常加动词不定式作为宾语。

例：Many rural residents have decided move to cities.

错误：move 是动词，不能充当 decide 的宾语。

改正：Many rural residents have decided to move to cities.

翻译：很多农村的居民已经决定搬到城市。

C. 不及物动词和系动词没有被动语态

不及物动词后不能直接加任何名词或者名词性质的成分作宾语；如果要加宾语，则要加介词；不及物动词没有被动语态，如 happen, appear, disappear, rise, emerge, occur, take place 等词都没有被动语态。

例 1：The accident was similar to the one that was happened last year.

错误：happen 是不及物动词，没有被动语态。

改正：The accident was similar to the one that happened last year.

翻译：这个事故和去年发生的那个类似。

例 2：I disagree many points made by the supporters of globalisation.

错误：disagree 是不及物动词，不能直接加宾语 points。

改正：I disagree with many points made by the supporters of globalisation.

翻译：我不同意全球化支持者所提出的很多观点。

D. 有一些动词词组如 consist of, belong to, take place, benefit from 也没有被动语态

例：The curriculum is consisted of core courses and optional courses.

错误：consist of 没有被动语态。

改正：The curriculum consists of core courses and optional courses.

翻译：教学大纲由主课和选修课组成。

E. 准系动词如 seem, remain, prove, appear, look, smell, taste 等一般不用被动语态

例 1：Most children are seemed to be better at remembering bad habits, instead of good ones.

错误：seem 是系动词，没有被动语态。

改正：Most children seem to be better at remembering bad habits, instead of good ones.

翻译：大部分孩子看来都比较容易记得坏习惯，而不是好习惯。

例 2：Teamwork has been proven effective in improving students' performance.

错误：prove 是系动词，没有被动语态。

改正：Teamwork has proven effective in improving students' performance.

翻译：团队工作在提高学生表现方面已经被证明是有效的。

F. 及物动词的使用错误

a. 及物动词后一定要加名词或者名词性质的成分作宾语，构成主语 + 谓语动词 + 宾语的基本句型；否则就是错误的。

例 1：I will discuss in some detail.

错误：discuss 是及物动词，后面必须有宾语，而 in some detail 只是状语。

改正：I will discuss this topic in some detail.

翻译：我会比较详细地讨论这个话题。

例 2：In many countries, salaries remain unchanged and even reduce.

错误：reduce 是及物动词。

改正：In many countries, salaries remain unchanged and even drop.

翻译：在很多国家，收入一般不变，甚至下跌。

b. 有一些及物动词后面跟宾语和宾语补足语，构成主语 + 谓语动词 + 宾语 + 宾语补足语的基本句型，如 make, see, have, let，这些词后面跟的动词常用不加 to 的动词不定式形式。

例 1：Education can let young people to find jobs easily after they finish their education.

错误：to 是多余的。

改正：Education can let young people find jobs easily after they finish their education.

翻译：教育能够让年轻人在完成学业后很容易找到工作。

例 2：Whether we like it or not, our families shape our lives and make us to be what we are.

错误：to be 是多余的。

改正：Whether we like it or not, our families shape our lives and make us what we are.

翻译：不管我们是否喜欢，我们的家庭决定我们的生活，让我们成为不同的个人。

c. 有一些及物动词后面跟宾语和不定式，构成主语 + 谓语动词 + 宾语 + 宾语补足语的基本句型，如 **enable, encourage, allow, prompt**。

例：Private sponsorship has allowed the academic community survive.

错误：allow somebody to do something 是固定表达，to 不能省略。

改正：Private sponsorship has allowed the academic community to survive.

翻译：私人赞助让学术界可以生存下去。

d. 有一些及物动词同时也是不及物动词，注意在语境中确定其词性。

例：Consumer confidence should improve, as it is crucial to an economic recovery.

错误：消费者信心应该是被提高。

改正：Consumer confidence should be improved, as it is crucial to an economic recovery.

翻译：消费者信心应该被提高，这对经济复苏是至关重要的。

G. 介词的使用错误

a. 介词不是连词，一般后面只接名词或者具备名词性质的短语或者带连词的宾语从句，因此不能加句子。比较容易被当作连词的介词（短语）有 **despite, in spite of, during, because of, due to**，也不能加动词。

例 1：Many smokers are unwilling to cease smoking despite they have knowledge of ill health effects.

错误：despite 不是 although，不是连词。

改正：Many smokers are unwilling to cease smoking despite their knowledge of ill health effects.

翻译：很多抽烟者不愿意停止抽烟，尽管他们知道这有害健康。

例 2：Many children depend on their parents give support.

错误：on 是介词，后面不能加句子。

改正：Many children depend on their parents' support.

翻译：很多小孩依赖他们父母的支持。

b. to 在某些情况下（如词组 **give rise to, contribute to, pay attention to, conform to,**

lead to（中）作介词，需要加名词或者具备名词性质的成分充当宾语，而不是加动词原形充当不定式。

例1：Public disorder can lead to damage a country's economy.

错误：to 是介词，后面不能加动词。

改正：Public disorder can lead to a country's economic crisis.

翻译：社会的无秩序状态可能导致一个国家的经济灾难。

例2：There are many solutions to deal with the problem.

错误：to 是介词，后面不能加动词。

改正：There are many solutions to the problem.

翻译：这个问题有很多解决方法。

c. 有一些词既可以作介词，也可以作连词（跟句子），考生需根据语境进行判断，如 **for, since, after, before, as。**

例：Traditional buildings are desired sometimes, for the simple reason is that they are of commercial and cultural values.

错误：for 在这里是介词，不是连词，后面不能加句子，that they are... 是表语从句。

改正：Traditional buildings are desired sometimes, for the simple reason that they are of commercial and cultural values.

翻译：传统建筑有时候是受人喜爱的，因为一个简单的原因——它们有经济和文化价值。

d. 介词在很多情况下用法是固定的，考生除了熟背之外，好像并无他法，如 **aware of, damage to，preference for。**

例：People have different attitudes for life.

错误：与 attitude 搭配的介词一般是 towards。

改正：People have different attitudes towards life.

翻译：人们对生活有不同的态度。

H. 副词的使用错误

a. 副词或者名词短语充当状语时，前面不能加介词。

例1：Students are more likely to do homework on the computer in today.

错误：today 作状语时是一个副词，前面不能加介词。

改正：Today, students are more likely to do homework on the computer.

翻译：学生如今更有可能在电脑上做作业。

例2：People can travel to and from duty in every day on foot or by bike.

错误：every day 作状语，前面不能加介词。

改正：People can travel to and from duty every day on foot or by bike.

翻译：人们可以每天步行或者骑自行车上下班。

b. 副词几乎可以修饰所有语法成分，但是不能修饰名词或者代词，形容词只可以修饰名词或者代词。

例 1：There are not easy answers to the problems facing this country.

错误：not 是副词，不能修饰名词 answers，应该用具备形容词性质的 no，等于 not any, not one 或者 not a。

改正：There are no easy answers to the problems facing this country.

翻译：这个国家面临的问题没那么容易解决。

例 2：A balanced diet is an integral part of a healthily lifestyle.

错误：healthily 是副词，不能修饰名词。

改正：A balanced diet is an integral part of a healthy lifestyle.

翻译：饮食平衡是健康生活的重要部分。

c. 副词一般很少充当表语，而只有形容词才可以。

例 1：Young drivers are more possibly to have accidents than old drivers.

错误：possibly 是副词，不能作表语。

改正：Young drivers are more likely to have accidents than old drivers.

翻译：年轻的驾驶者比年长的驾车者更容易出车祸。

例 2：Cycling is beneficially to our health.

错误：beneficially 是副词，不能作表语。

改正：Cycling is beneficial to our health.

翻译：骑车对我们的健康是有益的。

d. 副词在 have/has been 这个结构中一般出现在这两个词的中间。

例：The importance of education for one's success has been long recognised in society.

错误：这里 long 是副词。

改正：The importance of education for one's success has long been recognised in society.

翻译：教育对一个人成功的重要性在社会上一直都被大家认同。

2.2.4 句子结构的错误

A. 一个完整的句子不能充当另外一个句子的主语

在这种情况下，需要将其中一个句子改成从句，或者使用形式主语 it。

例 1：Students receive job training is important.

错误：students receive job training 是一个句子，不能充当另外一个句子的主语。

改正：It is important for students to receive job training.

翻译：学生接受工作训练是重要的。

例 2：Students receive job training can become competitive in the labour market.

错误：students receive job training 是一个句子，不能充当另外一个句子的主语。

改正：Students can become competitive in the labour market if they receive job training.

翻译：如果学生接受工作培训的话，他们在劳动力市场上会变得非常有竞争力。

B. 连词的使用错误

a. 一般来说，两个连词不能同时用在一个句子当中，典型的例子包括 because 和 so，although 和 but。

例：Although the crime rate is falling in many parts of the world, but violent crimes are constantly rampant.

错误：although 和 but 不能连用。

改正：Although the crime rate is falling in many parts of the world, violent crimes are constantly rampant.

翻译：虽然在世界上很多地方犯罪率在下降，暴力犯罪仍然是非常猖獗的。

b. 标点符号中，分号 semi-colon (;) 类似于连词，而逗号 comma (,) 不具备连词的功能。

例：Education has been made available to more people nowadays, however, many adults have some problems with literacy and numeracy.

错误：however 是副词，不是连词，前后都是完整的句子，因此不能用逗号连接。

改正：Education has been made available to more people nowadays; however, many adults have some problems with literacy and numeracy.

翻译：如今，更多的人可以获得教育；然而，很多成年人仍然有读写和计算的问题。

c. 有一些副词，如 however, therefore, otherwise, thus, hence，常被误认为是连词，实际上这些词是不可以连接句子的。试看下面四个准确的句子。

句 1：He studied hard; therefore, he passed the test. (分号等于句号)

句 2：He studied hard. Therefore, he passed the test. (句号连接句子)

句 3：He studied hard, so he passed the test. (so 是连词)

句 4：He studied hard, and therefore, he passed the test. (and 是连词)

例：People like to think that being on a diet is healthy, however, there is considerable evidence to the contrary.

错误：however 是副词，不能连接两个句子。

改正：People like to think that being on a diet is healthy; however, there is considerable evidence to the contrary.

翻译： 人们总是喜欢认为节食是健康的；然而，有大量的证据证明这是错误的。

d. 多于一个的名词、动词、形容词等出现的时候，需要使用并列连词 and, but 或者 or。

例 1：Smoking, drinking are banned in many places of work.

错误： smoking 和 drinking 都是主语，要用连词。

改正： Smoking and drinking are banned in many places of work.

翻译： 抽烟和喝酒在很多工作场所都是被禁止的。

例 2：More people would prefer cycling, walking if conditions were right.

错误： cycling 和 walking 都是宾语，应该用连词。

改正： More people would prefer cycling or walking if conditions were right.

翻译： 如果条件适当的话，更多人会喜欢骑自行车或者走路。

C. 句子残缺

a. 从属连词（because, although 等）一定要连接两个句子。状语从句一般是由从属连词（because, although, since, as 等）引导的。

例 1：Because it is not serious. Many countries do not take any real countermeasure.

错误： because 引导的是一个从句，缺一个主句。

改正： Because it is not serious, many countries do not take any real countermeasure.

翻译： 因为这不是很严重，很多国家没有采取任何实质性的对策。

例 2：Some countries are not able to solve environmental problems. Although these countries have realised these problems' devastating effect.

错误： although 引导的是一个从句，缺一个主句。

改正： Some countries are not able to solve environmental problems, although these countries have realised these problems' devastating effect.

翻译： 有一些国家不能解决环境问题，尽管这些国家意识到这些问题的影响。

b. 完整的句子一定要有谓语。

例：Tourism has instead of agriculture as the main industry in many places.

错误： instead of 是介词词组，不能充当谓语动词。

改正： Tourism has replaced agriculture as the main industry in many places.

翻译： 旅游业在很多地方已经代替农业成为支柱产业。

c. 完整的句子一定要有主语。

例：In China has more than 100 million subscribers to cable television.

错误： in China 是介宾短语，不能充当主语。

改正：China has more than 100 million subscribers to cable television.

翻译：中国有超过一亿的有线电视观众。

D. 名词性从句的使用错误

a. whether 和 that 不能同时使用。

例：The question remains whether that it was a serious love affair or a passing fancy.

错误：whether 和 that 不能同时使用。

改正：The question remains whether it was a serious love affair or a passing fancy.

翻译：这究竟是严肃的感情，还是一时的好感，这个问题仍然存在。

b. 名词性从句可以用 how, what, why, when, where 等词引导，但不能与 that 同时使用。

例：Many people do not realise that how serious environmental problems can be.

错误：that 和 how 不能同时使用。

改正：Many people do not realise how serious environmental problems can be.

翻译：很多人意识不到环境问题可以多么的严重。

c. that 引导名词性从句时，从句一定是完整的句子，这和定语从句有显著的不同。

例：It is widely believed that people improving efficiency by using computers.

错误：improving 不是完整的谓语动词。

改正：It is widely believed that people can improve efficiency by using computers.

翻译：被广泛认可的事情是人们可以通过使用电脑提高效率。

d. 和状语从句、定语从句类似，名词性从句出现时，必须要有主句，否则句子不完整。

例：The fact that education is the key to a country's long-term success.

错误：the fact 引导同位语从句，但没有主句。

改正：Government funding is supported by the fact that education is the key to a country's long-term success.

翻译：政府的资助基于一个事实：教育是国家长期成功的关键。

第 3 章

雅思大作文（Task 2）攻略

3.1 雅思大作文的评分标准

学习雅思大作文，我们先要分析一下其评分标准。如果大家不知道剑桥雅思考试委员会的官方要求是什么，只顾自己一味地埋头按照国内英文考试的思维和套路写，就不太可能获得好成绩。

雅思大作文（Task 2）的评分标准有四项，分别是：

标准 *1*： Task Response（写作任务回应）

标准 *2*： Coherence and Cohesion（连贯与衔接）

标准 *3*： Lexical Resources（词汇丰富程度）

标准 *4*： Grammatical Range and Accuracy（语法多样性及准确性）

为了方便上课讲解，我一般都将四个评分标准缩写成 TR，CC，LR，GRA。大家要牢记这四个缩写词，我在这本书很多文章的点评中会不断使用。

剑桥雅思的官网上有不同分数作文的一些特点，我在这里节选了 6 分和 7 分作文描述的中英文对照，因为这两个分数段是大部分考生的目标分数段。

7 分作文的特点（中英对应）

Task Response (TR)	写作任务回应
● addresses all parts of the task	● 回应各部分写作任务
● presents a clear position throughout the response	● 回应写作任务过程中始终呈现一个清晰的观点
● presents, extends and supports main ideas, but there may be a tendency to overgeneralise and/ or supporting ideas may lack focus	● 呈现、发展主要论点并就其进行论证，但有时出现过于一概而论的倾向及 / 或论点缺乏重点的倾向
Coherence and Cohesion (CC)	连贯与衔接
● logically organises information and ideas; there is clear progression throughout	● 有逻辑地组织信息及论点；清晰的行文推进发展贯穿全文
● uses a range of cohesive devices appropriately although there may be some under-/over-use	● 恰当地使用一系列衔接手段，尽管有时使用不足或过多
● presents a clear central topic within each paragraph	● 每个段落均有一个清晰的中心主题

Lexical Resources (LR)	词汇丰富程度
• uses a sufficient range of vocabulary to allow some flexibility and precision • uses less common lexical items with some awareness of style and collocation • may produce occasional errors in word choice, spelling and/or word formation	• 使用足够的词汇，体现一定灵活性及准确性 • 使用不常见词汇，对语体及搭配有一定认识 • 在选择用词、拼写及／或构词方面可能偶尔出现错误
Grammatic Range and Accuracy (GRA)	**语法多样性及准确性**
• uses a variety of complex structures • produces frequent error-free sentences • has good control of grammar and punctuation but may make a few errors	• 运用各种复杂的语法结构 • 多数句子准确无误 • 对语法及标点符号掌握较好，但有时出现少许错误

6 分作文的特点（中英对应）

Task Response (TR)	写作任务回应
• addresses all parts of the task although some parts may be more fully covered than others • presents a relevant position although the conclusions may become unclear or repetitive • presents relevant main ideas but some may be inadequately developed/unclear	• 回应各部分写作任务，但某些部分的论证可能比其他部分更为充分 • 提出一个切题的观点，尽管各种结论有时不甚清晰或重复 • 提出多个相关的主要论点，但某些论点可能未能充分展开进行论证或不甚清晰
Coherence and Cohesion (CC)	**连贯与衔接**
• arranges information and ideas coherently and there is a clear overall progression • uses cohesive devices effectively, but cohesion within and/or between sentences may be faulty or mechanical • may not always use referencing clearly or appropriately • uses paragraphing, but not always logically	• 连贯地组织信息及论点，总体来说，能清晰地推进行文发展 • 有效地使用衔接手段，但句内及／或句间的衔接有时有误或过于刻板，不够灵活 • 有时无法保持一贯清晰或恰当地使用指代 • 使用段落写作，但未能保持段落间的逻辑
Lexical Resources (LR)	**词汇丰富程度**
• uses an adequate range of vocabulary for the task • attempts to use less common vocabulary but with some inaccuracy • makes some errors in spelling and/or word formation, but they do not impede communication	• 使用足够的词汇开展写作任务 • 试图使用不常用词汇，但有时使用不准确 • 在拼写及／或构词方面有错误，但不影响交流

Grammatic Range and Accuracy (GRA)	语法多样性及准确性
● uses a mix of simple and complex sentence forms ● makes some errors in grammar and punctuation but they rarely reduce communication	● 综合使用简单句式与复杂句式 ● 在语法及标点符号方面有一些错误，但这些错误很少影响交流

我们会在后面的范文里分别细致地解释这些评分标准，并且告诉大家具体应该怎么做，才可能获得比较好的成绩。

除了上面这些官方公布的评分标准之外，考生进入考场后，在你们的答题纸上会看到一些考官考虑的额外因素，这些因素的意义大致如下：

- Off-topic（偏题）：考生答卷和题目要求不符合。
- Underlength（字数不够）：Task 1 至少 150 字，Task 2 至少 250 字。
- No. of words（字数）：基本同上。
- Memorised（背诵）：考生需要用自己的语言和思路答题，而不是生搬硬套。这一点主要针对很多热衷套句的中国考生。
- Penalty（罚分）：主要是针对那些在考场违规，然后被记录的考生。
- Illegible（字迹潦草）：主要是惩罚那些不注意书写的考生。

从这几个评分点来看，考生切记不要死记硬背，这样很容易跑题，被考官认为是背诵。

3.2 《剑 10》考官范文的分析

我们下面通过分析《剑 10》中考官写的一篇范文 (9 分)，深入了解一下雅思作文的四个评分标准。初次备考雅思的同学，也可以通过这篇范文大致了解雅思大作文题目的模式和大概要写成什么样子。

注：因为《剑 11》和《剑 12》没有提供考官范文，因此我没有分析。

因为《版权法》的约束，下面的范文不能够全部显示，请大家去对照《剑 10》的范文原文。

题目

It is important for children to learn the difference between right and wrong at an early age. Punishment is necessary to help them learn this distinction. To what extent do you agree or disagree with this opinion?

What sort of punishment should parents and teachers be allowed to use to teach good behaviour to children?

题目大意

孩子从小知道对错是重要的。要让他们知道这一点，惩罚他们是必要的。在多大程度上你赞同或反对这个观点？

考官范文

旁边的标注是体现范文符合不同评分标准的一些具体的例子。

> LR：这个词是"良心、道德观"的意思，属于展示词汇量的表达。

> CC：使用限定词 this，增加两个句子间的联系。

> TR：扣题，因为这个题目讨论的是惩罚是否能够帮助年轻人分辨对错。

...child's growth is c... ...pment of a conscience, which is linked to the ... ...from wrong. This skill comes with time and good parenting ... ...at punishment does not have much of a role to play in t... ...sagree almost entirely with the given statement.

> TR：使用代词指代前面的 infant。

> GRA：比较句和定语从句构成复杂句，展示运用复杂语法的能力。

> CC：使用 however 这个连接词代表不同教育方法的对比。

To so... ...the question depends on the age... ...ish a very yo... ...wrong and foolish, as an ... what is happening or why he or she is being punis... reason is reached, however, a ... for good behaviour and discouraged from bad. This kind ... ...hieve more than harsh punishments, which might entail many negative consequences unintended by the par...

> LR：sanction 替换前面的 punishment，体现了用词的变化。"好的榜样"，整段话的目的很清晰。

> CC：使用代词指代前面的 physical punishment。

> TR：段落第一句话明确说清楚这段话的观点是"父母可以树立好的榜样"，整段话的目的很清晰。

> GRA：这是一个名词同位语，引导一个定语从句。

...fference between right and wrong, teachers ... ...provide good role modeling in their own behaviour. After that, if sanctions are needed, the punishment sho... ...that merely sends the message tha... ...smaller ones—an outcome which may ... starting to bully others ... ...hment be in any ...

> CC：连接词，突出本段和上段话的 punishment 进行转折。

> LR：这是"留堂"的意思，这种词汇体现了用词能力。

> TR：这里使用很多例子，让观点的论述更加具体。

> CC：连接词，增加句子的紧凑性。

> GRA：比较句和定语从句构成复杂句，展示运用复杂语法的能力。

Rather, teachers a... ...a variety of methods to discipline ... such as detention ... ...ges, and time-out. ...nt fit the crime is ... ...ould see children being made to pick up rubbish they have dropped, clean up graffiti they have drawn, or apo... ...hey have hurt. In these ways responsibility is developed in ... ...s to ... ...ture behaviour than does punishment.

范文大意

孩子成长中最重要的一个阶段是道德观的形成，这和分辨对错的能力有关系。这个技能随着年龄而增长，也和父母的教育有关。我坚定地认为惩罚对这个没有什么作用。因此，我差不多完全不同意这个看法。

在某种程度上，惩罚取决于孩子的年龄。惩罚一个年幼的孩子是错误和愚蠢的，因为一个婴儿不知道发生什么事情，也不知道为什么自己被惩罚。一旦到了明白事理的年龄，孩子因为好的行为而得到奖励，从而不去做坏事。这种慈爱的但是非常坚定的做法效果比严厉的惩罚要管用，而惩罚会有很多意想不到的后果。

为了帮助一个小孩知道对错，老师和父母首先要提供好的榜样。然后，如果需要惩罚，不应该是体罚，因为这会传递一个信息，那就是大人可以打小孩，结果就是小孩开始欺负别人。惩罚不应该是残忍的。

反之，父母和老师应该使用不同的方法去管束年轻人，比如留堂，取消一些福利，不让他们出去玩。按照犯的错误去惩罚是一个很好的概念，让孩子去捡起他们扔的垃圾，清理自己乱涂乱画的东西，向自己伤害过的人道歉。这样，他们就有责任感，以后塑造的行为会比惩罚所形成的行为要好。

3.3 《剑 12》范文 (5.5 分和 7.5 分范文对比)

很多考生经常问 5.5 和 6 分的作文有什么区别，高分作文长什么样。下面我给出一篇考生文章(题目来自《剑 12》)，大家可以对比一下。最后是我写的 7.5～8 分范文。

题目

> *Some people believe that it is good to share as much information as possible in scientific research, business and the academic world. others believe that some information is too important or too valuable to be shared freely. Discuss both these views and give your own opinion.*

我先让一些考生写了关于这个题目的观点。很多考生的观点要么跑题，要么不够有逻辑。观点不好，会影响 Task Response 的分数。

考生的观点	错误的原因
收费信息，研究人员得到回报，培养科研兴趣。	跑题。这个题目讨论的是要不要给信息，而不是是否要收费。
不分享信息，公司、国家保持自己的优势，促进社会进步。	逻辑不好。保持优势可以理解，为什么因此就促进社会进步？
不免费分享信息，不会失去个人财富，创造信息价值，带动行业发展。	逻辑不好。为什么不免费分享信息就不会失去财富？为什么不分享反而会带动行业发展？
信息根据目的分类，保持安全共同进步。	跑题。这个题目不关心如何使用信息。
分享重要信息，重要信息泄露，危害国家安全。	太具体。这只是一个例子，而不是观点。

可以接受的观点

分享信息，让大众了解知识，培养人才。

尽可能多地分享信息，了解最新的动态，促进跨学科交流，有利于发展最新的科技。

分享信息，研究成果泄露，打击研究者的动力。

考生的作文

　　The time we are now in is an information era where more information means more possibility to succeed, especially in scientific field. Though it is of great sense to share cutting-edge scientific information, some core technologies deserve being kept secrets for a period to stimulate a better development of science.

　　An open and transparent scientific information environment will be beneficial to the improvement of individual's living conditions. Science in this modern society is a popular field where the more information is shared the more novel ideas can be created, acting as the sources of direction of further scientific researches, the results from which can be applied for the public. For example, the invention of vaccines for some epidemics should be released to the whole world to protect everybody on this planet from contracting the diseases. If only a minority of people can have access to the vaccines, the world would be unimaginably a disaster.

　　Notwithstanding, it is reasonable some scientific information to be classified for protecting the security of the whole society. Usually scientific researches and technologies, those about military in particular, are highly confidential as they matter a lot for the nation as well as the whole world, so they are too dangerous for sharing. If everyone knows how to build a gun, the individual safety can never exist, let along the peaceful life we are now living. The best way to prevent such situation is keep those kinds of information known within a small group of experts, thus the wellbeing of ordinary people will be maintained.

非常啰唆的表达。

没有冠词，表达也不好。

没有这个说法。

没有这个说法。

中式表达。

生活环境？

没有这些表达，分词结构也非常奇怪。

没有 applied for 这个说法。

没有这个表达。

用词错误，这是个介词。

不大清楚这是什么意思。

不能说 researches，因为 research 是不可数名词。

produce weapons 更恰当。

let alone 后面一般不加句子，而且这个表达也不好。

be + do 是错的。

thus 不是连词。

In my view the scientific information should be categorised according to its purpose and then it can be decided as shared or classified. As it talked above, it is not suitable for all the information shared without any restrictions. So if releasing some particular information would cause chaos to the society, the government should not let it happen, and if not, the sharing is fine to be done.

没有这个说法。

状语从句一般不用 would。

没有这个表达。

To sum up, whether the scientific information should be shared or not is decided by its own purpose.

点评

从很多考生的角度来看，这篇文章肯定是不错的文章。首先，字数很多，感觉就很强！

其次，各种从句、倒装句，还有分词，肯定是强强强！

最后，还有不少表达看上去很炫。

然而，这篇文章最后考场的分数只有 5.5 分。

Task Response　6 分	这个考生讨论的是"信息应该被分类"，其实题目不关心这个。
Cohesion and Coherence　6 分	句子连接不错。
Lexical Resources　5 分	很多表达都是中式表达。
Grammatical Range and Accuracy　6 分	定语从句存在很多问题，as it talked above 是什么东西？
总分 5.5 分	

我写的作文

考官评分 7.5~8 分，TR 8 分，CC 8 分，LR 7~8 分，GRA 8 分。

Globalisation, along with the extensive use of digital technology, has facilitated information sharing among academics and businesspeople, regardless of nationality and race. I agree that the easy access to valuable information can foster innovation and address some global problems, despite the risk that some information can be misused.

We can find solutions to problems easily if we have unlimited access to different databases, such as those which contain information about how to cure diseases, prevent famines and mitigate pollution. This kind of knowledge is not available for people living in some poorest sections of the world, and this is why they are still afflicted by some preventable diseases and problems that can otherwise be avoided.

Some people are reluctant to share their know-how because they are afraid that their knowledge and intellectual properties can be exploited. This is particularly understandable in the business world, where companies are not willing to provide information about their managerial skills, software and patented products on the Internet. Their competitiveness would be undermined if their global competitors could acquire such information.

I would, however, view this issue in a positive light. While it is up to business owners to decide what information is withheld, they should exchange their ideas with their peers in the same industry. It can create an atmosphere worldwide, in which designers, inventors and engineers can mine each other's information with permissions and come up with creative solutions, without having to advance their research alone through trial and error.

In conclusion, it may not be practical to require all people to give up the ownership of their essential knowledge, but they should accept that sharing in a globalised world is better than concealing information.

3.4 国内英文考试和雅思考试的区别

雅思作文是一项关注考生交流能力的考试。

这几年，我通过网络教学接触了大量的国内考生，很多考生觉得很奇怪，自己以前在国内的语言考试，如专业八级和研究生考试中都没什么阻力，也获得了很好的成绩，而雅思作文总是考 5.5 分。也有很多写作能力比较弱的考生很奇怪，自己以前考大学英语四、六级时都是考前看看背背，最后就都过了，雅思作文却怎么考也考不过。

这主要是因为雅思作文的考官是英文母语者，他们非常精细，很多以前考生在国内考试中犯的错误，可能在国内的中国考官眼里没什么，但是在外国人眼里却是比较明显的、不可饶恕的。

我经常和考生说，你虽然通过了国内的考试，写作可能还是很烂，也不自信。但是如果你写作能力不提高，依然很烂，你就过不了雅思。简单地说，雅思作文成绩和你的写作能力直接挂钩。能力有多高，分数就多高。你不提高写作能力，不管花多少钱上课，考试都过不了。而有些写作能力比较强的学生，甚至可能从来没有接受过培训，在考场上按照自己的感觉写也能考过。

我再一次按照雅思大作文的评分标准，对比一下国内考试和雅思考试作文要求的不同。

评分标准	国内英文考试	雅思考试
Task Response (TR) 写作任务回应	论述有时候偏题没什么大碍，关键是字数写够。 因此，很多考生依赖背诵好的一些句子和段落，甚至文章，在考场上写上去，虽然和题目关系不大，但是也能够过关。	考官基本上是明察秋毫。不管考生写的句子如何漂亮和复杂，如果内容和题目关系不大，前后逻辑关系比较牵强，考官就会认为考生可能是背诵（memorised answer）的，会出现惩罚性扣分。

	很多考生不注意拓展观点，经常是一句话换不同的表达重复说明，目的是凑够字数。	语句重复考官很容易看出来，他们会认为考生缺乏讨论观点的能力，会给很差的分数。
Coherence and Cohesion (CC) 连贯与衔接	很多考生写作存在句子论述跳跃的问题，句子之间没有什么逻辑关系，而国内的考试对于论述的连贯性没太大关注。	考官关注连贯性。特别是需要拿 7 分的考生，不要妄想东说一句西说一句就可以考过。
	国内考试很注意连接词 firstly, secondly, what's more, furthermore 等的使用，还有这些词的替换词，哪怕是这些词使用得非常机械；不用反而扣分。	雅思作文对连接词的使用比较挑剔，滥用连接词和连接词使用错误都会导致丢分，特别是目标 7 分的考生，使用连接词一定要注意准确。除了连接词之外，雅思作文还考查代词在句子联系中的应用。
Lexical Resources (LR) 词汇丰富程度	国内考试认可考生追求词汇的变化，而不是恰当和准确，很多考生认为长的单词还有自己不熟悉的单词是最容易获得高分的。	雅思强调用词的恰当和准确。讲究单词的搭配，也就是词伙 (collocations)。如 acquire education 在国内考试中可能是加分的，但是在雅思中就会被扣分，因为这个搭配不对。
Grammatical Range and Accuracy (GRA) 语法多样性及准确性	国内考试鼓励考生使用定语从句、倒装句、虚拟语气、强调句、分词等，哪怕是写错，只要写了，分数都比不写好。	雅思考试不需要你写很复杂的句子，特别是目标只有 6~6.5 分的考生，如果从句和分词写错了，你就会被扣分。
	国内考试主要是看考生什么地方比较出彩，是否用了复杂的语法，而这些出彩的地方能够抵消小错误的扣分。	雅思考试中如果存在基本的句子结构和语法错误 (如句子缺乏谓语等)，你就很难拿 6 分。因为考官觉得你缺乏基本的语言表达能力。

因此，在我们一个个成功提分考生的背后，并非是因为他们写出了多么惊艳的作文，而是因为完成了准确和朴实的文章。

关于作文学习，我的建议是：

- 首先增加语法知识，减少语法错误，提高写句子的能力，包括简单句和从句的结构。
- 其次注意用词的积累，主要是词伙 (collocations) 的积累。
- 最后全面学习整篇文章的写作 (包括从审题到扣题和想观点、论述观点等)。

基础不好的考生 (事实上，90% 的考生基础都不是很好)，首先要做一下第 2 章 2.1 的的句子翻译练习，搞清楚句子结构，然后看一下语法常见的错误。

有了这些基础后，大家可以开始做全文翻译练习。每篇文章有 13~17 句中文，你可以逐句翻译，然后对照后面的英文答案。

在这个翻译的过程中，记得不要都闷自己写的英文和我的答案有所不同。因为我写的句子不是逐字翻译，而是使用比较地道的说法，去表达句子的主要意思。

关于每个句子的翻译，我选了一个考生的错误句子进行点评和纠错，大家也要看这个部分，这样可以提高自己的改错能力。

然后可以看整篇范文，还有点评，这样大家对文章有个整体的认识。最后有一个提升的范文，这些范文很长，很多时候超过 300 字。大家不要以为一定要写那么长才可以获得高分。我只是尽量拓展，帮助大家提高论述的能力，因为大部分中国考生的问题是没话可说，或者是重复，不知道如何有效地论述自己的观点。

在阅读范文的过程中，大家可以遵循 TELCCS 标准来分析范文。TELCCS 是我创造的一个单词。这个单词可以帮助大家更好地记忆和熟悉雅思大作文的评分标准。如果考生牢记这个单词，在写作中不断思考这些标准，满足这些条件，就可以获得更高的分数。

TELCCS 是六个单词的首字母缩写，分别是：

Task-oriented：每句话要注意扣题，尽量出现题目的关键词。

Extension：句子要懂得拓展，在简单的想法上增加信息，使句子变得丰富。

Linking devices：句子连接要紧密，连接方法灵活有变化，前后句子要保持很好的逻辑关系。

Consistency：每个句子要和中心句保持一致，和前面一句话论述保持逻辑一致。

Collocations：用词要尽量使用词伙，尊重单词的搭配习惯。

Syntax：句子结构要准确，变化要合理恰当。

3.5 本书 Task 2 关键学习点总结

因为雅思写作非常细致，所以我在每篇文章的后面，都有一个雅思作文关键点的讲解。大家要仔细阅读，增加对雅思作文的理解，清楚怎么在细节的地方满足雅思作文的要求。下面是所有关键学习点的汇总，方便大家查阅和复习。

论述类题目写作要点	A. 论述类题目主体部分头两段一定要说持有不同看法的人为什么是对的，不能质疑他们。 B. 论述类题目的中心句会经常出现一些字眼，如 some people argue that, it is sometimes argued that 等。 C. 论述类题目的中心句不需要写得很肯定。 D. 论述类题目讨论你自己看法的主体段（也就是主体部分的第三段）可以作为结尾段。
观点类题目（优缺点题目）写作要点	A. 你可以写一件事情全是好处，或者全是坏处；也可以说一件事情有好也有坏。 B. 写折中段的时候，用词可以变得含糊，这样不会转折太强烈。 C. 题目是讨论 effect 时，要注意题目的限定对象（如 individuals, family, society 等）。

观点类 (agree or disagree 题型) 写作要点	A. 有时候会限定某个动作的结果，很多考生容易写跑题。 B. 可以完全支持或者反对，也可以部分支持或者反对。 C. 尽量避免出现 some people think/argue/believe/hold the view that 这些表达。 D. 注意审题时和优缺点题目 (advantages/disadvantages, positive/negative effects) 的区别。 E. 题目出现 best, only 这种字眼也可以折中。
报告类题目写作要点	A. 主体部分可以分 2～3 段写。 B. 报告类文章的解决方法一般都是对应问题的原因，但是如果不对应，也可以接受。 C. 报告类文章的开头和主体段落一般不会出现 some people think that/argue that 这样的字眼。
混合类题目写作要点	A. 两个问题同等重要，都要回答。 B. 每个问题可以用 1～2 个观点回答，如果有 2 个观点可以分段，也可以写在一段。
开头段注意事项	A. 开头段不要写得很长，因为主体部分才是考官重点阅读的部分。 B. 开头段如果写得好，对你分数不会有大的影响; 但是如果写得不好，就会有很大的负面影响。所以开头段千万别犯语法错误。 C. 不要抄题，这样考官会把照抄的部分去掉，不算字数。 D. 不要使用大家用烂的一些表达 (如 there is a trend that... with the development of...)。 E. 改写题目的话不要改变题目的论述重心。
审题的要素	A. 题目里是否出现了一个行为 (action)，政策 (policy)，趋势 (trend)。 B. 题目里是否针对某个特定的结果 (outcome/consequence)。 C. 题目最关注的群体是什么 (最受影响的是谁)。 D. 题目的类型是什么。(报告? 论述? 观点? 混合?)
扣题的要素	A. 开头段表明立场的时候可以扣题。 B. 每个主体段落的中心句要出现题目的关键词，对应题目。 C. 举例的时候，尽量要和题目的问题对应。 D. 每个主体段落的结尾，如果题目出现两个对比的对象，可以用"对比"的方式扣题。 E. 不断出现关键词，特别是最后一句。 F. 结尾段扣题。

中心句的写作要素	A. 中心句一定要和段落的内容一致。
	B. 中心句要有连接词。
	C. 中心句要出现关键词或者关键词的替换表达。
	D. 中心句要对应题目。
举例的常见问题	A. 没头没尾的例子。
	B. 不相关的例子。
	C. 不符合题目论述对象的例子。
	D. 和前面观点或中心句不一致的例子。
	E. 虚假例子。
	F. 中国的例子。
对比的方法	A. 题目出现两个对立的事物，可以用 in contrast, by comparison 对比。
	B. 一件事情如果不发生，会产生什么情形和结果，可以用 otherwise 引导。
	C. 虚拟语气，尝试一个相反情况发生会出现的情况。
结尾的写作要素	A. 结尾段不要很长，1～2 句话即可，主要是总结立场。
	B. 如果愿意总结观点也可以，但是要注意不要用重复的表达。
	C. 不要出现新的信息，不要升华。
选择观点的要素	A. 观点要避免重复。
	B. 观点要具体，不只是表明立场。
	C. 观点不要太空泛。
	D. 观点要针对题目的第一关注人群。
	E. 观点不是例子。
前后一致的要素	A. 立场的前后一致。
	B. 每段话论述的内容一致。
如何避免重复和跳跃	A. 多想原因，多培养批判性的思维。
	B. 多思考结果，多思考某个东西对我们的影响。
段落连接的方法	A. 连接词。
	B. 状语从句。
	C. 一些名词性从句。
	D. 一些含有 this, these 的词组。
	E. 代词 they, this, their 等。
	F. 含有 another 的表达。
	G. 上下文两个句子本身的逻辑关系。
	H. 一些关键表达的重复。

代词使用的常见错误和注意事项	A. 连接词和代词重合使用。 B. 使用 you。 C. 在同一句话里重复使用可数名词复数，如 people，students，不会使用代词 they；或者重复使用不可数名词，但是不会使用代词 it。 D. 代词不一致，people 不能和 we, our 连用，单数名词不能和 they 一起用。 E. 前面有两个表示人的名词复数出现，还使用 they，导致指代不清。 F. 前面是不可数名词，但是后面用 they, them, us 这些表示复数的代词。 G. these, those 不能和不可数名词连用。 H. this, another 后面只能加可数名词单数，而不是加不可数名词或者名词复数。
中国考生用词的常见问题	A. 中文生硬地翻译为英文。 B. 使用长单词，不尊重词伙。
如何替换表达	A. 使用替换词或者词组。 B. 使用名词加形容词或者名词作修饰语。 C. 使用代词。 D. 使用定语从句。
如何将简单句转化成复杂句	A. 如果两个简单句没有因果关系，基本上是两件独立的事情，往往可以简单地用 and 相连。 B. 如果两个简单句有一定的因果关系，往往可以用状语从句相连。 C. 如果用状语从句怕重复，可以用 and (或者 ;) + 连接词的方式。 D. 如果第一个单句的最后一个单词和第二个单句的第一个单词重复，可以用定语从句连接。 E. 如果第二个单句是第一个单句的结果，有可能使用非限制性定语从句。
状语从句的使用要点	A. 状语从句提醒考生思考原因和结果。 B. 状语从句经常用在观点类和论述类的中心句中，表示条件 (if, when)。 C. 状语从句可以帮助考生避免一些中国式的表达。
并列句的写作要点	A. 要注意事情的先后顺序。 B. 要注意第二个分句的动词和主语是否匹配。 C. 要注意两个分句并列成分的清晰，避免语意不清。

定语从句的使用要点	A. 放在句首替换状语从句。
	B. 替换关键的名词（key words）。
	C. where 引导的定语从句解释地点所发生的事情。
	D. 非限制性定语从句表示结果。
	E. 前面一个单句的最后一个词如果和后面一个单句的第一个名词重复，可以用定语从句连接。
标点符号的使用要点	A. 分号和句号都类似于连词，连接两个独立的句子，而逗号不可以。
	B. 逗号如果连接两个独立的句子，中间要有并列连词 and 或者 or, but 等。
	C. 使用连接副词moreover, consequently, also, even, however 等的时候，只有前面加了分号或者句号，才可以连接独立的句子。
	D. 分号和句号前后一定是独立的句子，因此，如果后面只有一个状语从句，就是错误的。
	E. 逗号决定了限制性定语从句和非限制性定语从句的区别。

3.6 雅思评分标准 1：Task Response（写作任务回应）

雅思大作文的第一个评分标准是关于考生写的作文是否对应题目，是否针对题目进行很好的论述。

很多考生在备考雅思作文的过程中都忽略了这个评分标准，经常导致丢分。

本部分会首先告诉大家怎么审题。雅思大作文（Task 2）的题目通常由两部分组成。以我们之前分析的考官范文的题目为例：

It is important for children to learn the difference between right and wrong at an early age. Punishment is necessary to help them learn this distinction. To what extent do you agree or disagree with this opinion?

首先，会有 1~2 句陈述句，说一下发生的一个趋势，或者是对某个问题的一个描述，或者是一个假定或者观点。

例如这个题目的前两句，首先陈述了一个事实（孩子很小就会分辨对错很重要），然后说了一个假设和观点（要让孩子学会分辨对错，惩罚是必需的）。

其次，会有一个问句，这个问句基本上决定了你整篇文章的结构和写作的重点。

我将雅思大作文按照问句的不同分成了 4 种类型的作文：论述类、观点类、报告类、混合类。下面大家可以通过做全文翻译来了解这些类型的特点和区别。

再次，我会告诉大家其他的审题要素，还有如何扣题。扣题很重要，因此我会通过两篇文章来讲解。

最后，我会讲解一下如何拓展，避免重复。

3.6.1 全文翻译 1：遵守规则＋论述类题目写作要点

> *Some people think that children should obey rules or do what their parents and teachers want them to do. Other people think that children controlled too much cannot deal with problems themselves in adulthood. Discuss both views and state your own opinion.*

题目大意

有些人觉得小孩应该遵守规则，或者做父母和老师想要他们做的事情。另一些人觉得被过分控制的小孩不能够在成年后自己处理和解决问题。讨论这两个观点并阐述你个人的看法。

读者自学步骤 1

阅读题目后，写出三个观点。

下面是我学生写的一些错误或者不好的观点，大家可以看看自己是不是也犯了同样的错误。

学生的观点	点评
小孩要遵守规则，提升他们自己的个人素质，对他们成年后有好处。	太过空泛。个人素质太空泛，要特别说明表示人的行为、礼貌等。
限制太多，思维局限，缺少创新精神，难有创新成果。	跑题。这个题目的第二个立场关心的是处理成年人的问题，而创新成果和这个立场没有关系，属于跑题。
管得太多，没有机会尝试一些自己感兴趣的活动，对生活感到乏味。	跑题。这个题目的第二个立场关心的是处理成年人的问题，而生活有趣还是乏味和这个立场没有关系，属于跑题。
要约束小孩，但要培养其独立思考的能力，使其长大后能独立解决问题，更好地适应社会。	跑题。这个题目不需要提供建议，只需要讨论约束小孩的好处，或者是约束小孩是不是不能发展他们的解决问题的能力。

读者自学步骤 2

翻译下面的句子。在翻译过程中，记住先想词伙，再想句型，然后写出句子。相关词伙可以查阅微信公众号：gu_writing。

介绍段

改写题目	1. 小孩在家里或者是学校一般都要遵守一些规则。
阐述立场	2. 严格的管教有时可能很重要，但是我觉得可能会影响小孩处理问题的能力。

主体部分第一段

中心句	3. 规则的主要功能是让小孩对他们的行为负责，从小塑造好的行为。

解释	4. 小孩不像成年人一样知道自己行为产生的后果，而通过规则，小孩会逐渐意识到怎么做才可以在社会上被别人认可。
举例 1	5. 例如，小孩会学习怎么和人打招呼，怎么礼貌地请人帮忙，吃饭的时候注意什么礼节。
举例 2	6. 规则也会告诉他们欺负同学、说脏话、作弊、打断老师等行为是不对的。

主体部分第二段

中心句	7. 有些时候，规则未必会对小孩的成长有好的影响，如果那些制定严格规则的父母强调小孩的顺从的话。
解释	8. 小孩如此地依赖规则来做决定，以至于他们自己没有独立解决问题的能力。
举例	9. 家长规定孩子每天应该做什么，那么小孩长大后，就可能不知道如何独立安排时间，在工作中，如何应对工作要求。
结果	10. 他们很难在职业生涯中获得成功。

主体部分第三段

我的观点	11. 遵守规则会限制小孩的想象力，他们不能够用各种方法去解决问题。
解释	12. 小孩不敢实践自己的想法，因为他们怕不遵守规则会受到惩罚。
举例	13. 如果规定学生用一种方法去写作文，他们就不知道使用其他方法去描述自己的想法会有什么结果。
结果	14. 工作里遇到的问题是很复杂的，没有创造力的人会束手无策。

读者自学步骤 3

检查自己的翻译。先看正确句子的词伙和句子结构，然后看错误的句子，看是否能够发现问题。

句 1

正：Children are expected to obey different rules either at home or at school.

学生的句子：Children should obey rules when they at home or school.

改：when 引导状语从句，那么从句应该是独立的句子，这个从句缺少谓语动词。

句 2

正：Strict discipline is sometimes important, but it would have an adverse impact on children's problem-solving abilities.

学生的句子：Strict discipline sometimes is important, but it would have a impact on children's ability of solving problems.

改：impact 前的冠词应该是 an；ability to do something 是固定的表达。

句 3

正：The main function of rules is to hold children accountable for their behaviour and to help them develop good behaviour patterns from a young age.

学生的句子：The main function of discipline is to make children take responsible to their behaviours, and shape a good behaviour.

改：take 后面要加名词，而不是形容词；behaviour 一般是不可数名词，或者有时候用复数，很少用冠词 a。

句 4

正：Unlike adults, children are normally not aware of the consequences of bad behaviour, and setting rules can help them realise how to behave in a socially acceptable way.

学生的句子：Unlike adults, children are not aware of the results caused by their behaviour, but they will realize that how to be accepted by the society through discipline.

改：results caused by 这个搭配不是很地道；realise that 宾语从句后面应该是独立的句子。

句 5

正：For example, children can learn how to greet others, make polite requests and show table manners.

学生的句子：For instance, children may understand how to greet to others appropriately, how to ask for help in politeness and what manners they need to mind when having meals.

改：greet 是及物动词，不需要加介词；没有 in politeness 的说法。

句 6

正：Rules also forbid inappropriate behaviours, such as bullying, using profanity, cheating in exams and interrupting teachers during a lesson.

学生的句子：Rules can also teach them that some behaviour is definitely wrong, such as bullying, swearing or cheating.

改：后面那么多行为，behaviour 用单数不是很恰当。

句 7

正：Sometimes rules may not have a positive influence on children, if those parents who establish the strict rules give priority to children's obedience.

学生的句子：Sometimes rules may not have great influence for children, if those parents establish the strict rules emphasise children's obedience.

改：influence 后的介词用 on；从句中有 establish 和 emphasise 两个动词。

句 8

正：Children will rely heavily on rules and may not be able to solve problems independently.

学生的句子：Children rely on rules to so a degree that they are not able to solve problems independently.

改："so…that" 搭配里，so 一般修饰形容词或者副词，而 degree 是名词。

句 9

正：If parents dictate what children should do every day, children may not know how to manage time independently and cope with the demands of work in the future.

学生的句子：If parents make a plan to tell their children what should they do every day, then children will difficult to arrange their time when they grow up.

改：what they should do 才是正确的语序；主句没有谓语，difficult 是个形容词。

句 10

正：They are unlikely to achieve success in their careers.

学生的句子：They are unlikely to achieve a succeed career.

改：succeed 是动词；achieve career 搭配不对。

句 11

正：Strict rules can stifle children's creativity and they are not able to solve problems in different ways.

学生的句子：Their imagination are limited by obeying rules, thus failing to coming up good ideas which help to cope with problem effectively.

改：imagination are 主谓不一致；fail to do something 是常用表达。

句 12

正：They dare not put their ideas into practice, since they are afraid of being punished if they disobey rules.

学生的句子：Children refuse to put their thoughts in practice, since they are afraid of being punished if they against rules.

改：refuse 在这里不恰当；against 是介词，从句中没有谓语动词。

句 13

正：If they are required to abide by strict rules in essay-writing, they will not know the outcome of expressing their ideas in other ways.

学生的句子：If the rule regulate students to write essay in one approach, students will have no idea about the result of other methods to express their thoughts.

改：rule regulate 主谓不一致；essay 是可数名词，要用复数；other methods 前面用动名词，如 adopting 会通顺点。

句 14

正：The problems in the real world are complex and people cannot tackle these problems without using imagination.

学生的句子：The problems people are facing in their real life are complicated, and those who without creativity would find it difficult for them to tackle the problems.

改：前半句的主语写得太复杂，读起来不通顺；后半句的定语从句中没有动词。

读者自学步骤 4

整体学习和检查范文，看看是否符合 TELCCS 原则。

范文全文（7.5 分）

Children are expected to obey different rules either at home or at school. Strict discipline is sometimes important, but it would have an adverse impact on children's problem-solving abilities.

这里可以加入一些单词表明这是你自己的看法，如 but I think it would …。

The main function of rules is to hold children accountable for their behaviour and to help them develop good behaviour patterns from a young age. Unlike adults, children are normally not aware of the consequences of bad behaviour, and setting rules can help them realise how to behave in a socially acceptable way. For example, children can learn how to greet others, make polite requests and show table manners. Rules also forbid inappropriate behaviours, such as bullying, using profanity, cheating in exams and interrupting teachers during a lesson.

这里可以突出是某些人的想法。

和前面的 children 有点重复，可以用代词，提升 CC。

这里可以增加一些关于规则的内容，提高 TR 的分数。

这里可以增加一个连接的表达，提升 CC。

Sometimes rules may not have a positive influence on children, if those parents who establish the strict rules give priority to children's obedience. Children will rely heavily on rules and may not be able to solve problems independently. If parents dictate what children should do every day, children may not know how to manage time independently and cope with the demands of work in the future. They are unlikely to achieve success in their careers.

这里也可以出现 some other people argue that, an opposing view is that 等表达，突出这是另外一些人的看法。

这里没有连接词，没有代词，也没有关键词呼应，读起来很跳跃。

和前面的 independently 重复，影响 LR 的分数。

Strict rules can stifle children's creativity and they are not able to solve problems in different ways. They dare not put their ideas into practice, since they are afraid of being punished if they disobey rules. If they are required to abide by strict rules in essay-writing, they will not know the outcome of expressing their ideas in

这里可以给出提示词，说明这是"你的看法"。

这句话的前面已经有 if，再来一个 if，读起来非常重复，影响 CC 和 GRA 的成绩。

other ways. The problems in the real world are complex and people cannot tackle these problems without using imagination.

> 这里可以用 they，否则从前面的 children，突然到这句话的 people，会很跳跃。

本节关键学习点

我们首先说说论述类题目的结构和要点。所谓论述类题目，就是大作文的题目中出现"discuss both views and give your own opinion"这样的字眼。

这种题目一般都是提出某些人的看法，然后再提出另外一些人的看法。例如本节中的这个题目，第一批人的看法是"一定要遵守规则"，第二批人的看法是"遵守规则可能导致小孩以后不能解决问题"。一般来说，论述类题目的结构是：

介绍段	给出个人立场（你可以支持任何一批人的立场，也可以在某种情况下两方立场都支持）。
主体部分第一段	第一批人的看法（一定要说第一批人的看法为什么是对的，这一段不能质疑他们）。
主体部分第二段	第二批人的看法（一定要说第二批人的看法为什么是对的，这一段不能质疑他们）。
主体部分第三段	自己的看法。
结论段（可写可不写）	总结自己的看法，甚至可以总结双方的立场。

论述类题目有下面这些特点：

> 特点1：论述类题目主体部分前两段一定要说持有不同看法的人为什么是对的，不能质疑他们。
>
> 特点2：论述类题目的中心句会经常出现一些字眼，例如 some people argue that, it is sometimes argued that 等。
>
> 特点3：论述类题目的中心句不需要写得很肯定。
>
> 特点4：论述类题目讨论你自己看法的主体段（也就是主体部分的第三段）可以作为结尾段。

具体如下。

特点1：论述类题目主体部分前两段一定要说持有不同看法的人为什么是对的，不能质疑他们。例如，这篇作文的主体部分第一段，你不能讨论"遵守规则"有什么不好。因为第一批人的看法就是要遵守规则。既然他们觉得要遵守，那么必定有他们的道理。你只能讨论为什么他们那么认为。

特点2：论述类题目的中心句会经常出现一些字眼，例如 some people argue that, it is sometimes argued that 等。

这些表达会让读者知道，你现在不是在写自己的立场，而是在引述别人的看法。

特点3：论述类题目的中心句不需要写得很肯定。

在论述类文章主体部分的第一段和第二段，在引述别人的看法时，你可以经常写一些如 may, might, are likely to, sometimes, in some cases, can be 这样不确定的表达。尽量不要用 should, must, certainly, definitely, clearly 等比较肯定的表达，因为这些表达给人感觉这是你最后的立场。

特点 4：论述类题目讨论你自己看法的主体段 (也就是主体部分的第三段) 可以作为结尾段。

因为论述类题目的问法是 "discuss both views and give your own opinion"，也就意味着既然你在主体部分第三段给出了个人的看法，那么这一段本身就可以作为结尾段。

很多考生特别害怕写两边讨论的文章或者折中类文章 (就是主体部分说了一件事情的好处，也说了坏处) 的结尾段，觉得这样会 "立场不坚定"，这其实是一种多虑。

我们生活中大部分的事情都有好和坏，认定它有坏处并不代表就不好。例如，我们认为网络购物是件好事，很方便，比较便宜，但是缺点就是假货多。我们很多人看好网络学习，因为很方便、很自由，自己可以掌握进度，但是缺点就是考生没有人监督就很难学习等。

雅思考试的很多作文需要考生说清楚立场 (一般这个立场要在结尾段亮明，然后是开头段)，但是这不代表考生一定要完全支持或者完全反对一件事情。

例如本书的第一篇文章是关于校规对孩子的影响。主体部分第一段说了严格的管教可以塑造好的行为，主体部分第二段说的是严格的管教会让孩子缺乏自己解决问题的能力，主体部分第三段说的是规则会限制孩子的想象力。

如果总体来说，你觉得规则是不好的，那么在结尾段你可以说清楚这是你的立场，然后折中一下。例句下面这个结尾段，前半部分突出我的立场是反对规则，后面用 despite the fact that 来引出折中的内容，这样的连词还有 although, while。

For the reasons mentioned above, I would suggest that parents and teachers relax rules to allow children to develop problem-solving skills and use imagination, despite the fact that strict discipline can reduce poor behaviour.

当然，在时间不够的情况下，只写你支持的一方，不写折中的观点也是可以的。

For the reasons mentioned above, I would suggest that parents and teachers relax rules to allow children to develop problem-solving skills and use imagination.

简而言之，作文要求你说自己的 view, opinion，不是非要完全支持或者反对一件事情，你可以主要支持或者反对一件事情。

提升的范文

标色的部分是和原文有差异的地方，下划线部分是词伙。

Children are expected to obey different rules either at home or at school. Strict discipline is sometimes important, but I would argue that it would have an adverse impact on children's problem-solving abilities.

Some people are strong advocates of imposing rules because rules can hold children accountable for their behaviour and help them develop good behaviour patterns from a young age. Unlike adults, children are normally not aware of the consequences of bad behaviour, and setting rules can help them realise how to behave in a socially acceptable way. For example, they can learn how to greet others, make polite requests and <u>show table manners</u>, if they are required by adults to do so. In addition, rules can also forbid inappropriate behaviours, such as bullying, using profanity, <u>cheating in exams</u> and interrupting teachers during a lesson.

Opponents, however, argue that rules can limit the development of problem-solving skills, if those parents who establish strict rules give priority to children's obedience. Children will rely heavily on rules and may not be able to solve problems independently. For instance, some rules may dictate what children should do every day, but when children enter the workforce, they may not know how to manage time without the instructions of their parents and cope with the demands of work themselves. They are unlikely to <u>achieve success</u> in their careers.

In my view, strict rules can <u>stifle children's creativity</u> and they are not able to solve problems in different ways. They dare not put their ideas into practice, since they are afraid of being punished if they <u>disobey rules</u>. Some teachers, for example, require students to abide by strict essay writing rules, and the consequence is that children will not know the outcome of expressing their ideas in other ways. The problems <u>in the real world</u> are complex and they cannot tackle these problems without <u>using imagination</u>.

3.6.2 全文翻译2：老龄化社会＋观点类题目（advantages/disadvantages 题型）写作要点＋段落的数目

> *In many countries, the proportion of older people is steadily increasing. Does this trend have positive or negative effects on society?*

题目大意

在很多国家，老年人的比例不断增加。这个趋势对社会是有积极还是负面的影响？

读者自学步骤1

阅读题目后，写出三个观点。

下面是我学生写的一些错误或者不好的观点，大家可以看看自己是不是也犯了同样的错误。

学生的观点	点评
父母、爷爷奶奶长寿，能在你遇到困难的时候给你提出建议，家庭和谐，感到幸福。	没有逻辑。能给你建议不代表和谐，和谐和社会发展有什么联系？题目里有个关键词是society，确定了题目讨论的范围是社会。
老年人口比例上升，医疗卫生设施建设的支出增多，有利于社会医疗卫生的进步。	观点牵强。如果要投资医疗卫生，直接投资就好，未必要等到老年人比例上升才投资。
老年人比例增加好，提供了更多的岗位，促进社会发展。	观点牵强。和我们的常识相反，老年人越多，应该是会推迟退休，因而占据很多岗位，年轻人机会更少。

老年人增多，老年人掌握的技艺得以传承，减少文化流失。	观点牵强。人不用变老也可以传承手艺，传承手艺并不是说肯定对社会好。如，有些地方做棺材也是手艺，但是未必对社会好。

读者自学步骤 2

翻译下面的句子：在翻译过程中，记住先想词伙，再想句型，然后写出句子。相关词伙可以查阅微信公众号：gu_writing。

介绍段

背景句	1. 因为科技的发展和人们财富的增加，人口寿命一直在延长。
阐述立场或者说明文章讨论内容	2. 虽然老年人可以为社会做贡献，但是这个人口的变化可能会导致很多问题。

主体部分第一段

中心句（经济：资源）	3. 一个和老龄化相关的问题是健康医疗的费用会激增，会对纳税人施加负担。
解释	4. 众所周知，大部分的医疗需求和费用都是在晚年出现。
结果	5. 因此，政府需要花更多钱在照顾老年人上，而其他的一些关键服务如教育就有资金不足的问题。
观点（经济：效率）	6. 随着年纪较大的工作者数目增加，工作的慢节奏可能是另外一个问题。
原因	7. 随着年龄增长，人们吸收信息和处理工作的能力通常会下降。
结果	8. 如果老年人推迟退休，他们可能会影响公司的效率和盈利。

主体部分第二段

中心句（经济）	9. 另一方面，很多人会推迟退休和延长职业生涯，而他们的经验和智慧是宝贵的社会财富。
原因	10. 因为人们现在非常注意饮食健康和运动，他们往往可以活得更健康、更长。
结果	11. 他们可以作为顾问将自己的知识和技能传授给年轻人。
举例	12. 例如，一些资深的管理人员会教年轻人如何管理一个公司，和如何更好地服务客户。

结论段

再次表明立场	13. 总之，寿命的急剧延长已经给很多国家的健康医疗施加了压力，也会影响劳动力的产出。
总结观点	14. 这会影响经济发展，虽然我们可以充分利用老年人的智慧。

读者自学步骤 3

检查自己的翻译：先看正确句子的词伙和句子结构，然后看错误的句子，看是否能够发现问题。

句 1

正：People's life expectancy has increased in many societies, possibly because of improvements in technology and the increase in personal wealth.

学生的句子：As the development of science and technology and people's increasing wealth, people's life expectancy have been prolonged.

改：as 表示"因为"时是连词，要接句子。

句 2

正：Although senior citizens can contribute extraordinarily to society, I would argue that this demographic change can bring about some problems.

学生的句子：Although old people can contribute to the society, demographic trend maybe lead to many problems.

改：trend 是可数名词，不能没有冠词，或者要变成复数；maybe 是副词，这里应该用情态动词 may。

句 3

正：One problem associated with an ageing population is that health care costs will escalate, imposing a burden on taxpayers.

学生的句子：A problem related to ageing population which will escalate the health care costs, it will exert a burden on taxpayers.

改：a problem is that 是习惯表达，用于描述具体问题；escalate 一般用作不及物动词；impose a burden 是习惯表达。

句 4

正：It is widely known that most medical needs and costs occur in the last years of life.

学生的句子：It is wide known that most of medical needs and fees are appeared in the last years of life.

改：wide 是形容词，不能修饰 known（过去分词）；most of 一般在后面的名词需要特指的时候使用；appear 是不及物动词，没有被动语态。

句 5

正：Governments have to pour more money in caring for the elderly, but other essential services like education will be underfunded.

学生的句子：Therefore, the government need to spend more money on taking care of older people, but other essential services like education will face the lack of funds.

改：government need 主谓不一致；应该是 spend money in doing something。

句 6

正：The slow pace of work is another problem，as the number of senior workers increases.

学生的句子：The other problem is the slow pace of work with the growing number of workers who are old people.

改：一般来说，"另外一个"是 another，"两者之中的另外一个"才用 the other；who are old people 这个定语从句太啰唆，多余，典型的中国考生，以为使用定语从句就可以加分。

句 7

正：The ability to absorb information and complete work normally declines with age.

学生的句子：With age grows, people's ability of absorbing information and dealing with jobs will decline.

改：with 是介词，后面不能加句子；ability to do something 是习惯表达。

句 8

正：If senior workers delay retirement, they may not perform as well as younger employees and this can influence companies' productivity and profitability.

学生的句子：If the senior workers postponed their retirement, they would influence the company's efficiency and profits.

改：senior workers 是可数名词的复数，不需要再用 the，因为不是特指；这句话不需要用虚拟语气，因为并不是不可能发生的事情。

句 9

正：On the other hand, many people will postpone retirement and extend their working life, and it is true that their experience and wisdom are a valuable asset to the whole society.

学生的句子：On the other hand, many people will postpone retirement and prone their working life, therefore, their experiences and wisdom will be fortune.

改：therefore 是副词，不是连词，不能连接两个独立的句子；而且这两句话并没有因果关系，属于连接词的误用。

句 10

正：People today can live healthier and longer, since they pay closer attention to healthy eating and sports.

学生的句子：For people more concentrate on healthy diet and sports, they will live more healthy and long.

改：for 表示原因，引导状语从句的时候，往往放在句中，而且是表示猜测，这里使用不恰当。

句 11

正：They can work as consultants and impart their knowledge and skills to the younger generation.

学生的句子：They can work as a consultant and impart their knowledge and skills on the younger generation.

改：consultant 和前面的 they 数不一致；impart something to somebody 是习惯表达。

句 12

正：For example, some senior managers can teach young people how to manage a company, and how to provide better services for clients.

学生的句子：For example, some managerments can teach young people how to manage a company, and how to provide better services for clients.

改：management 是表示"管理"这项工作，而不是说人。

句 13

正：In conclusion, the considerable extension of life expectancy has put strain on health care and made the workforce less productive.

学生的句子：In conclusion, the sharp extension of life expectancy has already exert a burden on many country's health care system. This tendency will influence the productivity of the labour force.

改：这里是完成时态，应该用 exert 的过去分词；many countries' 才是正确的所有格形式。

句 14

正：It will influence the economic development of a country, although we can make good use of senior workers' wisdom.

学生的句子：While it will influence economic development, we can still make good use of senior workers' wisdom.

改：while 不应该放在句首，因为这里有点类似于 although，这样就显得前半句是一个次要的内容，而后半句是主要的内容。而我们都知道，整篇文章目前是倾向于认为老龄社会导致问题。

读者自学步骤 4

整体学习和检查范文，看看是否符合 TELCCS 原则。

范文全文（7.5 分）

People's life expectancy has increased in many societies, possibly because of improvements in technology and the increase in personal wealth. Although senior citizens can contribute extraordinarily to society, I would argue that this demographic change can bring about some problems.

One problem associated with an ageing population is that health care costs will escalate, imposing a burden on taxpayers. It is widely known that most medical needs and costs occur in the last years of life. Governments have to pour more money in caring for the elderly, but other essential services like education will be underfunded. The slow pace of work is another problem，as the number of senior workers increases. The ability to absorb information and complete work normally declines with age. If senior workers delay retirement, they may not perform as well as younger employees and this can influence companies' productivity and profitability.

这个词有点太大，改成 increase 或者 climb。

这句话和上面一句话的主语和说的事情完全不同，所以要加连接词，例如 this means that。

这里应该突出对社会的影响。而且要和中心句的 impose a burden on taxpayers 对应，否则影响 CC 的分数。

这个句子的逻辑关系不强，不能因为推迟退休，老人就不能有良好的工作表现。

这里应该突出对社会的影响。

On the other hand, many people will postpone retirement and extend their working life, and it is true that their experience and wisdom are a valuable asset to the whole society. People today can live healthier and longer, since they pay closer attention to healthy eating and sports. They can work as consultants and impart their knowledge and skills to the younger generation. For example, some senior managers can teach young people how to manage a company, and how to provide better services for clients.

可以改成 may，might 等，这样语气不是很坚定。

这个套句有点多余。

这里的 they 没有说得很清楚是老年人还是普通人，这样会影响 CC 的分数。

这里可以稍微突出一下对社会的影响，去提高 TR 的分数，因为题目是强调对社会的影响。

In conclusion, the considerable extension of life expectancy has put strain on health care and made the workforce less productive. It will influence the economic development of a country, although we can make good use of senior workers' wisdom.

本节关键学习点

这一节我们讨论雅思大作文第二种常见的话题：观点类话题。观点类话题的问法比较多变，常见的有下面五种问法：

问法 1：Is it a positive or negative development?

问法 2：Do advantages of this outweigh disadvantages?

问法 3：Does it have positive or negative effects? (或者 What are the effects?)

问法4：To what extent do you agree or disagree？（或者 Do you agree or disagree？）

问法5：What is your opinion？

其中前三个问法的文章比较简单，只需要说好处或坏处。这种题目一般描述一个动作或者现象（例如这篇文章的老龄化，还有其他一些常见话题，如在家里上班、用手机购物、越来越多人开车等），主体部分你就讨论这些动作和现象的影响即可。

后面两种相对比较复杂，我们下一节再去讨论。

前三种观点类题目，我们要注意下面一些事项：

> 注意1：你可以写一件事情全是好处，或者全是坏处；也可以说一件事情有好也有坏。
>
> 注意2：写折中段的时候，用词可以变得含糊，这样不会转折太强烈。
>
> 注意3：题目是讨论 effect 时，要注意题目的限定对象（如 individuals, family, society 等）。

注意1：你可以写一件事情全是好处，或者全是坏处；也可以说一件事情有好也有坏。

一些学生在写这篇文章的时候，问我：老师，前面不是说老年人带来问题吗？后来怎么又说老年人有贡献？

在英语国家的文化里，这是很正常的。当你觉得老年社会有很多问题的时候，不代表你不可以认同老年人的贡献。

这不是立场不坚定，而是体现你思维的客观。

注意2：写折中段的时候，用词可以变得含糊，这样不会转折太强烈。

在写折中段的时候，如果你的用词语气很坚定，如 should，那么会与前面的立场形成直接的反驳，导致前后不一致。

因此，要用一些语气不是很确定的词，如 some, may, might, be likely to, sometimes, in some cases 等。这样一来，折中段说了和前面段落不同观点，也不至于转折很强烈。

注意3：题目是讨论 effect 时，要注意题目的限定对象（如 individuals, family, society 等）。

在最近几年的雅思考试里，遇到问 effect 的题目，剑桥雅思会增加一些限定词，用来考查学生的审题和扣题能力。如这个题目就出现了 effect on society。那么整篇文章在讨论影响的时候，一定要阐述到社会的层面，否则就是跑题。同样地，有些题目会出现 effect on individuals，那么就一定要讨论对个人的影响。

这一节我们还会讲一下关于段落的问题。

这篇文章我们原本是写了主体部分两段，比较符合很多中国老师的口味，就是主体部分每一段写两个观点以上。然而，这种写法在目前的雅思考试中已经慢慢不适用了。因为现在的题目比以前的抽象，比较难想观点，一般来说，一篇文章考生很少能够想到四个观点，能想到三个观点就很厉害了，这就意味着每个观点都要拓展得特别仔细，才可能写够字数。

那么如何拓展呢？

我的方法很简单，就是每个观点多想原因和结果，还有举例。

例如第一个观点是政府没有钱支付其他的公共服务，那么你就稍微拓展一下结果：没有教育和其他公共服务，社会进步很慢。

第二个观点是关于老年人工作节奏慢，那么你可以举个例子，说他们接受先进科技的速度比较慢，就可以很好地拓展了。

这样我们就可以将传统的一段话写两个观点，分开写成两段话两个观点。

提升的范文

标色的部分是和原文有差异的地方，下划线部分是词伙。

People's life expectancy has improved in many societies, possibly because of improvements in technology and the increase in personal wealth. Although senior citizens can contribute extraordinarily to society, I would argue that this demographic change can bring about some problems.

One problem associated with an ageing population is that health care costs will increase, imposing a burden on taxpayers. It is widely known that most medical needs and costs occur in the last years of life. This means that governments have to pour more money in caring for the elderly and in medical services. This is normally achieved by requiring working people to pay higher income tax and cutting funds for other essential services like education.

The slow pace of work is another problem, as the number of senior workers increases. The ability to absorb information and complete work normally declines with age. Many elderly people have a conservative attitude towards technology and struggle to learn how to use hi-tech devices and the latest software at work. If they choose to delay retirement, their presence in the workforce can influence companies' productivity and endanger the whole economy.

On the other hand, the experience and wisdom of senior citizens can be a valuable asset to society. People today can live healthier and longer lives, as they pay closer attention to healthy eating and sports. They can work as consultants even after leaving the workforce, and impart their knowledge and skills to the younger generation. For example, some senior managers can teach young people how to manage a company, and how to provide better services for clients. Our society can draw upon the expertise of these older people.

In conclusion, the considerable extension of life expectancy has put strain on health care and made the workforce less productive. It will influence the economic development of a country, although we can make good use of senior workers' wisdom.

3.6.3 全文翻译 3：看电视学习＋观点类题目 (agree or disagree 题型) 写作要点

> *Some people believe that children can learn effectively by watching TV and they should be encouraged to watch TV both at home and at school. To what extent do you agree or disagree?*

题目大意

一些人相信小孩可以通过看电视有效地学习，我们因此可以鼓励小孩在家里和学校看电视。在多大程度上你同意或者反对这个看法？

读者自学步骤 1

阅读题目后，写出三个观点。

下面是我学生写的一些错误或者不好的观点，大家可以看看自己是不是也犯了同样的错误。

学生的观点	点评
学生在家里和学校都看电视，会占用在学校学习的时间，导致学习分心，学习氛围不浓厚，学习效率下降。	逻辑不好。占用时间可以导致分心，为什么分心会破坏学习氛围？
鼓励在家和学校看电视，拓展课余生活，了解国家大事，全面发展。	空泛，而且跑题。这个题目关注的是学习效果，而不是全面发展。
看电视过多会影响休息和锻炼的时间，不利于孩子的身体和视力发展。	跑题。这个题目关注的是学习效果，而不是身体和视力。
看电视会占据其他活动的时间，儿童不进行室外活动和社交活动。	跑题。这个题目关注的是学习效果，而不是室外活动和社交活动。
看太多电视会影响身心健康，电视偶有暴力血腥情节，学生会模仿，养成不好的习惯。	跑题。这个题目关注的是学习效果，而不是孩子的行为。
孩子们可以更有效地通过电视来学习，可以获取很多学校里学习不到的知识，可以开阔视野，促进身心更好的发展。	没有逻辑。为什么开阔视野对身心发展有帮助？

读者自学步骤 2

翻译下面的句子：在翻译过程中，记住先想词伙，再想句型，然后写出句子。 相关词伙可以查阅微信公众号：gu_writing。

介绍段

背景句	1. 看电视（特别是资讯性的节目）被认为是一种有效的学习方法，因为声像信息很容易吸引学生的注意和培养他们的兴趣。
阐述立场	2. 尽管很多电视节目现在都具有教育价值，但是我不赞同学生应该多看电视。

主体部分第一段

中心句	3. 看电视会影响小孩的学习，还有参加其他有益于他们成长的活动。
解释	4. 看电视会分散孩子的注意力，特别是大人不在身边监督的话。
结果	5. 经常看电视的学生可能不能够专注于学习任务，这会导致他们考试成绩的下降。
并列的一个结果	6. 而且小孩很难进行那些促进大脑发育的互动式的活动，如阅读、唱歌和交流。

主体部分第二段

中心句	7. 此外，孩子看电视的时间加长会影响他们的交流能力。

原因	8. 他们会每天坐在电视前几个小时，而不去和小伙伴玩游戏，和老师交流。
结果	9. 他们会变得孤僻，不愿意和别人表达自己的看法，或者是理解别人的话。
拓展结果	10. 没有好的语言能力，他们很难学习知识，借鉴别人的想法，学业上很难有成就。

主体部分第三段 (折中段)

中心句	11. 另外一方面，我也知道电视让小孩接触知识的世界 (a world of knowledge)。
原因	12. 很多教育类的电视节目都是针对小孩的，让他们增加对不同科目的了解。
举例	13. 例如，历史纪录片可以让小孩懂得历史事件，而一些外语频道可以让他们学会外语。
对比	14. 这些知识是对他们在学校里学的知识的一个补充。

结论段

再次表明立场	15. 综上所述，家长和老师应该对小孩看电视加以限制，而不是鼓励这个习惯。
总结观点	16. 过多看电视会影响他们的学习，而不是提升他们的成绩。

读者自学步骤 3

检查自己的翻译：先看正确句子的词伙和句子结构，然后看错误的句子，看是否能够发现问题。

句 1

正：Watching television (especially informative television) has been recognised as an effective method of learning, because audio-visual information can attract students' attention and engage their interest.

学生的句子：Watching TV (especially informative television) is regarded as a effective learning method, because audio-visual information readily attract student's attention and raise their interests.

改：effective 是以元音发音开头的单词，不定冠词用 an；"information…attract…and raise…" 主谓不一致，因为 information 是不可数名词。

句 2

正：Although many TV programmes have educational value, I do not agree that increasing screen time is a good idea.

学生的句子：Although many TV programmes have highly educational valued, I disagree that students increase their screen-time.

改：valued 是分词，不能充当 have 的宾语。

句 3

正：Television viewing can interfere with children's studies and other activities which can benefit these children's development.

学生的句子：Watching TV may have an adverse impact on their study and their attending to other beneficial activities.

改：their attending（代词＋动名词）的结构很不自然；attend 是及物动词，不需要加 to。

句 4

正：Children can get distracted easily, especially when they watch TV without adults' supervision.

学生的句子：It is easy for children to get distracted, especially when they do not under their parents' surveillance.

改：it is easy 表示"容易的"，而这里我们要说的是"轻易地"；under 是介词，从句没有谓语动词。

句 5

正：Students who watch television frequently may not be able to concentrate on learning tasks, a problem which can lead to poor grades.

学生的句子：Students who often watching television may not able to focus on learning tasks, it will lead to a drop in students' test score.

改：定语从句 watching 谓语不完整；may not able to 主句谓语不完整；it will lead to… 是一个新的独立的单句，两个句子间没有连词。

句 6

正：It is also difficult for children to attend those interactive activities which promote brain development, such as reading, singing and communication.

学生的句子：These interactive activities which are used to promoting brain development, e.g., reading, singing and communicating which become difficult because of watching TV.

改：句中有 which are used to 和 which become 两个定语从句，整句话没有主句；be used to do something 是固定表达。

句 7

正：Another problem is that long screen time can have an adverse impact on children's social development.

学生的句子：In addition, an increasing screen time will affect their communication skills.

改：time 是不可数名词；their 指代不清楚。

句 8

正：They will sit in front of TV many hours, instead of playing games with their peers and communicating with teachers.

学生的句子: They may spent hours on watching TV rather than play games with friends or have talks with teachers.

改: may 后面加动词原形; spend...in doing, 介词不准确; talks 往往是 "长谈" 的意思。

句 9

正: They will become unsociable and unwilling to express their views and understand the thoughts of other people.

学生的句子: They will get solitary, this means they are not willing to show their ideas with others or understand the meaning others said.

改: 两个句子间没有连词连接; meaning said 搭配不当。

句 10

正: Without good communication skills, they will have difficulty in gaining knowledge, drawing upon the ideas of classmates or teachers, and achieving academic success.

学生的句子: Without language skills, they will have difficulties in gaining knowledge, borrowing others' ideas as well as improving academic achievement.

改: have difficulty in, 不需要用复数; improve achievement 搭配不当。

句 11

正: On the other hand, I understand that television has exposed children to a world of knowledge.

学生的句子: On the other hand, we also realise that television enable children connect with a world of knowledge.

改: 从句主谓不一致; enable somebody to do something 是习惯表达。

句 12

正: There are many educational programmes aimed for children, allowing them to gain an insight into different subjects.

学生的句子: Many educational television programs are designed for children, which allow them to develop further understanding of different subjects.

改: 定语从句指代不清楚, 不知道是修饰 children, 还是 programmes。

句 13

正: For example, documentaries can help children learn about historical events while foreign language channels can help them acquire foreign languages.

学生的句子: For example, historical documentary can promote the child to understand the historical events, and some foreign language can help them to learn foreign language.

改: documentary 是可数名词, 要用复数形式; 没有 promote somebody to do something 的表达; language 也是可数名词, 要用复数形式。

14

正：This kind of knowledge can complement what they learn at school.

学生的句子：These knowledge is a supplement to their curriculum.

改：knowledge 是不可数名词，前面不该有 these。

15

正：To summarise, parents and teachers should impose restrictions on children's television viewing, rather than endorse this habit.

学生的句子：In conclusion, parents and teachers should impose restriction on kids watching television but not encourage this habit.

改：restriction 是可数名词，这里应该用复数形式；kids 是口语化的表达。

16

正：Watching TV can have an adverse impact on children's grades, rather than improve their academic performance.

学生的句子：Excessive screen time affect children's grades, rather than promoting their academic performance.

改：主谓不一致。

读者自学步骤 4

整体学习和检查范文，看看是否符合 TELCCS 原则。

范文全文（7～7.5 分）

Watching television (especially informative television) has been recognised as an effective method of learning, because audio-visual information can attract students' attention and engage their interest. Although many TV programmes have educational value, I do not agree that increasing screen time is a good idea.

这句话读起来有点多余，为了用从句而用从句的感觉。

Television viewing can interfere with children's studies and other activities which can benefit these children's development. Children can get distracted easily, especially when they watch TV without adults' supervision. Students who watch television frequently may not be able to concentrate on learning tasks, a problem which can lead to poor grades. It is also difficult for children to attend those interactive activities which promote brain development,

这里有点重复。

这里和前面的 distracted 也是重复的。

和前面的 children 也是有点重复，可以用代词 them。

such as reading, singing and communication.

Another problem is that long screen time can have an adverse impact on children's social development. They will sit in front of TV many hours, instead of playing games with their peers and communicating with teachers. They will become unsociable and unwilling to express their views and understand the thoughts of other people. Without good communication skills, they will have difficulty in gaining knowledge, drawing upon the ideas of classmates or teachers, and achieving academic success.

On the other hand, I understand that television has exposed children to a world of knowledge. There are many educational programmes aimed for children, allowing them to gain an insight into different subjects. For example, documentaries can help children learn about historical events while foreign language channels can help them acquire foreign languages. This kind of knowledge can complement what they learn at school.

To summarise, parents and teachers should impose restrictions on children's television viewing, rather than endorse this habit. Watching TV can have an adverse impact on children's grades, rather than improve their academic performance.

这些不是 interactive activities，影响 CC 的分数。

这个表达和结尾的最后一句类似，可以替换一下，避免 LR 丢分。

这里不是特别合理，不是每个小孩都看那么长时间，可能加点限定会好一些，不那么跳跃，否则会影响 CC 的分数。

两个句子都是用 they 开头，感觉有点重复，影响 CC 和 GRA 的分数。

这里可以加标志词，表明你正在说自己个人的看法。

突然说到 endorse this habit 有点突兀，毕竟题目没有这么说。

主体段落不只是讨论学习，还讨论交流技能。

本节关键学习点

观点类文章里 (degree/disagree) 这一类题目比较难。这种 Do you agree or disagree 或者 What is your opinion 的题目有以下一些注意点：

注意 *1*：有时候会限定某个动作的结果，很多考生容易跑题。

注意 *2*：可以完全支持或者反对，也可以部分支持或者反对。

注意 *3*：尽量避免出现 some people think/argue/believe/hold the view that 这些表达。

注意 *4*：注意审题时和优缺点题目 (advantages/disadvantages, positive/negative effects) 的区别。

注意 *5*：题目出现 best, only 这种字眼也可以折中。

注意 *6*：题目已经认定的内容不需要去论述。

注意 *7*：观点类题目和论述类题目有两大区别。

下面我们讲解一下细节。

注意1：有时候会限定某个动作的结果，很多考生容易跑题。

这个时候你的论述一定要围绕这个结果进行，不能讨论其他东西。例如本题虽然说的是看电视，但是题目出现了 learn effectively 的字眼。这也就是为什么当讨论到看电视产生健康问题，如视力下降，你也要继续说这影响学习，确保和学习有一定联系，否则就属于跑题。

注意2：可以完全支持或者反对，也可以部分支持或者反对。

国内很多雅思培训老师在讲到观点类题目时总是要求学生一定要完全支持或者反对，而不能写折中段，因为他们觉得那样显得"立场不坚定"。其实这是对西方写作和思想特点的了解不够。英语国家的学术英文非常强调 critical thinking（批判性思维，一分为二地思考）。当你支持一方的时候，你当然可以同时认可它的缺点。

例如本文，你的立场可以是"大人要控制小孩看电视的时间"，同时你也可以说"电视可以让小孩增加知识"。

世界上没有什么东西是非黑即白的，因此不要担心自己的"立场不坚定"。

当考官问你 What is your opinion 的时候，不是说只有完全支持和反对才叫 opinion。部分支持和反对也可以是你的 opinion。

注意3：尽量避免出现 some people think/argue/believe/hold the view that 这些表达。

这些表达都是论述类题目（Discuss both views and give your own opinion）的表达，不适合观点类题目。

注意4：注意审题时和优缺点题目（advantages/disadvantages, positive/negative effects）的区别。

同意反对类题目 Do you agree or disagree 可以否定题目里设定的一个动作，而优缺点类题目只能讨论题目设定的趋势或者动作的优缺点。

对比下面这两个题目因为问法不同而带来的文章内容的差异性。

例1

优缺点类：People like watching sports on television, rather than take part in sports themselves. Do you think this is a positive or negative development?	这个题目只能讨论在电视上看体育的好处或坏处，不能讨论参加体育的好处或坏处（不能作为独立的段落讨论）。
同意反对类：People are very busy with work today, so it is appropriate for them to watch sports on television, rather than take part in sports themselves. Do you agree or disagree?	这个题目如果你支持，就讨论看电视体育节目的好处；如果你反对，就讨论参加体育的好处，或者是看电视体育节目的坏处。

例2

优缺点类：As well as making money, many businesses have tried to undertake other social responsibilities. Do you think this is a positive or negative development?	这个题目只能讨论承担社会责任的好处或坏处，不能讨论只关注赚钱的好处或坏处（不能作为独立的段落讨论）。

同意反对类: As well as making money, businesses should have other social responsibilities. Do you agree or disagree?	这个题目如果你支持,就讨论关注社会责任的好处;如果你反对,就讨论企业不关注社会责任(只关注赚钱)的好处。

注意5:题目出现 best, only 这种字眼也可以折中。

有时候观点类题目会出现表示唯一的字眼,如 best, only 这样的表达,这时你也可以部分支持。例如下面这个题目:

例1: The best way to study something is to go to school. To what extent do you agree or disagree?

你可以支持上学是最好的办法,但是你在主体段也可以说其他的方法,如上网,在家让父母教,或者是通过看电视学习。不是说你一旦支持上学是最好的办法,其他方法就肯定不行。你也可以说上学是学到东西的好方法,但是未必是最好的办法,其他方法某些时候也很好。

例2: Environmental problems are too big for individual countries and individual persons to address. In other words, we have reached the stage where the only way to protect the environment is at an international level. To what extent do you agree or disagree with this opinion?

这个题目的大意是环境问题那么大,个人和单个国家解决不了,所以唯一的解决办法是国际合作。

你可以支持说国际合作有好处,但是不一定是 only 的,然后,你还可以继续讨论个人和单个国家可以做什么去保护环境。

换言之,国际合作和个人或者单个国家都可以在同一篇文章里讨论,不用担心“立场不坚定”。

注意6:题目已经认定的内容不需要去论述。

有时候题目的论题包括两个部分,其中一个部分题目已经确定了,就不需要讨论了。

例1: Many employees may work from home with modern technology. Some people claim that it can benefit workers only, not the employers. Do you agree or disagree?

这个题目只需要讨论员工在家里工作是不是 benefit employers,你可以说对雇主好,也可以说对雇主不好,也可以说“对雇主既有好处,也有坏处”,但是不需要去讨论是不是对员工好 (benefit workers)。

例2: Air travel can only benefit the richest people in the world. Ordinary people can get no advantage with the development of air travel. To what extent do you agree or disagree?

这个题目的重心是讨论普通人是不是从航空业发展中获得好处,你可以说普通人获得好处,也可以说“有些地方获益,有些地方并没有得益”,但是并不需要去讨论有钱人是不是获益,因为你讨论有钱人获益还是不获益,都和普通人无关。

例 3：It is the responsibility of schools to teach good behaviours in addition to providing formal education. To what extent do you agree or disagree?

这个题目的论述重心是学校教 good behaviour，你可以说学校有责任让小孩的行为良好，也可以说"有责任，但是这不是学校的首要任务"，但是你不需要去讨论学校是不是应该 "provide formal education"（提供正式教育），因为即便你论述了学校确实应该提供正式教育，也还是没有论述"学校要提高学生行为"这个话题。

很多考生在写观点类题目，出现折中观点（就是既说优点，也说缺点）的时候，会经常问两个问题，①如果反对一个事物，是不是一定要缺点多过优点？②是否一定要把缺点写在前面，优点写在后面？

第一个问题，大部分时候是的，但是也未必。

第二个问题，写在前写在后都无所谓，关键是你的文字处理。

例如下面这篇文章：

我的主体部分第一段说看电视影响学习，第二段说影响健康，第三段说优点，电视可以传播知识。

事实上也可以倒过来，先写优点再写缺点。下面这是主体段的三个中心句：

I understand that television may benefit children by exposing them to a world of knowledge.

However, in most cases, television viewing can interfere with children's studies and other activities which can benefit these children's development.

Another problem is that excessive screen time can affect children's health.

看完后，你就知道，即便换了位置，最后的立场还是说看电视对孩子不好。

注意 7：观点类题目和论述类题目有两大区别。

区别 1：观点类题目可以完全支持，或者完全反对，论述类题目不可以。

区别 2：观点类题目的主体段落可能是两正一反，或者是两反一正，但是论述类题目的主体段头两段必定是一正一反。

对比一下下面两个题目：

Topic 1: Some people believe that children can learn effectively by watching TV and they should be encouraged to watch TV both at home and at school. To what extent do you agree or disagree?

这是观点类题目，主体段落结构如下：

	主体段落 1	主体段落 2	主体段落 3
如果完全支持看电视	支持的第一个观点	支持的第二个观点	支持的第三个观点
如果完全反对看电视	反对的第一个观点	反对的第二个观点	反对的第三个观点
如果主要支持看电视	支持的第一个观点	支持的第二个观点	反对的一个观点
如果主要反对看电视	反对的第一个观点	反对的第二个观点	支持的一个观点

Topic 2: Some people believe that children should be encouraged to watch TV both at home and at school, while other people argue that television viewing should be restricted. Discuss both views and give

your own opinion.

这是论述类题目，主体段落结构如下：

	主体段落 1	主体段落 2	主体段落 3
如果主要支持看电视	支持的第一个观点	反对的一个观点	支持的第二个观点
如果主要反对看电视	支持的一个观点	反对的第一个观点	反对的第二个观点

提升的范文

标色的部分是和原文有差异的地方，下划线部分是词伙。

Watching television (especially <u>informative television</u>) has been recognised as an effective <u>method of learning</u>, because <u>audio-visual information</u> can attract students' attention and <u>engage their interest</u>. Although many TV programmes have <u>educational value</u>, I do not agree with the idea of increasing screen time.

Television viewing can <u>interfere with children's studies</u> and other activities which can benefit these children's <u>intellectual development</u>. They may not be able to <u>achieve good grades</u> in exams because screen time displaces the time they could spend doing homework. It is also worrying to see that <u>television viewing</u> can <u>crowd out those activities</u> which can <u>improve children's intellectual skills</u>, such as reading, playing chess and <u>board games</u>.

Another problem is that long screen time can limit children's social development. Those children who sit in front of their TV for many hours, instead of playing games with their peers and communicating with teachers, will become unsociable and unwilling to express their views and understand the thoughts of other people. Without good communication skills, they will have difficulty in gaining knowledge, drawing upon the ideas of classmates or teachers, and achieving academic success.

On the other hand, I understand that television has exposed children to <u>a world of knowledge</u>. There are many <u>educational programmes</u> aimed for children, allowing them to gain an insight into different subjects. For example, documentaries can help children learn about <u>historical events</u> while foreign language channels can help them <u>acquire foreign languages</u>. This kind of knowledge can complement what they learn at school.

To summarise, I would argue that parents and teachers should impose restrictions on children's television viewing, although television shows are a source of knowledge. Watching TV can have an adverse impact on exam grades and social skills.

3.6.4 全文翻译 4：消费社会＋报告类题目写作要点

> *It is argued that we are living in a throw-away society: people throw away what they use in daily life, instead of recycling or reusing them. Why has this happened and how to address this issue?*

题目大意

有人说我们现在住在一个不珍惜东西的社会里。人们将自己日常生活中使用的东西不断扔掉，而不是循环利用。为什么发生了这样的事情？如何解决这个问题？

读者自学步骤 1

阅读题目后，写出三个观点。

下面是我学生写的一些错误或者不好的观点，大家可以看看自己是不是也犯了同样的错误。

学生的观点	点评
科技发展快，人们收入高，即扔社会。	没有逻辑。科技发展快，很多人还失业呢，为什么收入高？
政府管理少，基础设施跟不上，即扔社会。	不够有力。人喜欢东西用不久就扔，和基础设施没什么关系。如果你真想扔，垃圾桶要是多了，你更加愿意扔。
政府加强基础设施建设，增加便民服务点，减少浪费。	跑题。这个题目的重心不是怎么回收垃圾，而是怎么让大家珍惜东西，不要用不久就扔掉。

读者自学步骤 2

翻译下面的句子：在翻译过程中，记住先想词伙，再想句型，然后写出句子。 相关词伙可以查阅微信公众号：gu_writing。

介绍段

改写题目	1. 人们现在喜欢用东西只用一次，而不是使用很长的时间。
阐述立场或者说明文章讨论内容	2. 了解这个问题为什么发生和如何解决这个问题是重要的。

主体部分第一段

中心句（经济发展）	3. 人们现在的收入不断增加，因此他们可以购买大量的产品。
解释	4. 技术的革新和产品的批量生产降低了成本，也提高了人们的生产力。
举例	5. 一些电子产品，如手机和电脑，现在很低的价格就可以买到，所以当这些产品坏了的时候，人们很少去修理它们。
拓展	6. 特别是年轻人，他们喜欢购买带有新功能的最新手机，同时扔掉旧的。

主体部分第二段

附加观点（社会文化）	7. 人们缺乏环境意识也是另外一个原因。

解释	8. 很多人没有意识到他们的消费习惯会导致能源消耗，产生垃圾和污染。
举例	9. 他们不知道家用电器最终成为垃圾，而这些电器是很难分解的，对环境会有很大的伤害。
拓展	10. 他们不知道回收利用很多产品可以让我们的生活方式更加环保。

主体部分第三段

中心句	11. 因为产品的过度消费很普遍，采取一些措施去减少污染是很重要的。
观点 1	12. 我们需要提高人们的环保意识，因为这会改变人们使用和处理产品的方式。
解释	13. 环保团体应该传播关于如何回收利用一次性物品以及家电产品的知识。
观点 2	14. 政府也可以颁布一些法律，去抑制人们过分使用消费品。
举例	15. 例如，政府可以对一些一次性产品，如塑料袋收税，那么就会鼓励人们使用环保的购物袋。

结论段

总结观点	16. 人们对消费的态度和可支配收入的增加是过度消费的主要原因。
	17. 要成功地解决这个问题，首要的事情是提高人们对环境保护的意识，这样才会引起他们生活方式的改变。

读者自学步骤 3

检查自己的翻译：先看正确句子的词伙和句子结构，然后看错误的句子，看是否能够发现问题。

句 1

正：People are likely to use products only once instead of keeping these items for a long time.

学生的句子：People are likely to use products only once instead of using for a long time.

改：use 是及物动词，后面要加宾语。

句 2

正：It is important to understand why this throw-away culture has developed and how to reverse this trend.

学生的句子：It is of crucial importance to figure out the reasons and measurements to solve this problem.

改：of crucial importance to 一般后面加 something; measurement 是"测量"的意思。

句 3

正：People have increased wealth significantly and can afford many products.

学生的句子：As people have more disposable income nowadays, they are affordable for large amount of products.

改：人不能说 affordable; large amount 前少了冠词 a。

句 4

正：Technological innovations and mass production have reduced the cost of production and improved the productivity of the workforce.

学生的句子：Technological innovation and massive production of products lead to the low cost of production and also boost people's productivity.

改：应该是 mass production；用完成时态表示结果比较好。

句 5

正：Some electronic products such as mobile phones and computers are now sold at low prices, and this is why few people would fix broken items.

学生的句子：Some electronic devices such as mobile phones and computers are selling at low price, that is why fewer people would like to fix them when they are broken.

改：sell 是及物动词，这里用被动比较恰当；price 是可数名词，要用复数；两个句子间没有连词；them 指代不清楚。

句 6

正：Young people in particular, prefer to purchase the latest mobile phones with up-to-date features and throw old ones away.

学生的句子：Especially the young people prefer to purchase the latest designed mobile phones with new function and throw the old ones away.

改：especially 一般不在句首；没有 latest designed 这个表达；function 是可数名词，要用复数。

句 7

正：Another reason is that people lack environmental awareness.

学生的句子：People lack environmental awareness that is also another reason.

改：两个句子间没有连词。

句 8

正：People have not yet realised that their ways of life will lead to energy consumption and cause waste as well as pollution.

学生的句子：People have not realised that their consuming habits will lead to energy consumption, which results in wastes and pollutions.

改：consuming habits 不是习惯表达；waste 和 pollution 都是不可数名词。

句 9

正：They do not know that household appliances can end up in landfill sites and these non-biodegradable products can have a destructive effect on the environment.

学生的句子：They do not know that home appliance will end up in landfill sites as trash, which is very hard to degrade by themselves, imposing enormous damages on the environment.

改：appliance 是可数名词；定语从句不知道修饰什么；damage 是不可数名词。

句 10

正：They are not aware that recycling can make their lifestyles more sustainable.

学生的句子：They do not know that recycling these products can help us live in a environmentally friendly lifestyle.

改：一般说 live a...life，不需要加 in；environmenally 是以元音发音开头的单词，不定冠词用 an。

句 11

正：As the overconsumption of consumer goods is pervasive, it is important to take some measures to mitigate this problem.

学生的句子：Since the overconsumption of products is pervasive, it is crucial to take measures to mitigate the pollution.

改：crucial 后面的 to 是介词，不能加动词；pollution 前面的 the 多余，这里不需要特指。

句 12

正：Raising environmental awareness is important, because this can change the ways people use and dispose of different products.

学生的句子：Raising environmental awareness is important, because this can change ways that people use and dispose their products.

改：可以说 the ways in which，或者直接说 the ways；dispose of 是习惯表达。

句 13

正：Environmental groups can disseminate the knowledge of how to recycle disposable goods and household appliances.

学生的句子：Environmental groups should disseminate the knowledges about how to recycle disposable goods and household appliances.

改：knowledge 是不可数名词。

句 14

正：Governments can also enforce some laws to deter consumers from throwing away goods.

学生的句子：The government could announce some rules to forbid citizens from excessive use of consumption goods.

改：forbid somebody to do something 是习惯表达。

句 15

正：For example, the tax penalty can be imposed on some disposable products, including plastic bags, thereby encouraging people to use eco-friendly shopping bags.

学生的句子：For example, governments can pose taxes on some disposable products like plastic bags, then it can encourage people to use environmentally-friendly bags.

改：一般说 impose taxes on；then 是副词，不是连词。

句 16

正：People's attitude toward consumption and the increase in disposable income are main reasons behind excessive consumption of disposable items.

学生的句子：People's attitude of consumption and disposable income increase is the important reasons for overconsumption.

改：attitude 后面的介词一般是 to 或者 toward；主语是两个名词，因此谓语动词要用复数；increase 应该是主语，而不是 disposable income。

句 17

正：To address this problem successfully, the top priority is to raise people's awareness of environmental protection, which can lead to a change to their lifestyles.

学生的句子：The priority of solving the problem successfully is to increase the awareness of environmental problems thus will lead to the change of their lifestyles.

改：句中有 is 和 will lead to 两个谓语，应该引入一个从句。

读者自学步骤 4

整体学习和检查范文，看看是否符合 TELCCS 原则。

范文全文（7~7.5 分）

People are likely to use products only once instead of keeping these items for a long time. It is important to understand why this throw-away culture has developed and how to reverse this trend.

People have increased wealth significantly and can afford many products. Technological innovations and mass production have reduced the cost of production and improved the productivity of the workforce. Some electronic products such as mobile phones and computers are now sold at low prices, and this is why few people would fix broken items. Young people in particular, prefer to purchase the latest mobile phones with up-to-date features and throw old ones away.

中心句说的是增加财富，但是后面说的是商品价格下降。

这里出现了跳跃，应该先说买东西。

Another reason is that people lack environmental

awareness. People have not yet realised that their ways of life will lead to energy consumption and cause waste as well as pollution. They do not know that household appliances can end up in landfill sites and these non-biodegradable products can have a destructive effect on the environment. They are not aware that recycling can make their lifestyles more sustainable.

如果还用 they are... 和前面的句子有点重复。

As the overconsumption of consumer goods is pervasive, it is important to take some measures to mitigate this problem. Raising environmental awareness is important, because this can change the ways people use and dispose of different products. Environmental groups can disseminate the knowledge of how to recycle disposable goods and household appliances. Governments can also enforce some laws to deter consumers from throwing away goods. For example, the tax penalty can be imposed on some disposable products, including plastic bags, thereby encouraging people to use eco-friendly shopping bags.

前面已经说了 important，再说就重复了，影响 LR 的分数。

这句话和上面一句话有点重复，内容大致类似，可以去掉；否则，影响 CC 的成绩。

这里不明确是和 disposable products 还是和 plastic bags 对称。

People's attitude toward consumption and the increase in disposable income are main reasons behind excessive consumption of disposable items. To address this problem successfully, the top priority is to raise people's awareness of environmental protection, which can lead to a change to their lifestyles.

这里缺一个连接词。

主体段落说的是价格，这里说收入，不一致，影响 CC 的分数。

disposable items 是"一次性产品"的意思，不能够指代主体部分说的产品，影响 CC 的分数。

这个句子前面 to do 表示目的，这里定语从句 which lead to 表示结果，读起来很不舒服，会影响 GRA 的分数。

本节关键学习点

这篇文章属于雅思写作第三种常见的话题：报告类题目。报告类题目一般就是描述一个问题，然后问这个问题怎么产生的，应该怎么解决。

报告类题目有以下需要注意的要点：

注意 1：主体部分可以分 2～3 段写。

注意 2：报告类文章的解决方法一般都是对应问题的原因，但是如果不对应，也可以接受。

注意 3：报告类文章的开头和主体段一般不要出现 some people think that/argue that 这样的字眼。

下面我会解释一下这些要点的意义。

注意 1：主体部分可以分 2 ～ 3 段写。

以本文为例，关于结构有下面三种选择。

	throw-away society 的原因	throw-away society 的解决方法
选择 1：主体部分 2 段	1 段，写 2 个原因。	1 段，写 2 个解决方法。
选择 2：主体部分 3 段	2 段，每段各写 1 个原因。	1 段，写 2 个解决方法。
选择 3：主体部分 3 段	1 段，写 2 个原因。	2 段，每段各写 1 个解决方法。

注意 2：报告类文章的解决方法一般都是对应问题的原因，但是如果不对应，也可以接受。

例如这个题目的第一个观点是技术革新导致商品价格下降，大家愿意大量购买。显然科技革新本身并不是一个问题，我们不可能去阻碍技术革新。所以后面提出的"政府实施严格的法律"其实并不是一个对应的方法，但是也可以接受。

注意 3：报告类文章的开头和主体段一般不要出现 some people think that/argue that 这样的字眼。

理由很简单，因为不是论述类文章，不需要论述不同的人的看法，只需要描述客观发生的事情。

提升的范文

标色的部分是和原文有差异的地方，下划线部分是词伙。

People are likely to use products only once instead of keeping these items for a long time. It is important to understand why this throw-away culture has developed and how to reverse this trend.

Consumers today do not keep many goods for a long period of time because these products are not as expensive as before. Technological innovations and mass production have reduced the cost of production and improved the productivity of the workforce. Some electronic products such as mobile phones and computers are now sold at low prices, and this is why many people would purchase the newest products, instead of fixing broken ones. Young people in particular, prefer to purchase the latest mobile phones with up-to-date features and throw old ones away.

Another reason is that people lack environmental awareness. People have not yet realised that their ways of life will lead to energy consumption and cause waste as well as pollution. They do not know that household appliances can end up in landfill sites and these non-biodegradable products can have a destructive effect on the environment. If they are aware that recycling can make their lifestyles more sustainable, they will possibly try to reuse products.

As the overconsumption of consumer goods is pervasive, it is important to take some measures to mitigate this problem. The first one is to raise environmental awareness, educating people to change the ways they use and dispose of different products. Governments can also enforce some laws to deter consumers from throwing away goods. For example, the tax penalty can be imposed on the use of some disposable products, including plastic bags, thereby encouraging people to use eco-friendly alternatives.

To summarise, people's changing attitude toward consumption and price cuts are main reasons behind excessive consumption of consumer goods. To address this problem successfully, the top priority is to raise people's awareness of environmental protection and motivate them to change their lifestyles.

3.6.5 全文翻译 5：城乡转移＋混合类题目写作要点＋开头段的写作

Many people are moving from rural areas to big cities. Why has this happened? To what extent do you think it is a good trend?

题目大意

很多人现在从农村移居到城市。为什么如此？多大程度上你觉得这是一个好的趋势？

读者自学步骤 1

阅读题目后，写出三个观点。

下面是我学生写的一些错误或者不好的观点，大家可以看看自己是不是也犯了同样的错误。

学生的观点	点评
城市工作多，工资可观，就业人口增加，搬到城市，城市压力变大，地区发展不平衡。	两个观点混在一起。混合类题目的两个问题最好分开写。
很多人选择从乡村移居到城市生活，大城市生活条件更好，工作机会更多，人们可以有一个更好的生活，从而可以更好地为社会做贡献。	两个观点混在一起。工作机会更多，有更好的生活是原因，回答第一问。更好地为社会做贡献，这是结果，回答第二问。两个问题要分开回答。
大面积的人口流动造成城市交通紧张，人口分布不均，容易导致一些社会问题，城市化进程过快。	太过空泛。为什么城市化进程过快？会导致一些社会问题，什么社会问题？
城市比起乡村有更便捷的交通方式，为人们出行提供便利，节约时间，更高效率办公。	跑题。这个题目讨论的是人们移居城市的优缺点，不是城市居住的优缺点。

读者自学步骤 2

翻译下面的句子：在翻译过程中，记住先想词伙，再想句型，然后写出句子。相关词伙可以查阅微信公众号：gu_writing。

介绍段

背景句	1. 目前，很多人从农村移居到城市。
改写题目	2. 他们可能认为在城市更好找工作，生活也更加舒适，不过，这个趋势会带来很多问题。

主体部分第一段

中心句	3. 人们会选择去城市居住有两个主要原因。
原因 1	4. 首先，城市人口比较密集，工作机会比较多，相对来说，人们比较容易获得较高的收入。
结果	5. 这就意味着人们的生活水平提高，可以购买更多的产品。
对比	6. 相比之下，乡村地区的工作机会很少，因为很多行业发展不完善，消费力比较低。
原因 2	7. 另外一个原因是城市居民比乡村居民更加容易获得公共服务，包括教育和医疗保健并享有更好的生活水平。
结果	8. 年轻夫妇希望孩子在城市接受良好的教育，从而可以摆脱贫穷。

主体部分第二段

附加观点	9. 城市居民的数量增加会对城市的设施和住房造成压力。
原因	10. 一些城市土地比较稀缺，很难容纳大量的人口。
举例 1	11. 很多移居者最后要住在贫民窟并忍受恶劣的生活条件，因为他们买不起房子。
举例 2	12. 人们更加容易生病，因为城市的设施不能够满足清洁水的供应、家庭垃圾的处理、污水的处理等。

主体部分第三段

中心句（社会）	13. 乡村转移的一个主要问题是城乡收入差距变大，而不是减少。
解释	14. 有野心的、精力充沛的、勤奋的和有创造力的年轻人会去城市上学和找工作。
结果	15. 乡村地区的劳动力不足，重新振兴乡村经济就变得很难。
拓展结果	16. 而在城市，有些年轻人因为贫富差距的问题会选择犯罪。

结论段

总结观点	17. 总之，农村的就业前景不好和经济落后导致了人口迁移。
表明立场	18. 这是一个让人担心的趋势。

读者自学步骤 3

检查自己的翻译：先看正确句子的词伙和句子结构，然后看错误的句子，看是否能够发现问题。

句 1

正：These days many people from rural areas have chosen to migrate to cities.

学生的句子：These days many people immigrate from rural places to cities.

改：immigrate 一般指国际的移民；rural places 也不是一个恰当的表达。

句 2

正：They may believe that they are more likely to find employment and enjoy a better quality of life, but the movement of population to urban areas can cause many problems.

学生的句子：They may believe that cities provide them with more working opportunities and high quality lives, however, this trend may cause many problems.

改：没有 high quality lives 这个表达；however 不是连词，不能连接独立的句子。

句 3

正：There are two main reasons why these people have flocked to cities.

学生的句子：There are two main reasons why people would choose to settle in cities.

改：would 时态不对，毕竟这些人已经移居，用完成时态比较好。

句 4

正：Firstly, cities are more densely populated and there are more job opportunities available, so people may earn more money.

学生的句子：This is because cities are normally have a larger population and more employment, and people are more likely to find a well-paid job.

改："are + 动词原形"永远是错的；employment 是不可数名词，在这里表达不是很好。

句 5

正：This means that they can improve living standards and afford more consumer goods than ever before.

学生的句子：This means that people's living standards increase, so they are able to purchase more products.

改：这两个句子没有因果关系，而是并列关系，所以用 so 不恰当。

句 6

正：By contrast, employment opportunities are scarce in rural areas, due to the fact that many industries are underdeveloped and many inhabitants' buying power is limited.

学生的句子：By contrast, employment opportunities are not enough in rural areas, due to many industries remain underdeveloped and buying power is weak.

改：not enough 是非正式表达；due to 是介词，后面不能加句子。

句 7

正：Another reason is that city dwellers have easy access to public services, including education and health care, and enjoy better standards of living.

学生的句子：Another reason is that city dwellers gain broader access to public services including education and health care and enjoy better standard of living.

改：standard 是可数名词，要么加冠词，要么改为复数形式；health care 后面要加逗号，否则会产生歧义。

句8

正：Young couples intend to send their children to good schools in urban areas, so as to break the cycle of poverty.

学生的句子：Young couples expect their children receive quality education in urban settings, so they can break the cycle of poverty.

改：主句里有两个动词；expect somebody to do something 是固定表达。

句9

正：The increased number of urban dwellers can put huge pressure on housing and facilities in cities.

学生的句子：An increasing number of city dwellers will pose extra pressure on the infrastructure and housing in cities.

改：an increasing number of city dwellers 的重心是在 city dwellers，而人是不能造成压力的，只有 number 可以构成压力；pose pressure on 不是习惯表达。

句10

正：Some cities are unable to accommodate a large population because of the shortage of land.

学生的句子：Some cities which lack of land are hard to accommodate a huge number of population.

改：lack of 的 lack 是名词；不能说城市或者人 are hard to...；a number of 后面只能加名词复数。

句11

正：Many migrants end up living in slums and enduring poor living conditions, because they cannot afford home ownership.

学生的句子：Many migrants end up living in slum and bearing horrible living conditions because they cannot afford house price.

改：price 是可数名词，要改为复数形式；afford prices 这个搭配也不是很好。

句12

正：People are prone to poor health because urban facilities fail to meet the growing demand for clean water, dispose of household waste effectively and manage sewage.

学生的句子：People are prone to poor health because the urban facilities cannot meet the growing demand for clean water, and dispose household waste as well as manage sewage.

改：dispose of 是习惯表达；and 和 as well as 在这里同时使用没必要。

句13

正：Another problem associated with a rural-to-urban shift is that rural-urban income disparity will grow, instead of diminishing.

学生的句子：Another associated with rural-to-urban shift is that rural-urban income disparity will grow up, instead of diminishing.

改：shift 是可数名词，应该加不定冠词；grow up 表示人或者植物的成长。

句 14

正：Young people who are ambitious, energetic, hardworking and creative prefer to go to the cities in search of educational and employment opportunities.

学生的句子：Young people who are ambitious, energetic, hardworking are prefer to go to the cities to attend school and find employment.

改：三个形容词间没有连词是不可以的；"are + 动词原形"永远是错的。

句 15

正：The shortage of labour has become a problem in rural communities and it is not easy to revitalise the local economy.

学生的句子：It is hard to revitalize the economy in rural areas as there are probably short of workforce.

改：short 是形容词，不能作主语。

句 16

正：In cities, some young people may choose to commit crimes because of the widening gap between rich and poor.

学生的句子：While in cities, some young people may choose to commit crimes because of the widening gap between rich and poor.

改：while 这个词是从属连词，一定要连接两个独立的句子。

句 17

正：In conclusion, poor employment prospects and sluggish local economies have caused the population shift to cities.

学生的句子：In conclusion, the poor employment prospects and economic backwardness are the main reasons accounted for population shift.

改：account for 一般没有被动语态，而且一般不和 reasons 搭配。

句 18

正：This is a worrying trend.

学生的句子：This is worrying trend.

改：trend 是可数名词，要有冠词。

读者自学步骤 4

整体学习和检查范文，看看是否符合 TELCCS 原则。

范文全文 (大概 7.5 分)

These days many people from rural areas have chosen to migrate to cities. They may believe that they are more likely to find employment and enjoy a better quality of life, but the movement of population to urban areas can cause many problems.

连续两个 they，读起来不是很舒服。

There are two main reasons why these people have flocked to cities. Firstly, cities are more densely populated and there are more job opportunities available, so people may earn more money. This means that they can improve living standards and afford more consumer goods than ever before. By contrast, employment opportunities are scarce in rural areas, due to the fact that many industries are underdeveloped and many inhabitants' buying power is limited. Another reason is that city dwellers have easy access to public services, including education and health care, and enjoy better standards of living. Young couples intend to send their children to good schools in urban areas so as to break the cycle of poverty.

和前面的 migrate to cities 重复。

前面也有 people，可以用代词。

这个表达和上面的 due to the fact that 放在一起，有点重复的感觉。影响 CC。

和前面的 living standards 重复，可以去掉，提高 CC 的分数。

这里可能突出乡村的夫妇比较好。

这里有点跳跃，难道去好学校就可以摆脱贫穷？那么快？影响 CC 的分数。

The increased number of urban dwellers can put huge pressure on housing and facilities in cities. Some cities are unable to accommodate a large population because of the shortage of land. Many migrants end up living in slums and enduring poor living conditions, because they cannot afford home ownership. People are prone to poor health because urban facilities fail to meet the growing demand for clean water, dispose of household waste effectively and manage sewage.

这个 people 有点指代不清楚，可以说 all city dwellers。

这里读起来有点不通顺，不清楚 dispose of 是和 meet 对称，还是和 fail to 对称。

Another problem associated with a rural-to-urban shift is that rural-urban income disparity will grow, instead of diminishing. Young people who are ambitious, energetic, hardworking and creative prefer to go to the cities in search of educational and employment opportunities. The shortage of labour has become a problem in rural communities and it is not easy to revitalise the local

这两个句子的主语没有直接的关系，可以加连接词 thus。

economy. In cities, some young people may choose to commit crimes because of the widening gap between rich and poor.

这句话可以去掉，有歧义，前面说的是城乡的贫富差距，这里又变成了城市的贫富差距。

In conclusion, poor employment prospects and sluggish local economies have caused the population shift to cities. This is a worrying trend.

本节关键学习点

所谓的混合类题目就是题目有两个问题，一个问题属于报告类（问原因或者是解决方法），一个问题属于观点类（问影响），如下面两个例子：

What problems does it cause? What measures can be taken to deal with this?

What has caused this to happen? Does it have a positive or negative effect on society?

第一个例子的前半部分是问 "产生什么问题"，也就是问影响，而第二部分是问解决方法。

第二个例子的前半部分是问原因，第二部分问影响。

混合类题目在最近两年雅思考试中屡有出现，因为剑桥雅思考试委员会知道一些中国考生用模板来备考，因此会经常采用这种比较异类的问法来考查考生的审题和扣题能力。

混合类题目有下面一些要点：

> 要点 **1**：两个问题同等重要，都要回答。
>
> 要点 **2**：每个问题可以用一到两个观点回答，如果是两个观点，可以分两段写，也可以写在一段。

要点 **1**：两个问题同等重要，都要回答。

很多考生经常问我这个问题。混合类题目的两个问题都重要，都要回答，缺一不可。当然同等重要，不代表论述的字数和长度差不多。你可以一个问题只写一个观点，另外一个问题写两个观点。考官不会因为你观点的多寡而认为你论述有倾向性。

要点 **2**：每个问题可以用一到两个观点回答，如果是两个观点，可以分两段写，也可以写在一段。

正如本文一样，我在解释人们去城市的时候，两个原因写在了一段。而在讨论其问题的时候，两个问题分开写了。

雅思作文大部分题目都比较常规，也就是书里讲过的观点类、论述类、报告类和混合类题目。然而，有些时候也会出现比较 unusual 的题目。遇到这些题目的时候要注意三点：

注意 **1**：如果题目出现两个问题，那么两个问题都要用不同的段落回应。

注意 **2**：每个问题可以用一到两段回答，不需要做到类似长度。

注意 **3**：每段话中心句一定要直接回答题目，确保考官知道你在扣题。

例 1：Competitiveness is regarded as a positive quality for people in most societies. How does competitiveness affect individuals? Is it a positive or negative trend?

主体部分可以写三段，其中一段对应一个问题，其他两段对应另一个问题。

第一段的中心句可以说（对应第一个问题）：People who have a competitive mentality may work hard to achieve their ambitions.

第二段的中心句可以说（对应第二个问题）：The trend towards viewing competitiveness as a good trait can be positive, as long as people can improve skills to reach their potential.

第三段的中心句可以说（对应第二个问题）：On the other hand, competitiveness can be detrimental to us, if we become overambitious and selfish.

例2：Some people who failed at school can be highly successful in their adult life. Why does this happen? And what are the main factors to get a successful life?

主体部分可以写三段，其中一段对应一个问题，其他两段对应另一个问题。

第一段的中心句可以说（对应第一个问题）：Some people who successfully turn their ideas into profitable businesses can also become rich, even though they drop out of school.

第二段的中心句可以说（对应第一个问题）：Some people may have exceptional social skills and benefit from personal resources, although they do not have good qualifications.

第三段的中心句可以说（对应第二个问题）：I think good character and knowledge are among factors contributing to one's career success.

我们这一节也说说开头段的写法。关于作文的开头段，大家要注意下面几点。

注意1：开头段不要写很长，因为主体部分才是考官的重点阅读部分。

注意2：开头段如果写得好，对你分数不会有很大的影响；但是写得不好，就会有很大的负面影响。所以在开头段千万别犯语法错误。

注意3：不要抄题，这样考官会把照抄的部分去掉，不算字数。

注意4：不要使用大家用烂的一些表达（如 There is a trend that… With the development of…）。

注意5：改写题目的话不要改变题目的论述重心。

我自己在写开头段的时候，一般写两句。第一句一般是背景句，第二句表明立场或者告诉读者文章大概会说什么。

就本文而言，我的背景句有如下三种可能：

可能1：描述一个客观发生的事实或者趋势。	Many countries have experienced a significant movement of population to large cities in the past few decades.
可能2：强调某个事物对我们有影响。	The rural-to-urban shift has an impact not only on rural people, but also on those living in cities.
可能3：改写题目。	Many people have chosen to migrate to cities.

而第二句话有如下两种可能：

| 可能 *1*：表明自己的立场。 | In my view, this has presented a challenge to many cities. |
| 可能 *2*：大概说一下主体部分会讲什么。 | There are a number of factors behind this trend and this trend can cause various problems. |

然后将这两个句子组合一下，就成为开头段：

例 1：Many countries have experienced a significant movement of population to large cities in the past few decades. In my view, this has presented a challenge to many cities.

例 2：The rural-to-urban shift has an impact not only on rural people, but also on those living in cities. There are a number of factors behind this trend and this trend can cause various problems.

还有一些考生比较痛苦的是不知道背景该写什么，毕竟习惯了不管什么话题，都会说"随着社会的发展"。解决的方法是：平时在复习中有意识地根据不同话题，先思考一个比较概括性的现象。

例如：

常考话题，环境类：Many environmental problems such as air pollution have become serious.

常考话题，电脑和网络：We live in the Internet age and depend on the Internet technology to deal with many problems in our daily lives.

常考话题，教育：Many parents today spend a large proportion of their income on their children's education.

常考话题，旅游：It is clear that many people today have chosen foreign countries when they decide where to take a vacation.

常考话题，电视：Watching TV has been the most popular form of entertainment for most households in the world.

有些考生会质疑，假如我写这些，会不会成为新的套句，和其他考生类似？

核心是使用词伙，围绕词伙去写背景句。

如环境问题，你可以说 environmental issues, environmental protection, preserve the environment, environmental degradation 等。

- Many environmental issues can affect our health and the wellbeing of future generations.
- There are many challenges we have to overcome in environmental protection.
- It is clear that we should take concrete action to preserve the environment.
- Environmental degradation has been a cause of preventable diseases in the world.

这样，是不是背景句就很难重复了？

我出国前，看到过很多培训材料都是以套句开头，而十多年后，我回来了，大家还是用那么几个句子开头。英文只是一种语言，并不是深奥的学问。我们经济和科技发展那么快，但是语言学习和教育止步不前，真是值得大家检讨和反思。

当然，也有很多考生特别不喜欢写背景句，觉得很难想出来一个和话题相关的现象，所以倾向于改写题目。改写题目的难点是很多考生缺乏替换词汇的积累，很多时候会照抄题目。这也是一个难点。

那么有什么方法改写题目？

我们使用这个题目的背景句 Many people are moving from rural areas to big cities 作为例子，改写一下题目。

方法1：改表达。

改表达包括 ① 改词性；② 换说法。

① 改词性。

如 moving 可以改成 movement，这是改词性。

那么这句话可以写成 The movement of people from the countryside to the city has been a clear trend in many parts of the world.

② 换说法。

如 rural areas 的替换表达有 rural communities, the countryside, farming areas。big cities 的替换表达有 large cities, megacities, metropolitan areas 等。move 的替换表达有 relocate to, migrate to 等。也可以是一些词伙的使用，如 rural residents, the rural-to-urban shift。

那么这句话可以写成：Many rural residents have migrated to metropolitan areas.

方法2：改结构。

改结构主要是通过一些关键词的位置变换。例如将句子后面的信息移到前面去。

那么这句话可以写成：Big cities have attracted many people who used to lived in rural areas.

方法3：内容稍稍拓展。

这个方法涉及两个方式：① 名词可以用例子去具体化；② 通过状语来拓展。

① 名词可以用例子去具体化。

来自乡村的人，可以说本来是务农的, work in farms。大城市，可以说是工业特别发达的 manufacturing jobs。

那么这句话可以写成：Many people from rural areas, who previously worked in farms, have chosen to move to big cities, especially those which provide numerous manufacturing jobs.

② 通过状语来拓展。

状语可以是条件、时间、原因状语等，例如当他们失去工作的时候。

Many people are moving from rural areas to big cities, possibly because they have lost their traditional livelihoods in their hometown.

很多考生在写开头段的时候，总是喜欢用 with 开头。这种千篇一律的写法，会让考官非常反感。此外，很多时候，with 是"有了……"的意思，因此也不符合一些语境，例如：

With the high cost of fast food, people pay closer attention on healthy eating.

因为有了快餐的高价，人们会更加注意健康的饮食。（好像人们蓄意提高价格一样）

那么如何减少对 with 的依赖？如何减少 with 的使用？

方法 1：如果表示原因的话，可以用 because of, due to, as a result of... 等。

Because of the lack of well-paid jobs in rural communities, many people have chosen to migrate to cities.

大意：因为农村地区缺乏好的就业机会，很多人选择移居城市。

对比：With the development of cities, many people have chosen to migrate to cities.

方法 2：如果表示一个同时发生的状况或者情形，可以用 as 引导的状语从句。

As many cities have become prosperous, a growing number of people from rural communities have chosen to move to urban areas for a better standard of living.

大意：随着许多城市变得富裕，越来越多的人从农村移居城市，为了过上更好的生活。

方法 3：有时候可以直接去掉 with，将 with 后的宾语和后面的句子合成一句话。

The economic growth of many cities has driven people from rural communities to move to urban areas in search of jobs.

大意：很多城市的经济发展已经鼓励乡村的人移居城市去找工作。

对比：With the economic growth of many cities, people from rural communities to move to urban areas in search of jobs.

提升的范文

标色的部分是和原文有差异的地方，下划线部分是词伙。

These days many people from rural areas have chosen to migrate to cities, believing that they are more likely to find employment and enjoy a better quality of life in urban areas, but the movement of population can cause many problems.

There are two main reasons why these people have made this decision. Firstly, cities are more densely populated and there are more job opportunities available, so they may earn more money. This means that they can improve living standards and afford more consumer goods than ever before. By contrast, employment opportunities are scarce in rural areas, due to the fact that many industries are underdeveloped and many inhabitants' buying power is limited. Another advantage of urban life is that city dwellers have easy access to public services, including education and health care, and young couples who used to live in the countryside intend to send their children to urban schools to get prepared for better job opportunities in the future.

The increased number of urban dwellers can put huge pressure on housing and facilities in cities. Some cities are unable to accommodate a large population because of the shortage of land. Many migrants end up living in slums and enduring poor living conditions, because they cannot afford home ownership. All city dwellers are prone to poor health because urban facilities do not have the capacity to manage waste and sewage effectively and to match the growing demand for clean water.

Another problem associated with a rural-to-urban shift is that rural-urban income disparity will grow, instead of diminishing. Young people who are ambitious, energetic, hardworking and creative prefer to go to the cities in search of educational and employment opportunities. The shortage of labour has thus become a problem in rural communities and it is not easy to revitalise the local economy.

In conclusion, poor employment prospects and sluggish local economies have caused the population shift to cities. This is a worrying trend.

3.6.6 全文翻译 6：廉价航空服务＋审题的要素

> *Many people think cheap air travel should be encouraged because it gives ordinary people freedom to travel further. However, others think this leads to environmental problems, so air travel should be more expensive in order to discourage people from travelling by air. Discuss both sides and give your own opinion.*

题目大意

很多人认为便宜的空航应该被鼓励，因为它给普通人机会去更远的地方旅游。但是，另一些人认为这会导致环境问题，因此空航应该更加的昂贵，这样人们就会打消乘飞机出行的念头。讨论这两个观点并给出你个人的看法。

读者自学步骤 1

阅读题目后，写出三个观点。

下面是我学生写的一些错误或者不好的观点，大家可以看看自己是不是也犯了同样的错误。

学生的观点	点评
空中旅行非常方便，可以很好地解决偏远地区人们的出行困难，便宜的空航应该被鼓励。	观点不够有力。为什么需要解决出行困难的问题？解决这个问题有什么好处？
机票便宜 / 越来越多人乘飞机出行 / 方便人们出行，促进经济发展。产生大量二氧化碳，污染环境。	两个观点混在一起。经济发展是优点，产生二氧化碳是缺点。

小幅度提高票价，票价一部分用于环境治理，环境污染得到控制。	跑题。这个题目的第二个立场要求讨论的是提高票价可以减少人们使用空航，而不是去讨论钱怎么使用。
降低机票价格，飞机噪声污染增加，影响机场附近居民的生活水平和健康。	跑题。这个题目的第二个立场要求讨论的是提高票价可以减少人们使用空航，而不是讨论机票价格便宜的坏处。
机票钱便宜，更多普通人有能力支付，提高人们的幸福感。	不够有力。为什么有能力支付就可以提高幸福感？
廉价空航给人们提供了更多的旅行机会，对于商务人士来说可以开拓更广阔的市场，从而带动经济的发展，所以应该鼓励发展廉价空航。	轻微跑题。商业人士不是普通人，普通人应该是打工族。
机票降价，同预算选择空间大，可飞更远。	不够有力。飞得更远的好处是什么？为什么要飞得更远？
鼓励飞机票贵，提供的服务水平及质量会更好。鼓励人们努力工作挣钱，享受生活。	跑题。这个题目的第二个立场要求讨论的是提高票价可以减少人们使用空航，而不是讨论提高票价的其他好处。

读者自学步骤 2

翻译下面的句子：在翻译过程中，记住先想词伙，再想句型，然后写出句子。相关词伙可以查阅微信公众号：gu_writing。

介绍段

背景句	1. 廉价空航让我们可以更便宜地跨越国界旅行。
我的立场	2. 我觉得廉价的航空服务有利于大众，虽然我们需要减少不必要的旅行。

主体部分第一段

中心句	3. 人们可以通过航空旅行去不同的国家旅游，增加对不同国家的了解，获得更多就业机会。
举例 1	4. 一些人可能去到别的国家，找到更好的工作机会，获得更高的收入。
举例 2	5. 有些小生意人在旅行中可能会发现一些商机，通过出口或者进口产品来赚取利润。
对比	6. 如果机票价格上升，他们就会失去这些机会。

主体部分第二段

中心句 （环境）	7. 与此同时，有人认为航空服务提价可以减少航空业的环境影响。

解释	8. 价格较高让人们打消去其他地方旅游的念头。
结果 1	9. 如果航班减少，那么飞机每年产生的温室气体就会减少。
结果 2	10. 其他和空航相关的问题包括噪声污染、修建机场和相关的设施所造成的环境破坏（也会得到改善）。

主体部分第三段

中心句（健康）	11. 我个人觉得提高价格没有必要，因为人们应该有机会去其他地方旅游，休闲放松。
解释	12. 人们现在都很忙，压力很大，特别那些生活在大都市的打工族。
结果	13. 如果机票便宜，他们可以去远一点的地方度假。
举例	14. 例如，中国的游客可以去一些热带国家旅游，品尝当地的美食，而不是在家里度假。

结论段

总结观点	15. 总的来说，我的观点是限制空航的看法并不合理，毕竟便宜的航班对于大众是好的。
	16. 航空公司可以通过技术革新来减少空航产生的环境压力。

读者自学步骤 3

检查自己的翻译：先看正确句子的词伙和句子结构，然后看错误的句子，看是否能够发现问题。

句 1

正：Low-cost air travel has enabled us to travel across borders at a lower cost.

学生的句子：Cheap air travel can make us travel across borders expend less than before.

改：句中有 travel 和 expend 两个动词。

句 2

正：I think cheap flights can benefit the masses, although we should avoid unnecessary journeys.

学生的句子：I think cheap air travel benefit the public, although we need reduce unnecessary travels.

改：air travel benefit 主谓不一致；need to do something 是常用的表达；travel 是不可数名词。

句 3

正：People who travel to different countries can have a better understanding of these countries and explore more career opportunities.

学生的句子：People can travel to different countries by air to have a better understanding of those countries. This can help improve job prospects.

改：中心句最好写成一句话。

句 4

正：Some people can visit other countries where they can find better jobs and earn higher salaries.

学生的句子：Some people are likely to travel to other countries where there have better job opportunities and higher salaries.

改：没有 there have 这个表达，只有 there be（如 there is/are, there have been 等）。

句 5

正：Some small business owners can discover business opportunities during their trips and earn profits by exporting or importing products.

学生的句子：In addition, some business men will find some opportunities, which bring benefits to them by export or import products.

改：by 是介词，后面要加名词或者动名词。

句 6

正：They are likely to miss out on these opportunities, if the cost of flights is higher.

学生的句子：They are more likely to loss those opportunities if the cost of tickets continue growing.

改：loss 是名词；从句的主谓不一致。

句 7

正：At the same time, some people argue that raising airfares can help reduce the environmental impact of the airline industry.

学生的句子：On the other hand, some people consider that the adverse impact to the environment can be reduced by improving airfare.

改：impact 一般与介词 on 搭配；improve 一般是指提高质量和标准，而不是东西的价格和数量。

句 8

正：Higher prices have discouraged people from travelling great distances to other places.

学生的句子：High price always discourages people to travel around to other places.

改：price 是可数名词，要加冠词或者改为复数形式；discourage somebody from doing something 是习惯表达。

句 9

正：Greenhouse gases produced by airplanes can decrease if the number of air flights drops.

学生的句子：The greenhouse gas produced by airplanes can decrease if the amount of airflights can be limited.

改：amount of 后面不能加可数名词复数。

句 10

正：Other problems related to the aviation sector, including noise pollution and the environmental destruction caused by the construction of airports and other facilities, will also be mitigated.

学生的句子：Other problems about air flights can be improved, for example, the environmental destruction caused by building airports and other facilities.

改：for example 后面这些名词应该是作为同位语去解释前面的 problems 的，但是离得太远了。

□ 11

正：Personally, I do not think it is necessary to make air services expensive to potential passengers, because they deserve an affordable holiday to relax.

学生的句子：I personally think that it is not necessary to raise the prices of air flights, because people should be given the opportunities to relax themselves in other places.

改：一般来说，I think that 后面不要用否定；relax themselves 也没有这个表达。

□ 12

正：Many people, especially working people living in large cities, lead a hectic life and feel stressed.

学生的句子：Most people today are busy with work and they are easily to feel stressed out especially those who live in the megacities.

改：easily 是副词，不能充当表语。

□ 13

正：If air tickets are highly affordable, they can travel to some exotic locations on holiday.

学生的句子：If airfares are enough cheap, they are able to travel further and enjoy their happy holidays.

改：一般 enough 修饰形容词的时候，会放在形容词的后面。

□ 14

正：For example, tourists in China can spend a holiday some tropical countries where they can sample local food, instead of staying at home.

学生的句子：For example, tourists in China can go to some tropical countries and taste the food in local places, instead of relaxing at home.

改：没有 in local places 的说法。

□ 15

正：Overall, it would be wrong to impose restrictions on air travel, and above all, cheap airlines can benefit the public.

学生的句子：In conclusion, my view is that restricting air travel is not reasonable, above all cheap flights are benefit to the public.

改：above all 不是连词，不能连接句子。

□ 16

正：Air companies can turn to technological innovations as part of the effort to reduce the strain of the whole industry on the environment.

学生的句子：A airline company can reduce the strain on environment by using new technologies.

改：airline 前面应该用 an；一个公司是不能减少压力的，这也不恰当；environment 是可数名词，要用冠词 the 或者复数。

读者自学步骤 4

整体学习和检查范文，看看是否符合 TELCCS 原则。

范文全文 (7~7.5 分)

Low-cost air travel has enabled us to travel across borders at a lower cost. I think cheap flights can benefit the masses, although we should avoid unnecessary journeys.

> 和前面的 low cost 重复。

People who travel to different countries can have a better understanding of these countries and explore more career opportunities. Some people can visit other countries where they can find better jobs and earn higher salaries. Some small business owners can discover business opportunities during their trips and earn profits by exporting or importing products. They are likely to miss out on these opportunities, if the cost of flights is higher.

> 后面一个例子是关于商业的机会的，不属于工作机会；CC 分数会有影响。

> 前面有一个 people，这里又有一个，重复。

> 这里有跳跃，为什么价格高就失去了这些机会。CC 分数会受影响。

At the same time, some people argue that raising airfares can help reduce the environmental impact of the airline industry. Higher prices have discouraged people from travelling great distances to other places. Greenhouse gases produced by airplanes can decrease if the number of air flights drops. Other problems related to the aviation sector, including noise pollution and the environmental destruction caused by the construction of airports and other facilities, will also be mitigated.

> 这里可以说 some may，不用再说 people。

> 时态不恰当。如果用完成时，表示飞机票已经提价，和题目不符合。影响 TR 的分数。

Personally, I do not think it is necessary to make air services expensive to potential passengers, because they deserve an affordable holiday to relax. Many people, especially working people living in large cities, lead a hectic life and feel stressed. If air tickets are highly affordable, they can travel to some exotic locations on holiday. For example, tourists in China can spend a holiday some tropical countries where they can sample local food, instead of staying at home.

> can 表示能力，这里不恰当。

> travel to 说了很多次，会影响 LR 的分数。

> 这里可以稍微强调一下去其他地方的好处。

> 这句话和上面一句话内容有点重复，可以整合到一起，否则会影响 TR 的分数。

> 这里少了一个介词。

Overall, it would be wrong to impose restrictions on air travel, and above all, cheap airlines can benefit the public. Air companies can turn to technological innovations as part of the effort to reduce the strain of the whole industry on the environment.

 有点多余。

本节关键学习点

审题在雅思考试里是非常重要的，决定了 Task Response 的分数（占总成绩的 25%）。大部分中国老师在教学中都注意单词和句子结构，但是很少注意审题和扣题的讲解，这也是大部分中国考生在考场上做得最不好的一个部分。

在大作文里，大家要注意下面几个审题要素：

要素 1：题目里是否出现了一个行为（action）、政策（policy）、趋势（trend）。

要素 2：题目里是否针对某个特定的结果（outcome/consequence）。

要素 3：题目最关注的群体是什么（最受影响的是谁）。

要素 4：题目的类型是什么。（报告？论述？观点？混合？）

我们用下面的题目来解释一下这几个要点。

Many people think cheap air travel should be encouraged because it gives ordinary people freedom to travel further. However, others think this leads to environmental problems, so air travel should be more expensive in order to discourage people from having it. Discuss both sides and give your own opinion.

要素 1：题目里是否出现了一个行为（action）、政策（policy）、趋势（trend）。

这个题目确定的行为是比较便宜地乘坐航班旅行，还有航班是否应该加价。换言之，你只能讨论航班的事情，不能讨论其他的行为或者趋势等。

例如，你不能说增加油价，或者减少人开车也可以解决环境问题，那就跑题了。

要素 2：题目里是否针对某个特定的结果（outcome/consequence）。

这个题目的第二句话指定了论述的结果，就是减少环境问题。那么当提高空航的价格，你就一定要讨论环境问题一定程度上得以解决。

如果你说，提高空航的价格会导致经常出国公干的人增加费用，减少他们公司的收入，那就跑题了。因为第二句话只关注环境。

我在网络课程中提到的一个概念是 ABC，有时候我叫它 ARE。A 就是 action，R 是 result，也就是 action 的结果，E 是 end result，也就是 action 结果的结果。在审题的时候，我们需要确定题目到底是确定了 A（也就是动作），还是 C 或者 E（也就是结果的结果）。

本题就是既确定了动作，也确定了动作的最终结果。

要素 3：题目最关注的群体是什么（最受影响的是谁）。

这个题目最关注的群体是普通人 (ordinary people)，而不是航空公司，也不是政府，也不是普通人去的国家，因此下面这些观点都是错误的。

•增加航班价格，会增加航空公司的收入。

•减少航班价格，鼓励人们旅行和消费，增加政府收入。

•减少航班价格，鼓励人们旅行，促进某些国家的旅游业发展。

要素 4：题目的类型是什么。（报告？论述？观点？混合？）

学生最常见的问题是报告类和论述类题目混清。

这个题目是论述类，那么第一个立场（廉价空航让人们更加自由地旅行）只能讨论其好处。因为既然这是某些人的看法，那么必定是这些人觉得这件事情有好处，才会这么认为。

如果有考生主体部分第一段写廉价空航的坏处（如导致消耗大量汽油），那么就跑题了。

上述的审题要素里，前三点在题目里出现的相关词都是关键词，在整篇文章中需要不断出现，确保扣题。

例 1：Many people believe that the main aim of university education is to help graduates to find better jobs, while some people believe that university education has benefits for individuals and society. Discuss both views and give your own opinion.

这个论述类题目的第一个立场出现了一个动作，university education，这是关键词；也出现了一个影响，find better jobs，也是关键词。第二个立场出现了限定词，individuals and society，规定了论述的范围，也是关键词。这些关键词在文章里都要不断出现。

有时候题目里会通过 such as, including 这些词给出例子，这些例子方便考生清楚了解一个名词的含义，也可以在文章中不断出现，从而扣题。

例 2：Fossil fuels, such as coal, oil and natural gas, are used in many countries. But in some countries, the use of alternative sources of energy, including wind and solar power, has been encouraged. Is this trend a positive or a negative development?

这个题目里出现了 coal, oil, natural gas, wind power, solar power 等例子，那么尽可能使用这些例子，而题目没有提到的例子，如 nuclear power，就要慎重使用。

例 3：Some people think that the government should provide assistance to all kinds of artists including painters, musicians and poets. However, other people think that is a waste of money. Discuss both views and give your own opinion.

这个题目出现了 painters, musicians, poets 的例子，可以让考生更好地把握 artists（艺术家）这个词的概念，艺术不仅包括视觉艺术，如绘画，也包括其他艺术形式，包括音乐和诗歌。然而，最好避免 filmmakers, film directors，因为电影是否一种纯艺术还很难说。

提升的范文

标色的部分是和原文有差异的地方，下划线部分是词伙。

Low-cost <u>air travel</u> has enabled us to travel <u>across borders</u> more frequently than before. I think cheap flights can benefit the masses, although we should avoid <u>unnecessary journeys</u>.

People who travel to different countries can have a better understanding of these countries and explore some opportunities to advance their careers or increase wealth. Some young people can visit other countries where they can find better jobs and <u>earn higher salaries</u>. Some small <u>business owners</u> can <u>discover business opportunities</u> during their trips in foreign countries and earn profits by exporting or importing products. If air tickets are expensive, these businesspeople will fly less frequently to other countries and miss out on some opportunities to grow their business.

At the same time, some may argue that <u>raising airfares</u> can help <u>reduce the environmental impact</u> of <u>the airline industry</u>. Higher prices will deter people from <u>travelling great distances</u> to other locations to go on holiday or travel for business. Greenhouse gases produced by airplanes can decrease if the number of air flights drops. Other problems related to the <u>aviation sector</u>, including <u>noise pollution</u> and the <u>environmental destruction</u> caused by the construction of airports and other facilities, will also be mitigated.

Personally, I do not think it is necessary to make air services expensive to potential passengers, because they deserve an affordable holiday to relax. Many people, especially working people living in large cities, <u>lead a hectic life</u> and feel stressed. If <u>air tickets</u> are highly affordable, they may choose to take a vacation in some <u>exotic locations</u>, such as <u>tropical countries</u> where they can <u>sample local food</u> and experience a different way of life, and <u>get away from everyday life</u> of their own countries.

Overall, it would be wrong to impose restrictions on air travel, and above all, cheap airlines can benefit the public. <u>Air companies</u> can turn to <u>technological innovations</u> as part of the effort to <u>reduce the strain on</u> the environment.

3.6.7 全文翻译 7：法律和社会 + 如何扣题 I

> *The society is based on rules and laws. The society would not function well if individuals were free to do whatever they want. To what extent do you agree or disagree?*

题目大意

社会的基础是规则和法律。如果每个人都为所欲为，那么社会就不能够很好的运转。在多大程度上你同意这个看法？

读者自学步骤 1

阅读题目后，写出三个观点。

下面是我学生写的一些错误或者不好的观点，大家可以看看自己是不是也犯了同样的错误。

学生的观点	点评
人们随心所欲，交通瘫痪，人们生活不便。	例子当观点。交通瘫痪是一个例子，而不是观点。

存在规则制度，便于企业及其他单位管理，有利于经济发展。	轻微跑题。这个题目的关键词是 individuals, the society, function well，如果说企业和经济发展，一定要最后和这些关键词关联。
没有法规限制行为，人们生活方式不健康，社会医疗负担加重。	例子当观点。生活方式是一个例子，而不是观点。更何况政府未必有规则去影响人们的生活方式。
人们随心所欲，滥用资源，生态环境遭破坏。	轻微跑题。这个观点不错，但是最好要说以后社会的资源越来越少，不能很好地运转，就可以扣题。
人们的行为不受限制，损害他人和国家利益，扰乱社会秩序。	太过空泛。这个题目不是单纯讨论没有规则的坏处，要具体解释为什么社会不能很好地运转。
人们自由生活，选择自己喜欢的事情去做，人们可以生活得开心，得到满足感。	跑题。这个题目不能讨论满足感的事情，只能讨论社会的运转问题。

读者自学步骤 2

翻译下面的句子：在翻译过程中，记住先想词伙，再想句型，然后写出句子。相关词伙可以查阅微信公众号：gu_writing。

介绍段

背景句	1. 法律指的是那些实施在人们身上的规则。
改写题目	2. 虽然法律在规范人们行为上非常重要，但是我认为它约束个人的自由。

主体部分第一段

中心句 （社会）	3. 如果社会成员不遵守法律，社会就没有秩序，经济很难发展。
举例 1	4. 如果一些人不遵守交通规则，交通事故就会增加，交通堵塞也会成为一个问题。
举例 2	5. 在网络上卖假货的人不受惩罚，消费者就不敢买东西，经济就会受影响。

主体部分第二段

中心句 （个人：福利）	6. 人们如果不遵守道德准则和社会规范，人和人之间就会缺乏尊重和信任。
解释	7. 人们有时候会因为自己的利益驱使去做一些伤害别人的事情。

举例 1	8. 如果人们出卖朋友，他们就不会合作做事情，社会就会缺乏凝聚力。
举例 2	9. 如果人们不守信用，他们就很难一起做生意，而争执会影响生产力。

主体部分第三段

中心句 （个人: 福利）	10. 然而，有时候，法律不可避免地会抑制个人自由，甚至会阻碍社会发展。
举例 1	11. 例如，一个国家如果对商业实施很多的限制，商业活动就会不够活跃。
举例 2	12. 如果高收入人群要交很高的收入税，他们可能没有动力去付出更多的努力，提高他们的收入。
结果	13. 政府可以放松一些限制，鼓励大家创新，这样有利于社会发展。

结论段

再次表明立场	14. 认为社会没有了法律和规则就不能够很好地运转是合理的。
总结观点	15. 尽管法律不能让人随心所欲地行为，其主要目的是创造一个大家可以和谐生活的社会。

读者自学步骤 3

检查自己的翻译：先看正确句子的词伙和句子结构，然后看错误的句子，看是否能够发现问题。

句 1

正：Laws refer to the rules imposed on human beings.

学生的句子：Law is that the rule imposed on human beings.

改：law 和 rule 都是可数名词，要么用复数，要么加定冠词 the。

句 2

正：Although laws play an important role in regulating our behaviour, I believe that strict laws can also restrict our freedom.

学生的句子：Although laws are important to regulate human behaviours, I believe that it also restricts personal freedom.

改：没有 something is important to do something 的说法；it 是单数，指代不了 laws。

句 3

正：If no law regulated people's behaviour, a country would be in chaos and the economy would collapse.

学生的句子：If people do not abide by laws, it is difficult for government to maintain social order and these countries will miss out on many opportunities for economic growth.

改：government 是可数名词，不能没有冠词，或者改为复数形式；opportunities 一般搭配 to do something。

句 4

正：If people do not obey traffic regulations, traffic accidents will increase and traffic congestion will become a problem.

学生的句子：For instance, if some people do not follow traffic rules, there would be an increase in the number of traffic congestion which may also become a social problem.

改：number of 后面只能加可数名词复数，congestion 是不可数名词。

句 5

正：If people who sell fake products online are not punished, consumers will stop shopping on the Internet and a country will suffer economically.

学生的句子：Similarly, if the people who sell fake products online without being punished, other people will not dare to buy any items on the online shopping mall.

改：状语从句里没有动词，without 是介词。

句 6

正：If people do not follow moral principles and conform to social norms, they will not be able to develop a respectful and trusting relationship.

学生的句子：If people do not obey moral principles and social norms, they are not likely to respect and trust each other.

改：条件状语从句一般来说，主句用将来时比较多。

句 7

正：People are sometimes motivated by self-interest to do something that would be harmful to others.

学生的句子：Sometimes people may be motivated by self-interest and pose a threat to others' well-being.

改：people 不可能 pose a threat to others' wellbeing，不搭配。

句 8

正：If people betray the trust of friends, they will not work together and social cohesion will be under threat.

学生的句子：Those who betray their friends to make fast money are unable to work closely with their coworkers. It may damage community cohesion because of the lack of mutual trust.

改：it 指代前面的事情，事实上和 lack of mutual trust 重复。

句 9

正：If people do not fulfil their promises, they will find it difficult to conduct business together, and arguments will reduce productivity.

学生的句子：Similarly, if business people cannot keep their words, they would have difficulty in making a deal. Without basic regulation in business world, they may have a lot of conflicts which may affect productivity.

改：world 是可数名词，要用冠词 the； conflicts 后面应该用非限制定语从句，因为任何 conflict 都可以影响 productivity。

句 10

正：Nevertheless, laws sometimes inevitably restrain human's freedom and even hamper/hinder/obstruct social progress.

学生的句子：Nevertheless, laws sometimes are inevitable to restrain human's freedom, even to obstruct the development of society.

改：副词 inevitably 修饰动词 restrain，如果使用形容词 inevitable，修饰的是 laws，很明显不恰当。

句 11

正：For instance, if one country has many restrictions on the business world, the business activity will not thrive.

学生的句子：For instance, if one country has many limits on the business activities so that the business market cannot be active.

改：if 和 so that 两个连词不应该出现在同一句子里；cannot（表示"不能够"）应该改成 will not（表示"不会"）。

句 12

正：If high income earners are subject to high income tax rates, they may lack motivation to make greater efforts to increase their income.

学生的句子：If high income earners have to pay a large amount of income tax, they are unlikely to have motivation to work harder and raise income.

改：raise 表示"提升"，一般搭配 price/rate/money 这样的词。

句 13

正：The government can relax regulations to foster innovations, which can contribute to social progress.

学生的句子：The government should reduce restrictions to encourage people to create and it has positive impact on the social development.

改：create 是及物动词，后面要加宾语；impact 是可数名词，前面要有冠词。

句 14

正：It is reasonable to conclude that the society cannot operate well without laws and rules.

学生的句子：It is reasonable to conclude that society cannot operate well without the laws and rules.

改：society 是可数名词，要加冠词；laws 这里没有特指，所以不需要加 the。

句 15

正：Even though the law does not allow people to act at will, the main purpose is to create a society where people can live in harmony.

学生的句子：Even though the law does not allow people to act at will, the main purpose is to create a harmonious society for everyone.

改：原文说的是：可以和谐生活的"社会"，应该用定语从句去表达。

读者自学步骤 4

整体学习和检查范文，看看是否符合 TELCCS 原则。

范文全文（大概 7 分）

Laws refer to the rules imposed on human beings. Although laws play an important role in regulating our behaviour, I believe that strict laws can also restrict our freedom.

If no law regulated people's behaviour, a country would be in chaos and the economy would collapse. If people do not obey traffic regulations, traffic accidents will increase and traffic congestion will become a problem. If people who sell fake products online are not punished, consumers will stop shopping on the Internet and a country will suffer economically.

If people do not follow moral principles and conform to social norms, they will not be able to develop a respectful and trusting relationship. People are sometimes motivated by self-interest to do something that would be harmful to others. If people betray the trust of friends, they will not work together and social cohesion will be under threat. If people do not fulfil their promises, they will find it difficult to conduct business together, and arguments will reduce productivity.

Nevertheless, laws sometimes inevitably restrain human's freedom and even hinder social progress. For instance, if one country has many restrictions on the

这句话和前面一句话都是以 if 开头，不仅影响 GRA 的成绩，也会影响 CC 的成绩。

这句话应该说一下交通堵塞对经济的影响，和中心句保持一致，否则会影响 CC 的成绩。

这句话和前面一句话都是以 if 开头，不仅影响 GRA 的成绩，也会影响 CC 的成绩。

又来一个 if，而且段落间没有连接词，影响 CC 的分数。

这个表达一般是表示行为的规范，和后面说的人和人的相处没有什么联系，会影响 CC 的分数。

前面也是 people，可以用代词连接。

这里应该有个表示例子的连接词，不能再用 if 了，CC 的分数要扣没了。

这里出现了跳跃，为什么不在一起工作就会影响社会凝聚力。

这里可以增加一些信息来扣题，以提升 TR 的成绩。

转折太厉害了，影响 CC 的分数。

business world, the business activity will not thrive. If high income earners are subject to high income tax rates, they may lack motivation to make greater efforts to increase their income. The government can relax regulations to foster innovations, which can contribute to social progress.

这里又来一个 if，影响 GRA 和 CC 的成绩。

不大清楚为什么突然说到革新，影响 CC 的成绩。

It is reasonable to conclude that the society cannot operate well without laws and rules. Even though the law does not allow people to act at will, the main purpose is to create a society where people can live in harmony.

这里和上段话连接不够。

结尾段和开头段不一致。

本节关键学习点

扣题是雅思作文评分标准 1 (Task Response) 的一个重要事项。

很多考生在考场上以终极目标就是字数写够，在写作的过程中没有看题目，也没有任何的组织，想到哪写到哪，字数凑够后交卷，看看能拿几分。

雅思的考官可谓洞察秋毫，因为英文是他们的母语，他们看考生的段落很快，很容易看出考生的文章是否和题目相关。

不相关、不扣题的文章，哪怕是用词多好，句子多复杂，字数再多，分数最多就是 5.5 分。

那么考生在考场的高压情况下，如何能够在最大限度上确保扣题呢？我觉得扣题大概有四个要点可以注意。

> 要点 1：每个主体段的中心句要出现题目的关键词，对应题目。
>
> 要点 2：举例的时候，尽量要和题目的问题对应。
>
> 要点 3：在每个主体段的结尾，如果题目是两个对比的对象，可以用"对比"的方式扣题。
>
> 要点 4：结尾段扣题。

下面我们用这篇文章做例子，分开解释这几个要点。

要点 1：每个主体段的中心句要出现题目的关键词，对应题目。

这个题目的关键词是 function well（很好地运转），还有 rules and laws（规则和法律），那么主体部分第二段和第三段的中心句最好都要出现这些关键词。

第二段的中心句可以改成：

People can also enjoy their lives in a peaceful, closely-knit society, where they follow social rules and behave in a socially responsible way. (这个句子里出现了 social rules，社会规则，去扣题目的关键词 rules。)

第三段的中心句可以改成：

Nevertheless, laws and rules can sometimes limit freedom and stifle creativity, which can prevent us from building a prosperous society. (这个句子里出现了 laws，也出现了 prosperous society，富裕的社会，这样就和题目的社会运转联系起来。)

要点 2：举例的时候，尽量要和题目的问题对应。

主体部分第二段的例子：

Taking on the phone can disturb other people's work.

简单说用电话影响别人工作有点莫名其妙，最好说清楚工作时不要大声说话是一个好的 rule，并且说清楚影响别人工作，会影响社会运转。

这个例子可以改成：

People who are conscious of business etiquette may keep their voices down when talking on the phone in the workplace, so their colleagues can concentrate on their work and the company can operate effectively. This also applies to the whole society.

要点 3：在每个主体段的结尾，如果题目是两个对比的对象，可以用"对比"的方式扣题。

第一个主体段最后一句话可以说在一个没有法律的社会里，人们缺乏安全感，社会运转不好。

如 In contrast, in a lawless society, people do not have a sense of security when they do business, drive to work and buy products, which can have a negative impact on the economy.

要点 4：结尾段扣题。

虽然主体段一般是最重要的扣题地方，但是如果主体段已经有点偏题，你也没办法再去大改，结尾段可能是你最后的一个机会。

最后结尾段你可以说，如果法律太过严厉，整个社会很难进步。

The society cannot advance easily, if laws are too restrictive.

提升的范文

标色的部分是和原文有差异的地方，下划线部分是词伙。

Laws refer to the rules imposed on human beings. Although laws play an important role in regulating our behaviour, I believe that strict laws can also restrict our freedom.

If no law regulated people's behaviour, a country would be in chaos and the economy would collapse. For example, if people do not obey traffic regulations, traffic accidents will increase and traffic congestion will become a problem. The revenue of numerous businesses will be affected because their products cannot be delivered efficiently. Similarly, in a country where there are no laws to punish those merchants who sell fake products online, consumers will stop shopping on the Internet and this country will suffer economically.

Following moral principles is also important; otherwise, people will not be able to develop a respectful and trusting relationship. They are sometimes motivated by self-interest to do something that would be harmful to others, such as betraying the trust of their business partners, but this would cause damage to their relationship. If people do not fulfil their promises, they will find it difficult to conduct business together, and arguments will reduce productivity. It is fair to say that no society could function well when people lack mutual trust.

On the other hand, laws sometimes inevitably <u>restrain human's freedom</u> and even <u>hinder social progress</u>. For instance, if one country has many restrictions on the <u>business world</u>, the <u>business activity</u> will not thrive. <u>High income earners</u> who are subject to <u>high income tax rates</u> may lack motivation to make greater efforts to increase their income. The government can <u>relax regulations</u> to <u>unlock potential</u> of these people, which can contribute to social progress.

From what has been discussed, it is reasonable to argue that a country cannot operate well without laws and rules. Alternatively, our <u>society cannot advance</u> easily, if laws are too restrictive.

3.6.8 全文翻译 8：传统教育和网络教育＋如何扣题 II

> *Nowadays, distance-learning programs have gained in popularity (those teaching programmes that involve the use of written materials, videos, televised lessons and the Internet), but some people argue that courses can never be taken as good as those by attending a college or university in person. To what extent do you agree or disagree?*

题目大意

远程教育项目（也就是那些用书面材料、视频、电视还有网络教授知识的项目）如今越来越流行，但是有些人认为上这些课程不如自己亲自去上大学那么好。在多大程度上你赞同或者反对这个看法？

读者自学步骤 1

阅读题目后，写出三个观点。

下面是我学生写的一些错误或者不好的观点，大家可以看看自己是不是也犯了同样的错误。

学生的观点	点评
参加大学课程，与同学交流学习，扩大社交网络。	重心不对。这个题目论述的重心是 distance learning programmes，而不是大学课程。
远程教育上课时间内容灵活，依个人情况而定，节约时间成本。	略微跑题。这个题目不是简单地讨论远程教育的好处，还是强调是不是和上大学一样好。
接受大学教育，获得文凭或资格证，有利于找到好工作。	观点没有唯一性。网络教育也有给文凭的。
大学课程好，面对面学习，师生互动多，发展社交，也是交友的一种有效方式。	跑题。这个题目只关心学习效果，不关心社交。
选择远程教育，不受时间地点限制，自主安排学习时间。	略微跑题。这个时候最好要说自己安排时间，学习效果比在大学里好。
远程上课，授课内容精简，了解学生弱项，查漏补缺效果好。	观点不够有力。为什么远程教育比传统教育更能够查漏补缺？

远程教育容易获得，让更多人获得教育资源，获得高人气。	跑题。这个题目只关心学习效果，不关心远程教育是否流行。

读者自学步骤 2

翻译下面的句子：在翻译过程中，记住先想词伙，再想句型，然后写出句子。 相关词伙可以查阅微信公众号：gu_writing。

介绍段

背景句	1. 因特网的到来已经改变了人们工作和生活的方式。
改写题目	2. 越来越多的人现在考虑远程教育，这种教育系统可以让他们在家里完成一个学位。
阐述立场	3. 尽管远程教育有别于传统大学教育，远程教育在某些方面是有优势的。

主体部分第一段

中心句（科技发展）	4. 与传统教育相比，远程教育更加灵活，从而使更多的人接受教育成为可能。
解释	5. 学生需要阅读相关的材料，也可以看视频上课。
	6. 当他们有问题的时候，可以按暂停，回放课程，直到他们完全理解内容。
拓展	7. 这些远程教育课程每天 24 小时、每星期 7 天都开放，因此对于那些生活方式很忙的人非常理想，只要他们可以上网。

主体部分第二段

中心句（学习能力）	8. 远程教育的发展也允许学生和讲师之间有互动的机会。
解释	9. 学生可以在虚拟课堂里使用互动工具问问题，也可以发电子邮件。
结果	10. 这样一来，他们可以得到讲师的指导，更好地完成所有的课程。
拓展	11. 有时候，他们甚至可以和世界名校的学者交流，尽管他们身在自己的国家。

主体部分第三段

观点（社会发展）	12. 远程教育的一个主要的缺陷是学生的交流技能也不能够提高，因为远程教育一般没有小组作业。
结果	13. 学生是独立完成学业，很难认识其他同学。
拓展结果	14. 他们没有机会拓展人脉，这对于他们职业发展有影响。

结论段

再次表明立场	15. 远程教育让大学教育更加的普及，因为其灵活性。

总结观点	16. 然而，它也有一些缺点，如，缺乏互动，所以它不能够像传统大学教育那样产生同等的学习效果。

读者自学步骤 3

检查自己的翻译：先看正确句子的词伙和句子结构，然后看错误的句子，看是否能够发现问题。

句 1

正：The advent of the Internet has changed the ways people live their lives and complete work.

学生的句子：Internet has changed ours life, including the way how to working and living.

改：ours 不能作定语，应该是 our; how to 后面要加动词原形。

句 2

正：A growing number of people are now considering distance education, which allows them to complete a degree at home.

学生的句子：A growing number of people are now consider distance education, which allow them to complete a degree at home.

改：are considering 是现在进行时；education 是不可数名词，allow 是动词的复数形式，主谓不一致。

句 3

正：Even though distance learning is different from traditional college education, distance learning has some advantages in some aspects.

学生的句子：Even though distance learning has difference from traditional college education, distance learning has some advantages in some aspects.

改：has difference from 不是习惯表达，习惯表达是 be different from 和 differ from。

句 4

正：Distance education is more flexible than the traditional way of receiving education, thereby offering learners more educational opportunities.

学生的句子：Compared with traditional education, learning online is more flexible so that it is possible for more people to gain an access to education.

改：一般来说，如果有比较级，一般要用 than；access 是不可数名词，不能加 an。

句 5

正：Students can read relevant materials and attend lectures by watching videos.

学生的句子：Students need read related materials and also watch videos to take lessons.

改：need read 是两个动词连用；take lessons 也不适用于大学，应该是 attend lectures。

句 6

正：When they have problems in digesting information, they can click the pause button and replay the video until they fully understand the content.

学生的句子：When having problems, they could pause and replay the course until they fully understand the content

改：分词结构 when having problems 不恰当，因为经常有进行时的意味，这里描述的是一个普遍存在的条件，而不是一个正在进行的问题。

句 7

正：These distance education courses are available 24 hours a day, 7 days a week, and therefore suitable for those who lead a hectic life, as long as they have Internet access.

学生的句子：These distance education courses are available for 24 hours and 7 days in a week, so it is suitable for those who have a busy lifestyle as long as they have internet access.

改：it 指代不了前面的 courses。

句 8

正：The improvements in online education also make it possible for students to communicate with their lecturers whenever necessary.

学生的句子：Advanced distance education also make it possible for students to have opportunities to communicate with their lecturers.

改：主谓不一致；make it possible to do 这个 do 最好不要用 have，因为 have 是 "拥有" 的意思，表示的是一种状态。

句 9

正：Students can use interactive communication tools to ask questions in virtual classes or talk to lecturers via email.

学生的句子：In virtual classes, students could use interactive tools or send emails to ask questions.

改：could 一般是表示不确定的一种可能性，而这里是比较肯定的，用 can 比较好。

句 10

正：In this way, these learners can get lecturers' guidance immediately, thereby completing all courses more effectively.

学生的句子：By this way, learners could get lecturers' guidance thereby completing their courses successfully.

改：没有 by this way 的说法。

句 11

正：Despite living in their own countries, they can even communicate with scholars from top universities around the world.

学生的句子：They sometimes with famous universities scholars exchange ideas despite they have been living motherland.

改：exchange ideas 的位置太奇怪；despite 后面只能加名词；they 指代不清楚，不知道是指代前面的 they，还是名校的学者。

句 12

正：A main drawback of online education is that students have found it difficult to improve their social skills because there are few group assignments.

学生的句子：A main drawback of online education is that students' communication skill cannot be improved because there is no group assignments for them.

改：skill 是可数名词，要用复数形式；there is assignments 主谓不一致。

句 13

正：Students complete their degree independently and do not have opportunities to meet each other and socialise together.

学生的句子：Students complete their degree independently; therefore, it is difficult for them to meet other people.

改：people 在这里有歧义，是同学，还是社会上的其他人？

句 14

正：They do not have opportunities to build up a network of contacts, which can have a negative impact on their career development.

学生的句子：They do not have opportunities to built up a network of contacts, which has a negative impact on their career development.

改：built 是过去时，而 opportunities to do 要用原形；has 的主语不清楚是 network，还是 contacts。

句 15

正：Distance learning has made university education more accessible, because of its flexibility.

学生的句子：Distance education could make university education more pervasive because of its flexibility.

改：could 强调可能性。

句 16

正：However, it has some drawbacks, such as lack of interaction, so it is not able to achieve the same learning outcomes as traditional college education.

学生的句子：However, it also has some deficiencies, such as, lack of interaction, so it cannot produce the same effect as traditional tertiary education.

改：such as 后面一般不用加逗号。

读者自学步骤 4

整体学习和检查范文，看看是否符合 TELCCS 原则。

范文全文（大概 7 分）

The advent of the Internet has changed the ways people live their lives and complete work. A growing number of people are now considering distance education, which allows them to complete a degree at home. Even though distance learning is different from traditional college education, distance learning has some advantages in some aspects.

可以用代词，避免和前面表达重复。

文章不是问远程教育的好处和坏处，而是问是否和传统上大学的效果一样。

Distance education is more flexible than the traditional way of receiving education, thereby offering learners more educational opportunities. Students can read relevant materials and attend lectures by watching videos. When they have problems in digesting information, they can click the pause button and replay the video until they fully understand the content. These distance education courses are available 24 hours a day, 7 days a week, and therefore suitable for those who lead a hectic life, as long as they have Internet access.

这也是 distance education 的优点，并没有回答是否和传统上大学一样。这样会影响 TR 的分数。

这里可以具体化，增加细节，提升 TR 的分数。

这个句子说的是远程教育的好处，并不体现是否和传统上大学的效果一样，所以不恰当，去掉。

The improvements in online education also make it possible for students to communicate with their lecturers whenever necessary. Students can use interactive communication tools to ask questions in virtual classes or talk to lecturers via email. In this way, these learners can get lecturers' guidance immediately, thereby completing all courses more effectively. Despite living in their own countries, they can even communicate with scholars from top universities around the world.

A main drawback of online education is that students have found it difficult to improve their social skills because there are few group assignments. Students complete their degree independently and do not have opportunities to meet each other and socialise together. They do not have opportunities to build up a network of contacts, which can have a negative impact on their career development.

这也是 distance education 的缺点，并没有回答是否和传统上大学一样。

这个定语从句有点歧义，不知道是修饰前面整个句子还是先行词，影响 GRA 的分数。

Distance learning has made university education more accessible, because of its flexibility. However, it has some drawbacks, such as lack of interaction, so it is not able to achieve the same learning outcomes as traditional college education.

结尾也没有对应题目。

本节关键学习点

我们上一篇文章说到了扣题的四种方法。

方法1：每个主体段的中心句要出现题目的关键词，对应题目。

方法2：举例的时候，尽量要和题目的问题对应。

方法3：每个主体段的结尾，如果题目是两个对比的对象，可以用"对比"的方式扣题。

方法4：结尾段扣题。

我们这一节会增加两个方法：一个是开头段的扣题，另一个就是不断出现关键词。

> 方法1：开头段表明立场的时候可以扣题。
>
> 方法2：每个主体段的中心句要出现题目的关键词，对应题目。
>
> 方法3：举例的时候，尽量要和题目的问题对应。
>
> 方法4：每个主体段的结尾，如果题目是两个对比的对象，可以用"对比"的方式扣题。
>
> 方法5：不断出现关键词，特别是最后一句。
>
> 方法6：结尾段扣题。

方法1：开头段表明立场的时候可以扣题。

开头段的第二句话可以改变一下，尽量和题目相配。

Although distance learning differs from traditional college education in some aspects, learners will possibly find that they can gain as much knowledge from an online course as they do at university.

意思是说"虽然远程教育和传统教育在某些方面有差别，学习者可能会发现他们在网络教育上获得的知识和大学的知识是一样的"。

方法2：每个主体段的中心句要出现题目的关键词，对应题目。

如主体部分第一段的第一句话，我们可以改成：

Distance education is flexible and offers learners educational opportunities to attend lectures without having to travel to university.

意思是说"远程教育非常灵活，给学习者机会去参加课程，而不一定要去大学"。也就是说，他们还是可以参加课程，只是不用出席。这样就更加扣题。

还有主体部分第三段的第一句话，我们可以改成：

In spite of these facts, distance education may not offer students the networking experience which they can get in a bricks and mortar college.

意思是"尽管上述这些事实,远程教育提供不了学生在传统大学里可以获得的交友经历"。

方法 3:举例的时候,尽量要和题目的问题对应。

这篇文章我没有举例,所以不讨论这一点。

方法 4:每个主体段的结尾,如果题目是两个对比的对象,可以用"对比"的方式扣题。

主体部分第三段的最后一句话可以加上上传统大学的对比,这样可以更加扣题。

In contrast, those who study at university can do a wide range of activities on campus such as playing sport and joining clubs, which can help them build close relationships.

大意是"对比而言,那些在大学学习的人可以参加很多活动,如体育和参加俱乐部,有助于他们建立非常紧密的社会关系"。

方法 5:不断出现关键词。

很多考生在段落写作中,前两句还能扣题,后面就越写越远,使用一些关键词或者关键词的替换词,可以有助于扣题。

如主体部分第三段,第一句话用了 a bricks and mortar college,第二句话用了 complete a degree independently,第四句话用了 on campus, study at university,这些表达都是在不断地扣题,突出远程教育和大学上课这些关键词。

方法 6:结尾段扣题。

结尾段是扣题的最后一道防线,正如我在上一篇文章中说过的。结尾段你可以说:

In conclusion, interactive technology has enabled learners to communicate with lecturers easily and benefit from the opportunities presented by distance education, so I believe that distance education is now as good as traditional ways of completing a degree at university.

提升的范文

标色的部分是和原文有差异的地方,下划线部分是词伙。

The advent of the Internet has changed the ways people live their lives and complete work. A growing number of people are now considering distance education, which allows them to complete a degree at home. Although distance learning differs from traditional college education in some aspects, learners will possibly find that they can gain as much knowledge from an online course as they do at university.

In distance learning programmes, students can access the same content of degree courses as those who attend lectures in person. They can read relevant materials, such as textbooks and class notes, and attend video lessons, which are recorded lectures of reputable professors. When they have problems in comprehending some key concepts, they can click the pause button and replay the video until they fully digest information.

The improvements in online education also make it possible for students to communicate with their lecturers whenever necessary. Students can use interactive communication tools to ask questions in virtual classes or talk to lecturers <u>via email</u>. In this way, these learners can get lecturers' guidance immediately, thereby <u>completing all courses</u> more effectively. This is exactly the same as the interaction with professors in lecture rooms. Despite living in their own countries, students can even communicate with scholars from top universities around the world.

While distance education has clear advantages, it may not offer participants the same networking experience they can get in <u>a bricks and mortar college</u>. Students complete their degree independently and do not have opportunities to meet each other and socialise together. This can have a negative impact on their career development in view of the importance of building up a network of contacts. In contrast, those who study at university can <u>do a wide range of activities</u> on campus such as playing sport and joining clubs, which can help them <u>build close relationships</u>.

In conclusion, <u>interactive technology</u> has enabled learners to communicate with lecturers easily and <u>gain qualifications</u>, so I believe that distance education is now as good as traditional ways of completing a degree at university.

3.6.9 全文翻译 9：交税＋如何写中心句

> *Some people believe that they should be able to keep all the money they earn and should not pay any tax to the state. To what extent do you agree or disagree?*

题目大意

一些人相信他们应该可以将自己赚的钱都留着，不应给国家交任何税。在多大程度上你同意或者反对这个看法？

读者自学步骤 1

阅读题目后，写出三个观点。

下面是我学生写的一些错误或者不好的观点，大家可以看看自己是不是也犯了同样的错误。

学生的观点	点评
不交税，政府没有资金发展国防工程，国家安全危机。	不够有力。很多小国家没有国防预算，也没有什么问题。
不交税，官员贪污腐败，不利于社会和谐发展。	没有逻辑。为什么不交税官员就腐败？
交税，政府有钱招聘优秀人员，有助于人们改善生活。	不够有力。为什么要招聘优秀人员？什么人是优秀人员？
不交税，可支配收入增大，有更多的钱实现自我价值。	比较空泛。为什么钱多了就可以实现自我价值？

读者自学步骤 2

翻译下面的句子：在翻译过程中，记住先想词伙，再想句型，然后写出句子。 相关词伙可以查阅微信公众号：gu_writing。

介绍段

背景句	1. 很多人可能抱怨税是一个沉重的负担，因为税减少他们的可支配收入。
阐述立场	2. 我觉得我们需要交税，因为没有税的话，社会很难运转。

主体部分第一段

中心句 （经济资源）	3. 有了税收，政府可以资助公共设施项目，包括道路、学校，还有医院。
举例 1	4. 没有一个好的公共交通系统，人们上下班很困难，而交通堵塞会影响效率。
举例 2	5. 公立学校可以给小孩提供教育机会，让他们获得知识，这对经济也有好处。
对比	6. 这些公共项目一般不会得到私企的资助，因为利润不高。
附加观点 （个人福利）	7. 我们也需要意识到：政府通过税收可以达到财富再分配的目的。
举例	8. 例如，在很多国家，高收入的人一般要交很高的税，而低收入群体甚至会得到国家的资助。

主体部分第二段

中心句	9. 政府收税，可以规范人的行为。
解释	10. 人们很多时候不能表现自制，很难改变一些不好的习惯。
举例	11. 例如，对香烟和酒征收重税可以减少人们在这些方面的消费。
结果	12. 人们可以更加健康，医疗系统的压力也会减少。

主体部分第三段

中心句	13. 人们没有动力勤奋工作，而创业者也不想创业。
解释	14. 钱对很多人来说是一个动力，因为人们可以过更好的生活，也可以获得成就感。
举例	15. 没有这些人的勤奋工作，展现自己的才华，一个国家不可能变得富裕，福利系统也难以为继。

结论段

再次表明立场	16. 我深信 (I am convinced that) 税是经济的命脉，虽然过高的税对经济有一定的负面影响。

读者自学步骤 3

检查自己的翻译：先看正确句子的词伙和句子结构，然后看错误的句子，看是否能够发现问题。

句1

正：Many people regard tax as a burden, because it can reduce their disposable income.

学生的句子：Many people maybe complain that tax is a heavy burden, because it reduce their disposable income.

改：maybe 类似于 possibly，不是 may 的意思；it reduce 主谓不一致。

句2

正：I think that we need to pay tax, because without tax revenue, the society cannot function appropriately.

学生的句子：I think we need to pay tax, because our society is difficult to operate without the tax revenue.

改：一般不要说人或者一个机构非常 difficult。

句3

正：If the government has tax revenue, public facilities such as roads, schools and hospitals can receive more funds from the state.

学生的句子：If the government have tax source, which can finance public facilities such as road, school and hospital.

改：government have 主谓不一致；这个句子有条件状语从句，也有定语从句，但是没有主句；后面 road, school, hospital 这些词都是可数名词，要用复数。

句4

正：Without a great public transport system, commuters find it difficult to travel to and from work, and traffic congestion could reduce work efficiency.

学生的句子：Without a great public transportation system, people commute become difficult and traffic congestion could reduce the work efficiency.

改：commute become 两个动词连用；efficiency 是不可数名词，不需要特指。

句5

正：Public schools can provide children with educational opportunities and enable these young students to gain knowledge, which is beneficial to economic growth.

学生的句子：Public schools can provide children with education opportunities and thus enable to gain knowledge, which is beneficial to economic growth.

改：enable 前面缺主语，而且 enable 后面要有名词作宾语。

句6

正：These projects or services are normally not funded by the private sector, because of the low profit margin.

学生的句子：This public project usually not get fund from private company, because of the low profits.

改：project 不可能是单数，因为前面说了两个 project；company 也不可能是单数，因为私营企业不可能只有一个。

句 7

正：We should also recognise that the government can achieve the goal of income redistribution by taxation.

学生的句子：Last, we should recognize that government can achieve the goal of the income redistribution via the revenue.

改：recognize 是美式拼写；government 前面没加定冠词；via 后面接工具、人或者地方，用在这里不恰当，用 by 就可以。

句 8

正：For example, in many countries, the high income group needs to pay high tax, while the low income group can get assistance from the government.

学生的句子：For example, in many countries, the group of high income people need to pay high tax, on the contrary, the group of low income people can get assistance from the government.

改：on the contrary 是副词短语，不能连接两个独立的句子。

句 9

正：Levying taxes can regulate people's behaviour.

学生的句子：It can regulate people's behaviour through levy taxes.

改：through 是介词，后面要加动名词，而且应该放在句首，否则那个 it 指代不清楚。

句 10

正：People fail to show self-restraint sometimes and cannot change some bad habits.

学生的句子：People cannot show restraint in many conditions, it is difficult to change some bad habits.

改：cannot 表示"不能"，而这里应该是 do not 或者 fail to，因为人永远是"可能或者可以"表现自制的，只是某些时候做不到；两个句子间没有连词。

句 11

正：For example, the heavy tax on cigarette and alcohol discourages people from spending on these items.

学生的句子：For instance, the heavy tax of the cigarette and alcohol greatly decrease people's consumption.

改：tax…decrease 主谓不一致；for instance 之前已经使用过，重复。

句 12

正：This change can improve the well-being of people and ease the pressure on the medical system.

学生的句子：People may become healthier, which will reduce the pressures on medical system.

改：healthier 这个比较级不恰当，意思是你原本就健康，现在更加健康；system 是可数名词，要有冠词。

句 13

正：People may not have the incentive to work hard and entrepreneurs are also not willing to set up a business.

学生的句子：People are lack of motivation of work and business men also do not want to set up a business.

改：人作主语的时候，不要用 be lack of 的结构，因为 lack=shortage, 人不是"缺乏"。

句 14

正：Money is a great motivator for most people because they can improve living standards and gain a sense of accomplishment.

学生的句子：Most of people believe that money is a motivation to make a better life and a sense of accomplishment.

改：除非名词是特指，否则一般不需要用 most of；这句话也没有很好地表现原意，不是金钱是过上好生活的动力，而是过上好生活是赚钱的动力。

句 15

正：Without the hard work of these people and their willingness to show their talents, a country would not become prosperous and the welfare system could not be sustained.

学生的句子：If not for their diligence and trying to show their talent, a country cannot become rich and sustain the welfare system.

改：if 引导状语从句，句子不完整。

句 16

正：I am convinced that taxes are the lifeblood of the economy although high taxes can have an adverse effect on economic growth.

学生的句子：I am convinced that taxes are the lifeblood of economy although high tax rates can have negative influence on economy.

改：influence 和 economy 都是可数名词，要加冠词。

读者自学步骤 4

整体学习和检查范文，看看是否符合 TELCCS 原则。

范文全文（大概 7 分）

Many people regard tax as a burden, because it can reduce their disposable income. I think that we need to pay tax, because without tax revenue, the society cannot function appropriately.

If the government has tax revenue, public facilities such as roads, schools and hospitals can receive more funds from the state. Without a great public transport

state 和 government 有点重复，读起来不够通顺，影响 CC 的分数。

system, commuters find it difficult to travel to and from work, and traffic congestion could reduce work efficiency. Public schools can provide children with educational opportunities and enable these young students to gain knowledge, which is beneficial to economic growth. These projects or services are normally not funded by the private sector, because of the low profit margin. We should also recognise that the government can achieve the goal of income redistribution by taxation. For example, in many countries, the high income group needs to pay high tax, while the low income group can get assistance from the government.

Levying taxes can regulate people's behaviour. People fail to show self-restraint sometimes and cannot change some bad habits. For example, the heavy tax on cigarette and alcohol discourages people from spending on these items. This change can improve the well-being of people and ease the pressure on the medical system.

People may not have the incentive to work hard and entrepreneurs are also not willing to set up a business. Money is a great motivator for most people because they can improve living standards and gain a sense of accomplishment. Without the hard work of these people and their willingness to show their talents, a country would not become prosperous and the welfare system could not be sustained.

I am convinced that taxes are the lifeblood of the economy although high taxes can have an adverse effect on economic growth.

这句话和教育机会有点重复。

知识对经济发展有好处，有点跳跃，影响 CC 的分数。

有点指代不清楚前面的 schools 或 transport，因为 schools 不是 projects，影响 CC 的分数。

这里出现了一个新的观点，但是中心句没有体现这一点。这样会影响 CC 的分数。

可以说 people on low incomes，这样不至于和前面的 group 重复。

可以用词伙 financial support。

没有连接词，和上面一段的联系不够强，不够连贯。

这个连接词不恰当，解释的其实是中心句，而不是前一句话。影响 CC 分数。

可以改成 the public。

有点指代不清楚，影响 CC 分数。

这里有点跳跃，为什么突然说到医疗系统。

中心句没有提到税的事情。

这里最好要出现收入，这样前后一致，并且更加扣题。

这里和上面一段话没有什么太大的联系，可以加上 overall。

本节关键学习点

这一节我想讲讲中心句（也就是主体段每段话的第一句）。中心句在西方的书面语里是很重要的。这多少和他们的论述习惯有关系。他们喜欢演绎式的表达（deduction），简单来说，就是先总结，后解释。

举个简单的例子：

就这篇文章，关于"是否要交税"，我们中国的说话习惯是：

① 我们交税，② 政府就有钱，③ 有钱就可以资助一些公共设施，如学校和交通，④ 人们生活就更好，社会经济发展。

他们的习惯是：

① 我们交税，④ 大家生活就更好，社会经济发展，② 因为政府有钱，③ 有钱就可以资助一些公共设施，如学校和交通。

所以，他们总是在中心句会把整段话的主要观点给说出来。

在雅思考试里，中心句的写作决定了两个评分标准的分数：Task Response 和 Coherence and Cohesion。

在写中心句的时候，你要注意下面几个要素：

> 要素 1：中心句一定要和段落的内容一致（决定了你的 Coherence and Cohesion 成绩）。
>
> 要素 2：中心句要有连接词（决定了 Coherence and Cohesion）。
>
> 要素 3：中心句要出现关键词或者关键词的替换表达（决定了 Task Response）。
>
> 要素 4：中心句要对应题目（决定了 Task Response）。

我们下面根据这些准则，提升一下前面的范文。

要素 1：中心句一定要和段落的内容一致（决定了你的 Coherence and Cohesion 成绩）。

主体部分第一段整段话讨论了两个分论点：一个是政府可以资助公共设施；二是政府可以重新分配社会财富。但是前面范文的第一句并没有体现这一点。

我会将中心句写成这样：Paying tax can have important implications to a country's economy. 这样读者就知道整段话会讨论税收对经济的意义。

要素 2：中心句要有连接词（决定了 Coherence and Cohesion）。

主体部分第二段是第二个交税的好处，但是原文没有任何的连接词和标志词。所以可以写成这样：

Levying taxes can also regulate people's behaviour.

要素 3：中心句要出现关键词或者关键词的替换表达（决定了 Task Response）。

主体部分第三段折中段的中心句，没有说清楚这是交税带来的影响。这样读者就云里雾里，不清楚为什么突然说到不想好好工作。

我可以加上关键词，如交税这样的表达：

On the other hand, if taxpayers are subject to high taxes, they may not have the incentive to work hard and entrepreneurs are also not willing to set up a business.

这样读者就会跟上你的思路，知道你在说高税收的问题。

要素 4：中心句要对应题目 (决定了 Task Response)。

这体现在两点。第一，中心句要对应题目的类型。例如本题是观点类题目，那么考生不能说 some people argue that, or some people hold the view that，因为这些表达是论述类文章中常见的套句。

第二，中心句要回答题目的问题。例如，这个题目讨论的是交税的好处和坏处，那么就要直接回答，不要去铺垫其他的信息和背景。

提升的范文

标色的部分是和原文有差异的地方，下划线部分是词伙。

Many people regard tax as a burden, because it can reduce their disposable income. I think that we need to pay tax, because without tax revenue, the society cannot function appropriately.

If the government has tax revenue, more funds can be used to build public facilities such as roads, schools and hospitals. Without a great public transport system, commuters find it difficult to travel to and from work, and traffic congestion could reduce work efficiency. Public schools can provide children with educational opportunities, and without a well-educated workforce, a country cannot sustain economic growth. Private investors are normally not interested in transport links and schools, which do not generate considerable profits.

Levying taxes can also regulate people's behaviour and encourage them, especially those who sometimes fail to show self-restraint, to break bad habits. For example, the heavy tax on cigarette and alcohol discourages the public from spending on these items. The resulting lifestyle changes can improve their health and reduce hospital visits, thereby easing the pressure on the medical system.

On the other hand, if taxpayers are subject to high taxes, they may not have the incentive to work hard and entrepreneurs are also not willing to set up a business. Money is a great motivator for most people because with high income, they can improve living standards and gain a sense of accomplishment. Without the hard work of these people and their willingness to show their talents, a country would not become prosperous and the welfare system could not be sustained.

Overall, I am convinced that taxes are the lifeblood of the economy although high taxes can have an adverse effect on economic growth.

3.6.10 全文翻译 10：道德教育 + 如何举例

> *Some people think schools should only teach students academic subjects. Others think schools should also teach students how to discriminate between right and wrong. Discuss both views and give your own opinion.*

题目大意

有些人认为学校应该只教授学生学术课程。另一些人则认为学校应该教学术怎么去分辨对错。

讨这两个观点并给出你个人的看法。

读者自学步骤1

阅读题目后，写出三个观点。

下面是我学生写的一些错误或者不好的观点，大家可以看看自己是不是也犯了同样的错误。

学生的观点	点评
只教文化课，学生的思维仅限于书本，不懂礼仪和其他社交技能。	空泛。为什么读书就不知道礼仪，中国的老话不是"知书达理"吗？为什么不懂礼仪就是一件坏事？
只教学术科目，学生思维局限、刻板，缺乏社会认识，不利于个人发展，走上社会后容易被错误观念误导。	空泛而且跑题。这个题目是论述类，如果讨论"教学术科目"，要说原因，而不是说缺点，而且思维刻板就被误导，也是比较站不住脚。
学校应该提供道德教育，学生应该全面发展，提高国家竞争力。	很空泛。为什么学生应该全面发展，为什么国家就有竞争力。
教授学术知识，培养专业化人才，为文化、科学、教育的发展做贡献。	很空泛。接受教育主要还是为了提升自己，为了职业，然后才是社会贡献。
学会明辨是非，尊老爱幼，社会更团结。	太过具体。尊老爱幼是一个例子，不是观点。

读者自学步骤2

翻译下面的句子：在翻译过程中，记住先想词伙，再想句型，然后写出句子。相关词伙可以查阅微信公众号：gu_writing。

介绍段

背景句	1. 学校一直被认为是一个帮助年轻人提高知识和增加就业能力的地方。
阐述立场	2. 在我看来，学术课程很重要，但是学生如果不懂得对错的区别，也很难事业成功。

主体部分第一段

中心句	3. 很多老师认为学生应该关注主科，因为这些课程决定了他们以后是否可以进大学。
解释	4. 这些课程学到的知识可以给大学打下良好的基础，以后可以找到好工作。
举例	5. 例如，如果在中学学好数学，那么他们以后可以在大学里建立模型去分析数据，成为金融分析师和工程师。
对比	6. 如果学生需要花时间学习道德准则和行为规范，他们可能就不能关注主科。

主体部分第二段

中心句 （社会）	7. 学校可以灌输一些重要的美德，让他们可以利用好自己的知识，成为对社会有用的人。
举例 1	8. 如果一个人懂得忠诚，那么就不会将公司的机密材料卖给竞争者。
举例 2	9. 如果一个工程师有社会责任，就会设计出能够让消费者安全使用的产品。
对比	10. 一个学生即便在学校的学习成绩很好，如果不能够遵循道德规则，他也很难取得成功。

主体部分第三段

中心句	11. 我个人觉得，学生能够分辨对错才可能取得成功。
举例 1	12. 学生在学校里要懂得尊重老师，和同学和睦相处。
举例 2	13. 一些小孩可能喜欢吃快餐，这样会引起肥胖。
对比	14. 如果他们不意识到这些问题，这些问题不仅影响学习，也影响以后的工作。

读者自学步骤 3

检查自己的翻译：先看正确句子的词伙和句子结构，然后看错误的句子，看是否能够发现问题。

句 1

正：Schools are normally seen as the place where the next generation can increase knowledge to improve employability.

学生的句子：School always be believed as a place where can increase knowledge and expand work skills of young people.

改：主句里没有谓语动词；从句里没有主语。

句 2

正：In my view, academic subjects are important to one's career achievement, but students who do not learn the difference between right and wrong cannot succeed in their working lives.

学生的句子：In my opinion, academic courses are very important, but students do not know how to distinguish between right and wrong, they are difficult to success in their future works.

改：人不能说 are difficult to；success 是名词；work 是不可数名词。

句 3

正：Many teachers suggest that students should concentrate on core subjects, because the performance in these courses can determine whether they can enter university in the future.

学生的句子：Many teachers think that students should give top priority to major courses, as those courses can be a key factor which can decide whether they can enter to university in the future.

改：enter 是及物动词；a key factor which can decide whether 也非常多余。

句 4

正：What students can learn in academic courses can provide a firm grounding for university and help them find decent jobs.

学生的句子：The knowledge which learned from these courses can lay a firm grounding for university and find a better job in the future.

改：which learned 少了一个助动词 is。

句 5

正：For example, students who acquire mathematical skills at school can build models to analyse data at university and work as financial analysts and engineers after they graduate.

学生的句子：For instance, if they study math well in middle schools, they can build models to analyze data in college and maybe become financial analysts or engineers.

改：analyze 是美式拼写，最好改成 analyse 英式拼写；maybe 是副词，应该改成情态动词 may。

句 6

正：They are less likely to focus on key disciplines if they are required to spend time in studying moral principles and behaviour norms.

学生的句子：If students need to spend time on studying ethics and behaviours, they are may not able to focus on core subjects.

改：spend time in doing something 才是正确的表达；are 助动词和 may 情态动词不能连用，这种错误是低级错误。

句 7

正：Schools can impart some important virtues into students, which enable them to make good use of their knowledge to contribute positively to society.

学生的句子：Schools can impart some important virtue into students, which enable these students to make good use of their knowledge and become active members of the society.

改：定语从句的谓语动词单复数不对，如果修饰前面整句话，谓语动词应该用单数。

句 8

正：If one understands the value of loyalty, he or she will not sell confidential documents of his or her employer to other companies.

学生的句子：If someone knows loyalty, they are not able to sell important documents of this company to other competitors.

改：someone 和 they 两个代词不搭配；not able to 也不恰当，这些人永远是"有能力"去出售，只是"去不去"出售。

句 9

正：Engineers who are conscious of social responsibilities are more likely to design safe products which benefit consumers.

学生的句子：If a engineer meet his or her social responsibility, there will be more products that are safe to use available to consumers.

改：engineer 前面应该用 an；从句主谓也不一致。

句 10

正：Students who do not have a moral compass cannot achieve success, even though they perform well at school.

学生的句子：Students who do not conform moral principles cannot achieve success, even they perform well in schools.

改：conform 是不及物动词，不能直接接宾语；even 是副词，不能连接句子。

句 11

正：In my opinion, students cannot be successful if they are not able to distinguish right from wrong.

学生的句子：In my opinion, students can get succeed when they are able to distinguish right and wrong.

改：succeed 是动词，不能和 get 连用。

句 12

正：Students should learn how to respect teachers and get along well with classmates.

学生的句子：Students should respect teachers and get a good relationship with classmates.

错：没有 get a good relationship 这个表达。

句 13

正：Some students like eating fast food, which can cause obesity.

学生的句子：Some students like eating fast foods, which can cause their overweight.

改：overweight 是形容词，不能充当宾语。

句 14

正：If they do not realise these problems, their education and career can be affected adversely.

学生的句子：If they are not able to realize these problems, their study and even future jobs will be affect negatively.

改："be + 动词原形" 永远是错的。

读者自学步骤 4

整体学习和检查范文，看看是否符合 TELCCS 原则。

范文的全文 (大概 7 分)

Schools are normally seen as the place where the next generation can increase knowledge to improve employability. In my view, academic subjects are important to one's career achievement, but students who do not learn the difference between right and wrong cannot succeed in their working lives.

Many teachers suggest that students should concentrate on core subjects, because the performance in these courses can determine whether they can enter the university in the future. What students can learn in academic courses can provide a firm grounding for university and help them find decent jobs. For example, students who acquire mathematical skills at school can build models to analyse data at university and work as financial analysts and engineers after they graduate. They are less likely to focus on key disciplines if they are required to spend time in studying moral principles and behaviour norms.

这里有一点跳跃，难道学了数学就会建模？

Schools can impart some important virtues into students, which enable them to make good use of their knowledge to contribute positively to society. If one understands the value of loyalty, he or she will not sell confidential documents of his or her employer to other companies. Engineers who are conscious of social responsibilities are more likely to design safe products which benefit consumers. Students who do not have a moral compass cannot achieve success, even though they perform well at school.

这里应该有个连接词，因为在说相反的观点。

最好不要用定语从句修饰整个句子，特别是 which 前面的先行词是人，影响 GRA 的分数。

这个例子和前面的 contribute positively to society 不匹配。

题目说的是学生，而不是 engineers。

In my opinion, students cannot be successful if they are not able to distinguish right from wrong. Students should learn how to respect teachers and get along well with classmates. Some students like eating fast food, which can cause obesity. If they do not realise these problems, their education and career can be affected adversely.

为什么不和同学好好相处，就不能成功？

这些生活习惯的问题不能算道德问题，和题目不相关，这样会影响 CC 的分数。

本节关键学习点

举例是雅思作文以及以后大学作业写作的重要拓展手段。举例可以让你的段落更加具体、有内容，增加可读性。恰当的例子也可以展示你对观点和理论的深入了解。

上面范文主体部分第一段的一个例子就是非常恰当。

For example, students who acquire mathematical skills at school can learn how to build models to analyse data at university and work as financial analysts and engineers after they graduate.

这个例子首先非常扣题。出现了 students, at school，也出现了 mathematical skills（数学能力）这样的字眼，对应题目里所说的学生、学校，还有学术课程。这个例子也和前面的观点非常地匹配。

这段话的前两句说的观点是关注主要学科可以读大学，可以找好工作。而这个例子说学好数学可以在大学里建模，以后可以做工程师，很好地解释了观点。

然而，举例并不是一件简单的事情，不是写个 for example 那么简单。很多考生举例都有问题。下面是一些常见的问题：

> 问题 1：没头没尾的例子。
>
> 问题 2：不相关的例子。
>
> 问题 3：不符合题目论述对象的例子。
>
> 问题 4：和前面观点和中心句不一致的例子。
>
> 问题 5：假例子。
>
> 问题 6：中国的例子。

我们下面详细解释这些问题。

问题 1：没头没尾的例子。

所谓没头没尾的例子，就是举例没有原因，没有结果，太过简单，读者不知道这个例子和观点以及题目有什么联系。

如文章最后一段话的例子：

Students should learn how to respect teachers and get along well with classmates.

学生知道如何尊重老师，和同学和睦相处，这和题目的"分辨对错"有什么联系呢？然后学生知道这些，对他们的成功又有什么帮助呢？文中对此都没有很好的解释。可以改成这样：

Students who learn politeness and social rules may understand how to respect teachers and get along well with classmates, and because of this, they will also be able to develop a strong working relationship with colleagues once they start working. This is the key to career achievement.

问题 2：不相关的例子。

不相关的例子就是这个例子和题目没什么联系。

例如，这个题目说的是分辨对错，这一般是指道德的判断，为人处世的好坏，遵守法律和社会惯例，但是文章最后一段的一个例子是关于肥胖和快餐的，这是生活习惯和方式的问题，并不恰当。只要不是过量地吃，或者不注意饮食均衡，吃快餐未必是坏事。

问题3：不符合题目论述对象的例子。

我们之前说过，举例是扣题的一个重要手段。在举例的时候，一定要注意题目的主要论述对象是什么。这个题目很明显是关于中学生的，那么主体部分第二段关于工程师的例子就不是很恰当。

Engineers who are conscious of social responsibilities are more likely to design safe products which benefit consumers.

可以改成：

Students who are conscious of social responsibilities are more likely to design safe products which benefit consumers, if they work as engineers for the manufacturing sector in the future.

问题4：和前面观点和中心句不一致的例子。

段落的例子一定要注意和前面观点和中心句的联系。很多考生写的例子经常和中心句意思有差距，甚至相反。

例如，主题部分第二段的中心句是说学生懂得美德，能够很好地为社会做贡献。但是后面的例子说的是年轻人将机密材料卖给其他公司赚钱，这和社会没什么联系。所以，前面的中心句可以稍微改一下：contribute positively to their future employers and even the whole society.

问题5：假例子。

很多考生经常是写了一个 for example, for instance，事实上后面一句话只是在重复观点，并不是具体的例子。

例如：For example, children who can tell right from wrong will earn respect from others in the workplace.

这句话说：懂得分辨对错的孩子能够在职场上获得别人的尊重。但是并没有说清楚分辨对错体现在哪里。你可以说孩子知道怎么尊重别人的付出，尊重别人的意见，提供及时的帮助等。

For example, children who can tell right from wrong will earn respect from others in the workplace, because they respect the input of their colleagues, appreciate other people's efforts and support other people whenever necessary.

问题6：中国的例子。

中国的例子有两点不好。

① 概括性不够。

有时候你如果说 in Asian countries 或者 in Asian cultures，可能就会好很多。

In China, children at school are required to be respectful to teachers, and this traditional value may benefit children in later life, since they will respect their supervisors in the workplace as well.

大概的意思就是"在中国，孩子一般被要求要尊重老师，这种传统的价值观对孩子以后会有好处，因为他们在职场上也会尊重上司"。

那么只说中国会不会有点狭隘，如果说 in some Asian countries, 会不会有种"通吃"的感觉。

② 考官未必能够有认同感。

很多考生在写作中经常用一些中国的拼音词，如 Li Na, Liu Xiang, Taobao 等，其实考官未必知道这些在中国家喻户晓的名字，这个时候一定要解释一下。

例如下面这句话，淘宝可能考官不知道，但是如果说是一个最大的电子商务公司，考官就懂了。

Taobao, one of the biggest E-commerce websites in China, has attracted many online shoppers.

提升的范文

标色的部分是和原文有差异的地方，下划线部分是词伙。

Schools are normally seen as the place where the next generation can increase knowledge to improve employability. In my view, academic subjects are important to one's career achievement, but students who do not learn the difference between right and wrong cannot succeed in their working lives.

Many teachers suggest that students should concentrate on core subjects, because the performance in these courses can determine whether they can enter university in the future. What students can learn in academic courses can provide a firm grounding for university and help them find decent jobs. For example, students who acquire mathematical skills at school can learn how to build models to analyse data at university and work as financial analysts and engineers after they graduate. They are less likely to focus on key disciplines if they are required to spend time in studying moral principles and behaviour norms.

On the other hand, some educationalists are in favour of imparting some important virtues and moral values into students, motivating the next generation to make good use of knowledge to contribute positively to their future employers and the whole society. Students who are conscious of social responsibilities are more likely to design safe products which benefit consumers, if they work as engineers for the manufacturing sector in the future. Students who do not have a moral compass cannot achieve success, even though they perform well at school.

In my opinion, the younger generation cannot be successful if they are not able to distinguish right from wrong. Students who learn politeness and social rules may understand how to respect teachers and get along well with classmates, and because of this, they will also be able to develop a strong working relationship with colleagues once they start working. This is the key to career achievement. If they do not realise this, their education and career can be affected adversely.

3.6.11 全文翻译 11：艺术投资＋对比／结尾

> *Many countries spend a lot of money in the arts. Some people think investment in the arts is necessary, but others say money is better spent on public services and facilities. Discuss both views and give your own opinion.*

题目大意

很多国家花大量的钱在艺术上。一些人认为艺术上的投资是必要的，但是另一些人认为钱最好花在公共服务和设施上。讨论两个观点和给出你个人的看法。

读者自学步骤 1

阅读题目后，写出三个观点。

下面是我学生写的一些错误或者不好的观点，大家可以看看自己是不是也犯了同样的错误。

学生的观点	点评
支持城市的文化艺术建设，有利于提高市民素质，营造城市文化氛围，建立城市文化名片。	太过空泛。应该具体说提高什么素质，文化氛围有什么好处等。
把钱投资在公众服务和设施上，公民生活有基本保障，社会更和谐。	太过空泛。为什么有了保障，社会就和谐？
投资公共设施，减少医疗成本，政府可投资其他设施，促进社会进步。	跑题和空泛。减少医疗成本为什么政府就投资其他设施，为什么社会就进步？
投资艺术，提高鉴赏能力和审美观，创造出杰出的作品。	不够有力。创造出杰出的艺术品有什么好处？
钱优先用于完善公共服务和基础设施，国家城市发展，吸引游客。	不够有力。基础设施好就可以吸引游客？
艺术的表现形式丰富，人们的思维被开拓，工作更有创造力，社会生产力提高。	逻辑不对。创造力和生产力不能混为一谈。
投资艺术必要，学校能开设艺术课增加学生艺术修养，短期内见不到收益。	跑题。投资艺术不见得是增设艺术课；这是论述类题目，第一个立场最好说投资艺术的好处。
投资艺术使人们得到更多的知识，开拓人们的思路，使人们发展更全面。	不够有力。为什么可以增加知识？为什么可以开拓思路？为什么发展更加全面？

投资公共服务，可以提高医疗服务水平，人们更健康、长寿。	太过具体。公共服务不只是医疗。
政府投资文化，文化产业发展居民更多享受文化成果，社会更具包容性。	观点不够有力。为什么艺术会增加社会的包容性？

读者自学步骤 2

翻译下面的句子：在翻译过程中，记住先想词伙，再想句型，然后写出句子。相关词伙可以查阅微信公众号：gu_writing。

介绍段

背景句	1. 人们对政府赞助艺术有不同的看法，特别在国家遇到预算问题的时候。
阐述立场	2. 我觉得我们应该优先注重基础设施，只有政府有盈余的时候才去投资艺术。

主体部分第一段

中心句	3. 很多人支持投资艺术，认为艺术可以使我们的城市更加吸引人。
原因 1	4. 艺术作品如雕塑、绘画、塑像，可以使我们的公共场所，例如图书馆、地铁站甚至公共厕所都变得漂亮。
原因 2	5. 如果艺术行业繁荣发展，城市建筑也有各种风格，我们可以更好地享受城市生活。
拓展的结果	6. 接触艺术让我们减少压力，也会让我们心情更好。

主体部分第二段

中心句（经济和社会）	7. 虽然艺术如此重要，但是很多人认为公共设施更加应该获得政府的资助。
解释	8. 普通公民对公共设施（如水电供应、学校、图书馆、道路）更感兴趣，这些设施对他们的生活质量有直接影响。
举例	9. 例如，好的卫生条件和干净的水可以促进大众的健康，减少疾病，而学校和图书馆可以普及知识，提高人们的工作前景。
对比	10. 相比之下，对于大部分人来说，雕塑、绘画或者歌剧是奢侈品，不可能给他们带来什么实际的好处。

主体部分第三段

中心句（经济）	11. 我自己的看法是公共设施促进经济发展，从而使政府有钱去资助艺术。

举例	12. 例如，投资交通系统可以使人们上下班更容易，提高生产力，而投资高铁和飞机场可以使物品运输更加方便。
结果	13. 有了这些设施，城市可以吸引投资，变得更加富裕，人们生活更好。
对比	14. 相比之下，投资艺术很多时候在短时间内很难获得一个好的经济回报。

结论段

再次表明立场	15. 因此我认为，即使艺术让我们的城市更加美丽，政府的重心也应该放在公共设施上。

读者自学步骤 3

检查自己的翻译：先看正确句子的词伙和句子结构，然后看错误的句子，看是否能够发现问题。

句 1

正：People have different views about government funding for the arts, especially when a country struggles with budget deficits.

学生的句子：Citizens hold different views about government sponsorship towards the art, especially when facing budget problems.

改：when facing 这个分词结构有歧义，不太清楚是修饰 government，还是 citizens。

句 2

正：I reckon that we should give priority to essential services and infrastructures and then fund the arts when governments have a budget surplus.

学生的句子：I reckon that we should give priority to infrastructures and then to invest in the art when having a surplus.

改：to invest 不清楚是否和前面的 to 对称，因为前面的 to 是介词。

句 3

正：Many people support the public funds for the arts, which can make our cities more visually attractive.

学生的句子：Many people support to provide funds on arts, which can make our cities more appealing and attractive.

改：没有 support to 这种表达；funds on 也不是习惯表达。

句 4

正：It is true that artworks, including sculptures, paintings and statues can decorate public facilities such as libraries, metro stations, or even toilets, and increase the artistic appeal of these places.

学生的句子：The work of art such as sculptures, painting and statues can make public places like library, metro station and even bathroom pretty.

改：library 等名词都是可数名词，要变成复数形式。

句 5

正：If the art industry prospers, cities have a mix of different architectural styles and we are more likely to enjoy urban life.

学生的句子：If the art industry developed prosperously, and the different buildings of cities also have the unique styles. And for the reason, we will enjoy the city life better.

改：developed 时态不对；第一句话没有主句；有两个连词。

句 6

正：Exposure to artworks can reduce our pressure and put us in a good mood.

学生的句子：If we are exposed to art, it can decrease our pressure and make our mood well.

改：well 是副词，一般搭配是 make something + 形容词。

句 7

正：Although the funding for the arts is important, many people would argue that public facilities deserve more of public money.

学生的句子：Though the art is very important, many people think the public facilities should be focused more and should get the government sponsorship firstly.

改：focused more 一般不这么表达；如果 art 单独写，不需要用定冠词。

句 8

正：Ordinary people are more interested in public facilities (such as water and electricity supply networks, schools, libraries and roads), which have a direct impact on their living standards.

学生的句子：Ordinary people are more interested in public facilities(such as water and electricity power, schools, libraries, roadways), which has a direct impact on their living standards.

改：一般当列举几个名词的时候，在最后一个名词前要用 and 相连；定语从句的谓语 has 和前面的名词不一致。

句 9

正：For example, good sanitation and clean water can improve people's health and reduce diseases, while schools and libraries can disseminate knowledge and improve young people's job prospects.

学生的句子：For example, good sanitation and clean water can improve people's fitness and reduce disease and schools and libraries can popularize knowledge and give people a promising career.

改：disease 是可数名词，最好用复数形式；schools 前面的 and 不恰当，因为有太多的并列成分。

句 10

正：In contrast, sculptures, paintings and operas are luxury items to most people and are not likely to bring tangible benefits to them.

学生的句子：In contrast, works of art, such as paintings and operas, are luxury items to most people and are not likely to bring them tangible benefits.

改：operas 不是 works of art，所以不能作为 works of art 的例子。

句 11

正：In my view, improvements in public facilities can promote economy development so that the government can have enough money to invest in art.

学生的句子：From my perspective, governments need to support the public facilities first, and this can promote the economic development.

改：public facilities, economic development 前面都不用加 the，因为不用特指。

句 12

正：For example, the investment in the transport system can improve the productivity of working people by making daily commuting easier, while the public spending on high-speed railway systems and airports can ensure that cargo can be delivered faster.

学生的句子：For example, investment in transport system make it easy for people to go to work, so the productivity can be improved, while investment in high-speed rails and airports can make transportation more easier.

改：system 是可数名词，前面要用冠词；investment...make 主谓不一致；没有 more easier 这个表达。

句 13

正：Cities can attract investment and become wealthy, so people's living standards can also be improved.

学生的句子：As a result, cities can attract investment and become wealthy, people's living standards can also be improved.

改：两个句子没有用连词连接。

句 14

正：By contrast, the investment in the arts cannot create such returns in a short time.

学生的句子：By contrast, people are hard to get a good economic feedback by investing arts in a short time.

改：人不能说 hard to；invest 是不及物动词，不能不加介词。

句 15

正：To sum up, I believe that the government should focus on services and facilities vital to the wellbeing of the general public, even though artistic projects have made our cities spectacular.

学生的句子：Therefore, I think the government should focus on developing public facilities rather than art even it is useful to make our city more charming.

改：even 是副词，不是连词；没有 something is useful to do something 的说法。

读者自学步骤 4

整体学习和检查范文，看看是否符合 TELCCS 原则。

范文全文（7～7.5 分）

People have different views about government funding for the arts, especially when a country struggles with budget deficits. I reckon that we should give priority to essential services and infrastructures and then fund the arts when governments have a budget surplus.

> 这个句子太多考生用了, 有套句的嫌疑, 考官可能会觉得你 memorised。

> 这里指代有点不清楚, 不知道是什么国家。

> governments 是复数, 与 a budget surplus 数不一致。

Many people support the public funds for the arts, which can make our cities more visually attractive. It is true that artworks, including sculptures, paintings and statues can decorate public facilities such as libraries, metro stations, or even toilets, and increase the artistic appeal of these places. If the art industry prospers, cities have a mix of different architectural styles and we are more likely to enjoy urban life. Exposure to artworks can reduce our pressure and put us in a good mood.

> 这里又说 people, 有点重复, 影响 LR 的分数。

> 这里突然说到建筑风格, 和前面的艺术品不一样, 影响 CC 的分数。

Although the funding for the arts is important, many people would argue that public facilities deserve more of public money. Ordinary people are more interested in public facilities (such as water and electricity supply networks, schools, libraries and roads), which have a direct impact on their living standards. For example, good sanitation and clean water can improve people's health and reduce diseases, while schools and libraries can disseminate knowledge and improve young people's job prospects. In contrast, sculptures, paintings and operas are luxury items to most people and are not likely to bring tangible benefits to them.

> 这样写有点啰唆。

In my view, improvements in public facilities can promote economy development so that the government can have enough money to invest in art. For example, the investment in the transport system can improve the productivity of working people by making daily commuting easier, while the public spending on high-speed railway systems and airports can ensure that cargo can be delivered faster. Cities can attract investment and

> 和后面的论述内容不一致。

become wealthy, so people's living standards can also be improved. By contrast, the investment in the arts cannot create such returns in a short time.

To sum up, I believe that the government should focus on services and facilities vital to the wellbeing of the general public, even though artistic projects have made our cities spectacular.

如果用完成时态，表示这件事情已经发生了，这和题目不符合。

本节关键学习点

对比在作文考试中是一种很常见的段落拓展方法。

首先，在某些题目中出现两个对比对象的时候，对比可以让你的论述更加扣题。其次，对比有时候是在论述没有想法的时候增加一点字数。当然，这也是对比这种论述方法的缺陷：有时候读起来感觉比较重复，这时候表达的替换就比较重要。

对比的三种方法分别是：

方法 1：题目中出现两个对立的事物，可以用 in contrast, by comparison 对比。

方法 2：一件事情如果不发生，会产生什么情形和结果，可以用 otherwise 引导。

方法 3：虚拟语气，尝试一个相反情况发生，会出现的情况。

以本文为例。

方法 1：题目中出现两个对立的事物，可以用 in contrast, by comparison 对比。

题目中出现了艺术和设施的对比，那么在主体部分第二段的最后一句话是这样写的：

In contrast, sculptures, paintings and operas are luxury items to most people and are not likely to bring tangible benefits to them. 这是艺术品的重要性和公共设施重要性的对比。

方法 2：一件事情如果不发生，会产生什么情形和结果，可以用 otherwise 引导。

例如，你可以说政府投资基础设施可以让城市居民更加舒服，否则，他们会去其他的地方居住。

The government spending on public services can attract and retain many professionals, skilled workers and entrepreneurs, because they can enjoy a higher quality of life. Otherwise, they may migrate to other cities or countries.

方法 3：虚拟语气，尝试一个相反情况发生，会出现的情况。

虚拟语气一般用于描述一个不可能发生的事情产生的结果。你可以说假如政府花大量的钱在艺术上，而忽略了公共设施（这是不可能的），说一下其产生的结果。

If public money were poured in artworks, rather than public facilities, facilities and essential services might not be well equipped to support business activity and economic slowdown would become a problem.

然后，我们再讲讲结论段。结论段大家需要注意以下几点：

注意 *1*：结尾段不要很长，一般 1～2 句话，主要是总结立场。

注意 *2*：如果考生愿意总结观点也可以，但是要注意不要用重复的表达。

注意 *3*：不要出现新的信息，不要升华。

很多考生都很纠结如何写结尾。事实上，结尾段是雅思大作文最不重要的部分。所以，我不会细致讲这个部分。

至此，关于 Task Response 的评分标准我们基本上讲解完了，从四种题目类型的应对到审题，到扣题的要点，到中心句的写作，还有拓展的两种比较重要的方法（举例和对比）。

开头和结尾我没有细说，因为不重要。

提升的范文

标色的部分是和原文有差异的地方，下划线部分是词伙。

The government sometimes faces opposition when spending its budget on public art, especially in economically tough times. I reckon that we should give priority to essential services and infrastructures and then fund the arts when there is a budget surplus.

The supporters of the public funds for the arts argue that cities can become more visually attractive because of art. It is true that artworks, including sculptures, paintings and statues can decorate public facilities such as libraries, metro stations, or even toilets, and increase the artistic appeal of these places. If the art industry prospers, cities will have art exhibitions, art festivals and other cultural activities which can make urban life dynamic and interesting. Exposure to artworks can reduce our pressure and put us in a good mood.

Despite this, many people would argue that public facilities deserve more of public money. Ordinary people are more interested in public facilities (such as water and electricity supply networks, schools, libraries and roads), which have a direct impact on their living standards. For example, good sanitation and clean water can improve people's health and reduce diseases, while schools and libraries can disseminate knowledge and improve young people's job prospects. In contrast, sculptures, paintings and operas are luxury items to most people and are not likely to bring tangible benefits to them.

In my view, improvements in public facilities can promote economy development, but the arts may be less important in economic terms. For example, the investment in the transport system can improve the productivity of working people by making daily commuting easier, while the public spending on high-speed railway systems and airports can ensure that cargo can be delivered faster. Cities can attract investment and become wealthy, so people's living standards can also be improved. By contrast, the investment in the arts cannot create such returns in a short time.

To sum up, I believe that the government should focus on services and facilities vital to the wellbeing of the general public, even though artistic projects can make our cities spectacular.

3.7 雅思评分标准 2：Coherence and Cohesion（连贯与衔接）

雅思大作文的第二个评分标准是连贯与衔接。很多学生很单纯地以为衔接就是一些连接词，如 furthermore, what's more, secondly, admittedly 等。事实上，雅思大作文的连贯与衔接比这些要精细得多。

除了立场的前后一致之外（不可以开始支持，最后反对，或者是开始反对，最后支持），还有每段话论述的逻辑性（每句话之间要有一定的逻辑关系和因果关系），最后就是代词、连接词。

3.7.1 全文翻译 12：志愿者工作＋观点的先后／前后一致

> *Volunteer work organised by middle schools brings more benefits than problems. To what extent do you agree or disagree?*

题目大意

中学组织的志愿者活动带来的好处多过问题。在多大程度上你同意或者是反对这一观点？

读者自学步骤 1

阅读题目后，写出三个观点。

下面是我学生写的一些错误或者不好的观点，大家可以看看自己是不是也犯了同样的错误。

学生的观点	点评
提前踏入社会锻炼自己，为以后性格塑造打下基础。	没有逻辑。难道性格塑造不是年轻的时候就可以开始的吗？
当志愿者，锻炼他们的人际交往能力，丰富他们的实践活动，培养乐于助人的品德。	多个观点写在一起。这是三个观点，应该分开写。
志愿者活动有利于学校创建一个良好的口碑，吸引更多学生家长为他们的孩子选择学校。	不够有力。这个题目主要是针对学生，而不是学校。
中学组织志愿服务，提供无偿服务，低成本改善当地社区。	不够有力。说得好像社区要利用中学生廉价劳动力似的。
中学生参加志愿者工作，学会做家务，理解父母的艰辛。	不够有力。义工不一定是做家务。
学校组织志愿者工作，能够动员学生参加，保证人手充足，利于志愿服务活动的顺利开展。	不够有力。活动的开展不是重点，重点是为什么要开展？有什么具体的好处？
中学组织志愿者活动，有体力活动，锻炼学生身体素质，有利身心健康发展。	不够有力。提高身体素质的东西很多，为什么用志愿者活动这个方式？

中学组织志愿者工作，学校能合理分配人员和资源，有利于提高志愿工作的效率。	跑题。这个题目不是问志愿者工作能不能做到，而是问要不要这么做，这样做好不好。
中学组织志愿者活动，占用学生一定学习时间，促使学生提高学习效率。	逻辑不好。占用时间应该是减少学生的学习效率，应该说鼓励中学生更好地安排和管理时间。

读者自学步骤 2

翻译下面的句子：在翻译过程中，记住先想词伙，再想句型，然后写出句子。相关词伙可以查阅微信公众号：gu_writing。

介绍段

背景句	1. 志愿工作已经在很多学校被广泛推广，甚至被确定为毕业的一个要求。
我的立场	2. 志愿工作有不好的一面，尽管它对参与其中的人还有整个社区都是有好处的。

主体部分第一段

中心句	3. 通过参加社区服务，学生可以提高自己的素质。
解释	4. 学生会遇到很多问题和挑战，在他们提供社区服务的时候，这些问题和挑战是在学校很少见的。
举例	5. 例如，当他们为慈善公司筹款的时候，他们需要懂得怎么和捐献人交流，怎么组织活动，怎么和别人合作。
结果	6. 这会提高他们的信心和解决问题的能力。

主体部分第二段

中心句	7. 与此同时，年轻人也会学到责任感，知道怎么为社区服务。
解释	8. 他们知道自己的工作可以给社会其他成员带来帮助，所以他们会有一种社区的感觉。
举例	9. 帮助贫穷的孩子学习是一种责任，中学生感觉到帮助别人接受教育可以让这个社会更加公平和快乐。
结果	10. 这样有助于我们建立起一个关系紧密的社会。

我的看法

中心句	11. 我们不能够忽略这么一个可能性 (we cannot rule out the possibility)：社区服务有时候没有很好的计划，浪费了志愿者的时间和精力。
解释	12. 志愿工作变成枯燥和辛苦，而不是有趣和有教育意义。
结果 1	13. 志愿者并不投入，可能因为他们看不到自己劳动的价值。
结果 2	14. 或者这些志愿者觉得志愿工作占用时间，影响他们的学习。
另外一个观点	15. 他们会懂得怎么管理时间，因为他们的时间很紧。

结论段

总结观点	16. 总的来说，我的观点是 (my view is that) 志愿服务对于学生的能力和就业前景以及社会发展都很重要。
	17. 但是，学校一定要确保志愿工作能够适合学生的需要。

读者自学步骤 3

检查自己的翻译，先看正确句子的词伙和句子结构，然后看错误的句子，看是否能够发现问题。

句 1

正：Volunteer work has been promoted by many schools and even accepted as a requirement for graduation.

学生的句子：Volunteer works have been popularized widely in many schools, and even regarded as a demand for graduation.

改：work "工作" 是不可数名词，没有复数形式；demand 是 "需求量" 的意思。

句 2

正：Unpaid work has its downside, although it is of great value for those young participants as well as the whole society.

学生的句子：The volunteer work has some disadvantages, although, it is beneficial to the participants and the whole community.

改：although 后面不需要用逗号；work "工作" 是不可数名词，前面不需要加定冠词 the。

句 3

正：By providing community services, students can develop some positive qualities.

学生的句子：By taking part in community services, students can always be develop some positive qualities.

改："be + 动词原形" 永远是错的。

句 4

正：Students may be confronted with many problems and challenges, most of which are rare at school, when they are involved in these voluntary services.

学生的句子：Students would run into many troubles and challenges which they hardly encounter at school when they are offering volunteer work.

改：offering 这里不应该用主动语态，因为不是这些学生提供工作，而是机构提供工作。

句 5

正：For example, when raising funds for charities, they should figure out how to communicate with benefactors, organise events or functions, and work closely with others.

学生的句子：For example, when they assist charity companies for donation, they need to know how to communicate with donators, how to organise activities and how to cooperate with others.

改：没有 donator 这个说法，可以说 patron，benefactors，donors。

句 6

正：These activities can boost their confidence and improve their problem-solving abilities.

学生的句子：It will boost their confidence and develop their capabilities of solving problems.

改：capability to do something 用得比较多，problem solving abilities 是常见表达。

句 7

正：The younger generation can meanwhile learn responsibility and find enjoyment in serving the community.

学生的句子：At the same time, young people can learn the sense of responsibility and know how to serve for community.

改：serve 是及物动词，后面不需要用 for。

句 8

正：They have a sense of community since they can see how their work can make a positive difference to other members of community.

学生的句子：Because they know their work can help other social residents, they will have a sense of community.

改：没有 social residents 这个说法。

句 9

正：It is a huge responsibility to support disadvantaged children in schooling, and middle school students will come to realise that helping others to receive a good education can make a fair and happy society.

学生的句子：It is a responsibility for young students to help disadvantaged children in order to create a peaceful and pleasant society.

改：在这里用 in order to 不恰当，因为 in order to 表示"目的"，这里应该强调"结果"。

句 10

正：It can help create a closely-knit community.

学生的句子：This is good for us to build up a closely-knit community.

改：这是一个常见的错误，"有助于"的表达是 help do something，不能说 it is good/important/helpful/ beneficial to do something（表示"做什么是重要的……"）。

句 11

正：On the other hand, we cannot rule out the possibility that unpaid work can lead to a wasteful use of volunteers' time and energy, if not well-organised.

学生的句子：However, we cannot rule out the possibility that community service do not have a better plan sometimes and thus waste volunteers' time and energy.

改：service do not 主谓不一致。

句 12

正：Volunteer work programmes are sometimes tedious and strenuous, and many students do not see unpaid work as a rewarding experience which has educational value.

学生的句子：Volunteer work becomes tedious and strenuous but not interesting and educational.

改：become 这个词一般用完成时或者将来时，很少用一般现在时。

句 13

正：Young volunteers are not willing to devote their time to unpaid work, since they do not discover the value of what they do.

学生的句子：Volunteers especially the young workers are not devoted for their work.

改：这篇文章里的 volunteers 都是年轻人，所以 young workers 多余。

句 14

正：They may also regard voluntary work as a service which can take away their study time and interfere with their studies.

学生的句子：It is also because some volunteers feel it not worth and will influence their studies if their time is taken up by volunteer work.

改：it is not worth doing something 是比较习惯的表达。

句 15

正：Some of them may learn how to manage time, because they have a tight timetable.

学生的句子：Some of them may learned how to manage time, because of have a tight timetable.

改：may 后面一定要加动词原形，而 because of 后面一定要加动名词或者名词。

句 16

正：Overall, my view is that volunteer work is of considerable importance to the next generation in terms of sharpening skills and improving job prospects, and also to social progress.

学生的句子：Generally, my view is that volunteer work is important to students social abilities and employment, which also benefit to the development of community.

改：定语从句 benefit 的主语不知道是什么，而且 benefit 是及物动词，后面应该直接加名词。

句 17

正：However, schools should make sure that it suits students' needs.

学生的句子：Schools must ensure the work is suit for students' needs.

改：suit 是动词，后面不能加 be 动词。

读者自学步骤 4

整体学习和检查范文，看看是否符合 TELCCS 原则。

范文全文（7.5分）

Volunteer work has been promoted by many schools and even accepted as a requirement for graduation. Unpaid work has its downside, although it is of great value for those young participants as well as the whole society.

By providing community services, students can develop some positive qualities. Students may be confronted with many problems and challenges, most of which are rare at school, when they are involved in these voluntary services. For example, when raising funds for charities, they should figure out how to communicate with benefactors, organise events or functions, and work closely with others. These activities can boost their confidence and improve their problem-solving abilities.

The younger generation can meanwhile learn responsibility and find enjoyment in serving the community. They have a sense of community since they can see how their work can make a positive difference to other members of community. It is a huge responsibility to support disadvantaged children in schooling, and middle school students will come to realise that helping others to receive a good education can make a fair and happy society. It can help create a closely-knit community.

On the other hand, we cannot rule out the possibility that unpaid work can lead to a wasteful use of volunteers' time and energy, if not well-organised. Volunteer work programmes are sometimes tedious and strenuous, and many students do not see unpaid work as a rewarding experience which has educational value. Young volunteers are not willing to devote their time to unpaid work, since they do not discover the value of what they do. They may also regard voluntary work as a service which can take away their study time and interfere with their studies. Some of them may learn how to manage time, because they have a tight timetable.

如果这么说，就意味着整篇文章立场是不支持义工，这和后面的论述不一致。

可以更具体一点，不要太空泛，而且 qualities 一般是性格方面的素质，和后面的论述不是很一致，影响 CC 的分数。

confidence 一般来说后面要加 in，有具体的宾语，否则影响 LR 的分数。

这段话这里有点跳跃，为什么接受教育可以创造公平和快乐的社会，为什么社会会有凝聚力？

这句话和前面有点重复，影响 CC 的分数。

这段话的主要意思是关于义工的坏处，而义工帮助学生增加管理时间的能力就是一个好处，出现了不一致的问题。

Overall, my view is that volunteer work is of considerable importance to the next generation in terms of sharpening skills and improving job prospects, and also to social progress. However, schools should make sure that it suits students' needs.

主体段落好像没有讨论工作的事情，这样会影响CC的分数。

本节关键学习点

雅思作文的观点选择和先后顺序也是比较讲究的一件事情。

如果观点选得不好，首先，拓展比较难，因此容易写不够字数；其次，不够有说服力，考官可能要看半天才大概知道你的观点想说什么；最惨的是，考官有些时候会觉得你写跑题了，写的观点不直接对应题目，也会直接扣分。

在写观点的时候，尽量注意下面一些问题：

> 问题 *1*：观点要避免重复。
>
> 问题 *2*：观点要具体，不只是立场。
>
> 问题 *3*：观点不要太空泛。
>
> 问题 *4*：观点要关注题目的第一关注人群。
>
> 问题 *5*：观点不是例子。

我们用本文细致解释一下这些问题。

问题 *1*：观点要避免重复。

观点要有区分度，否则考官会觉得你在凑字数。

本文第一个观点是学生可以提高技能，增加经验。这是关于能力培养的观点。如果你下一段写学生有了技能可以更好找工作，就重复了。

问题 *2*：观点要具体，不只是立场。

所谓的立场是你对一件事情的褒贬看法（如是否支持志愿工作）。

例：I believe that doing unpaid work is valuable to young people.

这种句子应该放在开头段，而不是主体部分的中心句。

中心句应该表达的是论述你立场的观点，也就是你为什么觉得 unpaid work 非常有价值的观点。

就好比你说你喜欢出国读书，这只是你的立场，你要去说观点，如以后更好找工作、阅历更多等。

问题 *3*：观点不要太空泛。

这是中国考生一个很普遍的问题，大家会说社区和谐，人们团结，提高个人素质等。这些观点对于外国人是陌生的。而且大家都这么写，考官会觉得考生只会死记硬背，没有丰富的表达和论述能力。

如果你说志愿者提高个人素质，那么你一定要具体说出那是什么素质。如果你说社区会更加和谐，你要解释什么是和谐，和谐的好处是什么。

问题 4：观点要关注题目的第一关注人群。

遇到一些简单的题目，如旅游业、志愿者工作等，你会有很多观点，但是一定要注意使用最有力的观点，观点也需要关注题目的第一关注人群，如这篇文章是关于年轻人的，那么主要就是讨论这对年轻人的好处。如果你写的观点是慈善机构可以减少费用，学校可以提高名声，这些观点都不够有力。

问题 5：观点不是例子。

很多考生喜欢用例子做观点，那样就太过具体。

例如，如果我们其中一个观点是：年轻人如果去帮助老人，会更加有同情心。同情心这个好处就过分具体。

另外一个大家要很注意的评分标准是 Coherence，这个评分标准有两个要点：

要点 1：立场的前后一致。

要点 2：每段话论述的内容一致。

我们还是用这篇文章稍微说说这两点。

要点 1：立场的前后一致。

整篇文章主要的立场是说年轻人应该做义工，但是开头段却说"虽然义工有好处，但是它有缺点"，那么和主体部分内容论述不一致，所以要修改。

要点 2：每段话论述的内容一致。

文章主体部分一般来说每段话有一个中心，而论述的内容都是围绕这个中心进行。中心句如果是说优点，论述就不能出现缺点。中心句如果确定范围是说经济，论述就不能出现其他方面的内容，如环境、文化。中心句如果描述的对象是年轻人，论述就不要描述其他年龄群体等。

这篇文章的主体部分第三段是折中段，说的是义工的坏处，那么最后一句话说义工可以帮助年轻人学会怎么管理时间就不恰当，因为这是一个明显的好处。

每段话不要因为字数不够就去随便写一句话，特别是一句破坏段落连续性的话。

提升的范文

标色的部分是和原文有差异的地方，下划线部分是词伙。

Volunteer work has been promoted by many schools and even accepted as a requirement for graduation. Unpaid work may have its downside, but it is of great value for those young participants as well as the whole society.

By providing community services, students can improve their skills and increase their practical experience. Students may be confronted with many problems and challenges, most of which are rare at school, when they are involved in these <u>voluntary services</u>. For example, when <u>raising funds</u> for charities, they should figure out how to communicate with benefactors, <u>organise events</u> or functions, and <u>work closely with</u> others. These activities can <u>boost their confidence</u> in cooperating with <u>people from all walks of life</u>, and <u>improve their problem-solving abilities</u>.

The younger generation can meanwhile <u>learn responsibility and find enjoyment</u> in serving the community. They have a <u>sense of community</u> since they can see how their work can <u>make a positive difference to</u> other members of community. Examples include helping disadvantaged children to improve exam grades, supporting caregivers in nursing homes, and assisting disabled people in overcoming difficulties in daily lives. If young people are all happy to give a helping hand to others, it will create a close-knit and happy society.

On the other hand, we cannot rule out the possibility that unpaid work can lead to a <u>wasteful use of</u> volunteers' time and energy, if not well-organised. Volunteer work programmes are sometimes tedious and strenuous, and many students do not see unpaid work as a <u>rewarding experience</u> which is of educational value. They may also regard voluntary work as a service which can <u>take away their study time and interfere with their studies</u>.

Overall, my view is that volunteer work is of considerable importance to the <u>next generation</u> in terms of <u>sharpening skills</u> and <u>fostering a sense of responsibility</u>, and also to <u>social progress</u>. However, schools should make sure that it <u>suits students' needs</u>.

3.7.2 全文翻译 13：刑罚＋如何避免重复和跳跃

> *A longer prison term as a way of punishing those who break the law is not as good as other methods. To what extent do you agree or disagree?*

题目大意

严厉的刑罚不像其他惩罚罪犯的方法那么好。在多大程度上你支持或者反对这个看法？

读者自学步骤 1

阅读题目后，写出三个观点。

下面是我学生写的一些错误或者不好的观点，大家可以看看自己是不是也犯了同样的错误。

学生的观点	点评
触犯法律的人要进监狱，在长时间的监狱生活中，他们可以重新改造，学习知识，锻炼劳动技能，有利于他们出狱后自力更生。	观点不唯一。为什么只有在监狱里才可以学习知识，提高技能？
更长的刑期，违法者面临长期的非自由状态，容易产生绝望的情绪。	不够有力。绝望的情绪有什么不好的呢？

长期服刑不比社区服务，不能从根本上改造犯罪分子，刑满后难免继续犯罪，无法为犯罪分子的将来负责。	不够有力。为什么不能改造？为什么不能为将来负责？要具体解释。
增加入狱时间，政府财务压力增加，税率增加，纳税人压力增加，生活水平下降。	不够有力。犯罪的人是少数，怎么会导致税率增加？
长期判刑，罪犯缺乏社会技能，易再次犯罪，危害社会。	不够有力。社会能力是交流能力，应该说的是工作能力。
其他手段，犯罪者反省自我的同时还能有益社会。	不够有力。为什么用其他手段就会反省？入狱就不可以？
长期监禁的犯罪分子可以做一些简单的劳动，提升社会整体生产力。	不够有力。这是利用罪犯做劳力？
让重大罪犯获得自己应有的惩罚，减少死刑。	没有逻辑。为什么获得惩罚，就减少死刑？

读者自学步骤2

翻译下面的句子：在翻译过程中，记住先想词伙，再想句型，然后写出句子。相关词伙可以查阅微信公众号：gu_writing。

介绍段

背景句	1. 判刑在很多社会被认为是惩罚犯下严重罪行的人的一种方法，有时候也被看作一种改造方法。
阐述立场	2. 这种方法可能有一些优点，但是我们需要考虑其他的一些方法去改造罪犯。

主体部分第一段

中心句（社会）	3. 支持严厉刑罚的人会认为这种惩罚方式有震慑的作用，无论是对于潜在的罪犯，还是对于惯犯。
解释	4. 刑罚意味着失去自由，这是理智的人所不能够接受的后果。
	5. 这同时也会对他们以后的人生，包括职业，产生影响。
结果	6. 他们因此就不会犯罪，因为担心受到惩罚。

主体部分第二段

中心句（个人权利）	7. 尽管一个长期的刑罚有它的优点，我们可以考虑社区服务。
解释	8. 社区服务可以让一些犯法的人，特别是犯轻微罪行的人，成为守法的公民。
对比	9. 如果他们入狱，那么出狱后可能再犯罪，对社会的其他成员构成威胁。

主体部分第三段

中心句 （个人）	10. 我们也可以提供通过教育和技能培训来提高犯罪人员的个人技能和工作能力。
解释	11. 青少年罪犯或者是初犯因为缺乏社会经验或者社会地位低而违犯法律。
结果	12. 如果他们可以找到工作，或者知道法律责任，他们就不会犯罪。
对比	13. 监狱将违法者和社会隔离，阻碍了违法者获得工作技能，重新回到社会。

结论段

再次表明立场	14. 总之，我认为长期的刑罚可能可以震慑犯罪，但是不是最好的办法。
总结观点	15. 通过一些其他的改造计划，我们可以建立一个更加快乐和稳定的社会。

读者自学步骤3

检查自己的翻译：先看正确句子的词伙和句子结构，然后看错误的句子，看是否能够发现问题。

句 1

正：Imposing sentences is widely accepted as a method to punish those who commit serious offence and sometimes as a correctional method.

学生的句子：In many societies, imposing sentence are recognised that it is a method to punish those people who crime serious offence, sometimes, it is also seemed to be a correctional method.

改：imposing sentences 是动名词作主语，动词应该用单数；recognised as something 是习惯表达；seem（看起来是）是系动词，没有被动语态，而 see 是及物动词，有被动语态。

句 2

正：This approach may be effective, but we should also consider other ways to reform offenders.

学生的句子：This approach may has a lot of merits, however, we need to consider other ways to reform offenders.

改：may 情态动词后面要加动词原形；however 是副词，不是连词。

句 3

正：The supporters of stiff sentences believe that this kind of punishment has a deterrent effect on either prospective offenders or habitual offenders.

学生的句子：People who support stiff sentence will regard that this kind of punishment has a deterrent effect to either for the prospective offenders, or for those habitual offenders.

改：regard 和 consider 差不多，一般不接宾语从句；effect 后面的介词是 on。

句 4

正：Imprisonment means that those who violate laws will lose freedom, a consequence that no rational person is willing to take.

学生的句子：Penalty means to lose free, this is unaccepted consequence by sensible people.

改：mean 是及物动词，加名词或从句作宾语；free 是形容词，其名词形式是 freedom；逗句连接两个句子，典型错误。

□ 5

正：The criminal record can have a lasting impact on their lives including their career.

学生的句子：It is also influence on their life, include job in the future.

改："具有影响"的惯用表达是 have an impact/influence on；include 是动词，而这里应该是 including，介词。

□ 6

正：They will not commit crimes because they are afraid of being punished.

学生的句子：Because worry about punishment，so they cannot commit crime.

改：because 和 so 不能连用；because 后面要接完整的句子；cannot 是错的，因为人是"可以"犯罪的。

□ 7

正：Although a long prison term may sometimes help us fight crime, we can consider community services as an alternative.

学生的句子：Although, a long-term sentence has benefits for offenders, we still can consider about community services.

改：although 之类的从属连词后面不需要加逗号；consider 是及物动词，应该直接加宾语。

□ 8

正：This form of punishment can make some offenders, especially those who committed minor crimes, law-abiding citizens.

学生的句子：Community services can make some people, especially those minor crimes, become law-abiding citizens.

改：minor crimes 是轻罪，不是"罪犯"的意思，不能够解释前面的 people；make somebody... become 是一个不自然的表达。

□ 9

正：If they are sentenced to prison, they are likely to reoffend after being released, which can pose a threat to other members of society.

学生的句子：The offenders maybe pose a threaten to other social members, if the government put offenders in prison.

改：maybe 是副词，应该用 may；pose a threat 才是正常的表达，threaten 是动词；government put 主谓不一致。

□ 10

正：We can also provide educational opportunities and vocational training for them, improving their interpersonal skills and job skills.

学生的句子：We can also offer educational and vocational training to criminals in order to improving their personal skills as well as working ability.

改：educational training 的表达不是很好；in order to + 动词原形是常用表达。

句 11

正：It is worth noting that many juvenile offenders or first-time offenders broke the law because of a lack of social experience or low socio-economic status.

学生的句子：Young offenders or first time offenders commit crimes because they are lack of social experience or in low social status.

改：lack = shortage，一般不能说人 are lack of，意思变成了"人是一种缺乏"。

句 12

正：Crime is no longer an option, if they can find work and understand legal responsibilities.

学生的句子：If they found a job and knew the responsibilities of law, they would not commit crimes.

改：这句话没有必要用虚拟语气，因为通过培训，他们还是可以找到工作的；那么多人只有 a job，也不恰当。

句 13

正：The prison can isolate criminals from society, preventing them acquiring practical skills and reintegrating into society.

学生的句子：Prisons isolate offenders and societies, preventing offenders from acquiring job skills, which decrease the opportunities that they can reintegrate into societies.

改：isolate somebody from... 是正常的表达；which decrease 如果是修饰前面整句话，动词应该用单数；opportunities 一般不引导同位语从句。

句 14

正：Overall, I agree that the harsh penalty can deter crime, but it is not the best approach.

学生的句子：Overall, I believe that long-term punishment may can deter criminals, but it is not the best method.

改：deter crime，而不是 criminals 罪犯；may 和 can 两个情态动词不可能连用。

句 15

正：Through other rehabilitation programs, we can build a happy and stable society.

学生的句子：We can built a more steady and happier society through some other rehabilitation programs.

改：can 后面要接动词原形；一般用 stable 修饰 society。

读者自学步骤 4

整体学习和检查范文，看看是否符合 TELCCS 原则。

范文全文（大概 7 分）

Imposing sentences is widely accepted as a method to punish those who commit serious offence and sometimes as a correctional method. This approach may be effective, but we should also consider other ways to reform offenders.

The supporters of stiff sentences believe that this kind of punishment has a deterrent effect on either prospective offenders or habitual offenders. Imprisonment means that those who violate laws will lose freedom, a consequence that no rational person is willing to take. The criminal record can have a lasting impact on their lives including their career. They will not commit crimes because they are afraid of being punished.

这是观点类的题目，用这些论述类的表达不恰当。

题目不只是判刑，还是长的刑期，要注意扣题。

再写"惩罚"就会很重复。

Although a long prison term may sometimes help us fight crime, we can consider community services as an alternative. This form of punishment can make some offenders, especially those who committed minor crimes, law-abiding citizens. If they are sentenced to prison, they are likely to reoffend after being released, which can pose a threat to other members of society.

这里连接不太好。

应该是 community service, service 不可数。如果可数的话，表示一些政府的社会服务。

这个 punishment 会产生歧义，有可能指代的是 a long prison term。

这句话出现跳跃，为什么社区服务会让人们遵纪守法？

这里也出现了跳跃，为什么坐牢就会再犯罪？

We can also provide educational opportunities and vocational training for them, improving their interpersonal skills and job skills. It is worth noting that many juvenile offenders or first-time offenders broke the law because of a lack of social experience or low socio-economic status. Crime is no longer an option, if they can find work and understand legal responsibilities. The prison can isolate criminals from society, preventing them acquiring practical skills and reintegrating into society.

再一次说了工作技能，比较重复。

Overall, I agree that the harsh penalty can deter crime, but it is not the best approach. Through other rehabilitation programs, we can build a happy and stable society.

这个词伙一般用于一些身体或者行为修复的项目，和主体部分论述不一致，影响 CC 的分数。

本节关键学习点

跳跃和重复都是中国考生常见的问题。两个问题的核心原因是考生不大习惯思考原因。

我们更加喜欢得出一个结论，坚持这个结论，而不是论述它。

我们喜欢背很多的观点，但是很少去思考这些观点的道理是什么，有什么站不住脚的地方。

解决这两个问题的方法有两个：

> 方法1：多想原因，多培养批判性思维。
>
> 方法2：多思考结果，多思考某件事情对我们的影响。

方法1：多想原因，多培养批判性思维。

所谓批判性思维，就是不要简单相信和背诵一个观点，要多想原因。

例如看暴力的电影，很多考生背诵的观点是年轻人会模仿，变得很暴力。然而，他们很少会问自己：为什么年轻人会模仿？是不是所有年轻人都会模仿？年轻人模仿的原因可能是电影里的暴力往往是一些明星角色实施的，所以年轻人可能觉得暴力是魅力的表现，而电影里的暴力也是解决问题的一种手段，年轻人以为暴力也可以解决生活中的问题。如果你能够想到这些原因，那么你的作文就不会重复，也不会跳跃。

方法2：多思考结果，多思考某件事情对我们的影响。

我们很多时候会说社会和谐，很多考生一写作文就会说社会和谐。那么社会和谐有什么好处呢？你可以稍微阐述一下，可能是人们相互友好、生活更加开心、有归属感等。

很多时候考生说促进经济发展，那么经济发展有什么好处呢？可能是人们收入更高、生活更好等。

很多考生说教育提高素质，那么提高素质有什么好处呢？可能是事业更加成功、和别人相处更好等。

下面用今天的文章作为例子，在那些跳跃和重复的地方，不断去思考为什么和产生的结果。这样文章就会避免重复和跳跃。

	原因	结果
第一段：they will not commit crime.	他们可以去找工作来赚钱。	社会会更加的安全。
第二段：punishment can make offenders law-abiding citizens	他们可以学会社会责任感，会考虑到别人的利益和感受。	社会上的人相互帮助。
第二段：they are likely to reoffend	坐牢的人会受到罪犯的影响，不思悔改。	
第三段：reintegrate into society	罪犯对于工作没有信心。	

提升的范文

标色的部分是和原文有差异的地方，下划线部分是词伙。

Imposing sentences is widely accepted as a method to punish those who commit serious offence and sometimes as a correctional method. This approach may be effective, but we should also consider other ways to reform offenders.

The prison sentence may have a deterrent effect on either prospective offenders or habitual offenders.

A long prison sentence means that those who <u>violate laws</u> will <u>lose freedom</u> for a prolonged period of time, a consequence that no rational person is willing to take. The <u>criminal record</u> can have a lasting impact on their lives including their career. They will not commit crimes when they realise the problems that ensue; instead, they will choose to find work or <u>run a small business</u> to <u>earn a living</u>. This can help create a peaceful and <u>safe community</u>.

While I agree that a long prison term may sometimes help us <u>fight crime</u>, we can consider community service as an alternative. This punishment can make some offenders, especially those who committed <u>minor crimes</u>, <u>law-abiding citizens</u>. They can learn how to act as meaningful members of community by cleaning streets, removing graffiti and tending gardens, and realise that they can contribute to society. If they are <u>sentenced to prison</u>, they will possibly make friends with other offenders. They will not repent or <u>take stock of their lives</u>, so they may reoffend after being released, which can pose a threat to other <u>members of society</u>.

We can also provide educational opportunities and <u>vocational training</u> for them, improving their <u>interpersonal skills</u> and <u>job skills</u>. It is worth noting that many <u>juvenile offenders</u> or <u>first-time offenders</u> broke the law because of a lack of <u>social experience</u> or <u>low socio-economic status</u>. Crime is no longer an option, if they can find work and understand <u>legal responsibilities</u>. The prison can isolate criminals from society, <u>shattering their confidence</u> in finding work and <u>reintegrating into society</u>.

Overall, I agree that the <u>harsh penalty</u> can <u>deter crime</u>, but it is not the best approach. The focus should be on changing the behaviour of offenders and helping them function as productive members of society.

3.7.3 全文翻译 14：学生自己居住＋段落句子连接的方法

> *It is better for students to live away from home while studying at university than living with parents. To what extent do you agree or disagree?*

题目大意

学生在大学学习的时候，最好是离家居住，而不是和父母一起居住。在多大程度上你同意或者是反对这个看法？

读者自学步骤 1

阅读题目后，写出三个观点。

下面是我学生写的一些错误或者不好的观点，大家可以看看自己是不是也犯了同样的错误。

学生的观点	点评
离开家住，更自由，自己的时间变多，培养兴趣爱好，生活有趣。	逻辑问题。自由可以理解，为什么自己住时间会变多？是不用每天回家吗？

大学时不住家里，没有父母的管制，有更多时间自由支配。	没有褒贬。没有父母的管制为什么是好事？为什么自由支配时间就是好处？
住家里，可以得到父母的照顾，而且省钱，不需要支付房租，减少对学习时间的占用，有更多时间学习。	两个观点写在一起。省时间和省钱是不同的概念。
读大学不住家里，和父母疏远，缺乏监督，不好好学习，而且容易出现心理问题。	概念混淆。疏远的是情感，监督的是学习，两者不能混谈，而且说出现心理问题太夸张。
跟父母住，家里条件比宿舍好，对家庭依赖。	观点牵强。家里条件未必比宿舍好，而对家庭依赖也未必是好事。
上大学期间与父母住在一起，在必要的时候可以得到指导和帮助，有利于身心健康。	逻辑跳跃。为什么父母给予指导就身心健康，万一是坏爸爸、坏妈妈呢？
不在家住，跟家人在一起的时间少了，懂得珍惜家人，更加孝顺。	逻辑问题。既然孝顺，就应该陪伴。难道因为珍惜生命，所以要自杀？

读者自学步骤 2

翻译下面的句子：在翻译过程中，记住先想词伙，再想句型，然后写出句子。 相关词伙可以查阅微信公众号：gu_writing。

介绍段

改写题目	1. 很多大学生现在要么住在学校的宿舍，要么和同学合租公寓。
阐述立场	2. 我觉得这是一个成长的标志，虽然年轻人很难和父母每天保持交流。

主体部分第一段

中心句（社会能力）	3. 离开父母居住意味着年轻人要学习如何独立地生活。
举例 1	4. 他们需要学会一些生活技能，如做家务、理财、和室友相处等。
结果	5. 有了这些技能，他们以后也可以很好地应对工作上的事情。
举例 2	6. 例如，他们可以懂得如何将一切都打理得井井有条，如果他们有整理房间的习惯。

主体部分第二段

中心句	7. 此外，大学生也可以在社会生活中享受更多的自由，交一些新的朋友。
解释	8. 他们不用每天都回家，因此有更多的时间参加很多活动。
举例	9. 他们可以和同学一起去健身，参加讲座，去图书馆做作业，甚至一起打工。
结果	10. 不仅他们可以提高社会技能，以后也有更多的人脉可用。

主体部分第三段 (折中段)

中心句 (情感健康)	11. 这个选择也有一定缺陷，就是孩子和父母的接触会减少，情感的联系变得脆弱。
解释	12. 他们很少和父母一起吃饭，而他们的父母也不太知道孩子的近况。
结果	13. 他们有时候会觉得无助，如果有一些问题不能解决。
结果的拓展	14. 这可能对于他们以后对家庭生活的态度也有影响。

结论段

表明立场	15. 总结一下，年轻人离开父母居住是一个好的决定，虽然这会影响到他们和父母的关系。

读者自学步骤 3

检查自己的翻译：先看正确句子的词伙和句子结构，然后看错误的句子，看是否能够发现问题。

句 1

正：Many university students today have either chosen university accommodation or shared a flat with their friends.

学生的句子：Now, a large amount of students live in dorm or in apartment with their classmates.

改：a large amount of 不能修饰人；apartment 是可数名词，要用复数。

句 2

正：I think it is a rite of passage though these young people may not be able to maintain day-to-day contact with their parents.

学生的句子：I think it is a rite of passage though young people are hardly to communicate with their parents.

改：hardly 是副词，不能充当表语。

句 3

正：Living away from parents means that young people have to learn how to live an independent life.

学生的句子：Leaving their parents, it means that these people have to learn how to live independently.

改：leaving their parents 是这个句子的主语，it 是多余的。

句 4

正：They have to develop some life skills, such as doing housekeeping, managing finances and getting along with flatmates.

学生的句子：They have to learn some life skills, such as housework, money management and get along with roommates.

改：such as 后面一般加名词或者动名词，而 get along with 是动词词组；而且最好后面的成分词性一致。

句 5

正：With these skills, they can handle many matters casily in the workplace.

学生的句子：With these skills, they can handle works easily in the future.

改：work "工作" 是不可数名词，没有复数。

句 6

正：For example, they are more likely to keep everything organized if they have the habit of cleaning their bedrooms.

学生的句子：For example, they can understand how to keep everything organized if they get used to clean their rooms.

改：get used to + doing 是习惯用法。

句 7

正：In addition, college students can enjoy more freedom in social life and make new friends.

学生的句子：In addition, the college students can enjoy more free on social life and make more friends.

改：students 没有必要加定冠词，不用特指；free 是形容词，不能充当宾语。

句 8

正：They do not need to go home every day, so they have more time to do a wide range of activities.

学生的句子：They do not need to return home everyday, so they have more time to participate other activities.

改：everyday 是形容词，不是副词；participate 是不及物动词，不能直接加宾语。

句 9

正：They can go to the gym with other students, attend lectures, do assignments in the library and even do part-time work together.

学生的句子：They can work out with their classmates, attend lectures, do homework in the library, even do some part-time job together.

改：homework 一般不用于大学生；even 不是连词，不可以连接句子；job 是可数名词，要用复数形式。

句 10

正：In addition to improving social skills, they also have more personal resources to draw upon in the future.

学生的句子：Not only they can improve their social skills, but also draw upon personal resource in the future.

改：not only 放在句首时句子要倒装。

句 11

正：The downside of this choice is that the contact with parents will decline and the emotional tie will suffer.

学生的句子: This choice also has faults, which is that children have less opportunities to keep in touch with parents, the relation between emotions will be fragile.

改: faults 是 "失误" 的意思,不恰当;which is that 也是很别扭的表达;后面两个句子间缺少连词。

句 12

正: They hardly have a meal with their parents and cannot keep up to date with the news about their family.

学生的句子: The young people seldom have eat together with their parents, while their parents are unlikely to know what happen to these people recently.

改: 没有 have eat 这个表达;what happen 主谓不一致,而且时态不对。

句 13

正: They may feel helpless, if they cannot solve some problems in their studies.

学生的句子: They may feel a sense of lonely because some problems cannot be solved.

改: of 是介词,后面不能加形容词;不应该用原因状语从句,应该用条件状语从句。

句 14

正: This may also affect their attitude towards family life.

学生的句子: This may has a significant impact on their attitudes towards their family lives.

改: 情态动词后面要加动词原形。

句 15

正: In conclusion, it is a good decision for university students to leave home, although it may have a damaging effect on their family relationship.

学生的句子: In conclusion, although young people leave alone is a good decision, it will influence relationship with their parents.

改: young people leave alone 是独立的句子,不能充当句子的主语;although 使用错误,这里的重点应该是年轻人自己居住,所以应该作为主句出现。

读者自学步骤 4

整体学习和检查范文,看看是否符合 TELCCS 原则。

范文全文 (7.5 分)

Many university students today have either chosen university accommodation or shared a flat with their friends. I think it is a rite of passage though these young people may not be able to maintain day-to-day contact with their parents.

Living away from parents means that young people have to learn how to live an independent life. They have to develop some life skills, such as doing housekeeping, managing finances and getting along with flatmates. With these skills, they can handle many matters easily in the workplace. For example, they are more likely to keep everything organised if they have the habit of cleaning their bedrooms.

这里突然说到工作，比较突兀，可以改成 once they enter the workforce。

In addition, college students can enjoy more freedom in social life and make new friends. They do not need to go home every day, so they have more time to do a wide range of activities. They can go to the gym with other students, attend lectures, do assignments in the library and even do part-time work together. In addition to improving social skills, they also have more personal resources to draw upon in the future.

这几个例子可以放在 activities 的后面，这样两句话不至于显得比较啰唆，影响 CC 的分数。

这几个例子一定要突出能够交新的朋友。

中心句说的是 social life，make new friends，最好要对应一下，确保 CC 分数不会丢。

The downside of this choice is that the contact with parents will decline and the emotional tie will suffer. They hardly have a meal with their parents and cannot keep up to date with the news about their family. They may feel helpless, if they cannot solve some problems in their studies. This may also affect their attitude towards family life.

突然说到作业和学习，和前面没什么联系，影响 CC 的分数。

In conclusion, it is a good decision for university students to leave home, although it may have a damaging effect on their family relationship.

本节关键学习点

这篇文章，包括我在网课指导学生写的很多范文，都出现了非常丰富和多变的句子连接方式。通过这篇文章里的一些例子，我们来梳理一下写作中可以用到的一些连接的技巧和方法。

> 方法 1：连接词。
>
> 方法 2：状语从句。
>
> 方法 3：一些名词性从句。
>
> 方法 4：一些含有 this，these 的词组。
>
> 方法 5：代词 they，this，their 等。
>
> 方法 6：含有 another 的表达。
>
> 方法 7：上下文两个句子本身的逻辑关系。
>
> 方法 8：一些关键表达的重复。

下面我开始具体解释一下这些连接方法。

方法 1：连接词。

连接词可能是中国考生最熟悉的一种连接方法，常用的连接词如下所示：

表示结果	therefore, thus, as a consequence, consequently, because of this, for this reason, as such, as a result of this
引起并列的观点	apart from this, in addition to this, besides, furthermore, moreover, on top of this, also
表示观点排列	firstly, first of all, secondly, thirdly 等
表示转折和对比	however/nevertheless, despite this, on the other hand, in contrast/by contrast, by comparison, conversely, on the positive/negative side, meanwhile
表示选择	alternatively, instead, rather
表示举例	for example, for instance
表示引言	in general, in most cases, as a general rule, more often than not

例如这篇文章的主体部分第二段，一开始就用了 in addition，显示这是第二个观点。

这些连接词固然重要，不管是在口语中，还是在写作中，但是，中国考生的普遍问题就是滥用和机械使用连接词。有时候没有举例，也把 for example 放在句首。

方法 2：状语从句。

引导状语从句的 because, since, as, if, when, so 都能够展示句子的逻辑关系。

例如下面这句话，事实上 if 代表一个原因 (有清洁房间的习惯)，而前面是结果 (让一切井井有条)。这样就是一个连词连接了两个单句，让句子有了逻辑性。

For example, they are more likely to keep everything organised if they have the habit of cleaning their bedrooms.

方法 3：一些名词性从句。

this means that, the consequence is that, it follows that, this explains why, due to the fact that 等也有连接关系。

例如文中这句话用了 means that，事实上就是表示结果，因为离开父母居住，所以他们可以学习怎么过独立的生活。

Living away from parents means that young people have to learn how to live an independent life.

方法 4：一些含有 this, these 的词组。

如 by doing this, in this way, in this case, in this circumstance, for this reason 等。

主体部分第一段就用了：With these skills, they can handle many matters easily...

这些表达可以比较简单地联系两个句子。

方法 5：代词 they, this, their 等。

主体部分第一段就用了 they 去指代前面的大学生：They have to develop some life skills...

代词也是避免重复的一种重要手段，我们会在其他学习点具体阐述。

还有，主体部分第三段用了 this choice 去指代大学生分开住。然后还有下面这一句中，their parents，their family 都可以增加句子联系：

They hardly have a meal with their parents and cannot keep up to date with the news about their family.

方法 6：含有 another 的表达。

可以经常用 another problem, another method, another benefit, another advantage 这样的表达去引出一个新的观点。

例如，主题部分第二段可以说：

Another benefit is that college students can enjoy more freedom in social life and make new friends.

方法 7：上下文两个句子间本身的逻辑关系。

主体部分第二段，首先说每天不用回家，因此有时间参加活动，可以去运动等。这些句子本身有表示同一个意思的因果关系。

方法 8：一些关键表达的重复。

段落某些表达的重复，也可以帮助衔接句子，当然，这需要大家有比较强的改写能力，否则就会显得啰唆。

例如主体部分第二段里的如下这些词伙都是表示社会生活、交友、人脉、社会技能，都在讨论关于社会活动和能力的事情，使句子间有呼应：social life, make new friends, with other students, social skills, personal resources。

提升的范文

标色的部分是和原文有差异的地方，下划线部分是词伙。

Many university students today have either chosen university accommodation or shared a flat with their friends. I think it is a rite of passage though these young people may not be able to maintain day-to-day contact with their parents.

Living away from parents means that young people have to learn how to live an independent life. They have to develop some life skills, such as doing housekeeping, managing finances and getting along with flatmates. With these skills, they can handle many matters easily once they enter the workforce. For example, they are more likely to keep everything organised if they have the habit of cleaning their bedrooms.

In addition, college students can enjoy more freedom in social life and make new friends. They do not need to go home every day, so they have more time to do a wide range of activities, including going to the gym with other students, doing group assignments and even do part-time work together. Moreover, partying, club activities and backpacking allows these young people to enlarge the circle of friends, so they have personal resources to draw upon in future careers.

The downside of this choice is that the contact with parents will decline and the emotional tie will suffer. They hardly have a meal with their parents and cannot keep up with the news about their family. As they can tackle problems independently, they do not feel the need to visit their family and take advice from parents. This may also affect their attitude towards family life.

In conclusion, it is a good decision for university students to leave home, although it may have a damaging effect on their family relationship.

3.7.4 全文翻译 15：快餐 + 代词的使用注意事项

> *In many countries traditional food is being replaced by international fast food. This has negative effects on both families and societies. To what extent do you agree or disagree?*

题目大意

在很多国家，传统食物被国际快餐取代。这个趋势对家庭和社会都有负面的影响。在多大程度上你同意还是反对这个看法？

读者自学步骤 1

阅读题目后，写出三个观点。

下面是我学生写的一些错误或者不好的观点，大家可以看看自己是不是也犯了同样的错误。

学生的观点	点评
快餐流行，没有营养，人们容易生病。	跑题。不能只说生病，要说对社会的影响。
传统食物被快餐替代，全球都有一样的食品，在其他地方也能适应。	观点不够有力。为什么要去其他地方适应？为什么要吃一样的食物才可以适应？
传统食物被国际快餐替代，传统食品餐饮店减少，很多人失业。	观点不够有力。国际快餐店也是要请人工作的。
吃快餐不吃传统食物，品尝不同国家的食物，享受更多的生活乐趣。	观点不够有力。国际快餐的种类也就 10 个，怎么会有很多乐趣？

快餐取代传统食物，人们总是选择快餐，家里不做饭。	观点不清晰。不做饭有什么坏处呢？
传统食物被快餐替代，吸收外来食物的优点，创新出更多美味的食物，对家庭和社会来说都是一种进步。	观点牵强。常识好像是相反的，国际快餐目前是本地化，localise，加入当地元素。
吃国际快餐，食物选择变多，餐饮行业发达，人们更容易感到幸福，经济发展。	观点牵强。题目都已经说传统食物被取代了，怎么可能选择还变多？

读者自学步骤 1

翻译下面的句子：在翻译过程中，记住先想词伙，再想句型，然后写出句子。相关词伙可以查阅微信公众号：gu_writing。

介绍段

| 背景句 | 1. 人们现在很喜欢光顾快餐店，因为快的生活节奏和工作时间不稳定。 |
| 阐述立场 | 2. 快餐在很多文化里已经威胁传统的烹饪方式，人们需要重视这一变化可能产生的问题。 |

主体部分第一段

中心句（个人福利）	3. 快餐在某些国家，如美国，已经成为一个健康问题，在那些国家，肥胖人口迅速增加。
解释	4. 这不仅因为快餐含高脂肪、糖分、盐分和卡路里，也因为快餐往往分量很大。
结果	5. 一般来说，患有肥胖症的人比普通体重的人更可能患有心脏病和其他健康疾病。
拓展	6. 这就意味着政府需要花更多钱在医疗系统上，这可能会影响经济发展。

主体部分第二段

中心句（社会文化）	7. 另外一个问题是它也会影响人们的生活方式，包括饮食习惯。
解释	8. 传统食物的特点是食料，烹饪方式和口味的多样性，体现了烹饪文化在不同地区的演变。
对比	9. 目前，绝大部分的快餐连锁都是提供美国或者欧洲的食品，包括汉堡包、炸鸡和比萨饼。
结果	10. 人们的饮食逐渐变得单调，而一些传统菜谱可能消失。

主体部分第三段

中心句 (社会关系)	11. 快餐对家庭关系也有负面的影响，因为人们不想以前那么频繁地参加家庭聚餐。
解释	12. 家庭聚餐一般来说提供家人一个相互交流、相互理解的机会。
结果	13. 人们经常在外面吃饭，可能就不大知道家人的近况，很少能够顾及家人的感情需要。
拓展	14. 家庭越来越分散，而很多人在生活遇到问题的时候感到孤独和无助。

结论段

再次表明立场	15. 因此，我赞同快餐的普及是一个很大的问题。
总结观点	16. 快餐不仅威胁人们的健康，也会破坏饮食文化和社会关系。

读者自学步骤 3

检查自己的翻译：先看正确句子的词伙和句子结构，然后看错误的句子，看是否能够发现问题。

句 1

正：Many people today frequent fast-food restaurants, because of the fast pace of life and irregular working hours.

学生的句子：People prefer to go to fast-food restaurant now, because of fast pace of life and irregular working hours.

改：restaurant 是可数名词，要用复数形式；pace 是可数名词，要用冠词。

句 2

正：Fast food has posed a threat to traditional cuisine in many cultures, and people should put emphasis on the problems that may arise from this change.

学生的句子：Fast food has posed a threat to different cuisines in many cultures, people should put emphasis on the problems that may arise from this change.

改：cuisine 是不可数名词；两个独立的句子间没有连词连接。

句 3

正：The fast food has become a health issue in countries like America, where the number of overweight people has increased dramatically.

学生的句子：The fast food has become a health issue, such as America, where the number of obese people is increasingly dramatic.

改：such as 后面的名词一般是前面名词的一个例子，这里很明显 America 和 a health issue 是两码事；number is dramatic 也是奇怪的表达。

句 4

正：It is not only because fast food is high in fat, sugar, salt and calories but also because fast food is served in large portions.

学生的句子：This is not only because the fast food contains high fat, sugar, salt and calories but also it is always served in large portions.

改：the 去掉，fast food 不需要特指；but also 后缺 because，否则不对称。

句 5

正：In general, people who suffer from obesity are more likely to contract heart diseases than normal-weight people.

学生的句子：Generally speaking, people who suffer from the obesity are more likely to suffer from the heart disease than the normal-weight ones.

改：obesity 和 heart disease 前面不需要加定冠词，因为不需要特指；ones 使用的时候一般强调个体，不恰当。

句 6

正：As a consequence, this means that governments have to pour more money in the medical system, which may have an adverse effect on the economic development.

学生的句子：This means that governments have to invest more money in medical system, which may exerts bad influence on economic development.

改：system 是可数名词，前面要加冠词，development 也是如此；may 是情态动词，后面要加动词原形。

句 7

正：Another problem is that it can affect people's ways of life, including dietary habits.

学生的句子：Another problem associated with fast food is that can affect people's ways of life, including eating habits.

改：that 引导的表语从句没有主语。

句 8

正：Traditional means of food preparation are known for the diversity of ingredients, cooking styles and flavours, and many traditional dishes show the evolution of cuisine in different regions.

学生的句子：Traditional food is characterised by ingredients, cooking styles and diversity of flavour, reflecting the development of cooking culture in different regions.

改：diversity 位置不对；flavour 和 culture 都是可数名词，要用复数形式。

句 9

正：Currently, a vast majority of fast food chains provide American or European food, including hamburgers, fried chicken and pizzas.

学生的句子：Recently, most of fast food chains provide American and European food, including hamburger，fired chicken，and pizza.

改："现在"一般是用 currently 或者 at present；hamburger 和 pizza 是可数名词，在这里应该用复数形式；fired 应为 fried。

句 10

正：People's diet is increasingly monotonous, while some traditional recipes may vanish.

学生的句子：People's diet is increasing monotonous, while some traditional recipes may be vanished.

改：increasing 是现在分词，不能修饰形容词；vanish = disappear，是不及物动词。

句 11

正：Fast food also has an adverse effect on your family relationship, as people do not participate in family meals as frequently as before.

学生的句子：Fast food also has an adverse effect on family relationship, as people do not participate family meals as frequent as before.

改：participate 是不及物动词，后面要加介词；frequent 是形容词，不能修饰动词，此处是 participate。

句 12

正：As a general rule, family meals provide family members with an opportunity to communicate with each other and improve mutual understanding.

学生的句子：Generally speaking, family meals provide family members with a chance to communicate and understand each other.

改：generally speaking 比较少用于书面语，最好用 in general 或者 as a general rule 替代；communicate with 是习惯表达。

句 13

正：People who always eat outside may not be able to keep up to date with family issues and respond to emotional needs of other family members.

学生的句子：People often eat outside, they may not know the recent situation of family members, and they may rarely respond to the needs of family members.

改：前面的句子间没有连词；第二个 they 指代不清楚。

句 14

正：Families have become more and more dispersed, and many of us feel lonely and helpless when they have problems in daily lives.

学生的句子：The family become more and more dispersed, many people feel lonely and helpless when they have problems in daily life.

改：第一个句子主谓不一致；两个句子间也没有连词。

句 15

正：I thus agree that the popularity of fast food is a menace.

学生的句子：Therefore, I agree with that eating fast food has become a common problem.

改：with 多余。

句 16

正：They not only pose a threat to people's health but also to our cuisine culture and social relationships.

学生的句子：Fast food not only pose a danger to people's health but also break cuisine culture and social relationship.

改：food pose 主谓不一致。

读者自学步骤 4

整体学习和检查范文，看看是否符合 TELCCS 原则。

范文全文（7～7.5 分）

Many people today frequent fast-food restaurants, because of the fast pace of life and irregular working hours. Fast food has posed a threat to traditional cuisine in many cultures, and people should put emphasis on the problems that may arise from this change.

> 用词不是很好，不应该强调问题，影响 LR 的分数。

The fast food has become a health issue in countries like America, where the number of overweight people has increased dramatically. It is not only because fast food is high in fat, sugar, salt and calories but also because fast food is served in large portions. In general, people who suffer from obesity are more likely to contract heart diseases than normal-weight people. As a consequence, this means that governments have to pour more money in the medical system, which may have an adverse effect on the economic development.

> 这里又来了一个 fast food。
>
> 一句话中出现了两个 fast food，太过重复。
> 这里出现了跳跃，没有解释为什么人变得肥胖。
>
> 一句话中出现了两个 people。
>
> 连接词和代词重复。

Another problem is that it can affect people's ways of life, including dietary habits. Traditional means of food preparation are known for the diversity of ingredients, cooking styles and flavours, and many traditional dishes show the evolution of cuisine in different regions. Currently, a vast majority of fast food chains provide

> 这样的中心句和上面一段话很类似，会影响 CC 的分数。
>
> 连接词不好，可能用 however 比较好。

American or European food, including hamburgers, fried chicken and pizzas. People's diet is increasingly monotonous, while some traditional recipes may vanish.

这里可以用一些替换词，如 pre-prepared food or processed food。

Fast food also has an adverse effect on your family relationship, as people do not participate in family meals as frequently as before. As a general rule, family meals provide family members with an opportunity to communicate with each other and improve mutual understanding. People who always eat outside may not be able to keep up to date with family issues and respond to emotional needs of other family members. Families have become more and more dispersed, and many of us feel lonely and helpless when they have problems in daily lives.

最好不要用第二人称。

这里出现了跳跃，不知道为什么突然会说到家庭 dispersed。

us 和后面的 they 不搭配。

I thus agree that the popularity of fast food is a menace. They not only pose a threat to people's health but also to our cuisine culture and social relationships.

前面 fast food 是不可数名词，这里不要用 they。

our 和前面的 people 不匹配。

本节关键学习点

代词在书面语和口语中有很重要的使用，也是很多考生忽视的地方。代词可以增加句子之间的联系，避免一些关键词的重复。代词本身很简单，但是使用准确不容易。

代词使用的常见错误如下。

> 错误 1：连接词和代词重合使用。
>
> 错误 2：使用 you。
>
> 错误 3：在同一句话中重复使用可数名词复数，如 people，students，不会使用代词 they；或者重复使用不可数名词，但是不会使用代词 it。
>
> 错误 4：代词不一致，people 不能和 we，our 连用，单数名词不能和 they 一起用。
>
> 错误 5：前面有两个表示人的名词复数出现，还使用 they，导致指代不清。
>
> 错误 6：前面是不可数名词，但是后面用 they，them，us 这些表示复数的代词。
>
> 错误 7：these，those 不能和不可数名词连用。
>
> 错误 8：this，another 后面只能加可数名词单数，而不是加不可数名词或者可数名词复数。

我们下面用这篇文章的一些错误来讲解这些问题。

错误 1：连接词和代词重合使用。

错误的句子：as a consequence, this means that...

这里的 as a consequence 是多余的，因为后面的 this 已经和前面一个句子有联系。

错误2：使用 you。

一般书面语不要用第二人称，因为第二人称比较口语化。

错误3：在同一句话中重复使用可数名词复数，如 people, students，不会使用代词 they；或者重复使用不可数名词，但是不会使用代词 it。

例如主体部分第一段可以改成：The fast food has become a health issue…this kind of food is high in fat.

错误4：代词不一致，people 不能和 we, our 连用，单数名词不能和 they 一起用。

一般来说，people 用 their, they；we 用 our；单数名词用 it, this。

错误5：前面有两个表示人的名词复数出现，还使用 they，导致指代不清。

例如：Many people hardly talk to other members of family, so they are lonely.

这里的 they 指代不清楚到底是 people，还是 members of family。

可以改成：Many people today feel lonely because they hardly talk to other members of family.

错误6：前面是不可数名词，但是后面用 they, them, us 这些表示复数的代词。

结尾段最后一句话 they 不能指代 fast food。

错误7：these, those 不能和不可数名词连用。

你不能说 these knowledge, these equipment, these work 等，因为这些词都是不可数名词。

错误8：this, another 后面只能加可数名词单数，而不是加不可数名词或者可数名词复数。

例如开头段用了 this change，第三段用了 another problem，都是对的，因为 change 和 problem 是可数名词单数。

提升的范文

标色的部分是和原文有差异的地方，下划线部分是词伙。

Many people today frequent fast-food restaurants, because of the fast pace of life and irregular working hours. Fast food has posed a threat to traditional cuisine in many cultures, and people should not overlook the problems that may arise from this change.

The strong appetite for fast food has become a health issue in countries like America, where the number of overweight people has increased dramatically. This kind of food is not only high in fat, sugar, salt and calories but also served in large portions. This is why it is known as junk food and linked to obesity epidemic. Those who suffer from obesity are more likely to contract heart diseases than normal-weight people. This means that governments have to pour more money in the medical system, which may have an adverse effect on the economic development.

Another problem is that it can threaten the diversity of the world's cuisine. Traditional means of food preparation are known for the diversity of ingredients, cooking styles and flavours, and many traditional dishes show the evolution of cuisine in different regions. If <u>fast food chains</u> which provide American or European food, including hamburgers, <u>fried chicken</u> and pizzas, dominate the market, people will find that their diet will become increasingly monotonous and that some traditional recipes may vanish.

The reliance on <u>pre-prepared food</u> also has an adverse effect on <u>family relationships</u>, as people do not eat family meals as frequently as before. As a general rule, <u>family meals</u> provide family members with an opportunity to communicate with each other and <u>improve mutual understanding</u>. People who always eat outside may not be able to <u>keep up to date with</u> family issues and respond to <u>emotional needs</u> of other family members. They no longer have a sense of closeness at home, and enjoy the company of their family.

I thus agree that the popularity of fast food is a menace. It not only poses a threat to people's health but also to their cuisine culture and social relationships.

3.8 雅思评分标准 3：Lexical Resources（词汇丰富程度）

雅思大作文词汇方面主要考查三个方面。

用词的准确性：

每个单词的使用要恰当和准确，不能为了追求变化而使用不合适的词。

用词的搭配：

也就是所谓的词伙（collocations），单词之间的常见搭配要非常重视。

主题相关的词：

雅思考查的是每个话题下你所具备的相关词汇，也就是 topic-specific vocabulary。很多考生经常背一些比较普遍的替换词，如 pros and cons 替换 advantages and disadvantages，supposed to do something 替换 should do something，initially 替换 firstly，都是没有意义的，因为这些替换不是和话题相关的。

总而言之，雅思作文对词汇的考查不是机械的，而是对词汇准确性、恰当性和灵活性的一个考量。大家要永远记住，雅思考官是英文母语者，所以很容易觉察用词的不恰当，千万不要机械地使用大词、难词、替换词。

3.8.1 全文翻译 16：教育对成功的意义＋词伙

> *Some people who have been successful in the society don't attribute their success to the theoretical knowledge they learned from their university. Do you agree that theoretical knowledge is not as valuable as expected?*

题目大意

一些社会上的成功人士并不将他们的成就归功于他们在大学里学到的理论知识。你是否同意理论知识不像预想的那么有用？

读者自学步骤 1

阅读题目后，写出三个观点。

下面是我学生写的一些错误或者不好的观点，大家可以看看自己是不是也犯了同样的错误。

学生的观点	点评
只有理论，从不实践，是纸上谈兵，没有实践经验，也很难成功。	过分空泛。要具体说明什么是纸上谈兵，为什么就很难成功。
学习理论，被动接受教育，缺乏创新思维能力。	不够有力。为什么学习理论就是被动教育，大学不是你自己选择去读的吗？为什么就缺乏创新能力？
学习理论知识，让学生对课本知识产生固化思维，扼杀学生的创造力。	不够有力。为什么会产生固化思维，而且题目问的是成功，而不是创造力。
学习理论知识，教书育人，为社会发展做贡献。	例子当观点。教书只是一个职业，不是所有人都教书。
大学学习，专业不对口或对所学专业没有丝毫兴趣，浪费精力与时间，对自己也是种折磨。	跑题。这个题目是在讨论学习理论，不是在讨论选择专业。
成功人士不能把他们的成功归因于他们在大学中所学的知识，大学学习成绩对以后影响不大。	空泛。只有立场，没有解释。

读者自学步骤 2

翻译下面的句子：在翻译过程中，记住先想词伙，再想句型，然后写出句子。相关词伙可以查阅微信公众号：gu_writing。

介绍段

背景句	1. 关于理论知识对职业成功的贡献，人们一直都有不同的看法。
改写题目	2. 这是可以理解的，因为很多在事业上获得成功的人士并没有完成大学教育。
阐述立场	3. 我认为大学学的东西对成功是至关重要的。

主体部分第一段

中心句 （学习能力）	4. 通过学习理论，人们知道某个科目的概念和原则，因此可以成为某个行业的专业人士。

举例	5. 例如，一个心理医生不可能确定有效的治疗，除非他（她）了解各种解释人们心理疾病的理论。
解释	6. 很多理论都是基于实践经验发展起来的，因此有现实的意义，而掌握这些理论的人可以有很好的工作前景，甚至因为革新而获得很多财富。

主体部分第二段

中心句	7. 学习理论还有一个好处，就是提高人们解决问题的能力，还有创新能力。
解释 1	8. 大学生可以提高研究能力，收集信息去了解不同的课题。
解释 2	9. 理论可以开拓人的思维，提高人的思辨能力，让人们可以使用不同理论去推动知识的进步。
对比	10. 相比之下，没有上过大学的人可以参加一些实践训练去处理一些普遍问题，但是在面对一些非常规问题的时候就束手无策。

主体部分第三段

中心句	11. 我们也需要承认一个事实 (recognise the fact that)：理论知识不是人们成功的唯一因素。
解释	12. 有趣的是 (it is interesting to note that) 很多成功人士被发现有类似的性格特点。
举例 1	13. 一个乐观、勤奋、积极、善于与人交往的人更加能够克服困难，和别人合作，从而能够获得成功。
附加观点	14. 另外一个因素可能是社会关系网，通过这个网络，人们可以获得信息、想法和资源。
举例 2	15. 例如，一些商业人士可以告诉他们怎么和政府保持良好的关系，而教科书上未必有这样的知识。

结论段

再次表明立场	16. 大学教育的价值没有被人们正确地认识，而人们可以更加有效地甚至有创意地解决问题。
总结观点	17. 我们同时需要承认，除了教育之外，人的性格和社会关系也是成功的因素。

读者自学步骤 3

检查自己的翻译：先看正确句子的词伙和句子结构，然后看错误的句子，看是否能够发现问题。

句 1

正：People have different views about the contribution of theoretical knowledge to one's achievement.

学生的句子：People have different views about the contribution of theoretical knowledge on success.

改：contribution 后面的介词要用 to。

句 2

正：This is understandable due to the fact that a considerable number of people who did not complete a university education have achieved success in their careers.

学生的句子：This can be understood as a variety of successful people who do not complete a university education.

改：a variety of 不能用来修饰人，只能修饰物；as 引导原因状语的时候，词性是连词，后面应该是完整的从句。

句 3

正：In my view, what students have learnt at university is vitally important to a fulfilling career.

学生的句子：I believe that the knowledge of university plays an significant role in success.

改：university 是可数名词，要用复数形式；significant 前面不应该加 an。

句 4

正：By learning theories, people can gain a full understanding of concepts and principles of different subjects, so they can build expertise in their professions.

学生的句子：People can have a well-rounded understanding with the concept and principle of one subject by learning theoretical knowledge, then they can become the leaders in some industry.

改：a well-rounded understanding 和 learn knowledge 都不是习惯表达；then 是副词，不能连接句子。

句 5

正：For example, a psychiatrist cannot identify effective therapies, unless he or she is well-informed about all theories about different mental health problems.

学生的句子：For example, a psychiatrist cannot identify effective therapy, unless he/she understanding all kinds of theories explaining mental health problems.

改：therapy 是可数名词，要么用复数形式，要么加冠词；unless 是连词，后面应该有独立的句子，而 understanding 和 explaining 都是现在分词。

句 6

正：Many theories have developed on the basis of empirical knowledge, so these theories have practical implications and people who are familiar with theories can have a good prospect and even earn a fortune with some innovations they have advanced.

学生的句子：Lots of theories develop on the basis of empirical knowledge, so they have practical meanings and people mastering these theories can get better career blueprint and earn a fortune due to innovations.

改：develop 一般不用一般现在时；practical meanings, master theories 和 career blueprint 都是中

国式英文。

句 7

正：Another advantage of learning theories is that students can improve problem-solving abilities and exercise creative potential.

学生的句子：There is another benefit of learning theories is to improve their practical skills and creativity.

改：这个句子里有两个动词。

句 8

正：University students can improve research skills and collect information on different subject matters.

学生的句子：Students studying at universities can increase in the ability of research and also collect information or materials to understand different projects.

改：ability of 是错误表达；projects 一般是指公司的项目，大学的课题一般不用这个词。

句 9

正：Theoretical knowledge could broaden people's minds and improve critical thinking skills, empowering them to push forward the boundaries of knowledge.

学生的句子：Theoretical knowledge could broaden people's minds and improve critical thinking skill, which also enables people to promote the growth of knowledge in different theories.

改：skill 是可数名词，没有用复数形式或者加冠词；定语从句不知是修饰前面一整句话，还是 skill；growth of knowledge 这个表达不是很好。

句 10

正：In contrast, some people who did not go to university can receive some practical training to deal with some general problems, but they may be helpless in the face of unusual problems.

学生的句子：In contrast, some people who are not go to universities can attend some practical exercises to deal with some regular problems, but they may have no idea when it comes to irregular difficulties.

改："are + 动词原形" 语法不对；practical exercises 和 irregular difficulties 都是错误的表达。

句 11

正：Meanwhile, we must recognise the fact that theoretical knowledge is not the only determinant of success.

学生的句子：We must recognize the fact that theoretical knowledge is not the unique determinant of success.

改：unique (独一无二) 不合适；recognize 是美式拼写。

句 12

正：It is interesting to note that many successful people have some personality traits in common.

学生的句子：It is interesting to note that many successful people are found that they have one shared personality trait.

改：be found to do something 是习惯用法。

句 13

正：An optimistic, hardworking and sociable person is able to overcome difficulties and cooperate with others to achieve success.

学生的句子：A person with positive, hardworking, friendly personality is able to overcome difficulty and cooperate with others to achieve success.

改：一个以上的修饰词要用 and 连接；difficulty 是可数名词。

句 14

正：Another factor might be the social network, by which people can receive information, draw upon ideas and gain access to resources.

学生的句子：Another factor might be the social network, by which people to receive information, draw upon ideas and gain access to resources.

改：which 前面应该有 by，而 to 应该去掉，从句事实上是 "people receive information, draw upon ideas and gain access to resources by the social network"。

句 15

正：For instance, some businesspeople can tell them how to maintain a good relationship with the government, and this kind of knowledge may not be available in textbooks.

学生的句子：For instance, some businessman can tell students how to maintain good relationship with governments, which may not be seen on textbooks.

改：businessman 和 relationship 都是可数名词，要注意冠词和复数的使用；非限制定语从句的先行词不清楚。

句 16

正：Higher education has been undervalued, and people can handle many problems effectively and creatively with knowledge they have acquired at university.

学生的句子：The value of university education has not been fully understanded，people could deal with problems more effectively and even more creatively by it.

改：understand 的过去分词是 understood；两个句子间没有连词；it 指代不清楚。

句 17

正：On the other hand, we need to admit that personality and social relationships are also essential to success.

学生的句子：At the same time, we need to admit that personality and social relationships are also essential to success.

改：on the other hand 和 at the same time 一般都用于引出相反的看法，只是前者在书面语上更加常见和普遍。

读者自学步骤 4

整体学习和检查范文，看看是否符合 TELCCS 原则。

范文全文 (7 分)

People have different views about the contribution of theoretical knowledge to one's achievement. This is understandable due to the fact that a considerable number of people who did not complete a university education have achieved success in their careers. In my view, what students have learnt at university is vitally important to a fulfilling career.

> 这个表达还是有点模板化，可以去掉，避免对 TR 分数产生影响。

By learning theories, people can gain a full understanding of concepts and principles of different subjects, so they can build expertise in their professions. For example, a psychiatrist cannot identify effective therapies, unless he or she is well-informed about all theories about different mental health problems. Many theories have developed on the basis of empirical knowledge, so these theories have practical implications and people who are familiar with theories can have a good prospect and even earn a fortune with some innovations they have advanced.

> 这里可以用一下关键词，说明是大学里学的。在大学外面也可以学习 theories。

> 在这里需要说一下原因，about the causes of。
>
> 最好先写解释，再举例，而不是反过来；否则 CC 会受到影响。

> job prospects 一般用复数。

> 这里突然说到了 innovations，有点突兀，影响 CC。

Another advantage of learning theories is that students can improve problem-solving abilities and exercise creative potential. University students can improve research skills and collect information on different subject matters. Theoretical knowledge could broaden people's minds and improve critical thinking skills, empowering them to push forward the boundaries of knowledge. In contrast, some people who did not go to university can receive some practical training to deal with some general problems, but they may be helpless in the face of unusual problems.

> 题目并不是关于学习理论，而是关于上大学，在这里最好还是要扣题，避免 TR 丢分。

> 这里突然出现 people，和前面的 students 冲突。

> 这里出现的几个概念，improve research skills, collect information on subject matters, broaden minds, critical thinking skills 和中心句的 problem solving, creative potential 都没有建立很强的联系，影响 CC 的分数。

> 不是"能够"，因为每个人都能够接受培训，may 可能更好。

Meanwhile, we must recognise the fact that theoretical knowledge is not the only determinant of success. It is interesting to note that many successful

> 这个套句比较多余。

people have some personality traits in common. An optimistic, hardworking and sociable person is able to overcome difficulties and cooperate with others to achieve success. Another factor might be the social network, by which people can receive information, draw upon ideas and gain access to resources. For instance, some businesspeople can tell them how to maintain a good relationship with the government, and this kind of knowledge may not be available in textbooks.

可以换个表达，如 achieve ambitions。

这句话没有说清楚从谁那里获得信息和建议，和 social network 联系不上。

这里突然出现一个 businesspeople，有点突兀，不清楚是不是人脉的一部分，影响 CC 的分数。

Higher education has been undervalued, and people can handle many problems effectively and creatively with knowledge they have acquired at university. On the other hand, we need to admit that personality and social relationships are also essential to success.

这里可以出现一些提示词，指出这是你的个人看法。

本节关键学习点

词伙（collocations）对于准备雅思写作的考生是很重要的，尤其是希望获得 7 分的考生，因为剑桥雅思的官方标准明确说明，考生需要展示词伙的能力。

很多雅思考生在写作中都很随心所欲，用词不够地道。常见的问题有两个：

> 问题 *1*：中翻译英。
>
> 问题 *2*：使用长单词，不重视词伙。

问题 *1*：中翻译英。

很多考生是将中文逐字翻译英文，而忽略了组合的地道性。

例如说学习知识，很多考生觉得学习是 learn，知识是 knowledge，两个单词一合并，就是 learn knowledge。

但是这个表达在英文里并不地道，常见的表达是 gain/increase/acquire knowledge。

另外一个例子是接受教育，很多考生认为接受是 accept，教育是 education，那么接受教育就是 accept education。但是这个表达也是不恰当的，常见的说法是 receive education。

问题 *2*：使用长单词，不重视词伙。

不少考生不重视单词的组合，觉得有些单词太简单，自以为是地改变这些组合，用一些自己觉得很复杂、很上档次的单词，最后反而分数很低。例如 a well-rounded understanding。

这个考生觉得 well-rounded 很新颖，很有趣，很长，比 a deep understanding，a full understanding，a good understanding 要高大上。事实上，在雅思中，后面三个表达的分数更高，因为更加地道，符合外国人的语言习惯。

词伙有很多意思。我将这篇文章出现的一些词伙分了类，大家可以看看，平时在阅读和学习中可以自己整理。然后，我自己也会在另外一本专门的词伙书《顾家北教你雅思词伙》中更加深入地介绍词伙怎么应用在写作和口语中。

形容词 + 名词	theoretical knowledge fulfilling career social networks
动词 + 名词	achieve success complete a degree gain a full understanding of build expertise
动词 + 形容词 + 名词	receive practical training exercise creative potential
名词 + 名词	health problems job prospect university students
名词 + 介词	expertise in understanding of well-informed about access to essential to

也有一些考生会说，词伙不就是我们常说的"搭配"吗？我自己觉得词伙包括"搭配"，但是很多时候比"搭配"要复杂。

例如 deal with problems（解决问题）是一个常用词伙，但是如果你只是这么学习还不够，因为在雅思里经常会出现 deal with problems creatively，有创意地解决问题。

词伙在这个意义上就是一些可以表达我们常用观点的单词组合，这个组合可能不只2～3个单词，也可能是很多单词。

本书所有的大作文范文的词伙都用下划线画了出来，方便大家复习。

提升的范文

标色的部分是和原文有差异的地方，下划线部分是词伙。

It is understandable that some young people today drop out of college, because there are successful entrepreneurs or business leaders who did not <u>complete a university degree</u>. In my view, what students have learnt at university is vitally important to a fulfilling career.

By learning theories at university, people can gain a full understanding of concepts and principles of different subjects, so they can build expertise in their professions. Many theories have developed on the basis of empirical knowledge, so these theories have practical implications and people who are familiar with theories can deal with practical problems at work. For example, a psychiatrist cannot identify effective therapies, unless he or she attends some university courses to gain an insight into all theories about the causes of different mental health problems.

Academic study can also improve the problem-solving abilities of learners and empower them to exercise creative potential. University students need to collect information on different subject matters to finish essays and reports, so they gain experience in analysing different unfamiliar matters and tackling these problems effectively. When they embark on their careers, they will show confidence in doing research when problems surface, and come up with corresponding solutions. In contrast, those people who did not go to university may receive some practical training to deal with some general tasks, but they may be helpless in the face of unusual problems.

Meanwhile, we must recognise the fact that theoretical knowledge is not the only determinant of success. Many successful people have some personality traits in common. An optimistic, hardworking and sociable person is able to overcome difficulties and cooperate with others to achieve success. Another factor might be the social network, by which people can draw upon ideas of experts, investors and business managers, such as those managers who understand how to maintain a good relationship with clients, suppliers and government officials. This kind of knowledge may not be available in textbooks.

In a word, higher education has been undervalued, and people can handle many problems effectively and creatively with knowledge they have acquired at university. On the other hand, we need to admit that personality and social relationships are also essential to success.

3.8.2 全文翻译 17：政府免学费＋如何换表达

> *Instead of asking the government to bear the cost of higher education, students should pay tuition fees themselves. Do you agree or disagree with this statement?*

题目大意

学生需要自己交学费，而不是让政府去承担大学教育的费用。你是同意还是反对这个观点？

读者自学步骤 1

阅读题目后，写出三个观点。

下面是我学生写的一些错误或者不好的观点，大家可以看看自己是不是也犯了同样的错误。

学生的观点	点评
政府付学费，家庭有钱可以改善生活，有利于学习。	逻辑不对。改善生活和有利于学习没有什么逻辑关系，除非你说大学生不用去打工。
自付，懂父母辛苦，家庭和睦。	观点牵强。如果真知道父母辛苦，可能会选择不上大学。
自付，压力大，不快乐。	比较牵强。每个人都有各种压力，不能说有压力，就要政府花钱。
学生自己交学费，减小学校开支，可以有更好的设备。	逻辑不对。交学费会让学校资金增加，而不是减少开支。
自己交学费，减轻教育的财政压力，财政支出更合理。	过分空泛。什么是支出合理、支出合理体现在哪里？
自费学习，培养社会技能，更好地融入社会。	逻辑跳跃。需要解释清楚为什么自费可以提升社会技能。不都说大学生不接地气吗？
学生出钱，学生自己承担学费，懂得承担责任。	观点不唯一。培养责任感的方法很多，未必要用出钱的方式。
政府应该承担费用，纳税人福利之一，保证税收政策正常推行。	观点不够有力。为什么是纳税人的福利？为什么推行税收政策很重要？
政府根据学生个人情况考虑是否资助，情况不同获得的资助力度不同，缓解财政支出。	改变题目。这个题目要么讨论政府给钱，要么说学生给钱，最好不要以"政府有些人给有些人不给"作为一个独立的观点。

读者自学步骤 2

翻译下面的句子：在翻译过程中，记住先想词伙，再想句型，然后写出句子。 相关词伙可以查阅微信公众号：gu_writing。

介绍段

背景句	1. 接受大学教育对很多人是重要的，因为他们找工作更加容易。
改写题目	2. 那些支持政府增加大学教育投资的人认为有一些学生因为学费高昂而不能上大学。
阐述立场	3. 我的个人看法是学生应该承担学费，而条件不好的同学可以获得金钱上的帮助。

主体部分第一段

中心句 （社会发展）	4. 学生如果交学费，他们会更加努力学习，认真对待这个学习机会。
解释	5. 他们知道读大学的成本很高，尽量完成所有的作业，通过考试，准时获得学位。
对比	6. 如果政府承担费用，很多学生会无所谓，经常挂科。

主体部分第二段

附加观点 （社会发展）	7. 交学费的另外一个好处就是减少政府的负担。
结果 1	8. 政府可以多花点钱去资助中学和小学教育，减少文盲率，让更多的年轻人有能力上大学。
结果 2	9. 政府也可以给读研究生课程的学生提供补助，促进科技的发展。

主体部分第三段

中心句 （个人局限）	10. 另外一方面，低收入家庭的学生可以免除学费。
结果	11. 这样可以鼓励这些年轻人读大学，提高知识和技能，最后找到好的工作。
结果的延伸	12. 这样可以减少贫富差距，建立一个公平的社会。
对比	13. 如果他们需要交学费，他们可能会放弃学业，这样很难挖掘自己的潜能。

结论段

再次表明立场	14. 综上所述，政府应该根据学生的需要提供资助，以确保他们有接受教育的机会。
总结观点	15. 贫困的学生应该免除学费，而废除学费不实际。

读者自学步骤 3

检查自己的翻译：先看正确句子的词伙和句子结构，然后看错误的句子，看是否能够发现问题。

句 1

正：Receiving a university education is important to many young people, because they can find employment easily in the future.

学生的句子：Receiving university education is important to many people, because they can find employment easier.

改：a university education 是习惯搭配；easier 是形容词，不修饰动词。

句 2

正：Those people who support government spending on education think that some students do not enrol because of learning costs.

学生的句子：These people who support the government increases college education investment think that the high tuition fee is the reason why some students cannot go to university.

改：support 是动词，后面只能加名词作宾语，而不可能加句子 the government increases...。

句 3

正：My personal view is that students should pay tuition, while the disadvantaged can receive financial assistance from the government.

学生的句子：In my view, students themselves should afford the tuition fee, but those from less well-off backgrounds can get financial support.

改：afford 不是 "支付" 的意思，而是 "负担得起" 的意思。

句 4

正：If higher education is not free of charge, students will study hard and take this educational opportunity seriously.

学生的句子：If students pay tuition fee, they are more likely to study hard and take this learning opportunity seriously.

改：fee 是可数名词，要有冠词，或者变为复数形式。

句 5

正：They understand the financial cost of completing a degree, so they make a conscious effort to finish all assignments and pass all exams in order to gain the qualification on time.

学生的句子：They know the cost of university is high, so they try them best to finish all homework, pass exams, and obtain degree on time.

改：try them best 应该是 try their best。

句 6

正：In contrast, in cases where young people have free access to education, they will possibly take it for granted and fail exams from time to time.

学生的句子：If governments undertake the cost, many students won't take it seriously and even fail to pass exams from time to time.

改：won't 是缩写形式，书面语中不要使用。

句 7

正：Another benefit of charging tuition fees is that it can lighten the burden on the government.

193

学生的句子：Another advantage is that it can ease the pressure of nations.

改：不大清楚 it 指代什么；pressure 后面的介词一般是 on。

句 8

正：More money can be used in primary and secondary education, which can reduce illiteracy and prepare the next generation for university-level courses.

学生的句子：The government can pour more money in primary and secondary education and reduce the rate of illiteracy, and this enables more young people to attend university.

改：reduce the rate of illiteracy 不应该和 pour money 并列。

句 9

正：Subsidies can be provided for those students who enrol in post-graduate courses to promote technological innovation.

学生的句子：Additionally, postgraduate students who have the potential on advancing technology should also be aided financially by the government.

改：potential to do 是习惯表达。

句 10

正：On the other hand, young people from less well-off backgrounds can be exempted from tuition.

学生的句子：On the other hand, students from low income family can be exempted from tuition fees.

改：family 是可数名词，要用复数形式，或者加冠词。

句 11

正：This can encourage these young people to attend college to acquire knowledge and skills, which can improve their career prospects.

学生的句子：This can help encourage these young people to enter university, improving knowledge and skills, finding good employment eventually.

改：improve knowledge 表达不好；finding 前面缺少连词。

句 12

正：This can close the gap between haves and have-nots and help build a fair society.

学生的句子：It will build a peaceful society to narrow the gap between the rich and the people living in poverty.

改：between rich and poor 是习惯表达。

句 13

正：Conversely, tuition fees may force them to drop out of college and make it difficult for them to reach their potential.

学生的句子：If disadvantaged students are asked to pay the costly fees, they are likely to drop out of school, which make it difficult to exploit their potential.

改：定语从句指代不清楚；如果修饰一句话，谓语动词应该用单数。

句 14

正：To summarise, the government should provide financial support according to students' needs to ensure that they have access to education.

学生的句子：To conclude, government should give support to students based on their own financial situations, so that everyone has a chance to receive education.

改：government 是可数名词，前面要加定冠词；own 这个形容词多余。

句 15

正：Students from deprived backgrounds should be exempt from tuition fees, while the abolition of tuition for all students is not realistic.

学生的句子：The students who live in poverty should attend school for free, it is unpractical to abolish education tuitions for all students.

改：attend school 不合适，因为这是大学；tuition 是不可数名词；两个句子间没有连词。

读者自学步骤 4

整体学习和检查范文，看看是否符合 TELCCS 原则。

范文全文（大概 7.5 分）

Receiving a university education is important to many young people, because they can find employment easily in the future. Those people who support government spending on education think that some students do not enrol because of learning costs. My personal view is that students should pay tuition, while the disadvantaged can receive financial assistance from the government.

If higher education is not free of charge, students will study hard and take this educational opportunity seriously. They understand the financial cost of completing a degree, so they make a conscious effort to finish all assignments and pass all exams in order to gain the qualification on time. In contrast, in cases where young people have free access to education, they will possibly take it for granted and fail exams from time to time.

这里突然说 young people，和前面句子连接不好。

Another benefit of charging tuition fees is that it can lighten the burden on the government. More money can be used in primary and secondary education, which can reduce illiteracy and prepare the next generation for university-level courses. Subsidies can be provided for those students who enrol in post-graduate courses to promote technological innovation.

这里应该加个连接词，否则CC有影响。

这里产生歧义，不大清楚逻辑主语是 subsidies 还是 students。

On the other hand, young people from less well-off backgrounds can be exempted from tuition. This can encourage these young people to attend college to acquire knowledge and skills, which can improve their career prospects. This can close the gap between haves and have-nots and help build a fair society. Conversely, tuition fees may force them to drop out of college and make it difficult for them to reach their potential.

这个句子的主语和下面句子的主语都是一样的，读起来不通顺，影响 CC 的分数。

To summarise, the government should provide financial support according to students' needs to ensure that they have access to education. Students from deprived backgrounds should be exempt from tuition fees, while the abolition of tuition for all students is not realistic.

结尾和主体段的立场不一致，影响 CC 的分数。

有点指代不清，到底是 government 还是 students？

本节关键学习点

很多考生在写雅思作文的时候，特别喜欢换词。使用同义词替换是一种比较简单，同时也很粗暴的方法。

例如，说到 children，大部分中国考生会马上会想到 kids（这不是书面表达），下面就会想到 pupils（也不恰当，因为 children 未必是小学生，也可以是中学生）。接下来就会想到 adolescents（也不是特别好，这个词经常是表示有行为问题的年轻人）。

很多考生一方面知道自己的替换比较别扭，一方面又担心重复使用某个单词会导致词汇丢分。怎么办呢？

我们可以简单用下面一些办法解决。

情况 1：如果要替换的是一个名词，如 students，有下面的一些办法。

使用替换词或者词组。	Many young people have chosen to go to college after leaving school.

名词加形容词或者名词作修饰语。	Some eligible students（合格的学生）have chosen to work, instead of going to college. Some university students may not be able to complete a degree.
使用代词。	Many students fail to find work after they graduate. Many students fail to find work. These students may choose to set up a business.
使用定语从句。	Students who have work experience can find work easily.

情况2：如果要替换的是一个动宾短语，如 go to university，有下面的一些办法。

替换名词或者动词。	Many young people have chosen to go to college after leaving school.
替换表达。	Many young people have chosen to pursue a degree at university after leaving school. Many young people have chosen to continue their studies after leaving school.
使用代词。	Many young people have chosen to go to college after leaving school. This decision can be expensive.
使用其他形式，如动名词、从句等。	Those who have decided to go to university may have to rely on their parents to pay tuition. Going to university can be unaffordable for many young people.

也有很多考生在写段落中心句的时候，因为要使用关键词扣题，不知道怎么去避免重复。

首先，关键词如果找不到直接替换词，如 tuition，education 这样的词，可以不替换。

其次，可以通过 another 这个表达来避免关键词重复。

例如：Another benefit of providing free education is that the workforce can be more productive.

最后，还是通过替换表达的方式去处理。

例如免费教育，可以替换为 free education, free access to education, exempt from tuition fees, funded by the government 等。

提升的范文

标色的部分是和原文有差异的地方，下划线部分是词伙。

Receiving a university education is important to many young people, because they can find employment easily in the future. Those people who support government spending on education think that some students do not enrol because of learning costs. My personal view is that students should pay tuition, while the disadvantaged can receive financial assistance from the government.

If higher education is not free of charge, students will study hard and take this educational opportunity seriously. They understand the financial cost of completing a degree, so they make a conscious effort to finish all assignments and pass all exams in order to gain the qualification on time. In contrast, in cases where they have free access to education, they will possibly take it for granted and fail their exams from time to time.

Another benefit of charging tuition fees is that it can lighten the burden on the government. More money can be used in primary and secondary education, which can reduce illiteracy and prepare the next generation for university-level courses. Additionally, subsidies can be provided for those students who enrol in post-graduate courses, and the investment in these talented young people can promote technological innovation.

On the other hand, young people from less well-off backgrounds can be exempted from tuition. They will have an incentive to attend college to acquire knowledge and skills, which can improve their career prospects. This can close the gap between haves and have-nots and help build a fair society. Conversely, tuition fees may force them to drop out of college and make it difficult for them to reach their potential.

To summarise, Students from deprived back grounds should be exempt from tuition fees, while the abolition of tuition for all students is not realistic.

3.9 雅思评分标准 4：Grammatical Range and Accuracy（语法多样性及准确性）

虽然雅思大作文的四个评分标准原则上各自的比重一样，都是 25%，但是，我在课堂上最为强调的评分标准是语法。道理很简单，语法不好不仅影响第四个评分标准的分数，也会影响其他标准的分数。

例如，如果学生搞不懂词性，写出 Wild animals have extinct. 这样的句子就错了，因为 extinct 是形容词，要说 become extinct。那么就会影响第三个评分标准，即关于词汇的分数。

如果学生的句子结构不对，会影响第二个评分标准 Coherence and Cohesion 的分数。例如：Many students have chosen to go abroad to complete a degree. Because they can find a job easily after graduation.

这里的第二句话只有一个状语从句，没有主句，不仅会导致语法的失分，也会影响句子的联系，不清楚这个从句属于段落的哪一部分。

这就是为什么我在课堂上永远和学生说，如果你希望雅思作文尽快考到 6 分，那么你大概 80% 的时间要花在语法上；如果你想考到 7 分的话，句子要基本上做到没有语法错误。

还有一个中国考生常见的问题是喜欢用一些他们觉得很高大上的语法，如虚拟语气、倒装句、强调句、分词结构等，但他们却经常不能正确使用这些句子结构，最后反而导致分数很低。这就是雅思考试的特点。如果考生在变化的时候不够准确，就会丢分。

我总结了一些雅思大作文学生常见的错误，大家可以查阅 3.10。

3.9.1 全文翻译 18：广告＋简单句

> *Advertising aimed at children should be banned. To what extent you agree or disagree?*

题目大意

针对孩子的广告应该被禁止。在多大程度上你支持或者反对 (这个观点)？

读者自学步骤 1

阅读题目后，写出三个观点。

下面是我学生写的一些错误或者不好的观点，大家可以看看自己是不是也犯了同样的错误。

学生的观点	点评
禁止广告，孩子专注学习，成绩进步。	广告那么短时间，怎么会影响孩子学习？除非你说广告鼓励小孩买东西，小孩总是惦记，所以影响学习。
不禁止广告，对家长进行指导，更好的教育孩子。	这个题目并没有说教育孩子，也没有说怎么教育，完全跑题了。
禁止儿童广告，减少广告收入，没有足够的钱帮助困难儿童。	比较牵强，难道广告收入就是去帮助困难儿童的？而且这个文章主要是针对消费者，而不是广告商。
禁止针对儿童的广告，儿童少吃垃圾食品，降低疾病风险。	太过具体，垃圾食品只是个例子，广告不只卖垃圾食品。
儿童广告也可以，倡导公益，形成良好的道德规范。	广告一般都是营利性的，公益广告是 awareness campaigns。
禁止对孩子的广告，很多厂商的销量会降低，这些公司会破产，导致很多人失业。	这个观点不是最有力的观点，不能因为公司要赚钱，就要牺牲孩子。
国家不用禁止广告，但是要引导他们不能以营利为目的过度宣传。	这个只是一个立场，没有具体的观点。
不禁止，一些有教育意义的广告开发智力，帮助孩子提高智商。	太过具体，这是例子，而不是观点，很多广告不是提高智商的。
禁止,可能会对小孩想象力影响,成长不好。	观点不是很有力，毕竟激发想象力的东西还有很多，靠广告不大可能。
播放儿童广告，接受新鲜信息，有助于儿童成长。	接收新鲜信息可以通过读书、看教育节目等，未必要看广告。

读者自学步骤 2

翻译下面的句子：在翻译过程中，记住先想词伙，再想句型，然后写出句子。 相关词伙可以查阅微信公众号：gu_writing。

介绍段

背景句	1. 如今，很多小孩每天都会接触到数目庞大的商业广告。
立场	2. 这些广告会鼓励小孩买很多零食、玩具和电子游戏。
阐述立场	3. 我因此觉得这些广告需要被限制，甚至禁止。

主体部分第一段

中心句	4. 如果针对小孩的广告被整顿，那么小孩就不会缠着父母买很多东西。
解释	5. 小孩对价格不敏感，而父母现在又喜欢满足小孩的物质需要。
举例	6. 例如，一些小孩喜欢很贵重的玩具，女孩喜欢买衣服。
结果	7. 这会给低收入的家庭带来经济压力。这个问题可以避免，如果小孩接触广告减少的话。

主体部分第二段

中心句	8. 很多小孩的行为问题和生活习惯问题都是因为广告。
举例 1	9. 有些孩子喜欢吃快餐，因为每天他们都看到快餐的广告。
举例 2	10. 有些孩子很容易发脾气，因为他们每天都打一些暴力游戏。这些游戏也是广告商推广的。
结果	11. 这些问题都会影响小孩的健康和成长。

主体部分第三段

中心句	12. 当然，有一些广告对小孩是有益的。
举例 1	13. 例如，有些广告推广一些营养食品，如牛奶、麦片等。
举例 2	14. 也有一些广告推广一些图书、游戏和有教育价值的玩具。
结果	15. 父母在不熟悉产品的情况下，通过广告可以购买到好的产品。

结论段

再次表明立场	16. 总之，我觉得政府应该禁止很多针对儿童的广告，如果产品对小孩有害。
总结观点	17. 而其他一些推销好的产品的广告就可以放行。

读者自学步骤 3

检查自己的翻译：先看正确句子的词伙和句子结构，然后看错误的句子，看是否能够发现问题。

句 1

正：Many children are exposed to a large number of advertisements in the modern world.

学生的句子：Nowadays, many children are exposed to large number of commercial advertisements.

改：number 是可数名词，前面要加冠词。

句 2

正：These advertisements have encouraged them to buy many snacks, toys and video games.

学生的句子：These advertisements will encourage kids to buy a lot of snacks, toys and electronic games.

改：kids 不要出现在书面语中；will 将来时态也不是很好，因为广告产生的影响已经发生了。

句 3

正：So I agree that advertisements aimed at children should be restricted or even banned.

学生的句子：So I agree that the advertisement should be constrained, even banned to the children.

改：advertisement 用复数比较合理；constrained 不恰当，法律的限制一般用 restrict。

句 4

正：If advertising campaigns directed at children are regulated, children will not pester their parents to buy many goods for them.

学生的句子：If commercial advertisements that aimed at children are regulated, children will not pester their parents to buy many goods for them.

改：定语从句少了个动词，应该是 that are aimed at。

句 5

正：Children are not sensitive to prices and parents prefer to satisfy their needs.

学生的句子：Children are not sensitive to price and parents prefer to satisfy their needs.

改：price 是可数名词，要用复数形式。

句 6

正：For example, many children like expensive toys, and girls are obsessed with fashionable clothes.

学生的句子：Many children like expensive toys, such as clothes.

改：clothes 不是 toys。

句 7

正：These behaviours can put low income families under pressure. This problem can be avoided if children are not bombarded with advertisements.

学生的句子：This brings pressure to the low-income families, which can, however, be avoided if children are not exposed to many advertisements.

改：定语从句指代不清楚，如果是 families 就不恰当。

句 8

正：Advertisements are also responsible for many behavioural problems and lifestyle issues among children.

学生的句子：The advertisement causes damages on children's behaviors and lifestyles.

改：cause damage to 是习惯表达；而且也不能说行为和生活方式被破坏 damage。

句 9

正：For instance, some children like fast food since they are overwhelmed by fast food advertisements every day.

学生的句子：For instance，some children like eating fast food as they come into contact with quick meal advertisings everyday.

改：quick meal 不是 fast food 的替换表达；advertising 不可数；everyday 是形容词，不能修饰句子。

句 10

正：Children are increasingly temperamental due to their addiction to violent electronic games. These games are also promoted by advertising firms.

学生的句子：Their children are easier to lose their temper due to playing violent electronic games every day, these advantages are also advocated by advertisers.

改：人不能说 easy；两个独立的句子间没有任何的连词。

句 11

正：All these problems may pose a threat to their health.

学生的句子：All these problems may pose a threat on their health.

改：pose a threat to 是习惯表达。

句 12

正：On the other hand, we should recognise the advantages of advertisements.

学生的句子：It is inevitable that some commercial advertisements are beneficial to children's growing,

改：it is inevitable that 这种套句很别扭；折中段没有用连接词。

句 13

正：For example, some advertisements disseminate information about nourishing food like milk and cereal.

学生的句子：For example, some advertisements disseminate some nutritious food like milk and oatmeal.

改：disseminate 一般加 information, knowledge 这类词。

句 14

正：There are also many commercials selling books, games and toys of educational value.

学生的句子：There are also many ads promote some books, games and toys with educational value.

改：there be 后面不能加独立的句子。

句 15

正：Parents can purchase the best products with information from commercials, when they do not have knowledge about the options available in the market.

学生的句子：Parents can buy good products through advertisements if they are not familiar to these products.

改：through advertisements 有歧义，毕竟不是通过广告买产品；familiar with 是习惯表达。

句 16

正：Overall, I support the tight control over advertisements directed at children, when the advertised products are harmful to children.

学生的句子：Overall, I think the government should ban many advertisements showed to children, which products in these advertisements have negative impact on children.

改：show 的过去分词是 shown；impact 是可数名词，要加冠词。

句 17

正：Meanwhile, those advertisements promoting good products can be accepted.

学生的句子：Meanwhile, the advertising which markets helpful goods can be allowed.

改：advertising 一般是指广告这个行业。

读者自学步骤 4

整体学习和检查范文，看看是否符合 TELCCS 原则。

范文全文 (7~7.5 分)

Many children are exposed to a large number of advertisements in the modern world. These advertisements have encouraged them to buy many snacks, toys and video games. So I agree that advertisements aimed at children should be restricted or even banned.

> 两句话可以相连，这样增加句子变化性，提高 GRA 的分数。

If advertising campaigns directed at children are regulated, children will not pester their parents to buy many goods for them. Children are not sensitive to prices and parents prefer to satisfy their needs. For example, many children like expensive toys, and girls are obsessed with fashionable clothes. These behaviours can put

> 这两个句子不清楚是解释前面句子的哪个部分，究竟是 satisfy needs，还是 prices。

low income families under pressure. This problem can be avoided if children are not bombarded with advertisements.

指代不清楚前面的整个事情。

Advertisements are also responsible for many behavioural problems and lifestyle issues among children. For instance, some children like fast food since they are overwhelmed by fast food advertisements every day. Children are increasingly temperamental due to their addiction to violent electronic games. These games are also promoted by advertising firms. All these problems may pose a threat to their health.

这里可以加个连接词，说明这是并列的例子。避免 CC 分数的丢失。

这里可以用定语从句连接。

这里可以加个 and，和前面的句子相连。

这个指代不了 temperamental。

On the other hand, we should recognise the advantages of advertisements. For example, some advertisements disseminate information about nourishing food like milk and cereal. There are also many commercials selling books, games and toys of educational value. Parents can purchase the best products with information from commercials, when they do not have knowledge about the options available in the market.

玩游戏影响健康有点牵强，会影响 CC 的分数。

下面只说了一个优点，这里用复数不恰当，影响 CC 的分数。

两个单句可以用 and 相连。

Overall, I support the tight control over advertisements directed at children, when the advertised products are harmful to children. Meanwhile, those advertisements promoting good products can be accepted.

有点啰唆，可以连在一起，然后和下面一句话相连。

可以换个表达，避免重复，影响 CC 的分数。

本节关键学习点

我在教学过程中，经常让学生多写单句，我说单句写好了，复杂句也会写。这个做法可能和大部分老师是相反的。我的教学方法基于一个简单的道理：雅思考官不好蒙骗。你一个复杂句如果写得不对，考官马上可以看出来，分数马上就会降低。因此，踏实写好简单句，分数更加容易提高。

基础不好的考生（包括不熟悉词性、句子成分的考生）可以做一下 2.1 的句子翻译。这是我为考生设计的一个翻译练习。这个练习在过去几年中帮助无数考生在短时间内提高了语法，在网络上也有很多考生在不断传播。

当你熟悉单句后，下一步可以将句子连接起来。

方法 1：如果两个简单句之间没有因果关系，基本上是两件独立的事情，往往可以简单地用 and 相连。

例如：Children are not sensitive to prices and parents prefer to satisfy their needs.

方法 2：如果两个简单句之间有一定的因果关系，往往可以用状语从句相连。

一般来说，if 和 when 引导条件状语从句（也有一定因果关系，只是不那么强）。

例如：If advertising campaigns directed at children are regulated, children will not pester their parents to buy many goods for them.

since, as, because, so 等引导原因或者结果状语从句，表示比较强的因果关系。

例如：Some children like fast food since they are overwhelmed by fast food advertisements every day.

方法 3：如果状语从句怕重复，可以用 and（或者 ;）+ 连接词的方式。

有很多连接词，如 because of this, as a result of this, consequently, as a consequence 等，都可以表示因果关系。

例如：Some children are addicted to violent video games, and because of this, they can show aggression and bully their peers at school.

方法 4：如果第一个单句的最后一个单词和第二个单句的第一个单词重复，可以用定语从句连接。

例如：Children are increasingly temperamental due to their addiction to violent electronic games. These games are normally promoted by advertising firms.

可以改成：Children are increasingly temperamental due to their addiction to violent electronic games, which are normally promoted by advertising firms.

方法 5：如果第二个单句是第一个单句的结果，有可能使用非限制性定语从句。

举例：Advertisements have given a lot of information about products. This enables parents to make well-informed buying decisions.

可以改成：Advertisements have given a lot of information about products, which can help parents to make well-informed buying decisions.

简而言之，不要嫌弃简单句，简单句写熟了，复杂句很容易写。

提升的范文

Many children are exposed to a large number of advertisements in the modern world. These advertisements have encouraged them to buy many snacks, toys and video games, and I agree that advertisements aimed at children should be restricted or even banned.

If advertising campaigns directed at children are regulated, children will not pester their parents to buy many goods for them. Children are not sensitive to prices, and do not realise that the products promoted by advertisements, such as toys and fashionable clothes, can cost a fortune. If they are not bombarded with advertisements, they will not nag their parents to purchase those expensive products. This is particularly important to low income families who have been living under enormous economic pressure.

Advertisements are also responsible for many behavioural problems and lifestyle issues among children. For instance, some children like fast food since they are overwhelmed by fast food advertisements every day. They are also addicted to violent electronic games, which are advertised on television, and playing these games can make them aggressive and temperamental. Imposing an outright ban on these advertisements can help reduce poor behaviour, such as bullying and cursing, on campus.

On the other hand, we should recognise one advantage of advertisements. For example, some advertisements disseminate information about nourishing food like milk and cereal, and there are also many commercials selling books, games and toys of educational value. Parents can purchase the best products with information from commercials, when they do not have knowledge about the options available in the market.

Overall, I agree that governments should regulate or even ban those advertisements which boost the sales of products harmful to the next generation.

3.9.2 全文翻译 19：进口产品＋并列句的写作

> *In some countries, it is now possible for people to buy products made in other countries. To what extent do the benefits of this development outweigh the problems?*

题目大意

在一些国家，人们现在有可能去买其他国家制造的产品。这个改变的好处在多大程度上大于其带来的问题？

读者自学步骤 1

阅读题目后，写出三个观点。

下面是我学生写的一些错误或者不好的观点，大家可以看看自己是不是也犯了同样的错误。

学生的观点	点评
购买其他国家的商品，用的商品来自全球，促进经济全球化进程。	不够有力。促进经济全球化的好处是什么？为什么要经济全球化？
购买他国产品，发生质量问题，跨境退换成本高，消费者权益难以保证。	不够有力。如果质量那么多问题，买外国的产品干吗？而且买外国的产品不代表代购。
不同国家的商品，尤其是一些特色产品中包含着许多文化背景，互通贸易可以借此传播文化，有利于旅游业发展，促进文化交流发展。	不够有力。这个题目针对的是本国的消费者和公司，而不是出口国的好处。
购买进口产品，出口国产品购买量增加，减少出口国失业率。	不够有力。这个题目主要是考虑对进口国的影响，而不是出口国。

买别国商品,不用出国就可买到,节约时间。	不够有力。关键是买有什么好处,而不是一定要买,一定要省时间。
购买其他国家产品,了解其他国家的文化,增加知识。	不够有力。购买产品不代表可以理解其他国家的文化。买麦当劳不代表知道美国的文化,买奔驰不代表知道德国的文化。
买别国生产的产品,本国生产产品的工厂减少,从而减少工厂排放的污染物,利于本国环境保护。	不够有力。进口产品也产生污染,而且一般不会有人因为污染问题而买外国的产品。

读者自学步骤 2

翻译下面的句子:在翻译过程中,记住先想词伙,再想句型,然后写出句子。 相关词伙可以查阅微信公众号: gu_writing。

介绍段

| 背景句 | 1. 随着世界越来越国际化,国家之间商品的流通以惊人的速度进行着。 |
| 阐述立场 | 2. 在我看来(from my point of view),这个趋势能够提高消费者的生活水准。 |

主体部分第一段

中心句 (经济: 成本)	3. 进口商品在好几个方面有益于消费者。其中一个好处是这些产品的价格很有竞争力。
解释	4. 主要的原因是出口这些商品的国家一般都有技术和知识去控制成本,确保这些产品很便宜。
举例	5. 例如,中国擅长生产纺织品,因此在世界上很多地方,中国的纺织品都比当地的同等货物便宜。
附加观点	6. 此外,进口商品挑战国内生产商的统治地位,激化竞争,从而迫使这些生产商砍价。
结果	7. 这对于本国的消费者也是有益的,因为可以减少生活成本。
附加观点	8. 还有值得强调的是 (it is worth noting that) 消费者在购物的时候也有了很多的选择。
举例	9. 例如,进口食物可以缓和在某些地区反常天气造成的食物短缺。

主体部分第二段

中心句	10. 另一方面,进口商品的负面因素 (downside is that) 是国家过分依赖进口品可能会导致某些国内行业的发展不足。
举例	11. 例如,很多国家进口电脑,导致本国制造商的破产。
附加观点	12. 对于发展自给自足的经济是有害的。

其他观点 （社会·环境）	13. 此外，运输会造成比较大的污染，因为它涉及空运。

结论段

再次表明 立场	14. 因此，我们可以理智地认为（it is reasonable to think that）从其他国家进口商品总体来说对消费者有好的影响。
总结观点	15. 消费者可以更便宜地获得商品，虽然当地企业有可能倒闭。

读者自学步骤 3

检查自己的翻译：先看正确句子的词伙和句子结构，然后看错误的句子，看是否能够发现问题。

句 1

正：As the world is increasingly globalised, the exchange of commodities across the border is proceeding at an astounding rate.

学生的句子：As world becomes increasingly globalised, the exchange of commodities among countries is going on at an astounding rate.

改：world 是可数名词，需要加冠词；going on 表达不正式。

句 2

正：From my point of view, this development can help improve living standards of consumers.

学生的句子：From my point of view, this development is improve the living standards of consumers.

改：improve 是动词，"is + 动词原形"永远是错的。

句 3

正：Goods imported from overseas can benefit consumers in different ways. The first benefit is that these imports are competitively priced.

学生的句子：Goods import from overseas can benefit consumers in different ways. The first benefit is that these goods are still highly competitive.

改：第一句话有 import 和 benefit 两个动词，一个句子在没有连词的情况下不能出现两个动词。

句 4

正：The main reason is that the countries that export these goods normally have technology and know-how to reduce the cost of production to ensure that these products are affordable.

学生的句子：The main reason is that the countries which export this goods own their technology and profession knowledge that reduce the cost of production and keep the prices cheaper.

改：goods 是复数，代词应该用 these。

句 5

正：For example, China specialises in the production of textile products so China-made textile products are cheaper than local counterparts in many parts of the world.

学生的句子: For example, China is good at producing textile products, in many parts of the wold, Chinese textile products are cheaper than local counterparts.

改: 两个独立的单句之间应该有一个连词。

句 6

正: Besides, imported goods have challenged domestic manufacturers' dominance and intensified competition, thereby pushing these producers to cut prices.

学生的句子: Importing goods have challenged the dominance of domestic manufacturers and intensified competitions, which means that this phenomenon might cause the decreasing of the price.

改: 如果动名词作主语 (此处是 importing), 那么谓语动词要用单数 has; competition 的从句后半句过于烦琐。

句 7

正: It is beneficial to domestic customers, because the cost of living will decline.

学生的句子: It is beneficial to the domestic customers, because this is able to reduce the cost of living.

改: this 一般指代前面叙述的一个事物, 在这里指代不清。

句 8

正: It is worth noting that consumers can have diverse options when shopping.

学生的句子: It is worth noting that consumers have various options when shop.

改: various 表示的是 "几个" 的意思, 如果表示 "不同的", 可以说 different, diverse, a great variety of; when 是从属连词, 后面要加独立的句子, shop 是个动词, 没有主语。

句 9

正: Food products imported from overseas can alleviate the food shortage caused by abnormal weather in some regions.

学生的句子: Food products imported from overseas can alleviate food shortage which caused by abnormal weather in some regions.

改: shortage 是可数名词, 要加冠词; 定语从句 which caused 中少了一个 be 动词。

句 10

正: On the other hand, the downside of importing goods is that the excessive reliance on imports may lead to the underdevelopment of some domestic industries.

学生的句子: On the other hand, the downside of importing commodities is that excessive dependence on importing from overseas is possible to lead to the underdevelopment of some domestic industries.

改: 没有 is possible to 这种表达, 应改成 is likely to。

句 11

正：For instance, many countries import computers, resulting in domestic manufacturers' bankruptcy.

学生的句子：For example, many countries import computers from overseas, result in the bankruptcy of many domestic manufacturers.

改：result in 这个动词词组应该改成分词结构，充当结果状语。

句 12

正：This is harmful/detrimental to the development of a self-contained economy.

学生的句子：This is harmful/detrimental to develop a self-contained economy.

改：essential/harmful/detrimental/vital 这些词后面的 to 都是介词，需要加名词。

句 13

正：In addition, transportation may create considerable pollution, because it involves air freight.

学生的句子：In addition, transportations are more likely to cause a considerable number of pollution, because it involves air freight.

改：transportation 是不可数名词；a considerable number of 修饰可数名词复数，而 pollution 是不可数名词。

句 14

正：It is therefore reasonable to think that the overall effect of importing products from other countries is positive.

学生的句子：Hence, it is reasonable to think that the overall effect of import products from other countries is positive.

改：of 是介词，后面不能加动词原形。

句 15

正：Consumers can buy something at a lower cost, although some local firms may be shut down.

学生的句子：Consumers can buy something at a lower cost, despite some local firms may be shut down.

改：despite 是介词，不是连词，不能连接句子。

读者自学步骤 4

整体学习和检查范文，看看是否符合 TELCCS 原则。

范文全文（大概 6.5 分）

As the world is increasingly globalised, the exchange of commodities across the border is proceeding at an astounding rate. From my point of view, this development can help improve living standards of consumers.

Goods imported from overseas can benefit consumers in different ways. The first benefit is that these imports are competitively priced. The main reason is that the countries that export these goods normally have technology and know-how to reduce the cost of production to ensure that these products are affordable. For example, China specialises in the production of textile products so China-made textile products are cheaper than local counterparts in many parts of the world. Besides, imported goods have challenged domestic manufacturers' dominance and intensified competition, thereby pushing these producers to cut prices. It is beneficial to domestic customers, because the cost of living will decline. It is worth noting that consumers can have diverse options when shopping. For example, food products imported from overseas can alleviate the food shortage caused by abnormal weather in some regions.

模板。

和前面的 products 重复，可以具体化，提高 LR 的分数。

模板。

这里可以增加一个并列句，解释为什么生活成本下降。

模板。

一段话不要写太多观点，尽量一个观点具体拓展和解释。

On the other hand, the downside of importing goods is that the excessive reliance on imports may lead to the underdevelopment of some domestic industries. For instance, many countries import computers, resulting in domestic manufacturers' bankruptcy. This is harmful to the development of a self-contained economy. In addition, transportation may create considerable pollution, because it involves air freight.

模板。

这里可以加一个并列句，解释为什么会导致某些行业的发展会受到影响。
这里可以解释一下中心句，再举例，提高 TR 的分数。

为了套 in addition，加一个观点，却没有很好地论述。

It is therefore reasonable to think that the overall effect of import products from other countries is positive. Consumers can buy something at a lower cost, although some local firms may be shut down.

这句话和上面一段话矛盾，影响 CC 的分数。

本节关键学习点

很多考生在备考的时候比较依赖一些模板和套句。这种备考方式主要是以前准备国内一些考试的陋习。考生习惯了熟悉一个模板后，背一些观点和表达，然后套到模板上。

这个方法有两个缺点：

> 缺点 *1*：模板的字数太多，内容太少，直接影响考生 (Task Response) 的成绩。
>
> 缺点 *2*：模板太过生硬，考官见得太多，觉得考生不具备自己独立写作的能力，会给一些超低的分数。

那么怎么解决呢？

增加内容。增加内容的方法主要有两个：①多写并列句；②多思考前因后果。

我们下面讨论并列句的问题。并列句在雅思作文和书面语上有非常广泛的应用。很多老师觉得并列句语法太简单，而事实上，native speakers 认为并列句也是复杂句型。

例 1：The first benefit is that these imports are competitively priced.

我们可以思考一下进口品的价格很有竞争力的原因或者结果是什么。我相信有竞争力，性价比就会很高。可以说一下结果。

提升的句子：

These imports are competitively priced and offer good value for customers.

例 2：It is beneficial to domestic customers, because the cost of living will decline.

这句话的状语从句比较短，我们可以思考一下"生活成本下降"的原因是什么。

提升的句子：It is beneficial to domestic customers, because they can spend less on some products essential to their lives such as food and the cost of living will decline.

例 3：It is worth noting that consumers can have diverse options when shopping.

并列句除了可以表示原因和结果外，还可以表示并列的事情和动作。例如，消费者有不同的选择，那么很明显不同的选择可以满足不同的需要。因此改为：

Consumers can have diverse options when shopping, and products from other countries can address some of their needs.

当一个句子里的两件事情可以用一个主语的时候，尽量争取使用并列句，这样语言会显得比较简练。

Imported goods have challenged domestic manufacturers' dominance and intensified competition.

（注：很多语法专家认为这种句子还是单句，因为后面的分句没有主语。）

我总结一下并列句使用的三种语境：

语境 *1*：前后两个分句有一定的因果关系。

语境 *2*：前后两个分句并列，相连增加句子复杂性。

语境 *3*：前后两个分句共用某个部分（如主语或者宾语），可以连接，变得简洁。

并列句的写作要注意三点：

注意 *1*：要注意事情的先后顺序。

并列句的前半句一般发生在后半句的事情之前，或者前半句的事情要比后半句次要。

例：Renting a house, instead of buying it, can improve living standards and reduce the burden on people.

错误的原因："减少负担"应该先发生，然后才是"提高生活标准"。

提高的句子：Renting a house can reduce the burden on people and help them save money to improve living standards.

注意 *2*：要注意第二个分句的动词和主语是否匹配。

很多考生写并列句时总是忘记主语和分句的动词是否搭配恰当。

例：By providing community services, students can improve skills and enrich their experience.

错误的原因：students 是句子的主语，而分句的动词是 enrich（使……变得丰富），这个词不能用人作主语。

提高的句子：By providing community services, students can improve skills and increase their experience.

注意 *3*：要注意两个分句并列成分的清晰，避免语意不清。

有时候第一个分句出现两个或者更多的动词，而第二个分句就可能产生歧义。

例：Domestic firms have to cut prices to overcome competition and invest heavily in research and development.

错误的原因：分句中的 invest heavily in 事实上和 cut prices 对应，这里却可能被理解成和 overcome competition 对应，从而产生歧义。

这时候可以在 and 前面加个逗号，这样读者就知道 invest heavily in 不和 overcome competition 对应。

提高的句子：Domestic firms have to cut prices to overcome competition, and invest heavily in research and development.

提升的范文

标色的部分是和原文有差异的地方，下划线部分是词伙。

As the world is increasingly globalised, the exchange of commodities across the border is proceeding at an astounding rate. From my point of view, this development can help improve living standards of consumers.

The products from foreign countries are competitively priced and offer good value for money. The main reason is that the countries that export these goods normally have technology and know-how to reduce the cost of production to ensure that these products are highly affordable. For example, China specialises in the production of textile products so China-made clothes, bed linen and footwear are cheaper than local counterparts in many parts of the world.

Another benefit is that imported goods have challenged domestic manufacturers' dominance and intensified competition, thereby pushing these producers to cut prices. It is beneficial to domestic customers because they can spend less on some products essential to their lives such as food, and the cost of living will decline. This is particularly important for people who live on a tight budget and those who need to feed a big family.

The downside of importing goods is that foreign brands may steal the market share from local companies and lead to the underdevelopment of some domestic industries. These brands have been in the global marketplace for many decades, and they have attracted local consumers with clear advantages in technology, packaging, functions and after-sales services. For instance, Dell, Apple, HP and other world famous producers of computers and electronic products have conquered many markets and the arrival of these international brands has resulted in domestic manufacturers' bankruptcy. This is harmful to the development of a self-contained economy.

In conclusion, the overall effect of import products from other countries is positive. Consumers can buy something at a lower cost, although some local firms may be shut down.

3.9.3 全文翻译 20：英文全球语言＋状语从句

> *The advantages brought by the spread of English as a "global language" will outweigh the disadvantages. To what extent do you agree or disagree with this view?*

题目大意

英文作为全球语言的扩展的优点超过缺点。在多大程度上你支持或者反对这个看法？

读者自学步骤 1

阅读题目后，写出三个观点。

下面是我学生写的一些错误或者不好的观点，大家可以看看自己是不是也犯了同样的错误。

学生的观点	点评
英语全球使用，科学技术资料交流无障碍，发展中国家科技得到进步。	不够有力。不应该只讨论对发展中国家的影响。
英语作为全球语言，更多的人教英语，增加就业岗位和经济收入。	不够有力。教其他语言也可以创造机会，更何况教语言未必需要人，计算机也可以。
英语作为全球语言，逻辑性强，语法简单，容易入门，人们日常生活使用很方便。	轻微跑题。不需要讨论为什么英文成为国际语言，讨论的重点应该是英文的普及有什么好处。
英语作为全球语言有助于建立跨国公司，提高生产力。	逻辑不好。为什么英文有助于建立跨国公司？要解释清楚。

英语传播，使全球人民可以交流，促进全球化。	不够有力。为什么可以促进全球化？为什么这是一个优点？
英语作为全球语言所带来的优点大于缺点，出国旅游可以减少语言障碍，更加方便，更好地与人交流。	不够有力。英文的意义不只是为了旅游，毕竟你可以在本国旅游，也会去不说英文的国家旅游。
将英语作为全球化语言，世界共同文化过于单一，不利于其他国家文化在世界的传播。	逻辑不好。如果有一个国际语言，不同国家文化可以通过英文传播。这个学生对观点思考还不够细致。
英语作为全球语言，母语英语的人具有先天优势，获得更广阔的发展空间。	跑题。这个题目是问英文普遍的好处，而不是问学习英文的好处。

读者自学步骤 2

翻译下面的句子：在翻译过程中，记住先想词伙，再想句型，然后写出句子。 相关词伙可以查阅微信公众号：gu_writing。

介绍段

背景句	1. 目前，英文作为世界语言的地位是无可比拟的。
改写题目或引出话题	2. 然而，值得一提的是 (it is worth noting that)，英文的普及可能也有它的负面影响。
阐述立场	3. 在我看来，英文的领导地位应该用积极的目光(in a positive light)去看待。

主体部分第一段

中心句(经济: 资源)	4. 毫无疑问的是(it is unquestionable that)，英文的广泛使用促进全球合作，因为一个通用的语言可以让人们在国际环境下克服语言障碍。
举例 1	5. 人们可以在一起做生意，讨论怎么开公司，怎么进口产品，不管他们的母语是什么。
举例 2	6. 英文已经被很多国际性会议、科研机构确定为主要的语言。
拓展	7. 这就意味着学者可以在一起分享知识和想法，甚至一起工作去做项目。

主体部分第二段

中心句(科技和知识)	8. 另外，毫不夸张地说 (it would be no exaggeration to say that)，英文的普及有利于人们增加知识和开阔视野。
解释 1	9. 世界上大概 80% 的网站是通过英文发布信息的；所以说，懂英文的人可以在网络上看新闻、读杂志、阅读书籍等，更好地了解世界。
解释 2	10. 那些能够熟练说两种语言 (母语和英语) 的人可以很容易在世界各地旅行，熟悉不同地方的风土人情。

主体部分第三段

中心句 (社会: 传统)	11. 尽管英文对于全球化的进程有巨大的贡献，但是它被认为是语言多元化消失的罪魁祸首。
解释 1	12. 这个看法主要基于一个事实 (this idea lies in the fact that)：越来越多的年轻人学习英文，而忘记了他们的母语。
解释 2	13. 同样应该注意的是 (equally noteworthy is the fact that) 英文作为国际媒体的主要语言，会将英文国家的生活方式、价值观和信仰传输到世界不同的地方。
结果	14. 这有可能会影响世界文化的多元化。
举例	15. 某些文化里的治疗方法、食谱、宗教的习惯、传统的庆祝仪式都因为语言的消失而消失。我们对世界的认识会很有限。

结论段

再次表明 立场	16. 综上所述，英文对于来自不同国家的人民的交流和合作有着至关重要的角色。
总结观点	17. 尽管有人怀疑 (suspect) 英文会危及一些小语种，但是这种怀疑未必有根据。

读者自学步骤 3

检查自己的翻译：先看正确句子的词伙和句子结构，然后看错误的句子，看是否能够发现问题。

句 1

正：Today/at the present time, the role of English as a global language is indispensable.

学生的句子：Present day, the role of English as a worldwide language is indispensable.

改：Present day 和 worldwide language 没有这些说法。

句 2

正：It is worth mentioning that the prevalence of English worldwide might have its negative effect.

学生的句子：It is worth noting that English might has its negative effect.

改：might 后要加动词原形。

句 3

正：In my opinion, English's dominance can be viewed in a positive light.

学生的句子：In my opinion, English's dominance can view in a positive light.

改：view 应该用被动语态。

句 4

正：It is unquestionable that the extensive use of English worldwide helps promote international cooperation, as a universal language enables people to overcome language barriers in the global setting.

学生的句子：It is unquestionable that the extensive use of English worldwide promotes international cooperate, as a universal language enables people overcome language barriers in the global setting.

改：cooperate 是动词，不能充当 promotes 的宾语；include 是动词；enables people overcome 两个动词连用。

句 5

正：People can conduct business together and discuss how to set up a company and import products, regardless of their native languages.

学生的句子：People can do business together, discuss how to operate a company and import food，no matter what their native languages are.

改：两个动词间没有连词。

句 6

正：That's why English has been identified/regarded/recognised/acknowledged as the main language by many international conferences and academic groups.

学生的句子：That's why English had been recognised as the first language by many international conferences and academic groups.

改：时态错误，应该使用现在完成时。

句 7

正：This means that scholars can share knowledge and ideas or even cooperate to complete projects.

学生的句子：It means that scholars can share knowledge and thoughts together，and even work together to do projects.

改：this 更能指代前面的句子；together 有点重复。

句 8

正：In addition, it would be no exaggeration to say that the dominance of English can help people expand knowledge and broaden horizons.

学生的句子：In addition，it would be no exaggeration to say that the popularity of English can help people expand knowledge and broaden their horizon.

改：horizon 应该用复数形式。

句 9

正：About 80% of the world's websites publish articles in English, so people who master this language can read news, magazines and books on the web and learn more about the world.

学生的句子：About 80% of the websites all over the world deliver information in English；so people who understand English can read news, magazines and books online to have a better understanding of the world.

改：分号等于句号，这里没有必要，用逗号就可以。

句 10

正：People who have proficiency in two languages (English plus their native language) can travel in different parts of the world with ease and deepen their understanding of customs of these places.

学生的句子：Those who speaks two languages (native language and English) are able to travel all around the world easily, and get familiar with the customs of different places.

改：从句主谓不一致，谓语应该是 speak。

句 11

正：Despite the contribution of the English language to globalisation, it is considered the main culprit of the loss of language diversity.

学生的句子：Although English has made remarkable contribution to globalisation, but it is considered the culprit of language diversity disappears.

改：although 和 but 不能连用；of 这个介词后面不能出现句子，而 disappears 是动词。

句 12

正：The idea lies in the fact that young people in many parts of the world make an effort to study English, instead of their mother tongue.

学生的句子：This argument is based on the fact that more and more people study English, then forget their mother tongue.

改：then 是副词，不是连词。

句 13

正：It should also be noted that English, as the favourite language for international media, conveys English-speaking countries' lifestyles, values and beliefs to different parts of the world.

学生的句子：It should also be noted that English, as the favourite language for international mediums, conveys English-speaking countries' lifestyles, values and beliefs to throughout the world.

改：mediums 应该是 media；to 在这里是介词，后面不可能加另外一个介词 throughout。

句 14

正：It might affect the world's cultural diversity.

学生的句子：It might be affect the world's cultural diversification.

改：be 去掉，多余。

句 15

正：Some traditional therapies, recipes, religious practices and ceremonies will possibly vanish, if languages disappear. Our knowledge about the world will be limited.

学生的句子：Some traditional therapies, recipes, religious practices and ceremonies will be vanished, if languages disappear. Our knowledge about the world will be limited.

改：vanish 是不及物动词，没有被动语态。

句 16

正：In conclusion, English plays a vital role in communication and cooperation among people from different countries.

学生的句子：In conclusion, English plays a vital role to communicate and cooperate.

改：play a vital role 后面一般加介词 in。

句 17

正：Although some people suspect that English will endanger some minority languages, this claim is not supported with evidence.

学生的句子：Despite people claim that English threats some minority languages, this claim is not supported with evidence.

改：despite 是介词，后面不能加句子。

读者自学步骤 4

范文全文 (大概 7 分)

At the present time, the role of English as a global language is indispensable. It is worth mentioning that the prevalence of English worldwide might have its negative effect. In my opinion, English's dominance can be viewed in a positive light.

> 套句，可以省略，和下面一句话连起来，而且这句话和背景句刚好相反且矛盾，影响 CC 的分数。

It is unquestionable that the extensive use of English worldwide helps promote international cooperation, as a universal language enables people to overcome language barriers in the global setting. People can conduct business together and discuss how to set up a company and import products, regardless of their native languages. That's why English has been identified as the main language by many international conferences and academic groups. This means that scholars can share knowledge and ideas or even cooperate to complete projects.

> 套句，有点多余。

> 两个 people 有点重复，影响 LR 的分数。

> 多余的连接词，影响 CC，这句话和前面的句子没联系。

In addition, it would be no exaggeration to say that the dominance of English can help people expand knowledge and broaden horizons. About 80% of the world's websites publish articles in English, so people who master this language can read news, magazines and books on the web and learn more about the world. People who have proficiency in two languages (English plus their native language) can travel in different parts of the world with ease and deepen their understanding of customs of these places.

套句，有点夸大其词。

和前面的内容有点重复，可以用代词 they，这样可以提升 CC 的分数。

Despite the contribution of the English language to globalisation, it is considered the main culprit of the loss of language diversity. The idea lies in the fact that young people in many parts of the world make an effort to study English, instead of their mother tongue. It should also be noted that English, as the favourite language for international media, conveys English-speaking countries' lifestyles, values and beliefs to different parts of the world. It might affect the world's cultural diversity. Some traditional therapies, recipes, religious practices and ceremonies will possibly vanish, if languages disappear. Our knowledge about the world will be limited.

中心句和后面的内容不一致，后面不只是说 language diversity，影响 CC 的分数。

这个套句读起来累赘，而且上面一句话也没有说到任何语言多样性的损失，和中心句不一致。

这句话和下面一句话事实上联系不大，可以去掉；否则，会影响 CC 的分数。

这里突然说到对世界的认识，也是和前面的句子没有什么联系，影响 CC 的分数。

In conclusion, English plays a vital role in communication and cooperation among people from different countries. Although some people suspect that English will endanger some minority languages, this claim is not supported with evidence. The reality is that English sometimes assists us protecting cultural heritage.

这些套句都让文章变得琐碎，不够紧凑。

和主体段讨论不一致，整篇文章没有说英文可以保护文化，影响 CC 的分数。

本节关键学习点

这篇文章的原文里有八个套句之多。

很多雅思老师喜欢给考生讲套句，很多考生也喜欢学套句。主要的原因是套句好像是一种不用大脑的方法，写上去就可以让简单的句子变得复杂。

这种想法是一厢情愿的，因为考官不喜欢这些冗长的句子，显得啰嗦，特别是很多考生写的具体内容很少的时候，套句尤其显得扎眼。

那么怎么解决套句的问题呢？

就是多考虑前因后果，例如可以用原因状语从句，也就是使用 since, because, as 等连词引导的从句。

例 1：It would be no exaggeration to say that those who do not speak English find it difficult to survive in this global community.

这个句子用了一个套句，那么如果去掉后，考生可以写什么去取代呢？

你可以思考原因，为什么不会说英文的人很难在全球社会生存。可能英文在很多大公司是工作语言，也是很多知名大学的学习语言等。

原句可以改成：

As English as a dominant language is used in many large companies and also in many leading universities around the world, those who do not speak English find it difficult to survive in this global community.

另外一种方法是多思考结果，使用结果状语从句，或者其他的引导结果的句子结构。

例 2：The idea lies in the fact that young people in many parts of the world make an effort to study English, instead of their mother tongue.

这个句子也用了套句，如果去掉后，学生可以除了思考原因，为什么年轻人喜欢学英文之外，还可以说年轻人学习英文产生的结果。

原句可以改成：

Young people in many parts of the world make an effort to study English, instead of their mother tongue, and this is why some minority languages have died out.

状语从句在作文里还有两大意义：

> 意义 1：状语从句经常用在观点类和论述类的中心句中，表示条件 (if, when)。
>
> 意义 2：状语从句可以帮助我们避免一些中国式的表达。

意义 1：状语从句经常用在观点类和论述类的中心句中，表示条件 (if, when)。

因为很多时候雅思作文只是假定一个条件，而不是描述一个事实，所以用这些条件状语从句比较合适。

意义 2：状语从句可以帮助我们避免一些中国式的表达。

中文习惯是句子可以充当句子的主语，如：

年轻人讲英文可以很容易找到工作。（Young people speak English can find a job easily.）

但是作为英文是有语法错误的，那么怎么办，用状语从句，可以写成 If young people can speak English well, they can find a job easily.

提升的范文

标色的部分是和原文有差异的地方，下划线部分是词伙。

English has developed into a global language, which has been used as a vehicle for cross-cultural communication all over the world. The prevalence of this language worldwide can be viewed in a positive light, although it might have its negative effect.

The extensive use of English worldwide helps promote international cooperation, as it enables people to overcome language barriers in the global setting. Entrepreneurs can conduct business together and discuss how to set up a company and import products, regardless of their native languages. Moreover, English has been identified as the main language by many international conferences and academic groups. This means that scholars can share knowledge and ideas or even cooperate to complete projects in different areas of studies.

In addition, the dominance of English can help people expand knowledge and broaden horizons. About 80% of the world's websites publish articles in English, so people who master this language can read news, magazines and books on the web and learn more about the world. They can travel in different parts of the world with ease and deepen their understanding of customs of these places.

Despite the contribution of the English langauge to globalisation, it is considered the main culprit of the loss of cultural diversity. The idea lies in the fact that young people in many parts of the world make an effort to study English, instead of their mother tongue. Some less spoken languages may eventually die out, so will those traditional therapies, recipes, religious practices and ceremonies which are preserved by people speaking these languages. Our knowledge about the world will be limited, if some cultures disappear.

In conclusion, English plays a vital role in communication and cooperation among people from different countries, although some people suspect that English will endanger some minority languages.

3.9.4 全文翻译 21：生活方式＋名词性从句／定语从句

> *Some people say that the government should ensure that people lead a healthy life, while others believe that individuals should have their own choices. Discuss both views and give your opinion.*

题目大意

一些人说政府应该保证人们的生活方式要健康，但是另一些人认为人们应该有自己的选择。讨论两个观点并给出你的看法。

读者自学步骤 1

阅读题目后，写出三个观点。

下面是我学生写的一些错误或者不好的观点，大家可以看看自己是不是也犯了同样的错误。

学生的观点	点评
个人选择，根据自己的爱好，身体好。	不够有力。为什么按照自己的爱好身体就可以好？

222

人们自由选择，适合他们的职业，提高社会生产力。	跑题。这个题目只关注健康，不关注其他话题，如职业。
人们可以有自己选择生活方式的权利，同时政府不应该过度关注，会减少对经济等方面的关注，导致社会失衡。	不够有力。政府不是说管理人们的生活方式，就会忽视经济。
政府投资，更多的福利和设施，人们看病花的钱少了，医疗更先进了。	跑题。这个题目说的生活方式，而不是医疗设施和福利。
政府负担，增加纳税人负担，导致移民。	完全跑题。这个题目说的是决定人们的生活方式。这可以通过立法来实现，不需要花多少钱。
政府确保健康生活，在高热量食品上加税，减少人们的使用，身体变好。	过分细节。食品只是生活方式的一方面。
政府拥有税收，可以研发专业方法，保证人的健康。	跑题。现在说的是生活方式，而不是如何提高健康的科技。
政府适当引导，增加基础设施，如体育馆，提供免费运动器材。	不够有力。政府做这些事情是好，好在什么地方呢？
政府约束，营造健康的生活环境，健康。	跑题。这个题目关心的是生活方式，而不是生活环境。生活方式是每天和健康有关系的生活习惯。

读者自学步骤 2

翻译下面的句子：在翻译过程中，记住先想词伙，再想句型，然后写出句子。相关词伙可以查阅微信公众号：gu_writing。

介绍段

背景句	1. 健康的生活方式之所以重要，是因为它和人们的尊严及幸福有很大的关系。
阐述立场	2. 虽然很多人觉得生活方式是个人的选择，我认为人们不大可能采纳健康的生活方式，除非政府采取一些行动。

主体部分第一段

中心句	3. 如果人们能够决定自己怎么生活，他们会更加快乐。
解释	4. 他们选择健康的生活习惯，因为他们觉得这些习惯会让自己更好地享受人生。
举例	5. 例如，有些人会选择多吃蔬菜和水果，因为这样会帮助他们保持好身材，让自己在工作和社交中更加自信。
对比	6. 如果一个人总要想着如何遵循政府规定，那么他们会生活在很大的压力之下。

主体部分第二段

中心句 （个人行为）	7. 另一方面，政府在某些行为上施加约束是非常重要的，特别是那些被公认为不健康的行为。
原因 1	8. 很多人很难约束自己。
原因 2	9. 例如，抽烟的危害一直广为人知，但是很多人还是抽烟。
拓展	10. 他们不会戒烟，除非政府对香烟加税，和禁止人们在公共场所抽烟。

主体部分第三段

中心句	11. 我个人觉得，政府的约束和指导很重要。
解释	12. 很多人对于一些生活习惯的危害并不清楚。
举例 1	13. 例如，办公室工作人员会尽量多运动，如果政府的宣传活动传递这么一个信息：久坐的工作会影响健康，减少寿命。
举例 2	14. 政府的宣传活动还需要提供关于吃快餐导致健康问题的信息，因此消费者会注意健康饮食，还有食品包装上的营养信息。

读者自学步骤 3

检查自己的翻译：先看正确句子的词伙和句子结构，然后看错误的句子，看是否能够发现问题。

句 1

正：The healthy lifestyle is important because it has a direct bearing on our dignity and well-being.

学生的句子：The reason why healthy lifestyle is important is that it has a close relationship with people's dignity and happiness.

改：lifestyle 是可数名词，要加冠词。

句 2

正：Although many people regard lifestyle choices as a personal matter, I do not think people are likely to adopt a healthy lifestyle unless the government intervenes.

学生的句子：Although many people think that the lifestyle is the personal choice, in my view, people do not adopt the healthy lifestyle, unless the government take some actions.

改：government take 主谓不一致。

句 3

正：If people decide how to live their lives, they will possibly be happier.

学生的句子：People will be more happier if they could decide lifestyle by themselves.

改：只有 happier，没有 more happier 的说法；lifestyle 是可数名词，要加冠词或者变为复数形式。

句 4

正：They choose to develop and maintain healthy habits because they believe these habits can bring enjoyment to their lives.

学生的句子：They choose to develop and remain healthy habits because they believe these habits can bring about enjoyment to their lives.

改：remain 是系动词，后面不能加名词；bring about 是 cause 的意思，在这里不恰当。

句 5

正：For example, some people may pay attention to fruit and vegetables in their diets, which can help them keep fit and increase their confidence in work and social lives.

学生的句子：For example, some people chose to eat more vegetables and fruits, which can help them keep figure and become more confident in work and social activities.

改：chose 没必要用过去时；keep figure 这个表达也不恰当。

句 6

正：They will live under enormous pressure, if they are obsessed with how to follow the government's lifestyle guideline.

学生的句子：However, if someone are always obsessed with the government law, they would live under high pressure.

改：someone are 主谓不一致。

句 7

正：On the other hand, it is important for the government to tighten regulation on some behaviours, especially those which have been proven to be damaging to health.

学生的句子：On the other side, it is important for governments to strain some behaviours，especially those are regarded as unhealthy behaviours.

改：strain behaviours 搭配错误；those are 是一个新的单句，两个句子间没有连词。

句 8

正：There are many people who lack self-discipline.

学生的句子：There are numerous people find it difficult to restrain themselves.

改：这个句子有两个动词，但没有连词；没有 restrain themselves 这个表达，可以说 show self-restraint。

句 9

正：For example, they smoke, although it is common knowledge that smoking endangers their health.

学生的句子：For example, it is a common sense that smoking is harmful but many people still keep smoking.

改：common sense 的 sense 是不可数名词。

句 10

正：They would not quit smoking, unless the government imposes the tobacco tax and forbids citizens to smoke publicly.

学生的句子：They would not stop smoking, unless the government levies taxes on cigarettes and forbids people smoking in the public places.

改：forbid 的用法一般是 forbid somebody to do something。

句 11

正：In my view, the government should be responsible for educating the public about what to do and offering guidance.

学生的句子：In my opinion, the constraints and instructions of governments is important.

改：主谓不一致；constraint 一般是表示空间和时间上的约束。

句 12

正：Many people are not well-informed about how damaging their ways of life can be.

学生的句子：Many people do not clearly know that the negative effects of some unhealthy lifestyle.

改：that 引导的宾语从句应该是独立的句子，这里却只有一个名词短语。

句 13

正：For example, office workers will try to exercise regularly, if the government launches campaigns to convey the message that a sedentary job can affect health adversely and reduce life expectancy.

学生的句子：For example, office workers would do more exercises if the government launch a campaign to deliver a message that a sedentary working lifestyle can affect health and reduce life expectancy.

改：government launch 主谓不一致。

句 14

正：Awareness campaigns should also provide information about the health problems caused by eating fast food, so consumers will pay attention to healthy eating and read the nutritional information on food packaging carefully.

学生的句子：The government's campaign also needs to provide information about health problems caused by fast food, so consumers will pay attention to healthy diet and nutritional information on food packaging.

改：diet 是可数名词，不可以没有冠词。

读者自学步骤 4

整体学习和检查范文，看看是否符合 TELCCS 原则。

范文全文 (7 分)

The healthy lifestyle is important because it has a direct bearing on our dignity and well-being.Although many people regard lifestyle choices as a personal matter, I do not think people are likely to adopt a healthy lifestyle unless the government intervenes.

前面也有一个 people, 可以用代词 they.

If people decide how to live their lives, they will possibly be happier. They choose to develop and maintain healthy habits because they believe these habits can bring enjoyment to their lives. For example, some people may pay attention to fruit and vegetables in their diets, which can help them keep fit and increase their confidence in work and social lives. They will live under enormous pressure, if they are obsessed with how to follow the government's lifestyle guideline.

去掉, 避免 people 的重复, 或者写成定语从句。

可以说 increase the intake of fruit and vegetables, 更加地道。

这里出现了跳跃, 为什么 keep fit 就可以提高自信？

用词不是很恰当, obsessed 是 "入迷" 的意思。

On the other hand, it is important for the government to tighten regulation on some behaviours, especially those which have been proven to be damaging to health. There are many people who lack self-discipline. For example, they smoke, although it is common knowledge that smoking endangers their health. They would not quit smoking, unless the government imposes the tobacco tax and forbids citizens to smoke publicly.

这样转折太强烈, 而且不像是论述类文章。

In my view, the government should be responsible for educating the public about what to do and offering guidance. Many people are not well-informed about how damaging their ways of life can be. For example, office workers will try to exercise regularly, if the government launches campaigns to convey the message that a sedentary job can affect health adversely and reduce life expectancy. Awareness campaigns should also provide information about the health problems caused by eating fast food, so consumers will pay attention to healthy eating and read the nutritional information on food packaging carefully.

前面的中心句说政府需要 educate, 而这里说人们不是 well-informed, 有点自相矛盾, 影响 CC 的成绩。

本节关键学习点

名词性从句在雅思作文里有很广泛的应用。关于名词性从句，我想强调两点：

> 强调 1：要尽量避免写传统套句，如果写也要写得灵活、恰当。
>
> 强调 2：追求高分，如目标为 7～7.5 分的考生要学习如何使用 Wh 词引导的名词性从句。

名词性从句的主要问题是被滥用，一些约定俗成的表达，如 there is no denying that, there is no doubt that, people hold the view that 等，已经被很多考生滥用。这是多年雅思培训行业发展留下的恶习，很多老师教这些句子，告诉考生只要写了就可以增加句子复杂性。问题是考官会觉得考生是生搬硬套，不够自然，反而会觉得你是在背诵，因而扣分。

那么怎么使用这些句子呢？

首先，尽可能不用，如果真要用，也要确保句子前后的内容非常具体，这样考官会觉得你不依赖这些句子，而是会使用这些句型。

其次，某些句子可以从句首的位置转移到句中，这样考官就会觉得你比较灵活，而不是死板地使用。

例如，主体部分第一段的第二句写了 because they believe that these habits can … 还有主体部分第三段的第三句写了 although it is common knowledge that… 这种名词性从句因为位置的变化，感觉就不像套句了。

下面我们说说 Wh 词引导的名词性从句，这些从句主要是以 how, when, what, where, why 引导的。

如主体部分第一段的最后一句话出现了 how to follow the government's lifestyle guideline，而最后一段的第二句出现了 How damaging their ways of life can be.

下面我们说说定语从句。定语从句在雅思考试中有五个主要的应用：

> 应用 1：放在句首替换状语从句。
>
> 应用 2：替换关键的名词（key words）。
>
> 应用 3：where 引导的定语从句解释地点所发生的事情。
>
> 应用 4：非限制性定语从句表示结果。
>
> 应用 5：前面一个单句的最后一个词如果和后面一个单句的第一个名词重复，可以连在一起。

我们下面用这篇文章的一些句子来解释一下：

应用 1：放在句首替换状语从句。

例：If people decide how to live their lives, they will possibly be happier.

可以改写成：People who decide how to live their lives will possibly be happier.

应用 2：替换关键的名词（key words）。

例如，题目说了 lead a healthy life，那么主语可以说 People who are conscious of health may pay attention to fruit and vegetables.

应用 3：where 引导的定语从句解释地点所发生的事情。

例：People may not be able live an active life in large cities where they have to spend most of their time working.

where 引导的定语从句的特点是从句是独立完整的句子。

应用 4：非限制性定语从句表示结果。

例：Some people may pay attention to fruit and vegetables in their diets, which can help them keep fit and increase their confidence in work and social lives.

应用 5：前面一个单句的最后一个词如果和后面一个单句的第一个名词重复，可以连在一起。

例：It is important to tighten regulation on some behaviours. Those behaviours have been proven to be damaging to health.

连在一起，就变成：

It is important to tighten regulation on those behaviours which have been proven to be damaging to health.

值得一提的是，定语从句的使用有很多限制，基础不好的考生如果处理不好，可以不写。我在网课过程中，发现很多学生不懂定语从句的语法，以为加个 which, where 就是定语从句，这是很悲哀的。如果你不写，考官不知道你不懂，还能给你一个 6 分；如果你写了，错了，考官就会扣分。

定语从句使用的常见错误如下。

常见错误 1：关系代词的正确选择对很多考生来说是个问题。初学者在选择关系代词或者关系副词的时候，需要参照下面的表格。

	充当主语	充当宾语
先行词是人	who (or that)	whom (or that) (经常可以省略)
先行词是物	which (or that)	which (or that) (经常可以省略)

例：Unlike the Government, which advocates increasing the amount of money spent on public housing, the private sector considers it inconsistent with the market principles.

错误：政府在这里具备人的性质，应该用 who，而不是用 which。

改正：Unlike the Government, who advocates increasing the amount of money spent on public housing, the private sector considers it inconsistent with the market principles.

翻译：和支持增加公共房屋投资的政府不同，私人机构觉得这和自由市场的规律不符。

常见错误 2：定语从句缺乏谓语动词。

例：Those who overweight or indulge in unhealthy diets are candidates for heart attacks.

错误：从句中的 overweight 是形容词，前面缺一个系动词。

改正：Those who are overweight or indulge in unhealthy diets are candidates for heart attacks.

翻译：那些体重过高或者喜欢不健康饮食的人很有可能会变成心脏病发作者。

常见错误3：如果先行词在从句当中充当主语的定语，那么要用 whose，而不是 which 或者 who。

例：Of those fast-growing countries, China, which economy has been growing at 9 per cent per year, is particularly successful.

错误：先行词 China 作从句主语 economy 的定语，不能用 which。

改正：Of those fast-growing countries, China, whose economy has been growing at 9 per cent per year, is particularly successful.

翻译：在那些快速发展的国家里，中国经济每年增长9%，尤其成功。

常见错误4：关系代词如果是在介词后面，只能用 which 或者 whom，不能用 that。

例：There are plenty of natural resources in China, most of that are unused.

错误：of 是介词，后面不能加 that。

改正：There are plenty of natural resources in China, most of which are unused.

翻译：在中国有很多自然资源，大部分都还没被使用。

常见错误5：定语从句中动词的数应该和先行词的人称保持一致。

例：The elderly, who is normally incapable of looking after themselves, need time and compassion from their family.

错误：先行词是 the elderly，指一类人，是复数名词，类似于 people。

改正：The elderly, who are normally incapable of looking after themselves, need time and compassion from their family.

翻译：老年人通常没有能力照顾自己，需要他们家人付出的时间和宽容。

常见错误6：关系代词 which, that, who, whom 后的句子不完整（缺主语或宾语）；而关系副词 where，when, why 后的句子必定完整。

例：People like shopping on the Boxing Day, when can buy very fashionable commodities at low cost.

错误：关系副词 when 后句子要完整。

改正：People like shopping on the Boxing Day, when they can buy very fashionable commodities at low cost.

翻译：人们喜欢在节礼日购物，那一天他们可以低价购买非常时尚的商品。

常见错误7：限制性定语从句和非限制性定语从句的区别。

标志意义的区别：限制性定语从句先行词后面没有逗号，特指所修饰名词（先行词）的某个部分；

非限制性定语从句先行词后面有逗号，对所修饰名词（先行词）不作任何限定。

例 1：These courses are not appropriate for children, who have learning difficulties.

错误：如果是非限制性定语从句，意味着世界上的小孩都有学习困难。

改正：These courses are not appropriate for children who have learning difficulties.

翻译：这些课程不适合那些有学习困难的小孩。

例 2：International aid should target those impoverished countries which cannot afford any disaster relief.

错误：如果是限制性定语从句，意味着世界上的贫穷国家有两种：一种是不能解决自然灾害的贫穷国家，一种是可以解决的贫穷国家。

改正：International aid should target those impoverished countries, which cannot afford any disaster relief.

翻译：国际援助应该面向那些贫穷国家，这些国家不能提供灾难救援。

常见错误 8：定语从句不能没有主句。

例：People who do not consider it necessary to reduce the use of disposable products.

错误：这句话是 who 引导的定语从句，缺乏主句。

改正：There are many people who do not consider it necessary to reduce the use of disposable products.

翻译：有很多人不觉得有必要去减少使用一次性的产品。

提升的范文

标色的部分是和原文有差异的地方，下划线部分是词伙。

The healthy lifestyle is important because it has a direct bearing on our dignity and well-being. Although many people regard lifestyle choices as a personal matter, I do not think they will adopt a healthy lifestyle unless the government intervenes.

Some people insist that they should have freedom to decide how to live their lives; otherwise, they will be unhappy. They have the incentive to develop and maintain healthy habits believing that these habits can bring enjoyment to their lives. For example, some may increase the intake of fruit and vegetables to keep fit, and if they are confident in their physical appearance, they will have a positive attitude towards life and enjoy a rich social life. Conversely, they will live under enormous pressure, if they are forced to follow the government's lifestyle guideline.

On the other hand, it is sometimes argued that tightening regulation on some behaviours, especially those which have been proven to be damaging to health, is more important. There are many people who lack self-discipline. For example, they smoke, although it is common knowledge that smoking endangers their health. They would not quit smoking, unless the government imposes the tobacco tax and forbids citizens to smoke publicly.

In my view, the government should be responsible for educating the public about what to do and offering guidance. People should be well-informed about how damaging their ways of life can be. For example, office workers will try to exercise regularly, if the government launches campaigns to convey the message that a sedentary job can affect health adversely and reduce life expectancy. Awareness campaigns should also provide information about the health problems caused by eating fast food, so consumers will pay attention to healthy eating and read the nutritional information on food packaging carefully.

3.9.5 全文翻译 22：工作稳定＋标点符号

> *Today, people do not always work for the same job. Why does it happen and how do people prepare for job insecurity?*

题目大意

如今，人们并非总是做一个工作。这个事情为什么发生？人们如何为工作不稳定准备？

读者自学步骤 1

阅读题目后，写出三个观点。

下面是我学生写的一些错误或者不好的观点，大家可以看看自己是不是也犯了同样的错误。

学生的观点	点评
科技迅速发展，信息传播快，工作机会增加，人们换工作容易。	逻辑不好。信息传播快，不代表工作机会就多，只是你知道更多的工作机会而已。
和同事关系不好，无法有效合作，工作不顺，换工作。	不够有力。关系不好是个人的行为，现在和过去都有可能存在。
公司招聘含有夸张成分，工作没有发展前景，换工作。	不够有力。观点最好不要用个例，最好是描述一个现象。
当前工作压力太大，换一份轻松的职业，有更多的时间陪伴家人。	跑题。这个题目不讨论换工作的好处或坏处。
选择稳定工作的人容易有安全感，与同事合作更为顺利和愉快，容易被公司提拔。	严重跑题。这个题目不讨论稳定工作的好处或坏处。
家庭原因，回家乡发展。	不够有力。有几个人是真正因为要回家发展，从而换工作的。
调整心态，增加技能，适应各种环境，找到好工作。	两个观点混在一起。心态马上就可以调节，增加技能需要时间，两者最好不要放在一起说。
签合同，保障员工的权益，保证工作稳定。	跑题。现在不是讨论雇主能做什么，而是讨论员工能做什么。
对工作有激情，以积极的态度面对工作，有保障。	不够有力。工作不是光有激情就可以的，而且激情也应该是必需的能力。

读者自学步骤 2

翻译下面的句子：在翻译过程中，记住先想词伙，再想句型，然后写出句子。 相关词伙可以查阅微信公众号：gu_writing。

介绍段

背景句	1. 在这个快速变化的世界里，似乎期望得到一份永久的工作不再是现实的。
阐述立场	2. 他们可能自己决定要换工作，或者是被解雇。他们需要做一些事情去为工作的变化做准备。

主体部分第一段

中心句（社会和经济）	3. 商业世界有那么多不可预测的因素，以至于很多公司，即便是那些曾经雇用上万员工的公司，也可能随时倒闭。
原因 1	4. 有时候，特别是经济衰退的时候，公司要裁员去减少运营成本，人们因此失业。
原因 2	5. 科技发展如此之快，以至于很多人的技能不能够及时提高去适应新的雇主要求。
举例	6. 例如，很多人因为不熟悉最新的软件而跟不上工作节奏，因此也可能失去工作。

主体部分第二段

附加观点（社会文化）	7. 人们现在也希望自己有一个比较丰富的职业生涯，所以他们不断换工作。
解释	8. 他们希望为不同的公司工作，发现自己的才能和优点，能够挖掘自己的潜能。
举例 1	9. 他们有时候也会希望在更大的公司工作，可以提高自己的技能，获得更高的收入。
举例 2	10. 他们或者选择为创业公司工作，在那里可以承担更多责任。

主体部分第三段

中心句	11. 因为工作前景的不稳定，在职人士需要注意两点。
观点	12. 我们需要不断提高自己的技能，接受教育和工作培训，确保自己可以适应一个不断改变的工作环境。
举例	13. 例如，很多人目前都学习第二语言，因为在很多公司，国际化是一个明显的趋势。

| 附加观点 | 14. 我们需要注意个人储蓄，以帮助我们更好地处理失业带来的经济问题。 |
| | 15. 事实上，如果有足够的储蓄，有些人甚至可以尝试自营，将自己的一些想法付诸实践。 |

结论段

| 总结观点 | 16. 简而言之，变化莫测的经济环境和不可停止的技术发展解释了工作机会的不可预测性。 |
| | 17. 比较好的解决方法包括在职培训和理财。 |

读者自学步骤 3

检查自己的翻译：先看正确句子的词伙和句子结构，然后看错误的句子，看是否能够发现问题。

句 1

正：In this rapidly changing world, it is no longer realistic to expect to have a permanent job.

学生的句子：In this rapid changing world, it is no longer realistic to expect to have a permanent job.

改：rapid 是形容词，不能修饰分词 changing。

句 2

正：They may decide to change their jobs or they may be dismissed. They should take action to cope with the challenges of job insecurity.

学生的句子：They normally make a decision to change their job or be fired by their employers. Thereby they need to take some action for their job insecurity.

改：thereby 一般放在句子中间，后面加分词结构。

句 3

正：There are so many unpredictable factors in the business world that large companies which used to employ thousands of people are likely to go bankrupt.

学生的句子：In commercial area, there are so many unpredicted factors that even large company which once employed thousands of people are likely to go bankrupt.

改：没有 commercial area 这个说法；company 是可数名词，要用复数形式。

句 4

正：Sometimes, especially in times of economic recession, companies have to lay off some employees in order to reduce the running cost, which means that a large number of people will lose their jobs.

学生的句子：Sometimes, especially during deep economic recession, companies have to reduce the staff in order to cut down running cost, which means that a large number of people would lose their jobs.

改：cost 是可数名词，要加冠词。

句 5

正：Technology has been developing so fast that many people have failed to upgrade their skills to meet the requirements of their employers.

学生的句子：The technology has been developing rapidly so that the skill of many people cannot adapt to the requirements of their employers in time.

改：一般 so that 的 so 会放在形容词或者副词前，而不是在后面；adapt to the requirements 搭配不当。

句 6

正：For example, many people lose employment because they do not have the knowledge about the newest generation of software and cannot keep pace with the changes in the workplace.

学生的句子：For example, many people cannot follow the working pace because they are not familiar with advanced softwares, thus losing their employments.

改：software 和 employment 都是不可数名词。

句 7

正：Many people today are also interested in a varied career, thereby switching jobs from time to time.

学生的句子：On the other hand, workforces change jobs frequently, as they are willing to have a colourful career.

改：workforce 这个词很少用复数形式。

句 8

正：They work for different companies in order to discover their own talents and fulfil their potential.

学生的句子：These people might find out their talent and advantages when they are working for different companies, which enables them to tap their potentials.

改：talent 在这里可以用复数；这里定语从句指代不清楚，不知是修饰整句话，还是 companies；potential 是不可数名词。

句 9

正：Sometimes, they work for large companies, where they can improve skills and increase earnings.

学生的句子：Sometimes, they also want to work at a giant business to further their skills and acquire higher incomes.

改：further skills, acquire income 都是错误的搭配，要注意词伙。

句 10

正：Meanwhile, some people may choose to work for start-ups, in which they are trusted with more responsibilities.

学生的句子：They may choose to work for startups where they can take more responsibilities.

改：这里用非限制性定语从句可能更好，形容所有的创业公司。

句 11

正：Because of the uncertainty about job prospects, working adults have to pay attention to two major issues.

学生的句子：Because of unstable job prospect, they need to pay attention to two things.

改：prospect 应该用复数形式。

句 12

正：We should sharpen our skills and receive education to ensure that we can adapt to an ever-changing world.

学生的句子：We need to boost our skills continually, such as receiving education and training, and ensure that we can adjust to this rapidly changing work situation.

改：boost skills 这个搭配不对；receiving education 不能够修饰 skills；ensure that 的主语不应该是 we。

句 13

正：For example, many people today have sought to acquire a second language because many companies operate in a globalised world.

学生的句子：For instance, many people are learning second language because the globalisation is a main trend in many companies.

改：language 是可数名词，要加冠词；globalisation 是不可数名词，不需要加定冠词。

句 14

正：We should also save money to cope with all financial matters arising from unemployment.

学生的句子：Meanwhile, we should have money saving awareness which could provide us with financial support when we are unemployed.

改：money saving awareness 用法很奇怪；限制性定语从句修饰不恰当。

句 15

正：In fact, with sufficient savings, some people can even run their own businesses to put their ideas into practice.

学生的句子：In fact, people can even start their own business if they have sufficient savings and put ideas into practice.

改：put ideas into practice 产生歧义，不知道是和 start 对称，还是和 have sufficient savings 对称。

句 16

正：To summarise, the turbulent business environment and the unstoppable technological progress have accounted for the unpredictability of the job market.

学生的句子：To put it simply, turbulent economic environment and unstoppable technological development have explained the unpredictability of job opportunities.

改：environment 是可数名词，要加冠词。

句 17

正：Solutions to these problems include job training and sound financial planning.

学生的句子: Some better ways are available, including the working trainings and the financial management.

改: training 一般不可数。

读者自学步骤 4

整体学习和检查范文, 看看是否符合 TELCCS 原则。

范文全文 (7~7.5 分)

In this rapidly changing world, it is no longer realistic to expect to have a permanent job. They may decide to change their jobs or they may be dismissed. They should take action to cope with the challenges of job insecurity.

> 这个 they 指代不清楚。

There are so many unpredictable factors in the business world that large companies which used to employ thousands of people are likely to go bankrupt. Sometimes, especially in times of economic recession, companies have to lay off some employees in order to reduce the running cost, which means that a large number of people will lose their jobs. Technology has been developing so fast that many people have failed to upgrade their skills to meet the requirements of their employers. For example, many people lose employment because they do not have the knowledge about the newest generation of software and cannot keep pace with the changes in the workplace.

> 这个中心句不能总结主体部分的内容, 影响 CC 的分数。

> 又说 many people, 和前面的重复。

Many people today are also interested in a varied career, thereby switching jobs from time to time. They work for different companies in order to discover their own talents and fulfil their potential. Sometimes, they work for large companies where they can improve skills and increase earnings. Meanwhile, some people may choose to work for start-ups, in which they are trusted with more responsibilities.

> 这里的分词结构有点牵强, 不是说对职业变化有兴趣, 就必然换工作。

> 这里的连接词不是很好, 影响 CC 分数。

Because of the uncertainty about job prospects, working adults have to pay attention to two major issues. We should sharpen our skills and receive education to ensure that we can adapt to an ever-changing world. For example, many people today have sought to acquire a

> 代词和前面的 working adults 不匹配。

> 第二段已经出现了 for example, 有点重复。

second language because many companies operate in a globalised world. We should also save money to cope with all financial matters arising from unemployment. In fact, with sufficient savings, some people can even run their own businesses to put their ideas into practice.

代词突然变成 we，而且说的是第二个分论点，最好要有连接词替换。

这里 CC 有问题，和中心句的 uncertainty 不够一致，影响 CC 的分数。

To summarise, the turbulent business environment and the unstoppable technological progress have accounted for the unpredictability of the job market. Solutions to these problems include job training and sound financial planning.

本节关键学习点

我们这一节说一下雅思大作文评分标准最后一件比较重要的事情，Punctuation，也就是标点符号。

雅思大作文常用的标点符号只有三个：逗号（，）、句号（。）和分号（；）。句号和分号在语法上功能差不多，都类似于连词，用于连接句子，区别在于分号在语气上停顿比较短，而句号停顿比较长。

而逗号用法差异比较大。差异主要体现在下面几点：

> 差异 1：分号和句号都类似于连词，连接两个独立的句子，而逗号不可以。
>
> 差异 2：逗号如果连接两个独立的句子，中间要有并列连词 and 或者 or, but 等。
>
> 差异 3：连接副词 moreover, consequently, also, even, however 等使用的时候，只有前面加了分号或者句号，才可以连接独立的句子。
>
> 差异 4：分号和句号前后一定是独立的句子，因此，如果后面只有一个状语从句，就是错误的。
>
> 差异 5：逗号决定了限制性定语从句和非限制性定语从句的区别。

差异 1：分号和句号都类似于连词，连接两个独立的句子，而逗号不可以。

换言之，独立的句子中间不能用逗号，只能用分号和句号连接。

例：Companies have to lay off some employees; it can reduce the running cost.

这两个句子是独立的主谓宾结构，中间只能用句号或者分号，用逗号就是错的。

差异 2：逗号如果连接两个独立的句子，中间要有并列连词 and 或者 or, but 等。

例：They may decide to change their jobs, or they may be dismissed.

这是两个独立的句子，如果中间的并列连词 or 去掉，只有逗号，这个句子就错了。

差异 3：连接副词 moreover, consequently, also, even, however 等使用的时候，只有前面加

了分号或者句号，才可以连接独立的句子。

例：In times of economic recession, companies have to lay off some employees in order to reduce the running cost; in addition, any people have failed to upgrade their skills.

这里有两个独立的句子，而 in addition 是连接副词，而不是连接词，因此前面如果用逗号就是错的，只能用分号或者是句号。

差异 4：分号和句号前后一定是独立的句子，因此，如果后面只有一个状语从句，就是错误的。

例：Many people lose employment. Because they do not have the knowledge about the newest generation of software.

这句话是错误的，because 引导的是一个状语从句，不是一个独立的句子，前面不能用句号，只能用逗号。

差异 5：逗号决定了限制性定语从句和非限制性定语从句的区别。

非限制性定语从句的标志就是从句前有个逗号，可能修饰前面整句话，也可能修饰前面的一个动词或者名词。

例：They may discover their talents and strengths when working for different companies, which can help them achieve potential.

这句话 which 前面加了逗号，是因为从句修饰的是前面的 discover talents and strengths，而不是限定 companies；如果不加逗号，就会产生歧义。

提升的范文

标色的部分是和原文有差异的地方，下划线部分是词伙。

In this rapidly changing world, it is no longer realistic to expect to have a permanent job. People should take action to cope with the challenges of job insecurity, whether they decide to change their jobs or they are dismissed by their employers.

There are so many unpredictable factors in the world of work that employers have to downsize the workforce. For example, in the times of economic recession, companies have to lay off some employees in order to reduce the running cost, which means that a large number of people will lose their jobs. Technology has been developing so fast that many people have failed to upgrade their skills to meet the requirements of their employers. Some of them may lose employment, for example, for the simple reason that they do not have the knowledge about the newest generation of software and cannot keep pace with the changes in the workplace.

Another reason why few people expect to stay in the same job for a lifetime is that they are interested in a varied career. They work for different companies in order to discover their own talents and fulfil their potential. While some prefer to work for large companies, where they can improve skills and increase earnings, some may choose to work for start-ups, in which they are trusted with more responsibilities.

Because of the uncertainty about job prospects, working adults have to pay attention to two major issues. They should sharpen their skills and receive education to ensure that they can adapt to an ever-changing world. One example is the popularity of attending courses to <u>acquire a second language</u> because many companies operate <u>in a globalised world</u>. In addition to this, they should save money to <u>cope with all financial matters</u> arising from unemployment. With sufficient savings, they can even run their own businesses, if they fail to find employment.

To summarise, the <u>turbulent business environment</u> and the unstoppable <u>technological progress</u> have accounted for the unpredictability of the job market. Solutions to these problems include job training and <u>sound financial planning</u>.

3.10 雅思大作文考生常问问题和误区

3.10.1 雅思大作文考生常问问题

雅思作文考试和国内的考试有很大区别。很多老师对雅思作文不了解，一直用国内考试的观念去教学生，导致中国很多考生对作文有很多误解，问的很多问题其实都不是雅思考查的重点。我在微博和微信上多次回答这些问题，在这里统一再回答一次。

问题1：开头段是不是要写三句话：背景、改写题目和自己的看法？

回答：不是。雅思从来不规定开头段写多少句话。背景可写可不写。

问题2：观点类或者论述类文章的开头段是不是一定要给出自己的看法？

回答：不是。但是我个人习惯和很多考官范文都是在首段给出自己的立场。

问题3：文章是不是要换一些词分数才更高？

回答：不是。单词首先要准确，然后才可以考虑变化。如果不确定，就不要变。我们上课的时候教学生换"表达"，而不是换"词"。

下表是一些我在教学过程中看到的学生常犯的错误。

proliferation 不是 increase 的同义词	proliferation 经常是形容可以复制和迅速扩展的东西，如 networks, weapons 等。
increment 不是 increased 的同义词	increment 常指幅度很小的改变。
teenager 不是 childen 的同义词	teenager 是十几岁的少年，而 children 是 12 岁以下的孩子。
along with 不是 with 的同义词	along with 是 "together with" 的意思。
contradiction 不是 conflict 的同义词	contradiction 常指言语的自相矛盾。
imperative 不是 important 的同义词	imperative 虽然有 "重要的" 意思，但是也常有 "迫切的" 意思。
perspective 不是 perception 的同义词	perspective 是 "角度" 的意思。
attributed to 不是 contribute to 的同义词	attributed to 是 "归咎于" 的意思。
requirement 不是 demand 的替换词	requirement 是 "要求" 的意思，而 demand 是 "需求" 的意思。

measurement 不是 measure 的替换词	measurement 是 "测量" 的意思。
propogate 不是 promote 的替换词	propogate 一般有贬义，指的是政治宣传。
conducive 不是 beneficial 的替换词	conducive 常用于形容环境或者条件方便人们做某事。
kids 不是 children 的替换词	kids 不是正式的表达。
demerit 不是 disadvantage 的替换词	demerit 一般和 merit 连用的时候，可以表达 "disadvantage" 的意思。
curriculum 不是 course 的替换词	curriculum 是 "教学大纲" 的意思。
technique 不是 technology 的替换词	technique 是 "技巧" 的意思，不是 "技术"。
prone 不是 likely 的替换词	prone to 后面可以加名词，加动词一般是加不好的事情，而 likely 没有这个限制。

问题 4：主体部分是不是一定要用连接词 firstly, secondly, thirdly, furthermore 等？

回答：不是。句子连接方法非常多样，请参考 3.7.3。

问题 5：观点类的文章 (do you agree or disagree) 是否只能支持或者反对，不能说两个不同的观点，否则就 "立场不坚定"？

回答：不是。你需要给出你的立场，但是你的立场不是说一定要完全支持或者完全反对。考官不会在乎你的立场，只要你的立场和主体部分的论述保持一致就可以。

问题 6：如果支持某个立场，是不是观点越多越好，而相反的观点越少越好？

回答：不是。观点数量一样也是可以的。雅思考官范文甚至有一篇文章是相反的观点比支持的观点要多。考官看的还是你的观点论述的质量，而不是数量。

问题 7：文章是不是字数越多，分数越高？字数不够，肯定不过？

回答：不是。考官在乎的是你写的文章的质量，而不是数量。字数不够，分数会有影响，但是不大。我们有很多考生字数不够，最后也获得 7 分的。

问题 8：文章主体段落的中心句是不是不能很长？

回答：不是。考官范文也有很长的中心句。只要句子清晰易懂就可以，长度不是考量的因素。

问题 9：结尾是不是应该要有一定的 "升华" 和展望，或者提出解决方法？

回答：不是。雅思作文和西方书面语结尾一般就是总结观点。你可以 "升华"，或者提出解决方法，但是这不是必须的。

问题 10：作文的格式到底是每段空一行的方式，还是第一句话空格的方式好？

回答：我自己考试的时候，比较喜欢空行的方式。这不重要。你雅思不通过，主要的问题在于主体部分内容，格式的影响微乎其微。

问题 11：大作文主体部分写几段为好？是不是 2 段比 3 段好？

回答：2～3段。

《剑8》和《剑9》的文章一般是主体部分3段，我们上课时也是要求3段为主。2段也是可以的。

雅思考试考查 paragraphing 的能力。换言之，如果你的主体部分只有1段，考官会扣分。

如果你分了很多段，但是不合理，段落之间又没有很好的连接，也会扣分。

问题 12：大作文主体部分是不是每段最后一句话要写个总结，去扣题？

回答：不一定。因为中心句已经扣题。

有时候，如果考生在段落末尾加一句总结，用词和中心句差不多，还会导致重复的问题，失去 CC 的分数。

问题 13：是不是 first and foremost 和 initially 比 firstly，nevertheless 比 however 更容易提高分数？

回答：不是。

雅思的连接词使用一般不影响词汇的分数，而是影响连接性的分数。换言之，考官只看连接词是否准确使用，而不看其是否复杂而多变。

问题 14：to summarise, in conclusion, to sum up 这样的词已经泛滥，是否需要创造新颖的表达？

回答：否。这种词组用于议论文已经几百年，中国考生没有必要创新。考官不会因为有一些新颖的表达而加分。

问题 15：是不是雅思作文最好不要用 we, I？

回答：不是。

在观点类和论述类的话题里，使用"I"基本上是不可避免的。使用"we"也可以。但一般不用第二人称。

问题 16：大作文是不是每段话都举例就不好了？

回答：不是。

考官对举例的个数不感兴趣，关键是例子的质量和扣题。

问题 17：雅思作文是不是观点最好标新立异，才可能获得高分？

回答：不是。

观点不需要很特别，只要论述细致，用词准确，表达清楚，语法正确就可以获得高分。如果一个特别的观点没有很好的论述，考官只会觉得很费解。

问题 18：字数不够的时候，可不可以杜撰一些数据或者调查结果作为论述手段？

回答：未必。这是一种投机取巧的作弊。假设这个方法行得通，那么全体考生都可以捏造数据来写够字数，就不用具体论述了。

问题 19：在报告类（cause & solution）的话题里，可以不可以把原因和解决方法写在一起？

回答：最好不要。

这样不好写中心句，而且扣题比较难。题目一般是问两个问题，那就分段落回答原因和解决方法。

问题 20：在报告类（cause & solution）的话题里，到底是原因还是解决方法重要？哪个该写多一点?

回答: 没有谁比谁重要, 只要两者都写了, 就是扣题。

问题 *21*: 雅思写作是用英式拼写, 还是美式? 例如是 personalise, 还是 personalize ?

回答: 最好用英式。如果真用了美式, 也不会很影响成绩。毕竟, 大部分考生有太多的作文问题会被扣分。

	American English	British English
-or vs. -our	color	colour
	favorite	favourite
-ze vs. -se	urbanize	urbanise
	industrialize	industrialise
-ll vs. -l	fulfill	fulfil
	skillful	skilful
-er vs. -re	center	centre
	theater	theatre
-ense vs. -ence	defense	defence
	license	licence
-ling vs. -lling	quarreling	quarrelling
	traveling	travelling
-ed vs. -t	leaped	leapt
	learned	learnt

问题 *22*: 雅思大作文是否可以使用 idiom ?

回答: 否。雅思大作文是考查书面写作的能力。idiom 一般用于口语交流。

问题 *23*: 雅思大作文使用 the more...the more... 句型是否可以加分?

回答: 否。雅思大作文考查复杂句的写作能力, 但是不代表一定要写倒装句, the more...the more... 句型, 还有强调句才可以得到好成绩。反之, 如果考生这些句子没有写对或者是写恰当, 就会被扣分。

问题 *24*: 使用被动语态是否可以加分?

回答: 否。被动语态是一种很普通的语法点, 也没有什么丰富的变化。而在书面语里, 主动语态是优于被动语态的。这和中国很多老师的观念不同。

问题 *25*: 雅思大作文是否需要使用感叹号和问号来增加句子的变化?

回答: 否。从剑桥雅思公布的历年范文来看, 很少出现感叹号和问号。

问题 *26*: 雅思大作文可否使用缩写?

回答: 否。don't 要改成 do not, isn't 要改成 is not 等。

3.10.2 中国考生写雅思作文的 10 大常见误区

误区 1：写够字数很重要，否则没机会通过。

事实：雅思作文确实对字数有要求，但是这只是很多量分因素中的一个，如果你写的作文其他方面都很好，如用词和内容，即便字数不够，拿 7 分也是可能的。老顾有太多的考生写的字数不够，但最后也通过的。

误区 2：字数越多，分数越高。

事实：雅思没有安慰分和奖励分一说。文章的质量决定分数。如果字数越多分数越高，那你下一次背好两篇文章，直接写上去，写 800 单词，看看能得几分。

误区 3：换词可以加分，不管怎么换。

事实：考官会看考生是否能够用不同方式去表达同一件事情，也就是表达的变化是写作能力的一个体现。但是前提是你的表达变化是准确的、地道的。否则，考官只会扣分。

例如 receive treatment，有些考生觉得 receive 太简单，写成 acquire treatment。这个考生就是 5.5 分级别的考生，为什么？因为英文很烂，烂到不知道 acquire 和 treatment 不能连用。

误区 4：写复杂句（包括 the more...the more... 句型）和分词结构可以加分。

事实：句子变化是能体现一个人的写作能力，但是如果你的复杂句有错误，考官会扣分，而不是加分。使用不恰当，例如套句，不该用的地方粗暴出现，那么也会被扣分。

很多同学喜欢用定语从句，如 "where have..."，这就是 5.5 分的水平。因为 where 引导的定语从句后面是独立的句子，不可能缺乏主语。考官不是因为你用了 where 就给分，而是看你用得对不对，恰当不恰当。

误区 5：语法不重要，关键是单词和内容够牛。

事实：句子结构不对，语法错误多，哪怕是你用多高端的词，多好的内容都是 5.5 分。道理很简单，哪怕中文也是如此。如果通篇白字，写的句法不通，虽然你用唐诗宋词，旁征博引，但是读者觉得你连基本的文化都没有，更不要说水平多高了。

误区 6：词伙和大词多用可以加分。

事实：作文不是单词比赛。作文的目的是交流。中文那些著名的小说、著名的诗歌、著名的议论文，哪一篇里面是一堆大词，一堆词伙，一堆成语？

好的文章是内容的充实，句子的流畅，用词的恰当。

考官永远不是看单词的"出现"而给分，而是看单词的"使用"而给分。

误区 7：一定要加上连接词 in addition, furthermore, for example 才可以满足雅思评分要求。

事实：雅思作文不是一个走形式的考试，考官不是机器，看到一些连接词就给分。如果你使用了不准确的连接词，考官会觉得使用得非常死板 mechanical，反而会扣分。

例如很多考生以为 furthermore 是表示递进、结果的连接词，事实上，这个连接词一般是引出一个并列的、新的分论点。

误区 8：结构很重要，只要结构好，基本上可以通过。

事实：雅思考查分段的能力，但是不是说一篇文章写了 2 段或者 3 段，又或者是什么段落长一点或者短一点分数会更高。

再次强调，雅思不是一个走形式的考试。

考官主要是看学生用词、论述、审题、扣题、灵活使用句子的能力。这些都是内功，不是表面的几个架势就可以替代的。

误区 9：背网络上的范文，比自己写的作文要好。

事实：雅思其实考到一个基本的分数如 6 分，6.5 分并不需要你有多大的词汇量，多复杂的语法，多惊人的观点。

很多网络上所谓"名师"写的范文，其实有很多小错误，只是用一些大词和复杂句骗一下基础不好的学生。这些文章往往逻辑不好，不扣题。这些"名师"其实本身都没有在雅思考试中考出过理想的成绩。

误区 10：雅思作文可以预测中原题，平时多背范文就可以。

事实：从 2005 年到 2017 年，雅思大作文出现过 500 多道题目，剑桥雅思每次出题大概 30% 是从这些旧题里抽，大概 30% 会出现新题（也就是历史上没考过的题目），还有 40% 是一些老题重新改变字眼之后再考（这种题目陷阱最多，往往考查考生审题和扣题的能力）。

在 2014 年和 2015 年，因为剑桥雅思怀疑中国大陆地区的考卷提前泄露，进行了大规模的学生答卷抽查，推迟了公布成绩。而澳大利亚和中国香港考区 2015 年开始和中国大陆地区使用不同的考卷，另外还有一些考场开始执行考前打印作文题，包括剑桥雅思酝酿的机考。所有这一切，目的都在于杜绝任何个人和机构提前获得作文题目。

换言之，预测到原题或者考前获得原题的机会基本上是零。请广大雅思考生拒绝被骗，不要再相信网络上盛传的预测必中，或者是考前漏题。

这也是为什么我现在的备考策略有所改变。在上课的时候，现在都不再预测题目，而是预测话题，因为雅思常考的话题相对来说还是比较少的，大概只有 48 个。考生只要熟悉这些话题的观点和相关词伙，然后提高审题和扣题的能力就可以了。

3.11 总结（手把手教你作文范例）（《剑 11》题目）

大作文部分我就讲到这里。

希望大家通过之前的内容，可以熟悉：① 雅思 Task 2 作文主要考什么？② 怎么做才可以达到这个标准？

通过句子翻译练习和 22 篇全文翻译练习，我也相信很多考生提高了语法，增加了词伙。

那么，现在我会使用《剑 11》的一个题目，写一篇作文，帮助大家复习一下之前的内容。与此同时，我尝试将自己的整个写作过程和思路写了下来，这样大家可以看到我在 40 分钟之内是怎么完成一篇高质量的文章的，也可以看到我是如何确保这篇文章满足雅思作文四个评分标准的。

> *Some people claim that not enough of the waste from homes is recycled. They say that the only way to increase recycling is for governments to make it a legal requirement. To what extent do you think laws are needed to make people recycle more of their waste?*

完成的思路和步骤：

第一步：审题 和评分标准 TR 有关	我首先确认这是一个观点类题目，因为有 to what extent do you think。 一般遇到观点类题目，我要看看题目主要讨论的观点是什么。标志词可能是 they think, they argue that, they say that。 这个题目主要关注的观点是 "the only way to increase recycling is for governments to make it a legal requirement"， 大概的意思 "政府只有立法才可能让大家回收利用垃圾"。 这个时候，我基本上确定题目关键词是 recycle waste, make laws。这些关键词将会不断在文章中出现，确保扣题。 注意：如果一些考生讨论 recycle waste 的好处，或者是 waste 的坏处，那就跑题了，因为这个题目只关心如何能够让大家去 recycle waste。
第二步：想观点 和评分标准 TR 有关 考场上大概 3 分钟	想观点不是这本书的内容，大家可以查阅《顾家北手把手教你雅思词伙》，我用的是里面的一个百搭观点。 支持的观点：立法，大量扔垃圾会有一定惩罚，人们因此会回收垃圾。 反对的观点 1：增加宣传，让大家知道垃圾的危害，大家努力回收垃圾。 反对的观点 2：增加设施，让大家很容易回收垃圾，从而促进这个行为。 大家会发现，每个观点我都关注回收垃圾，这是题目的重点。 其实，还有其他观点，如政府给大家一些奖励，大家因此去回收垃圾，但是我没有写，因为觉得不好拓展；在考场上，永远是写自己最熟悉和最容易拓展的观点。
第三步：写开头段/介绍段 和评分标准 TR, LR 和 GRA 有关 考场上大概 5 分钟	我准备写两句，一句是背景，毕竟垃圾问题是每个城市都有的大问题。第一句话背景，写完 threat to the environment，我觉得略显单调，所以通过 especially in cities 来引出一个定语从句，从而增加句子变化。 句 1：Household waste has become a threat to the environment, especially in large cities where many consumers now tend to buy more than they need. 第二句话把立场说一下。要注意扣题，出现关键词（或者替换词）household waste, recycle waste, legislation。 句 2：In order to encourage them to recycle waste, governments should adopt a number of approaches, in addition to legislation.

	大家会发现，在词汇方面，我一如既往地依赖词伙 household waste, a threat to the environment, recycle waste, adopt approaches。
第四步：写主体部分第一段 和四个评分标准都有直接关系 考场上大概 9 分钟	首先我要想一下先写什么观点，因为开头段我说了 legislation，我决定顺着写，然后下面一段再转折。 然后我要想拓展：为什么法律管用？什么样的法律管用？ 来个中心句，一定要说清楚法律这个观点，然后要围绕垃圾处理去写。 句 3：Laws can be enforced to punish those who do not dispose of rubbish in an environmentally friendly way, thereby prompting all people to reduce the waste they produce. 然后解释一下为什么，注意不能重复，要具体解释。 句 4：They would be more environmentally conscious in treating waste, because of the legal consequences. 然后举例，举例一定要具体，具体说什么样的法律，什么样的惩罚，不能够泛泛而谈。 句 5：For example, they may have to pay extra fees when they produce excessive waste, and those families who do not separate rubbish and put recyclable items, including paper, glass, bottles and electrical equipment, in respective rubbish bins, will be fined. 因为这两个例子写得比较长，我就没有继续往下写。 不难看到，我主要是通过代词 they 和连接词 for example 来连接句子。 在变化表达的过程中，我注意了扣题，每句话都出现关键词 dispose of rubbish, waste management, separate waste。 除了使用 rubbish 这个直接替换词，我还使用了一些具体的例子，如 plastic，来避免单词的重复。
第五步：写主体部分第二段 和四个评分标准都有直接关系	第二段上来要记住转折，要注意连接，因为我不否认法律的重要性，所以转折的时候避免用 however 这个比较强烈的词。 句 6：While tough rules can change behaviour, it is also important to educate the public about the impact of waste on the environment. 下面我会去解释一下为什么提高人们的意识很重要。很多同学会反复说提高意识很重要，但是并不解释为什么。

	句7：People would not make an effort to go green, if they did not realise that waste could cause pollution, contaminate water and damage the environment.
	你会发现，即便说环境的影响，我也会说得非常具体。
	下面就是举例，要举具体的例子，我会说什么垃圾可以回收，不回收会产生什么影响。
	句8：Everybody should be aware that plastic bottles and cans, if not recycled, will end up in landfill sites, and that the toxic substances contained in these items can cause serious environmental problems.
	在写这个句子的时候，我不仅注意关键词 recycled，还注意用替换词 environmental problems 替换之前的 environmental impact, damage the environment。
	同时，我还通过重复一些单词的方法来增加句子的连接，用 everybody 指代前面的 people, be aware 指代前面的 realise。
	当然还有代词 these，these items 指代前面的 bottles and cans，也增加了句子的联系。
第六步：写主体部分第三段 和四个评分标准都有直接关系	第三段和第二段是一个并列的观点，因此要注意有并列的连接词。
	句9：It is also necessary to increase recycling facilities in communities.
	然后你会发现我将 recycling 和 facilities 连在一起，既中心句扣题，也比较灵活地避免了 recycle waste 的重复。
	下面可以直接举例，因为我觉得有设施可以更好地回收垃圾是一个常识，没什么好解释的。
	句10：Supermarkets and shopping malls can put bottle banks in prominent positions to collect bottles from passers-by, while colour-coded recycling bins can help people separate waste more easily.
	这里我写了两个很具体的例子，bottle banks（玻璃瓶收集处），colour-coded bins（带颜色的垃圾箱），这些单词都属于主题相关词汇（topic specific vocabulary），考官是会额外加分的。
	这个时候，我觉得很难具体地说什么样的垃圾可以回收，会和前面内容重复。重复是低分考生最普遍的问题，也是希望获得7分的考生一定要避免的错误。因此，我决定对比一下题目所说的法律，从而做到扣题。

	句 11: Without these facilities, they could not play a bigger part in the waste pre-treatment process, even though they understand it is a legal requirement to recycle waste effectively.
	大家会发现我再一次使用 these, they 这些代词，悄无声息地完成了句子的连接。
第七步：写结尾段 / 结论段 和四个评分标准都有直接关系	结尾段 / 结论段主要是总结主要的立场，观点不需要全部总结，注意用词扣题之余，不要重复。
	句 12: To conclude, setting tougher standards is one effective way to promote recycling, but awareness campaigns and investment in facilities are equally important.
	结尾段不是很重要，如果时间不够，可以不写，也记住不要加入新的内容和信息。

下面是整篇范文，总共 291 个字，比较长，主要是我的例子比较具体。

Household waste has become a threat to the environment, especially in large cities where many consumers now tend to buy more than they need. In order to encourage them to recycle waste, governments should adopt a number of approaches, in addition to legislation.

Laws can be enforced to punish those who do not dispose of rubbish in an environmentally friendly way, thereby prompting all people to reduce the waste they produce. They would be more environmentally conscious in waste management, because of the legal consequences. For example, they may have to pay extra fees when they produce excessive waste, and those families who do not separate rubbish and put recyclable items, including paper, glass, bottles and electrical equipment, in respective rubbish bins, will be fined.

While tough rules can change behaviour, it is also important to educate the public about the impact of waste on the environment. People would not make an effort to go green, if they did not realise that waste could cause pollution, contaminate water and damage the environment. Everybody should be aware that plastic bottles and cans, if not recycled, will end up in landfill sites, and that the toxic substances contained in these items can cause serious environmental problems.

It is also necessary to increase recycling facilities in communities. Supermarkets and shopping malls can put bottle banks in prominent positions to collect bottles from passers-by, while colour-coded recycling bins can help people separate waste more easily. Without these facilities, they could not play a bigger part in the waste pre-treatment process, even though they understand it is a legal requirement to recycle waste effectively.

To conclude, setting tougher standards is one effective way to promote recycling, but awareness campaigns and investment in facilities are equally important.

大家也可以通过下面的中文思路，自己写一次，或者大声说一次英文，加深记忆，并且更加深入地学习范文。

介绍段

背景句	家庭垃圾已经成为一个环境问题，尤其是在大城市，人们购买的东西已经超越了他们的实际所需。
阐述立场或说明文章讨论内容	政府应该采取一些措施，包括立法，来鼓励他们回收废物。

主体部分第一段

中心句	政府可以出台法律去惩罚那些处理垃圾时不够环保的人，因此促进所有人减少他们制造的垃圾。
解释	因为法律后果，他们在处理垃圾的时候会更有环保意识。
举例	例如，当他们产生过量的垃圾时，他们需要额外付费；垃圾不分类的家庭，也就是不将可回收物品，包括纸、玻璃、瓶子和电子设备，放到不同的垃圾箱里的家庭，会被罚款。

主体部分第二段

中心句	严厉的法规可以改变行为，但是教育公众关于垃圾对环境的影响也很重要。
解释	如果人们不能意识到垃圾会导致污染、污染水源并且破坏环境，他们就不会致力于环保。
举例	所有人都应该意识到如果不回收塑料瓶、罐，这些物品最后会到达垃圾填埋场，这些物品里含有的有毒物质会造成严重的环境问题。

主体部分第三段

中心句	在社区增加回收设备也同样重要。
解释	超市和商场可以把瓶子收集箱放在显眼的位置，来收集路过人的瓶子，同时彩色标签的回收箱可以帮助人们更好地区分废物。
举例	没有这些设施，人们不能在垃圾预处理中发挥更大的作用，即使他们了解回收废物是法律规定。

结论段

再次表明立场 总结观点	总之，制定严格的标准是促进回收的有效方法，但是加强意识和在设施上投资也同样重要。

第4章

学术类图表作文 (Task 1) 攻略

4.1 图表作文考试简介和本书内容简介

雅思学术类 Task 1 作文（或者小作文）考试时间约 20 分钟，考查考生的数字分析、总结归纳和对比比较的能力。

一般来说，雅思小作文常会出现四种图表，分别是饼图 (pie chart)、线图 (line chart)、柱图 (bar chart) 和表格 (table)；另外还有两种图是流程图 (flow chart) 和地图 (map)。这两种图在过去两年大量出现，考生不能忽视。

学术类作文考查图表写作的主要用意在于引起考生对图表和数据分析的注意。参加雅思考试的考生一般日后都会进入英联邦国家。在这些国家的大学里读书的时候，不管所读专业是什么，学生时常被要求分析统计数据和判断可能趋势。图表写作有助于考生提高这一方面的能力，应付大学学业；考生在以后的留学过程中，可以慢慢体会雅思考试中心的这一用意。

本书图表作文的讲解大致分为三部分：第一部分是普通图表（动态图表和静态图表）的范文和知识点学习；第二部分是流程图写作的介绍；第三部分是地图写作的介绍。

在普通图表的写作中，我准备了 10 篇范文，每篇范文下面用表格的形式介绍文章的结构，描述内容的先后，让读者知道每篇范文的大概思路。

然后整体给出范文，让读者有个全面的认识，最后会给出一个知识点的详细讲解。这个知识点一般是图表作文比较重要的环节，如时态、分段、关键信息的选择、总结段的写作等，方便考生深入了解图表作文的写作技能。

图表作文 Task 1 相对于大作文 Task 2 来说简单得多，因为思路差不多，表达和句子结构也差不多，甚至连语法错误也差不多。我从事雅思教学超过 10 年，最近两年从事网络教学，发现中国考生在准备小作文的时候，小错误很多，为此，我归纳了雅思小作文常见错误，请大家查阅一下 4.6，那些错误都不知道积累了多少"烤鸭"的血和泪。

4.2 雅思图表作文的评分标准

4.2.1 雅思官方评分标准

很多考生备考雅思小作文时也是比较简单化地侧重表达的变化，读数据，然后增加复杂句的应用。其实这也是他们缺乏对图表作文评分标准的理解。我们还是从评分标准开始看起。

雅思大作文（Task 1）的评分标准有四项，分别是：

标准 5：Task Achievement（写作任务完成情况）

标准 6：Coherence and Cohesion（连贯与衔接）

标准 7：Lexical Resources（词汇丰富程度）

标准 8：Grammatical Range and Accuracy（语法多样性及准确性）

不难看出，这个评分标准和大作文的评分标准都是四项，后面三项的名称一样，第一项变成了 Task Achievement，而不是大作文的 Task Response，主要原因是图表作文给出了图，你只要描述就可以，不需要给出主观的看法和观点，而大作文不是这样。

7 分 Task 1 作文（图表作文）的特点（中英对照）

Task Achievement (TA)	写作任务完成情况
• covers the requirements of the task	• 写作内容涵盖写作任务的要求
• (Academic) presents a clear overview of main trends, differences or stages	• （学术类）清晰地呈现关于主要趋势、区别或不同阶段的概述
• clearly presents and highlights key features/ bullet points but could be more fully extended	• 能就主要内容 / 要点进行清晰的呈现与强调，但未能更为充分地展开
Coherence and Cohesion (CC)	连贯与衔接
• logically organises information and ideas; there is clear progression throughout	• 符合逻辑地组织信息及观点；清晰的行文推进贯穿全文
• uses a range of cohesive devices appropriately although thcrc may be some under-/over-use	• 恰当地使用一系列衔接手段，尽管有时使用不足或过多
Lexical Resources (LR)	词汇丰富程度
• uses a sufficient range of vocabulary to allow some flexibility and precision	• 使用足够的词汇，体现一定灵活性及准确性
• uses less common lexical items with some awareness of style and collocation	• 使用不常见词汇，对语体及搭配有一定认识
• may produce occasional errors in word choice, spelling and/or word formation	• 在选择用词、拼写及 / 或构词方面可能偶尔出现错误
Grammatical Range and Accuracy (GRA)	语法多样性及准确性
• uses a variety of complex structures	• 运用各种复杂的语法结构
• produces frequent error-free sentences	• 多数句子准确无误
• has good control of grammar and punctuation but may make a few errors	• 对语法及标点符号掌握较好，但有时出现少许错误

6 分 Task 1 作文（图表作文）的特点（中英对照）

Task Achievement (TA)	写作任务完成情况
• addresses the requirements of the task • (Academic) presents an overview with information appropriately selected • presents and adequately highlights key features/ bullet points but details may be irrelevant, inappropriate or inaccurate	• 根据写作任务要求写作文 • （学术类）选择恰当的信息进行概述 • 呈现并充分地强调了主要内容／要点，但有时含有不相关、不恰当或不准确的细节信息
Coherence and Cohesion (CC)	连贯与衔接
• arranges information and ideas coherently and there is a clear overall progression • uses cohesive devices effectively, but cohesion within and/or between sentences may be faulty or mechanical • may not always use referencing clearly or appropriately	• 连贯地组织信息及观点，总体来说，能清晰地推进行文发展 • 有效地使用衔接手段，但句内及／或句间的衔接有时有误或过于机械 • 有时无法保持一贯清晰或恰当地使用指代
Lexical Resources (LR)	词汇丰富程度
• uses an adequate range of vocabulary for the task • attempts to use less common vocabulary but with some inaccuracy • makes some errors in spelling and/or word formation, but they do not impede communication	• 使用足够的词汇开展写作任务 • 试图使用不常用词汇，但有时使用不准确 • 在拼写及／或构词方面有错误，但不影响交流
Grammatical Range and Accuracy (GRA)	语法多样性及准确性
• uses a mix of simple and complex sentence forms • makes some errors in grammar and punctuation but they rarely reduce communication	• 综合使用简单句式与复杂句式 • 在语法及标点符号方面有一些错误，但这些错误很少影响交流

4.2.2 《剑 12》图表范文（不同级别）

WRITING TASK 1

You should spend about 20 minutes on this task.

The bar chart below shows the percentage of Australian men and women in different age groups who did regular physical activity in 2010.

Summarise the information by selecting and reporting the main features, and make comparisons where relevant.

Write at least 150 words.

Percentage of Australian men and women doing regular physical activity: 2010

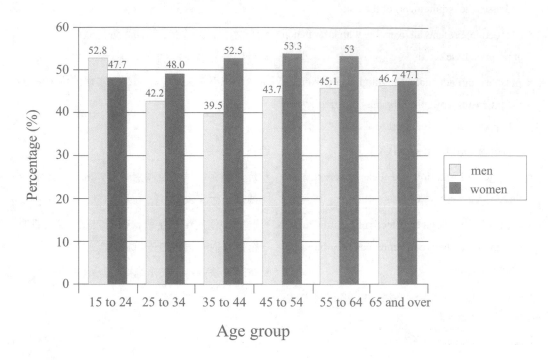

5 分学生作文

The graph presents information about the differences in terms of the number of males and females who are into exercise in Australia with various ages.

The percentage of women aged 45 to 54 was the highest, at 53.3%, around 10% higher than the figure for men with the same age. Similarly, both 35~44 and 55~64 female sport fans accounted for almost 53%, while the proportion of male counterparts was lower about 10% on average. Compared with other age groups, the number of female lovers was more than males, the individuals aged between 15 to 24 saw a different situation which the male enthusiasts sector (52.8%) surpassed the females (47.7%). In addition, it is not desirable that only 39.5% of the male population were keen to participating in workout, and there were two close percentages of females and males in the 65 and over group, at 47.1% and 46.7 respectively.

Overall, females are more able to recognize the significance of physical training, and they are likely to take part in those activities with age, while males neglect its benefits until they reach middle age.

点评：

评分标注 1 (TA)	从头到尾考生都没有搞清楚对象词是什么，不清楚数字代表什么。

评分标注2（CC）	没有分段，有些连接词如 similarly 使用错误，it is not desirable that 不知道是什么意思。
评分标注3（LR）	用词有很多问题，如 with the same age, female enthusiasts, close percentages 等。 不断换词，但是换的又都是错的，female lovers 是什么？
评分标注4（GRA）	错误百出，时态有时候用一般现在时。situation 引导定语从句？ age groups 和 number of female lovers 对比？

6分学生作文

The graph provides the data about the percentage of men and women of different ages in terms of doing exercise regularly in 2010.

Young boys were more passionate for physical activity, with up to 52.8% of those boys aged 15~24. This figure is slightly higher than the proportion of girls of the same ages. As people got older, the proportion of women who did exercise regularly saw a stead increase, and reached 53.3% of those aged 45~54 women, while it dropped to 47.1 when they aged over 64.

In contrast, a different trend was seen about men. The figure firstly dropped steadily with age, and only 39.5% of those aged 35 to 40 had interest about physical activity, and then saw an increasing trend as they got older.

Overall, women were more active than men in doing physical activity, and the most active age group of men and women is different, with the figure of men aged 15 to 24 and women aged 45 to 54 respectably.

点评：

评分标注1（TA）	基本上描述了图的主要信息，也非常注意对比。
评分标注2（CC）	句子连接和分段都比较恰当。
评分标注3（LR）	用词的问题比较多，包括 boys 使用不恰当。 interest 没有冠词，steady 拼错了。 graph 一般用于线图。
评分标注4（GRA）	of the same age, they were over the age of 64 才是准确的表达。

我写的作文（7.5分）

The chart compares the proportion of men and women who participated in physical activity regularly in Australia in the year 2010.

替换原图的题目，提升 LR 的分数。

As shown in the chart, women were more likely to exercise on a regular basis than their male counterparts in this country, with the exception of the 15-to-24 age group. The participation rate of women did not change significantly as they grew older, in contrast to the wider variance in that of men.

主体部分第一段就写了总结，这个比较少见，但是也是可以的。图表作文一定要写总结，决定了TA的分数。

Only 47.7% of 15-24-year-old women were regularly involved in physical activity, compared with 52.8% of men in the same age group, but they saw a different pattern with age. The figure for women rose steadily and reached a peak of 53.3% for those falling into the 45 to 54 age bracket, whereas the proportion of men who remained physically active fell to the lowest point at 39.5% for those aged 35～44.

改变年龄段的表达，提高LR的分数。

词性改变，提高LR的分数。

After women reached the age of 55, their participation in physical activity fell slightly (47.1% for those aged 65 or older), but the figure for men increased gradually. The smallest gender difference was seen in the 65-and-over age group.

句子结构变化，影响GRA的分数。

下面我会分析一下《剑10》的一篇考官范文，来深入阐述雅思的评分标准，我们也会通过其他范文具体解释怎样写才符合雅思的评分标准。

4.3 《剑10》考官范文的分析

后文题目中的表格是《剑10》的第二套题，我们可以用这个表格还有考官的范文来说说雅思图表作文大概的考点，考生一般要注意什么，写什么东西等。

这个表格是描述五个欧洲国家关于 coffee 和 bananas 两种产品的销售情况。

它是个动态表格，所谓的动态表格就是时间多于一个的表格（这个表格有两个时间点，1999和2004）。而静态表格一般来说只有一个时间点。

那么在写作的过程中，大家先要了解图表作文的评分标准：

1. Task Achievement（写作任务完成情况）

2. Coherence and Cohesion（连贯与衔接）

3. Lexical Resources（词汇丰富程度）

4. Grammatical Range and Accuracy（语法多样性及准确性）

那么根据这些评分标准，我们需要在写作中注意什么呢？下面是我对雅思图表作文评分标准的一个解读。考生只要做到这些，和侧重这些点，就可以在图表作文里获得不错的成绩。

评分标准	注意事项
Task Achievement	一定要明确表格里的数字代表什么 (也就是描述对象要确认)。很多考生经常写错。 一定要写总结和归纳段。 注意总结表格里的主要信息和趋势。 表格的最高值。 数值之间的比。 趋势 (如上升下降) 的归纳。
Coherence and Cohesion	连接词 (表示对比、比较、转折、相同趋势的一些连接表达)。 描述信息是否有一定合理的顺序 (如高值到低值，先总结上升幅度大的，然后再说小的等)。 分段恰当。
Lexical Resources	词性的变化 (一些词，如 increase 能否使用不同词性，包括名词、动词、分词)。 单词使用灵活。
Grammatical Range and Accuracy	句子结构准确、有变化。 写没有错误的句子。 时态准确。

例如，就《剑10》这个表格，一个考生在考场上比较合理的做法就是主体部分会分两段。

段落	重要的信息
第一段写 coffee：这段比较重要的信息是	1. Switzerland 销售比较大。 2. UK 增长最大。 3. 其他国家增长比较小。
第二段写 banana：这段比较重要的信息是	1. Switzerland 销售比较大，而且增长很大。 2. UK 和 Belgium 增长也很大。 3. Sweden 和 Denmark 的数字下降。

The tables below give information about sales of Fairtrade*-labelled coffee and bananas in 1999 and 2004 in five European countries.

Summarise the information by selecting and reporting the main features and make comparisons where relevant.

Write at least 150 words.

Sales of Fairtrade-labelled coffee and bananas (1999 & 2004)

Coffee	1999 (millions of euros)	2004 (millions of euros)
UK	1.5	20
Switzerland	3	6
Denmark	1.8	2
Belgium	1	1.7
Sweden	0.8	1

Banana	1999 (millions of euros)	2004 (millions of euros)
Switzerland	15	47
UK	1	5.5
Belgium	0.6	4
Sweden	1.8	1
Denmark	2	0.9

* Fairtrade: a category of products for which farmers from developing countries have been paid an officially agreed fair price.

我们现在看看考官的范文。

The two tables contain sales data for ... and bananas in 1999 and 2004, in five nations of Europe.

> LR: 替换题目中的 give information about。

> TA: 第一句话就总结出主要的趋势和特点。

... ows low-level coffee sales increasing in ... , albeit to widely varying de... es sales increased by the same small amount: 1.8—2 million eur... d 0.8—1 million in Sweden. The increment w... lgium, from 1—1.7 million euros. Meanwhile, in Switzerland ... 6 million euros. Fi... e was an enormous increase, from 1.5—20 million Euros ...

> LR: 替换题目中的 five European countries。

> GRA: 冒号引出解释。

> LR: 这个词一般指一些幅度不大的增长，替换常用的 increase。

> CC: 连接词的使用，增加句子之间的联系。

> GRA: 强调句，增加句子变化。

... le, it is Switzerland wh... ... as buying far more Fairtrade bananas than the other four countries. Swiss sales figures jumped fr... s across these five years, while i... sales ... 5.5 and from 0.6—4 million euros res... ... n and Denmark showed a different pattern, wi... sales from 1.8—1 and 2—0.9 million euros.

> LR: enormous 一个形容词，提高用词的变化性。

> CC: 使用代词 these，增加句子连接。

> LR: 去替换上面的 ... sales data。

> TA: 出现文字归纳，而不是直接读数据。

Comparing the two tables, it is clear that in 1999 Fairtrade coffee sales ranged from 0.8–3 million euros ~~~~~~~~ ountries, while banana sales also mostly clustered between 0.9 ~~~~~ os, with Switzerland the outlier at a huge 15 million euros. By ~~~~~ for both products had risen across the board, except for Sweden and Denmark, which ~~~~~ ns in banana sa~~~~~

> TA: 归纳了数字的区间。
>
> TA: 归纳了数字的区间, 而不是大量读数据。
>
> TA: 文字信息，指出特例。
>
> LR: 比较特别的表达, 表示"全面地"。

考官这篇范文有下面一些值得学习的地方，不难发现，考官的范文是严格按照剑桥雅思的评分标准写出来的。

学习点 1 (LR)	图表作文的开头段一般都是改写题目，确保不与题目重复。
学习点 2 (TA)	主体部分第一段的第一句话，考官总结了这个表格最核心的信息：销售量都上升，虽然幅度不一样。很多考生觉得图表题就是读数据，得分的手段是变换读取数据的方式，这是一个误区。
学习点 3 (CC)	从主体部分第一段可以看出来考官在 Coherence & Cohesion 这个评分标准上做得很好，从增幅比较小的数据到增幅比较大的数据，步步递进；其次，灵活使用一些连接词，如 meanwhile, finally。
学习点 4 (LR)	主体部分第一段，考官在 Lexical Resources 上也花了心思，如都是表示上升，第一句话用了分词 increasing，第二句话用了动词 increased，第三句话用了名词 increment，第四句话换了个说法，用了 doubled（增长两倍），最后一句话，没什么好换了，考官选择加了一个形容词 enormous。然后下面一段用了一些替换词，如 jumped, grew，和最后一段里的 rise 都是"上升"的意思。
学习点 5 (GRA)	主体部分第二段，考官在句子变化上 (Grammatical Range and Accuracy) 做得很好，第一句话使用了强调句，第二句话使用了 while 引导的状语从句，对比两个事物。
学习点 6 (TA)	范文的最后一段体现了考官对于 (Task Achievement) 的重视。我们之前说过，这主要体现在趋势的总结和数值的对比上。范文第一句话归纳了两个表的数字区间，第二句话归纳了两个产品的上升趋势。
学习点 7 (TA)	我们也要关注时态。整篇文章都是用一般过去时（因为 1999 年和 2004 年是过去），唯有到了 "by 2004"，才使用了过去完成时。

4.4 雅思普通图表作文的写作要点和顺序

普通图表作文指的是动态图表和静态图表。这两种图表在 Task 1 出现的概率比较大，大部分中国考生也比较熟悉。

我在课堂上授课的时候，给学生设定的普通图表作文步骤大概有 10 步，或者说有 10 个要点。

第 *1* 步：确定图表的类型（到底是动态图表，还是静态图表）。

第 *2* 步：确定时态（过去时、现在时、将来时）。

第 *3* 步：确定图表的主要信息（最高值、趋势、对比等）。

第 *4* 步：分段。

第 *5* 步：阅读信息的顺序（从大到小）。

第 *6* 步：确定对象词（描述对象）的准确性。

第 *7* 步：写的时候注意句子结构的变化。

第 *8* 步：句子之间要注意连接词。

第 *9* 步：词性有没有变化，对象词的变化是否正确、合理。

第 *10* 步：检查语法错误，确保不要犯错。

只要注意了这些要点和步骤，图表作文就可以满足雅思的评分标准。

与此同时，请大家关注 4.6 图表作文常见错误汇总。在教学过程中，我发现中国考生的通病是喜欢在图表作文中使用很多比较创新或者是变化的表达，而忽略了基本的小错误。图表作文只要减少小错误，拿 7 分并不难。

4.4.1 范文 1：动态图表＋动态图表描述要点（一个对比组）

> *Surveys conducted in 1982 and 2002 show different pictures of what motivate students to choose a college or university in the UK.*
>
> *Summarise the information by selecting and reporting the main features and make comparisons where relevant.*

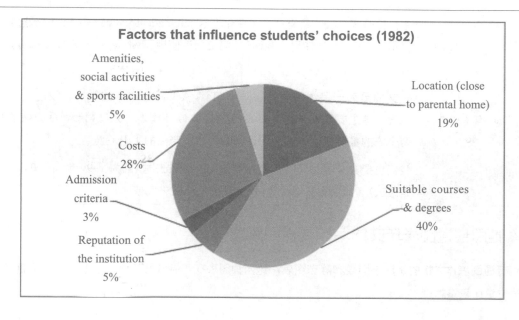

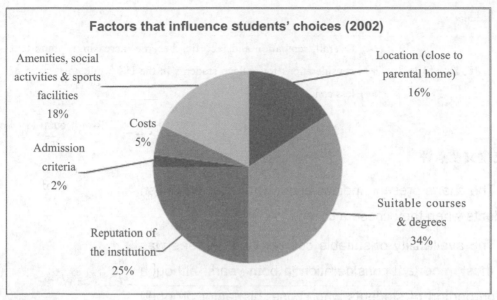

Factors that influence students' choices (2002)

Amenities, social activities & sports facilities 18%

Location (close to parental home) 16%

Costs 5%

Admission criteria 2%

Suitable courses & degrees 34%

Reputation of the institution 25%

首段

改写题目	The charts present findings about what affected British students when they chose a college.

主体部分第一段 (描述 2002 年比较高的值)

最高值 Suitable courses & degrees	The availability of suitable courses and degrees was the most important consideration in both years, although the proportion of students who chose this factor dropped from 40% to 34%.
第二最高值 Reputation of the institution	They were also more concerned with the reputation of the university, with one quarter of respondents rating this highly in 2002, in contrast to only 5% in 1982.
第三最高值 Amenities, social activities & sports facilities	The percentage of students who valued the access to amenities and sports facilities more than tripled from 5% to 18% in 2002, by which time this factor had become the third most common reason for choosing a university.

主体部分第二段 (描述其他的值)

Location	The location was also a significant consideration and the percentage of students who paid attention to this did not change remarkably (16% in 2002 and 19% in 1982)
Costs	In contrast, there was a dramatic decline in the percentage of students who considered the cost of education from 28% to 5%.
Admission criteria	Admission criteria, the least frequently mentioned reason, were chosen by a mere 2% and 3% respectively in these years.

总结段

总结趋势和主要特征	Overall, reputation and facilities became increasingly important considerations for college students in the UK while costs were of less concern.

(word count: 199 words)

范文全文及点评

The charts present findings about what affected British students when they chose a college.

The availability of suitable courses and degrees was the most important consideration in both years, although the proportion of students who chose this factor dropped from 40% to 34%. They were also more concerned with the reputation of the university, with one quarter of respondents rating this highly in 2002, in contrast to only 5% in 1982. The percentage of students who valued the access to amenities and sports facilities more than tripled from 5% to 18% in 2002, by which time this factor had become the third most common reason for choosing a university.

> 动态图要注意对比。
> 描述趋势。
> 描述趋势。
> 对比。

The location was also a significant consideration and the percentage of students who paid attention to this did not change remarkably (16% in 2002 and 19% in 1982). In contrast, there was a dramatic decline in the percentage of students who considered the cost of education from 28% to 5%. Admission criteria, the least frequently mentioned reason, were chosen by a mere 2% and 3% respectively in these years.

> 对比。
> 描述趋势。
> 描述趋势。
> 对比。

Overall, reputation and facilities became increasingly important considerations for college students in the UK while costs were of less concern.

学习要点

很多老师在讲解图表作文的时候，都喜欢按图表形状来分类，如线图、饼图、表格，还有柱图，事实上这样分类太过烦琐。

我更喜欢将图表按照时间来分类，如出现超过一个时间点(年代、月份等)的时候，我称之为"动态图表"。

前面这个图表面上是饼图，但是完全可以画成线图(一共有 6 根线，如 suitable courses 是一条从 40% 下降到 34% 的线)或者列成表格：

	Suitable courses	Reputation	Amenities	Location	Costs	Admission criteria
1982	40%	5%	5%	19%	28%	3%
2002	34%	25%	18%	16%	5%	2%

或者画成柱图：

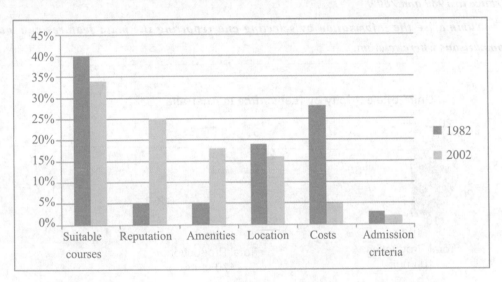

因此，不管图表形状怎么变，其本质是一样的，就是描述六个课程的变化趋势和对比。

那么动态图表怎么描述为好呢？什么是描述的重点？应该对比什么？结尾写什么？

我分析了过去几年雅思作文题中大部分的动态图表，发现大部分的动态图表只有一组对比对象。也就是说动态图表的本质就是对比一组不同对象(如年龄、性别、国家、课程等)的趋势(上升、下降或者保持不变)。

这篇文章的对比对象是学生选择大学的时候不同的考虑因素。整个文章的重点只有两个：

趋势对比，也就是谁上升了，谁下降了。

大小对比，谁比谁高。

动态图表(一组对比对象)的内容要点：

主体部分	主要是描述不同对象的各自趋势。描述它们的相对大小。	本文六个对象，每个对象都有其趋势，四个是下降，两个是上升。Suitable courses 一直很高。Reputation 在 2002 年很高。Costs 在 1982 年很高。
顺序	从数值比较高的对象开始说起。	也就是 Suitable courses，还有 Reputation。
结尾	关注比较高的数值的趋势对比。	结尾段不需要说所有对象的趋势，关注比较高的数值就可以。

4.4.2 范文 2：动态图表＋动态图表描述要点（两个对比组）

The pie charts below show units of electricity production by fuel source in Australia and France in 1980 and 2000.

Summarise the information by selecting and reporting the main features and make comparisons where relevant.

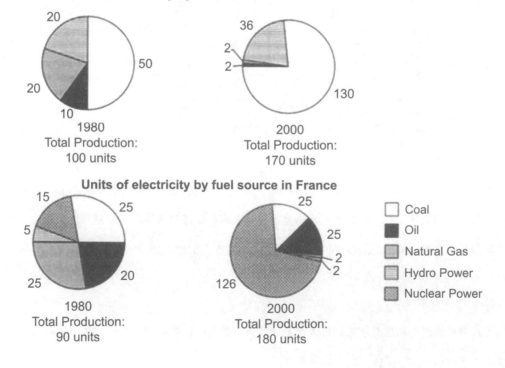

Units of electricity by fuel source in Australia

Units of electricity by fuel source in France

首段

改写题目	The charts compare the amounts of electricity created by different energy sources in two countries in 1980 and 2000.

主体部分第一段（描述比较主要的能源）

澳大利亚的最高值 Coal, 然后对比法国	The units of electricity created by coal, the main energy source in Australia, more than doubled to 130 in 2000, but this energy source was much less important in France, producing 25 units of electricity only in both years.
法国的最高值是 Nuclear Power	Nuclear power was the prominent energy source in France, with the figure rising more than eight fold to 126 units in 2000, but Australia did not use this energy source.

主体部分第二段（描述其他的能源）

Hydro Power	The amount of electricity created by hydro power also increased significantly from 20 to 36 units in Australia, while this fuel source was less important in France, creating 2 units of electricity only in 2000.
Natural Gas	The figures for natural gas declined in both countries to 2 units.
Oil	The proportion of electricity created by oil also saw a different trend in these two countries, increasing slightly to 25 units in France but falling steeply to 2 units in Australia.

总结段

总结趋势和主要特征	Overall, Australia and France relied on different fuel sources. While coal and hydro power were important in Australia, nuclear power dominated France's energy sector.

(word count: 190 words)

范文全文及点评

The charts compare the amounts of electricity created by different energy sources in two countries in 1980 and 2000.

The units of electricity created by coal, the main energy source in Australia, more than doubled to 130 in 2000, but this energy source was much less important in France, 对比法国。 producing 25 units of electricity only in both years. Nuclear power was the prominent energy source in France, with the figure rising more than eight fold to 126 units in 2000, but Australia did not use this energy source. 对比澳大利亚。

The amount of electricity created by hydro power also increased significantly from 20 to 36 units in Australia, while this fuel source was less important in France, creating 2 units of electricity only in 2000. The figures for natural gas declined in both countries to 2 units. The proportion of electricity created by oil also saw a different trend in these two countries, increasing slightly to 25 units in France but falling steeply to 2 units in Australia.

描述趋势。

对比法国。

描述趋势，顺便对比两个国家。

对比趋势。

Overall, Australia and France relied on different fuel sources. While coal and hydro power were important in Australia, nuclear power dominated France's energy sector.

学习要点

我们通过上一篇范文总结了只有一组对比对象的动态图表的写作要点，在这里我们看看两组对比对象的动态图表作文怎么写。这种动态图表有两组不同的对比对象。如本图除了每个国家有不同的能源对比之外，还有对两个国家进行对比。这种题目的对比会更加复杂一点，很多考生只关注能源的对比，最后就可能会忘记国家的对比。这样在 Task Achievement 上就有可能丢分。

我建议首先将对比对象进行一定的级别分类（如下图所示）。如果出现了国家，那么主要是对比国家，其他的对比对象其次。

本文侧重澳大利亚和法国所有能源的对比：不是先写澳大利亚的所有能源，再写法国的所有能源，而是在每种能源上对比澳大利亚和法国的情况。

趋势对比：主要是第二对比组对象的趋势（类似的或者相反的趋势）。

大小对比：第一对比组对象各自的高值；

第二对比组对象的相对大小。

动态图表（两组对比对象）的内容要点：

主体部分	主要是描述第二对比组不同对象的各自趋势。 对比第一对比组的对象。	主要是描述不同能源（第二对比组）的变化趋势。 然后每种能源分别对比国家（第一对比组）。
顺序	从第一对比组各自数值比较高的对象开始说起。	从澳大利亚和法国比较高的值开始说起。
结尾	关注比较高的值的趋势对比。	不需要说所有的对象的趋势，关注比较高的值就可以。

4.4.3 范文3：静态图表＋静态图表描述要点＋开头段的写法

The pie chart shows the main reasons why agricultural land becomes less productive. The table shows how these causes affected three regions of the world during the 1990s.

Summarise the information by selecting and reporting the main features and make comparisons where relevant.

Causes of worldwide land degradation

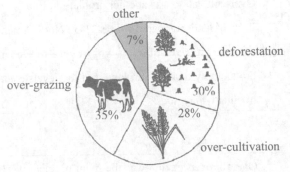

Causes of land degradation by region

Region	% land degraded by...			
	deforestation	over-cultivation	over-grazing	Total land degraded
North America	0.2	3.3	1.5	5%
Europe	9.8	7.7	5.5	23%
Oceania*	1.7	0	11.3	13%

*A large group of islands in the South Pacific including Australia and New Zealand

首段

改写题目	The pie chart presents information about the causes of land degradation in the world and the table shows how three regions of the world were affected by this problem.

主体部分第一段（第一个图，先说最高的 over-grazing，然后说其他值）

最高值	Over-grazing was the primary cause of the world's land degradation, with around 35% of land around the world degraded by this.
然后说一下其他值	Deforestation and over-cultivation were responsible for 30% and 28% of degradation respectively, while the remaining 7% was attributed to other problems.

主体部分第二段（第二个图，先说 Europe 的总量最高，然后分开说其他的值，注意国家／地区的对比）

最高值 23%，和其他两个地方相比	Europe had the largest proportion of unproductive land at 23%, nearly twice the figure for Oceania and more than four times the level of degradation in North America.
然后说一下 deforestation 里的 9.8%	Deforestation was the principal reason for land degradation in Europe (9.8%) and the proportions of land degraded by this cause in other two areas were significantly lower.
描述 over-cultivation	Over-cultivation was another problem in Europe, causing damage to 7.7% of land, compared with 3.3% in North America.
描述 Oceania	In contrast, over-grazing was severe in Oceania, reducing the productivity of 11.3% of land, but the levels of damage were lower in other two regions.

总结段

总结趋势和主要特征	Overall, over-grazing was the main problem worldwide in terms of land degradation. Europe had a higher proportion of degraded land than other two areas.

(word count: 193 words)

范文全文及点评

The pie chart presents information about the causes of land degradation in the world and the table shows how three regions of the world were affected by this problem.

Over-grazing was the primary cause of the world's land degradation, with around 35% of land around the world degraded by this. Deforestation and over-cultivation were responsible for 30% and 28% of degradation respectively,

对比，突出最主要的对象。

while the remaining 7% was attributed to other problems.

Europe had the largest proportion of unproductive land at 23%, nearly twice the figure for Oceania and more than four times the level of degradation in North America. Deforestation was the principal reason for land degradation in Europe (9.8%) and the proportions of land degraded by this cause in other two areas were significantly lower. Over-cultivation was another problem in Europe, causing damage to 7.7% of land, compared with 3.3% in North America. In contrast, over-grazing was severe in Oceania, reducing the productivity of 11.3% of land, but the levels of damage were lower in other two regions.

对比，突出最主要的对象。

通过倍数对比。

通过比较级对比。

再一次对比。

对比。

Overall, over-grazing was the main problem worldwide in terms of land degradation. Europe had a higher proportion of degraded land than other two areas.

学习要点

静态图表一般是那些图表里只有一个时间，或者没有任何时间的图表。

静态图表出现的频率不如动态图表多，但是普遍比动态图表要复杂和难写，因为静态图表没有上升和下降的趋势可描述，完全是对比。

范文3的这组图表由两个部分组成，第一个是图，只有一组对比对象（导致土地退化不同的原因），第二个是表，有两组对比对象（导致土地退化不同的原因和地区）。

只有一组对比对象的图表比较简单，直接对比数据，从高到低叙述就可以。

有两组对比对象图表我们还是参照下面的对比对象级别图。主要还是对照第一对比组的对象。

例如拿这篇文章第二个图来说，第一对比组的对象是地区，那么就应该是在每个土地退化的原因上对比不同的地区。

第一优先对比组：
国家／地区

第二对比组：
男女、年龄段等

其他对比组：
课程、能源等

然后我们看看开头段怎么写。图表作文的开头段主要是改写，只要是和题目的字眼不同，就是一个合格的开头段。

图表作文的开头段有四种改写方法：

方法 1：出现 "提供信息" 的字眼：The chart (or graph) provides (or presents) information (or data) about...

方法 2：出现 "show/illustrate + 名词"：The chart shows the changes in...

方法 3：出现 "how" 引导的宾语从句：The chart (or graph) shows (or illustrates) how...changed (or varied)...

方法 4：出现 "that" 引导的宾语从句，可能将总体趋势粗略地描述一下：The chart (or graph) shows (or reveals/indicates/suggests) that...

开头段很多考生的常犯错误有六个：

错误 1：有些考生开头段写得很复杂，其实没有必要。

例如 Given is the chart showing that... 没有必要用这种倒装。

错误 2：有些考生换错表达。

例如用 statistics 去替换 information 不恰当，因为 statistics 是一个国家的统计数据，一般很少会出现在图表作文里。

错误 3：有些考生喜欢详述很多年代或者国家的信息。

因为他们觉得这样可以凑字数，例如，如果图里有 5 个国家，他们就全部写出来，这会让内容很单调乏味。

错误 4：chart 和 graph 一般不用替换。

有些考生用 picture, image 去替换，这是错误的。

错误 5：show, compare, present 这些词不用过去时。

这个图是现在存在的，所以开头段第一句话不要用过去时，哪怕这个图里的数据是过去的数据。

错误 6：开头段不要照抄题目。

和大作文一样，如果抄题，这些抄的字数就会被扣除。

4.4.4 范文 4：半动态图表＋年龄的表达

The charts below show the main reasons for study among students of different age groups and the amount of support they received from employers.

Summarise the information by selecting and reporting the main features and make comparisons where relevant.

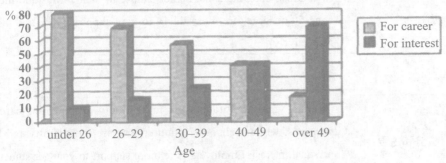

Reasons for study according to age of student

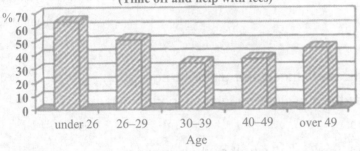

Employer support, by age group
(Time off and help with fees)

首段

改写题目	The bar chart compares students of different ages in terms of what motivates them to study and the support they receive from employers.

主体部分第一段 (第一个图，先说 for career 的情况，然后说 for interest)

最高值是年轻人为了职业学习的百分比	Young people study primarily to further their careers, with up to 80% of those under the age of 26 studying for this purpose. This figure is significantly higher than the proportion of those who study out of personal interest.
然后描述趋势	The gap between these two proportions narrows as students get older, and the figures for those aged 40 to 49 are the same (40%).
最后说一下 for interest	Students aged over 49 overwhelmingly study for interest (70%), rather than for career (under 20%).

主体部分第二段 (第二个图)

最高值和最低值	Around 60% of students aged under 26 receive support from employers for further education.
然后描述趋势	The figure drops steadily with age, and only one third of those 30-to-39-year-old students are supported by employers.

271

| 最后描述数据 | In contrast, older students, namely, those in their forties and those aged 50 or more, are more likely to gain support (35% and 42% respectively). |

总结段

| 总结趋势和主要特征 | Overall, younger students are more likely to study for career purposes, while their older counterparts are more motivated by personal interest. Employers give more support to younger students than to employees of other ages. |

(word count: 192 words)

范文全文及点评

The bar chart compares students of different ages in terms of what motivates them to study and the support they receive from employers.

Young people study primarily to further their careers, with up to 80% of those under the age of 26 studying for this purpose. This figure is significantly higher than the proportion of those who study out of personal interest. The gap between these two proportions narrows as students get older, and the figures for those aged 40 to 49 are the same (40%). Students aged over 49 overwhelmingly study for interest (70%), rather than for career (under 20%).

> 替换图里的 for career。

> 使用代词和比较级比较两个数据，突出对比，而不是枯燥地读数据。

> 文字信息，概括趋势。

Around 60% of students aged under 26 receive support from employers for further education. The figure drops steadily with age, and only one third of those 30-to-39-year-old students are supported by employers. In contrast, older students, namely, those in their forties and those aged 50 or more, are more likely to gain support (35% and 42% respectively).

> 文字信息，概括趋势。

Overall, younger students are more likely to study for career purposes, while their older counterparts are more motivated by personal interest. Employers give more support to younger students than to employees of other ages.

学习要点

我们之前讲过动态图表和静态图表的写作要点，我们利用这一篇文章讲一下半动态图表的写作要点。半动态图表一般出现在对比不同年龄段的文章里。

这种图表本来可以算是静态图表，因为图表里没有给出时间，或者只有一个时间点。

然而，因为涉及年龄增长中出现的趋势，那么我们还是有可能会用到关于上升和下降的表达，这就具备了动态图表的性质。

例如在这道题中，我们可以看到，随着年龄增长，为了兴趣读书的人在增加。

那么我们可以说：

With age, people are more likely to study out of interest.

或者说：

The proportion of people who study out of interest increases with age.

这样，事实上是在描述一个动态发生的事情，出现了关于上升或者下降的表达。这是动态图表的描述方法。

另一方面，可以换一种方式描述，就是年纪大的人比年轻人更加可能为了兴趣而读书。

Older people are more likely to study out of interest than younger people.

这样事实上是在对比不同年龄段的人，这是一种静态的对比。这是静态图表的描述方法。

这就是为什么我们可以把这种出现年龄群体的图表称为半动态图表。

我们同时也要学一有关年龄的一些表达：

表达的分类	24 岁以下的人	30 到 39 岁的人	超过 50 岁的人
aged...	people aged under 24	people aged 30–39 people aged between 30 and 39	people aged over 50
in...		people in their thirties	people in their fifties
age group	under-24 age group	30–39 age group	over-50 age group
...year-old	under-24-year-old people	30–39-year-old people	over-50-year-old people

4.4.5 范文 5：动态图表＋时态的选择

You should spend about 20 minutes on this task.

The graph below gives information from a 2008 report about consumption of energy in the USA since 1980 with projections until 2030.

Summarise the information by selecting and reporting the main features and make comparisons where relevant.

Write at least 150 words.

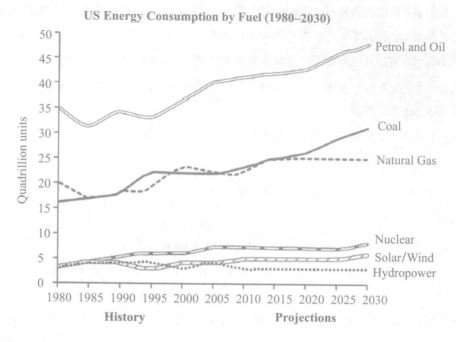

US Energy Consumption by Fuel (1980–2030)

首段

改写题目	The line graph shows the amount of energy consumed in the US from 1980 to 2015, as well as projected consumption to 2030.

主体部分第一段（从最高值 Petrol and Oil 说起，然后说 Coal 还有 Natural Gas）

最高值是 Petrol and Oil	Petrol and oil are the most important energy sources throughout the period: despite fluctuation in the first 15 years, the consumption of these two fuels rose steadily, and this is projected to persist, reaching 50 q in 2030.
然后说 Coal	Coal was as important as natural before 2015, but the gap between these two fuels is likely to widen. While the amount of coal consumed is predicted to climb to 30q in 2030, the figure for natural gas will possibly remain stable at 25q.

主体部分第二段（从剩下的最高值 Nuclear 开始说起，然后是其他能源）

Nuclear Power	Other fuel sources are less significant. Nuclear power consumption saw a steady increase to around 8q in 2005 and maintained this level until 2015, after which the level of consumption will not experience any remarkable change.
Solar/Wind and Hydropower	The use of solar/wind and hydropower is limited, and hydropower is the only fuel source which is predicted to fall back to the 1980 figure.

总结段

总结趋势和主要特征	Overall, fossil fuels will make up a large proportion of the energy consumption in the US, whereas renewable resources and nuclear energy will remain insignificant.

(word count: 192 words)

范文全文及点评

The line graph shows the amount of energy consumed in the US from 1980 to 2015, as well as projected consumption to 2030.

Petrol and oil are the most important energy sources throughout the period: despite fluctuation in the first 15 years, the consumption of these two fuels rose steadily, and this is projected to persist, reaching 50q in 2030. Coal was as important as natural gas before 2015, but the gap between these two fuels is likely to widen. While the amount of coal consumed is predicted to climb to 30q in 2030, the figure for natural gas will possibly remain stable at 25q.

这里用的是过去时，描述 2015 年之前的情形。

这是分词结构，只是表示主语的一个性质，和时态无关。

将来时。

Other fuel sources are less significant. Nuclear power consumption saw a steady increase to around 8q in 2005 and maintained this level until 2015, after which the level of consumption will not experience any remarkable change. The use of solar/wind and hydropower is limited, and hydropower is the only fuel source which is predicted to fall back to the 1980 figure.

描述的是从 1980 年到 2030 年整个时间段的特点，可以用一般现在时。

表示对将来情况的预测。

Overall, fossil fuels will make up a large proportion of the energy consumption in the US, whereas renewable resources and nuclear energy will remain insignificant.

学习要点

图表作文的主要时态是一般过去时，其他可能出现的时态有过去完成时和一般现在时。

A. 一般过去时

因为出现的数据一般都是以往的统计数据（例如今年是 2015 年，那么图里只要是 2015 年之前的数据，都用过去时），过去的情形和现在的情形很有可能完全不一样，因此用过去时比较恰当。

例如，这篇范文说到 2015 年之前的数据都用过去时。

B. 过去完成时

出现介词"by＋时间"的时候，使用过去完成时。

例：The divorce rate had dropped to 5% by the year 1999.

大意：离婚率在 1999 年之前跌到 5%。

C. 一般现在时

如果图表里并没有出现任何时间，用一般现在时比较理想。

例：Britain is responsible for 3% of the world's carbon dioxides emissions.

大意：英国制造世界上 3% 的二氧化碳排放量。（假设图里没有显示时间点）

另外一种情况，就是图表出现了过去、现在和未来的时间，如果你描述整个区间的一个特点，可以使用一般现在时。

例如本题描述 Petrol and Oil 的时候，说它们是最重要的能源来源，这是整个图里的一贯特征，就可以用一般现在时。

D. 一般将来时

有时候，图表作文会出现以后的时间，这个时候可以用 will 表示以后发生的事情。

但是，也有一些考官认为最好避免用 will 这种词，因为这样语气过分肯定，可以用其他的说法替代，如 be likely to，be projected/expected/predicted to。

4.4.6 范文 6：动态图表＋如何分段

> *The chart below shows information about changes in average house prices in five different cities between 1990 and 2002 compared with the average house prices in 1989.*

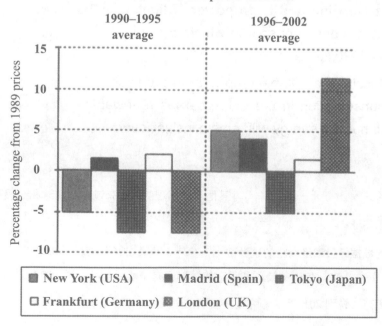

首段

改写题目	The bar chart compares five major cities in terms of the changes in the cost of an average house over a period of 13 years.

主体部分第一段 (从 London 开始说起，然后说 New York，两个城市第二个时间段的增长很大)

最高值是 London	Between 1996 and 2002, London saw the biggest increase in housing prices of these cities (over 10%), despite a drop of around 7% in the previous period.
然后说 New York	The figure for New York showed a similar pattern, declining by 5% during the first five year period but rising by 5% in the following 6 years.

主体部分第二段 (然后描述 Tokyo，下降一直很大)

Tokyo	Tokyo was the only city where the average house price dropped in both periods, around 7% in the five years and then another 5%.

主体部分第三段 (描述其他的城市)

Madrid and Frankfurt 的第一个阶段	The costs of an average home in both Madrid and Frankfurt climbed before the year 1996, 1% and 2% respectively.
第二个阶段	While prices in Madrid increased even faster over the six years after 1995, the growth in the housing market of Frankfurt slowed to approximately 1%.

总结段

总结趋势和主要特征	Overall, the property prices in London and New York were volatile during this 13-year period, in contrast to the consistently rising prices in Madrid and Frankfurt. Tokyo's houses were increasingly affordable.

范文全文及点评

The bar chart compares five major cities in terms of the changes in the cost of an average house over a period of 13 years.

Between 1996 and 2002, London saw the biggest increase in housing prices of these cities (over 10%), despite

从最高值开始描述，单图按照描述对象分段。

a drop of around 7% in the previous period. The figure for New York showed a similar pattern, declining by 5% during the first five-year period but rising by 5% in the following 6 years.

Tokyo was the only city where the average house price dropped in both periods, around 7% in the five years and then another 5%.

第三个对象可以单独写一段。

The costs of an average home in both Madrid and Frankfurt climbed before the year 1996, 1% and 2% respectively. While prices in Madrid increased even faster over the six years after 1995, the growth in the housing market of Frankfurt slowed to approximately 1%.

最后两个城市写一段。

Overall, the property prices in London and New York were volatile during this 13-year period, in contrast to the consistently rising prices in Madrid and Frankfurt. Tokyo's houses were increasingly affordable.

学习要点

我们说一下分段。图表作文的开头段一般独立一段，然后下面主体段分为2~3段，最后一段是结尾段。

开头段和结尾段是比较固定的，主要是主体部分的分段比较灵活，原则大概有三点，然后我们用之前的几篇范文作为例子解释一下。

主体部分的分段原则	例子
原则1：单图/表按照对象分段。	范文5是单图，反映6种能源的消耗量，那么就按照能源分段。
原则2：多图/表如果单位一致，描述的对象一致，那么当作单图/表来看，按照对象分段。	范文1是两个图，但是两个图的单位一致，都是不同百分比的学生选择大学考虑的六个因素，那么事实上这两个图可以看作一个单图。按照这六个考虑的因素来分段。
原则3：多图/表如果单位不一致，描述的对象不一致，那么按照图/表来分段。	范文3是一个图和一个表，分别描述了全世界土地退化的原因，和三个地区土地退化的原因，两者描述的东西不同，按照图/表来分段，每个图/表各写一段。

范文4是两个图，虽然这两个图的单位一致（都是百分比），但是描述的对象不一致（第一个图是关于人们为什么学习，第二个图是关于人们是否可以获得雇主的支持），属于上述的原则3。因

此按照图来分段。第一个图写一段，第二个图写一段。

而范文 6 这篇关于房价的文章，分两个时间段，本来算是两个图，但是因为描述的对象一致（5个城市的价格变化），而且单位也一致（都是百分比），所以就当作单图看。属于上述的原则 2。

因此，最后是按照城市分段。

下面的范文 7，是单图，属于原则 1，因此很简单，按照对象分段。

4.4.7 范文 7：动态图表＋文字信息和数字的选择

> *The table shows the amount of waste produced by different countries in 1980, 1990 and 2000.*
>
> *Summarise the information by selecting and reporting the main features, and make comparisons where relevant.*

Waste produced annually (millions of tonnes)

	1980	1990	2000
Ireland	0.2	*	3
Korea	*	31	19
Japan	44	49	52
Portugal	9.9	10.1	9.7
Poland	2	3	5
US	2003	3004	4005

首段

改写题目	The chart provides data about the waste production of six countries in the years 1980, 1990 and 2000.

主体部分第一段（从最高值美国开始说起，然后说比较高的值，包括 Japan, Korea）

最高值是 US	The US produced significantly more waste than other countries did and the amount of waste produced by this country nearly doubled from 2003 million tonnes to 4005 during the period.
然后说 Japan	The rising trend was also seen in Japan, where the waste rose from 44 to 52 million tonnes.
最后说 Korea	The waste output of Korea, in contrast, showed a marked decrease to 19 million in 2000, with no figure provided for the year 1980.

主体部分第二段 （然后说其他数值比较小的国家）

其他三个国家的特点	The waste production was noticeably lower in other countries.

其他三个国家的数字	While the figures for Ireland and Poland increased slightly to 3 and 5 million tonnes respectively, the waste produced in Portugal remained roughly unchanged at around 10 million.

总结段

总结趋势和主要特征	Overall, the US and Japan saw an increase in waste production and these two countries also produced much more waste than other countries did.

范文全文及点评

The chart provides data about the waste production of six countries in the years 1980, 1990 and 2000.

The US produced significantly more waste than other countries did and the amount of waste produced by this country nearly doubled from 2003 million tonnes to 4005 during the period. The rising trend was also seen in Japan, where the waste rose from 44 to 52 million tonnes. The waste output of Korea, in contrast, showed a marked decrease to 19 million in 2000, with no figure provided for the year 1980.

比较级，文字信息。

相同趋势的强调，文字信息。

不同趋势的强调，文字信息。

The waste production was noticeably lower in other countries. While the figures for Ireland and Poland increased slightly to 3 and 5 million tonnes respectively, the waste produced in Portugal remained roughly unchanged at around 10 million.

数值的比较归纳，文字信息。

Overall, the US and Japan saw an increase in waste production and these two countries also produced much more waste than other countries did.

学习要点

图表作文一个常见的问题是很多考生读取数据很多，而不注意总结和归纳，或者描述。雅思图表作文并不要求考生读取很多数据。大家不要担心因为少读几个数据而被扣分。

可能大家都发现，我写的范文，还有剑桥雅思上的官方范文，都有一个特点，就是文字信息总是很突出，而数字信息作为辅助说明。

每段话一般来说都有一些关键信息和主要特征的描述，写完这些特征后，再用相关数字去支持一下，作为辅助信息。

我们拿范文 7 的两个句子来讲解一下。

例 1：The rising trend was also seen in Japan（先说文字信息，突出日本的趋势也是上升），where the waste rose from 44 to 52 million tonnes（句子后半部分读数据）.

例 2：The waste output of Korea, in contrast, showed a marked decrease（先说文字信息，突出韩国的趋势是下降）to 19 million in 2000, with no figure provided for the year 1980（句子后半部分读数据）.

下面两个表格总结了动态图表和静态图表常见的一些文字信息。

动态图表的文字信息：

文字信息	常用单词
1. 最高值永远是最需要强调的文字信息（有时候也可以强调最低值）。	highest, main, major, the most, the lowest/smallest
2. 强调和归纳相同趋势（如上升和下降的趋势）。	similar, the same, likewise, similarly, also
3. 强调不同趋势（上升和下降的趋势）。	in contrast, on the other hand, different
4. 强调比较。	larger, lower, bigger, smaller 等

静态图表因为没有上升和下降这些趋势的归纳描述，所以文字信息主要是以数值对比为主：

文字信息	常用单词
1. 最高值永远是最需要强调的文字信息（有时候也可以强调最低值）。	highest, main, major, the most, the lowest/smallest
2. 比较数字。	往往有比较级 higher, lower, larger, smaller
3. 归纳具有相同特征的数字。	similar to, at a similar level
4. 归纳具有不同特征的数字。	Different from/distinct from, substantial/striking differences between, the gap between

那么图表里很多数据，很多考生会问：什么数据比较重要，需要列出，而什么数据不那么重要，可以不读呢？

动态图表的数据选择原则是：

最高值最重要，必定要读，也要强调。

其次是最后一个时间点的数据（如范文 7 这个表里的 2000 年的数据比较重要）。

然后是第一年的数据（因为第一年和最后一年的数据差别可以确定趋势到底是上升还是下降）

其他数据考生可以自己选择。

静态图表的数据选择原则是：

最高值最重要，必定要读，也要强调。

其他数据考生可以自己选择。

一般来说，我的范文中数据很少会超过 10 个。超过 10 个，数据就显得太多了，归纳和总结不够。

4.4.8 范文 8：动态图表＋图表作文如何替换表达

> *The charts give information about the proportions of boys and girls of a school who achieved high grades (A or B +) in respective courses.*
>
> *Summarise the information by selecting and reporting the main features, and make comparisons where relevant.*

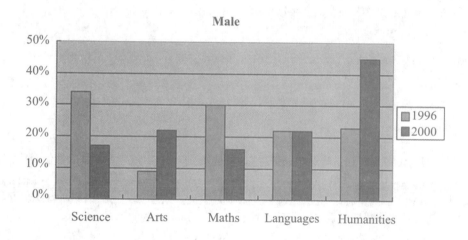

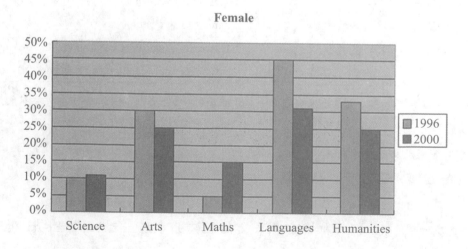

首段

改写题目	The charts show the changes in the performance of boys and girls in different subjects in 1996 and 2000.

主体部分第一段（从男性最高值开始说起，注意趋势的分类）

男性的最高值是 Humanities	Over 42% of boys achieved a high grade in humanities in 2000, up from 21%. The proportion of girls who achieved this standard in this subject was lower at 25% in 2000, although it was 32% in 1996.
然后说 Arts	Boys also improved their performance in the arts significantly with the figure rising from 9% to 21%, while the proportion of high-achieving girls dipped to 25%.

主体部分第二段（从女性最高值开始说起，注意趋势的分类）

女性的最高值是 Languages	Girls performed better than boys in languages, although the percentage of top achievers declined from 45% to 31%.
女性的其他上升的值 Science, Maths	There were also improvements in science and maths, in which the proportions of girls who achieved a good grade rose to 11% and 15% respectively.
对比男性	In contrast, the figures for boys in these two courses dropped.

总结段

总结趋势和主要特征	Overall, boys outperformed girls in science and maths, but the gap narrowed. While a larger proportion of boys reached higher standards in the arts, humanities as well as languages, the figures for girls saw a decline.

范文全文及点评

The charts show the changes in the performance of boys and girls in different subjects in 1996 and 2000.

Over 42% of boys achieved a high grade in humanities in 2000, up from 21%. The proportion of girls who achieved this standard in this subject was lower at 25% in 2000, although it was 32% in 1996. Boys also improved their performance in the arts significantly with the figure rising from 9% to 21%, while the proportion of high-achieving girls dipped to 25%.

Girls performed better than boys in languages, although the percentage of top achievers declined from 45% to 31%. There were also improvements in science and maths, in which the proportions of girls who achieved a good grade

代词，增强衔接度。

替换的表达。

替换的表达。

每个科目上进行男女对比。

文字信息和连接词的使用加强句子的连接。

rose to 11% and 15% respectively. In contrast, the figures for boys in these two courses dropped.

Overall, boys outperformed girls in science and maths, but the gap narrowed. While a larger proportion of boys reached higher standards in the arts, humanities as well as languages, the figures for girls saw a decline.

主体部分写了趋势，而结尾注意了对比。

学习要点

范文 8 这组图属于我们在范文 2 讨论过的动态图，出现了两个对比组，一个是男女，一个是科目。

这个时候，男女是优先对比组，而科目是第二对比组。尽量不要男孩和男孩对比自己的科目成绩，女孩和女孩对比。最好是在每个科目上对比男女的表现。

此外，借助这篇文章我也想讲一下单词替换的问题。

图表作文的单词替换主要体现在两个方面。

A. 常用单词的替换

常用单词一般就是涉及上升下降等表达的替换。

如下表所示：

	上升	下降
程度比较轻微	climb	dip, slide, fall
程度一般	increase, rise, grow	decline, drop, decrease, diminish
程度激烈	spiral, soar, rocket, surge, shoot up, leap	plumb, plunge, plummet, nosedive, tumble, slump

go up 这个表达过于口语化，应避免使用。

有时候，我们可以加上副词去增加变化。

常用的程度副词如下表所示：

轻微	slightly, modestly, moderately, marginally
显著	considerably, remarkably, notably, noticeably, markedly, substantially, significantly
极为显著	dramatically, radically, exponentially

这里值得一提的是，很多考生的误区是背很多替换词，包括复杂的替换词，其实这不是雅思官方要求和欣赏的写法。很多中国考生所使用的替换词不适合雅思的语境，也不够恰当，如 ascend, descend 等。

考官真正欣赏的反而是词性的变化，如 increase 这个动词可以用作名词，也可以用其分词结构 increasing。大家看看下面这个表格的变化。

	上升	下降
动词	The country's GDP increased by 5%.	This retail prices declined by between 5% and 9%.
名词加 of	There was an increase of 30% during the period.	There was a decline of 20% in car ownership.
名词在句首	The growth was significant during the period (around 4%).	The decline was dramatic in this country (about 3%).
使用 see	The 1990s saw a dramatic increase in the sales of videos.	Britain saw a steep drop in the sales of books in the 1990s.
使用 up 或者 down	The consumption of meat reached 45 thousand kilograms, up 40% from a year ago.	The trading volume dropped to 3 million a day, down 35%.
现在分词放在句中	The number of married people was 1.6 million, rising to 1.7 million in 1999.	The unemployment rate was 9% in 1990, dropping to 6% in 1995.
现在分词 showing 放在句中	The crime rate in 2000 was 15% compared to 10% in 1995, showing an increase of 5%.	The number of tourists was 3 million, showing a decrease of 14% compared with previous year's figures.
词组	The smoking rate in young girls was on the rise.	Motorcycle casualties were in decline.
趋势	There was an upward trend in sales.	The downward trend was significant during the period.

B. 与话题相关的单词的替换

这一部分比较难，能够更加真实地体现一个考生的水平。

就这篇文章而言，achieve high grades 是题目中的表达，而我在写作中换了很多种说法，如 achieve good grades, got high grades, performed well, reached high standards, top achievers, top-achieving students 等。

当然，这些表达对于一般的考生来说是很难的。我的建议是：如果考生拿不准怎么替换，那么就不要换。宁愿表达比较枯燥，也比换错的分数高。

关注总结，关注语法错误，关注句子变化，关注时态，你已经足够获得 7 分。

4.4.9 范文 9：动态图表＋总结段的写作

> *The charts below give information on the ages of the populations of Yemen and Italy in 2000 and projections for 2050.*
>
> *Summarise the information by selecting and reporting the main features and make comparisons where relevant.*

write at least 150 words.

YEMEN

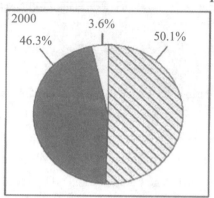 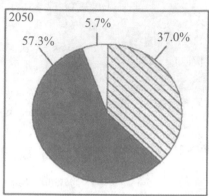

ITALY

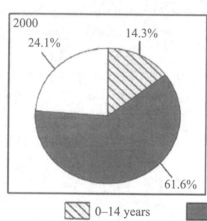 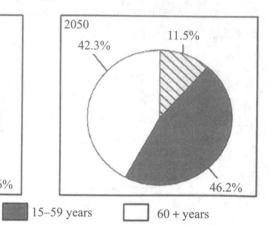

0–14 years　　15–59 years　　60 + years

首段

改写题目	The charts show the changes in the age profile of two countries in two separate years, 2000 and 2050.

主体部分第一段(先写 Yemen 2050 年的最高值 15 ～ 59 岁的人，其次是 14 岁以下的人，都要和意大利进行对比)

最高值是 15～59 岁的人	In Yemen, the proportion of people aged 15 to 59 is expected to rise significantly from 46.3% to 57.3% in 2050.
对比意大利的这一年龄段	This age group will also make up the largest proportion of Italy's population (46.2%) in 2050, despite a decline from 61.6% in 2000.
然后说 14 岁以下的人	The figures for those aged under 14 are likely to drop in both countries. Only 37% of Yemen's population is projected to fall into this age group, while the figure was much higher at 50.1% in 2000.
对比意大利	In Italy, the figure will decline to a lesser extent from 14.3% to 11.5%.

主体部分第二段：写老年人

最高值是意大利的老年人	Those aged 60 or above are projected to represent 42.3% of Italy's population in 2050, an increase of around 18%.
然后说 Yemen 的老年人	Yemen is also likely to see an increase in the proportion of elderly people in 2050 at 5.7%, although this age group will represent the smallest section of the population.

总结段

总结趋势和主要特征	Overall, the projection is that the populations of both countries will become older. Italy had an older population than Yemen in the year 2000, and the same is also predicted in 2050.

范文全文及点评

The charts show the changes in the age profile of two countries in two separate years, 2000 and 2050.

In Yemen, the proportion of people aged 15 to 59 is expected to rise significantly from 46.3% to 57.3% in 2050. This age group will also make up the largest proportion of Italy's population (46.2%) in 2050, despite a decline from 61.6% in 2000. The figures for those aged under 14 are likely to drop in both countries. Only 37% of Yemen's population is projected to fall into this age group, while the figure was much higher at 50.1% in 2000. In Italy, the figure will decline to a lesser extent from 14.3% to 11.5%.

预测值一般要用 expected to, likely to, projected to, estimated to 等表达进行提示。

连接词 also 和 this 增强句子的联系。

文字信息。

文字信息。

Those aged 60 or above are projected to represent 42.3% of Italy's population in 2050, an increase of around 18%. Yemen is also likely to see an increase in the proportion of elderly people to 5.7% in 2050, although this age group will represent the smallest section of the population.

文字信息。

Overall, the projection is that the populations of both countries will become older. Italy had an older population than Yemen in the year 2000, and the same is predicted in 2050.

学习要点

这组图表有两个对比组。第一个对比组是两个国家，Yemen 和 Italy，第二个对比组是三个不同的年龄组。因此我选择对比不同年龄群体两个国家的差异。

我们讲一下图表作文的总结。图表作文的总结是很重要的，因为雅思官方的评分标准有明确规定，不写总结会影响"Task Achievement"的分数。

这和 Task 2 大作文不同，大作文不写结尾段问题不大。

因此，我经常给考生的建议是：考场上如果时间不够，图表作文宁可主体段少写，也一定要把结尾段总结写了。

图表作文的结尾段总结要注意以下 7 点：

注意 1：动态图表和静态图表的总结各有重点。

注意 2：如果主体段没有比较，结尾段一定要比较。

注意 3：不要总结所有的信息，选择你觉得重要的信息（一般是 2～3 个）。

注意 4：不要出现数据。

注意 5：结尾段总结有时候可以写在开头段之后。

注意 6：不能使用 in conclusion 这样的字眼。

注意 7：不能表达个人观点、进行推测和预测。

下面详细讲一下。

注意 1：动态图表和静态图表的总结各有重点。

从下面这个表格可以看出动态图表和静态图表的主要总结的地方就是动态图表可以归纳趋势，而静态图表没有。例如这篇文章的图是动态图，那么总结段我就写了两个国家的人口都变老，这是一个趋势。

	动态图	静态图
最高值	√	√
趋势	√	
对比	√	√

注意 2：如果主体段没有比较，结尾段一定要比较。

我们可以看到这个动态图既有国家的对比，也有年龄段的对比。在主体部分，我写国家的趋势比较多，但是写国家的对比比较少。

因此，我在结尾段就非常注意国家的对比。第一句话说的是两个国家人口都变老，而第二句话说的是意大利的人口更加老一点。

注意 3：不要总结所有的信息，选择你觉得重要的信息（一般是 2～3 个）。

很多考生写结尾段总结时基本上把主体部分的内容又重新写了一遍，这样显得既重复又烦琐。

我这个结尾段就没有写最高值，也没有写 14 岁以下的年轻人如何变化，而是侧重了中老年人口的变化。

永远要记住，雅思图表作文考查的不是你芝麻西瓜都要检的能力，而是找出西瓜、不要芝麻的能力。

注意4：不要出现数据。

有些考生的结尾段出现数据的描述，那是不应该的。因为数据是细节，结尾段就应该是总结。

注意5：结尾段总结有时候可以写在开头段之后。

有些考官提倡结尾段总结写在开头段之后，然后再开始描述细节（也就是总结放在主体段前）。而剑桥雅思大部分的范文都是结尾段总结写在最后，所以我们的范文也都是总结在最后。

注意6：不能使用 in conclusion 这样的字眼。

图表作文没有讨论观点，只是陈述，所以没有conclusion（结论）这么一说。这也是为什么小作文中一般不会出现 however 和 therefore 这些单词（一般只用于观点论述）。

注意7：不能表达个人观点、进行推测和预测。

图表作文只需要根据数据进行总结和分析，图表里的数据不足以让你做任何的猜测。

4.4.10 范文 10：动态图表＋读数据的方法／连接词的使用

You should spend about 20 minutes on this task.

The graph below shows the quantities of goods transported in the UK between 1974 and 2002 by four different modes of transport.

Summarise the information by selecting and reporting the main features, and make comparisons where relevant.

Write at least 150 words.

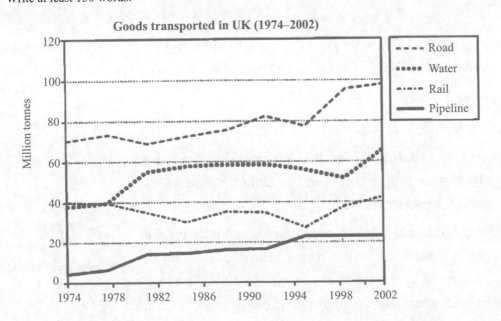

Goods transported in UK (1974–2002)

首段

改写题目	The line graph provides the information about the quantity of goods transported in the United Kingdom by four means of transport over the period 1974 to 2002.

主体部分第一段（先写最高值 Road，然后写 Water）

最高值是 Road	Shipping goods by road was the most popular choice throughout the period, with around 70 million tonnes of goods delivered by this mode of transport in 1974. The total amount had since then risen steadily, despite fluctuation, and reached about 100 million by 2002.
然后说 Water	The rising trend was also seen in transporting goods by water. The figure climbed to just under 60 million in 1982, after which it held steady at this level and then increased again to over 60 million tonnes in 2002.

主体部分第二段（先写 Rail，再写 Pipeline）

第三高值 Rail	There was an opposite trend in the use of trains for shipment. The amount of goods delivered by the railway system declined to 25 million tonnes in 1994, before increasing back to 40 million tonnes in 2002.
最后一个值是 Pipeline	At the same time, the figure for the pipeline was lowest, although it increased more than seven-fold from 3 million to 21 million tonnes.

总结段

总结趋势和主要特征	Overall, nearly all forms of transport saw an upward trend in the amounts of goods transported, while rail did not see any significant growth.

范文全文及点评

The line graph provides the information about the quantity of goods transported in the United Kingdom by four means of transport over the period 1974 to 2002.

Shipping goods by road was the most popular choice throughout the period, with around 70 million tonnes of goods delivered by this mode of transport in 1974. The total amount had since then risen steadily, despite fluctuation,

这句话的主语是 shipping goods，是一种运输方式，而不是数字。真正指代的东西是 the amount of goods transported by road，所以应该用介词 with。

and reached about 100 million by 2002. The rising trend was also seen in transporting goods by water. The figure climbed to just under 60 million in 1982, after which it held steady at this level and then grew again to over 60 million tonnes in 2002.

趋势类似的时候用 also。

表示上升或者下降到某种程度的时候用 to。

There was an opposite trend in the use of trains for shipment. The amount of goods delivered by the railway system declined to 25 million tonnes in 1994, before climbing back to 40 million tonnes in 2002. At the same time, the figure for the pipeline was lowest, although it increased more than seven-fold from 3 million to 21 million tonnes.

对比两个趋势的时候用 at the same time。

Overall, nearly all forms of transport saw an upward trend in the amounts of goods transported, while rail did not see any significant growth.

学习要点

我们稍微说一下图表作文的两个要点，包括连接词和描述数据的一些表达。

要点 1：连接词。

图表作文的连接词比较单调，但是也很重要。因为图表作文句子之间没有很强的逻辑关系和因果关系，基本上是一些事实的陈述。这些陈述如果没有连接词引导，就会感觉没有指导性。

表示类似趋势的连接词：also, similarly, likewise。

表示趋势对比的连接词：at the same time, on the other hand, in contrast/by contrast, by comparison。

虽然图表作文的连接词比大作文更为重要，但是不代表大家可以滥用这些连接词。很多考生每句话都写一个连接词，那是会被扣分的。

要点 2：描述数据的时候应该用的介词（或括号）。

	加什么数据	剑桥雅思真题例句
by	by 用于强调增加或者减少的幅度；可翻译成："增加了……"或"减少了……"	《剑5》Test 2 8 分考生作文 This percentage gradually declines by 10%–20% every decade（每 10 年下降的幅度是 10% 到 20%）.
at	at 基本上是描述数据最常用的一个介词，有三种可能。	1. 用于某个动词后面。 《剑9》Test 2 After peaking at 90 billion the following years, these calls had fallen back to the 1995 figure by 2002.

		《剑9》Test 2 Coal is predicted to increase steadily to 31q in 2030, whereas after 2014, gas will remain stable at 25q. 2. 用于句子的主语是 figure, number, proportion, amount 等词时。 《剑8》Test 2 The figure for resources was highest in 1991, at 20%. 3. 跟在所指代的数据后面。 《剑8》Test 1 North America had a lower proportion of degraded land at only 5% (指代前面的 proportion).
with	with + 数据经常用于句子的主语不是 figure, number, proportion, amount 等词时。	《剑9》Test 4 Petrol and oil are the dominant fuel sources throughout this period, with 35 quadrillion (35q) units used in 1980, rising to 42q in 2012.
to	to 后面常跟增加或者减少后最终的数值，这也是非常常用的介词。	《剑9》Test 2 There was a dramatic increase in mobile calls from 2 billion to 46 billion minutes. 《剑7》Test 2 By 2004 it had soared to almost 250 grams per person per week.
( )	括号比 at 和 with 的使用自由，经常跟在一个名词后面。括号主要是用在长句中，避免读数据使一个句子变得过分零散。	《剑8》Test 1 Europe, with the highest overall percentage of land degraded (23%), also suffered from over-cultivation (7.7%) and over-grazing (5.5%). 《剑7》Test 4 In 1980 Australia used coal as the main electricity source (50 units) and the remainder was produced from natural gas, hydro power (each producing 20 units) and oil (which produced only 10 units).

要点3：读数据的方法。

表达	例句
up to/as much as （多达）	The number of shoppers plunged by up to 23 per cent. House prices fell as much as 40% between 1980 and 1985.
only, a mere, no more than （仅仅）	The web economy represents a mere 1% of the country's GDP.

top, exceed （超过）	Exports topped (or exceeded) $ 10 billion in 2006.
in excess of （超过）	The turnover of the industry was in excess of $ 1.5 billion.
less than/more than （少于 / 多于）	More than one-third of the British population has trouble sleeping from time to time.
above/over/below （少于 / 多于）	The consumption of fish was just below 50 grams. Less beef was consumed (just over 50 grams).
a total of （总数）	A total of $900 million was spent on public transport.
remaining （剩余的）	Medicine represented 30 per cent of the company's revenues, merchandise 40 per cent and vehicles the remaining 30 per cent.
a(n) new/record/all-time high a new/all-time low [历史最高（低）值]	The enrolment rate dropped to an all-time low, 50%. The price of oil reached a new high in 2010. UK trade deficit with China rose almost 10% to 3 billion, a ten-year high.
ranging from...to... （在……范围内）	The price was volatile, ranging from $ 20 to $ 40.
respectively （分别地）	Animal grazing and tree clearance constituted 25 per cent and 40 per cent of the world's land degradation respectively.
peak at/amount to/equal （到达最高点，到达，等于……）	Britain's crime rate peaked at 9% or so in 1999. Time lost due to illness amounted to 1,200 working days.
versus （相比）	There was a steep decrease in the spending on education (223 million in 1989 versus 110 million in 1994).

要点 4：表示倍数的方法。

表达	例句
动词: double/triple/quadruple （升 2，3，4 倍）	Rent as a percentage of the household expenditure more than doubled between 1974 and 1998.
限定词: double/twice/triple/treble （是……的 2，3 倍）	This park will cover 1,400 surface acres, twice the size of the old park. This city had an accident rate triple the national average.
twofold, threefold... （2，3……倍）	There was a twofold increase in retail sales. The rent on average increased threefold in the past five years.

| twice/three times...as...as
（是……的 2，3 倍） | Television was twice as popular as washing machine in 1999.
Britons were twice as likely to die from heart attacks as Italians and three times as Chinese. |
| three/four...times more than
（是……的 3，4 倍） | An aggregate of 40,000 households bought new vehicles, three times more than the number in 2004. |

要点 5：读时间的方法。

表达	例句
during/over the period throughout... （整个时期之内）	Arable land diminished dramatically throughout the 1980s. The divorce rate remained high throughout the twenty-year period.
between...and..., from...to... （从……到……）	The growth accelerated during the period from 1995 to 2000.
...earlier （多长时间之前）	The proportion of homeowners was 78% in 1989, in marked contrast to a mere 35% three decades earlier.
at the beginning of ... （在……开始的时候）	At the beginning of the 1960s, around one third of the country's population were smokers.
by the middle of... （在……中期之前）	By the middle of the 20th century, the underground railway systems were built to serve more than one million passengers per year.
by the end of （在某一时间之前）	Expenditure on resources dropped by the end of the period.
by, until （直到）	The unemployment rate remains above 20% until at least 2020.
from...onwards （从……开始）	From the 1970s onwards, the volume of exports underwent a period of growth.
for at least... （最少多长时间）	The house prices remained high for at least five years.
in the following... （在随后的……年）	The investment fell to 5% per annum in the following five years.
the early.../the mid.../the late... （……年代的早期/中期/末期）	The crime rate rose from the mid-80s to the late 90s.
for the first time in... （多长时间内第一次）	Suicide rates declined for the first time in five years in 2010.

in a row （连续） for...consecutive years （连续……年）	The number of visitors increased for five years in a row.

4.4.11 范文 11：静态图表＋句型的变化

The chart below contains information provided by Australia's tertiary institutions about the percentage of male and female students who enrolled in different subjects in 1995.

Summarise the information by selecting and reporting the main features and make comparisons where relevant.

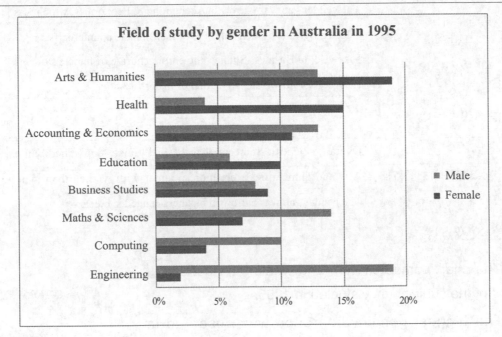

Field of study by gender in Australia in 1995

首段

改写题目	The chart compares men and women in Australia in terms of the subjects they studied in 1995.

主体部分第一段（从男性最高值开始说起，注意和女性的比较）

男性的最高值是 Engineering	The biggest gender difference was observed in Engineering, where 19% of male students chose this subject, in marked contrast to 2% of female students.
然后说 Computing 和 Math	The gender gap was also clear in Maths and Computing, with around 14% and 10% of males pursuing a degree in these two fields.

主体部分第二段（从女性的最高值开始描述，注意分组）

女性的最高值是 Arts & humanities	In contrast, female students' favourite subject was Arts & Humanities, where they outnumbered men (19% to 13%).
女性的第二最高值是 Health	Health was another popular subject, attracting 15% of female students, more than three times the figure for men (only 4%).
描述 Education，因为女性多过男性，和上面的两个科目性质比较类似	Women were also more likely to study education than men (10% and 6% respectively).

主体部分第三段（其余的科目）

第一个科目	The gender gap was narrow in Accounting & Economics, which was selected by 13% of men and 11% of their female counterparts.
第二个科目	Likewise, in Business Studies, the enrolment rate of female students (9%) was closely matched by that of males (8%).

总结段

总结趋势和主要特征	Overall, scientific subjects were basically male-dominated while Arts and Humanities were more popular with women than men. The gender gap was narrow in business-related subjects.

范文全文及点评

The chart compares men and women in Australia in terms of the subjects they studied in 1995.

The biggest gender difference was observed in Engineering, where 19% of male students chose this subject, in marked contrast to 2% of female students. The gender gap was also clear in Maths and Computing, with around 14% and 10% of males pursuing a degree in these two fields.

In contrast, female students' favourite subject was Arts & Humanities, where they outnumbered men (19% to 13%). Health was another popular subject, attracting 15% of female students, more than three times the figure for men

从最高值说起，gender difference 是个词伙。

also 这个连接词增强了句子的衔接度，让读者知道这几个科目的特点就是男性多过女性。

pursue a degree 这个词伙替换了前面的 study subjects, choose this subject 等，展现了词汇量。

文字信息，让读者知道这个科目在女生中非常流行。

代词 another 和下面一句话的 also 都可以增强句子之间的衔接度。

(only 4%). Women were also more likely to study education than men (10% and 6% respectively).

文字信息,让读者知道这一段描述的两个科目有什么特点。

The gender gap was narrow in Accounting & Economics, which was selected by 13% of men and 11% of their female counterparts. Likewise, in Business Studies, the enrolment rate of female students (9%) was closely matched by that of males (8%).

替换的表达。

Overall, scientific subjects were basically male-dominated while Arts and Humanities were more popular with women than men. The gender gap was narrow in business-related subjects.

学习要点

我们最后说一下句型变化。图表作文的主体段一般来说大概写 6 ~ 7 句话,所以我总结了一下常用的句型,熟练使用后基本上就可以应对主体部分的写作。

动态图表的必备句式:

必备句式 *1*:分词结构。

必备句式 *2*:while/whereas 或者 although 引导的状语从句,或者是 and/but 引导的并列句。

必备句式 *3*:after which, during which time, by which time, when, where 引导的定语从句。

必备句式 *4*:倍数。

必备句式 *5*:比较级和最高级。

必备句式 *6*:there be 句型。

静态图表的必备句式:

必备句式 *1*:while/whereas 引导的状语从句,有时候也可以用 and/but 并列连词连接。

必备句式 *2*:倍数。

必备句式 *3*:比较级。

必备句式 *4*:最高级。

必备句式 *5*: in comparison with, compared with/to。

有时候,如果图表里出现地点,如国家,有可能使用 where 引导的定语从句。

图表作文里切忌用定语从句描述数据。

4.5 图表作文其他学生常问问题的讲解

问题 *1*:雅思 Task 1 作文和 Task 2 作文哪个重要?如何安排考试时间?

回答：雅思作文考试的小作文部分比较简单，主要体现在以下两点：① 所用单词或句型相当单调，重复率大；② 图形大同小异，虽然描述对象不同（例如：人口、失业率、入学率等），叙述方法和写作思路基本一致。

因为上述两个原因，考生在备考过程中，主要注意力应该集中在大作文上。此外，剑桥雅思中心的官方网站屡次强调，大作文占分 2/3，而小作文占分 1/3；因此，即便考生在小作文中获得较好成绩，最终决定总成绩的还是大作文。在考试中，考生不妨先完成 Task 2（用时 40 分钟），然后开始写小作文（用时 20 分钟）。

问题 2：到底是 millions, thousands 还是 million, thousand？

回答：后者。只有"数字 + million or thousand"的说法。很多考生困惑的原因是很多图表的度量单位上写的是 millions 或者 thousands。在句子中出现的时候，这些词不能加复数。

问题 3：number 和 amount 可否互换？ proportion 和 percentage 可否替换？

回答：否。the number of 后面一般接可数名词的复数形式，the amount of, the quantity of 和 the volume of 类似，后面一般接不可数名词。

proportion 和 percentage 可以替换，结构都是 proportion of + 名词。The figure for... 是常用的名词替换方法。小作文一般用不到 data 这个词。

问题 4：雅思图表作文里是否可以出现第一人称 I 或者 we？

回答：否。雅思图表作文需要正式的书面语言，强调客观和准确。因此，在语言使用方面，要注意减少第一人称的使用，减少非正式的说法。

例：I believe that the graph shows a significant decline in the youth smoking rate.

改：吸烟率是否下降应该依据图表决定，不应该由你是否相信而决定。因此，应该把句子中的 I believe that 去掉。

问题 5：引用数据可否用括号以及定语从句？

回答：引用数据的时候可以使用括号。不需要用定语从句，直接引用数据便可。

例：Lamb was consumed in a lower quantity, which was around 50 grams.

改：which was 可以去掉，后面的数字作为同位语。

正：Lamb was consumed in a lower quantity, around 50 grams.

译：羊肉的消耗量小了一点，大概是 50 克。

问题 6：饼图里，表示"占据"的词（如 represent）用主动语态还是被动语态？

回答：主动语态。类似的词（组）有 account for, comprise, form, constitute, make up, take up.

问题 7：程度副词（如 dramatically）一般出现在什么位置？

回答：修饰上升、下降的副词一般放在动词的后面。

例：The number of obese people in the UK increased dramatically in at least ten years.

译：在至少 10 年中，英国患肥胖症的人数急剧上升。

常用的程度副词如下表所示：

低	slightly, modestly, moderately, marginally
显著	considerably, remarkably, notably, noticeably, markedly, substantially, significantly
极为显著	dramatically, radically, exponentially

问题 8：比较句中，到底是使用 that 还是 those 来指代前面的名词？

回答：取决于前面的名词是单数形式还是复数形式。

例：The crop yields worldwide in 1990 were 15% up on that of 1985.

改：that 错误，不能指代前面的名词复数 yields。

正：The crop yields worldwide in 1990 were 15% up on those of 1985.

译：1990 年，全世界的农作物产量比 1985 的产量高出 15%。

问题 9：描述数据时，表示"大约"的时候，使用 approximately 还是 approximate？

回答：一般都是使用副词 approximately，类似的词有 around, about 和 some。也可以用 or so 和 an estimated...。

例 1：The sales reached $ 4.5 million or so.

译：销售量到了大概 450 万美元。

例 2：The company controlled an estimated 90 per cent of the country's calls.

译：这个公司控制着这个国家大概 90% 的电话。

around, about 和 or so 也可以表示时间。

例 3：For twenty years or so, there was an upward trend in the number of deaths caused by heart disease.

译：从心脏病导致的死亡数字来看，上升的趋势差不多持续了 20 多年。

同理，表示"接近"的一些词，如 nearly, almost 也是副词。

问题 10：表示"2/3"的时候，用 two thirds 还是 two third？

回答：two-thirds 是正确的表达。其他的常用表达有 a quarter of, one third of, two-fifths of, half of。

例：African Americans make up two-thirds of the city's population.

译：非洲裔美国人占据这个城市 2/3 的人口。

问题 11：比较句最常见的错误是什么？

回答：比较句当中，比较的对象必须一致。

例：The proportion of commuters who used public transport was nearly 30% in 2010, much higher than 2000.

改：不清楚比较的是年代，还是人数。

正：The proportion of commuters who used public transport was nearly 30% in 2010, much higher than the figure in 2000.

译：使用公共交通工具上下班的人的比例在 2010 年差不多是 30%，比 2000 年的数据要高得多。

使用 in contrast to, in comparison with 和 compared with 的时候，一定要注意比较的对象一致。

例：In contrast to two-parent families, the income was much lower in single-parent families.

改：句子主语是 the income，不能和 two-parent families 相比。

正：In contrast to two-parent families, single-parent families had much lower incomes.

译：和双亲家庭相比，单亲家庭的收入要低得多。

使用 while 和 whereas 的时候，注意两个单句的结构一致。

例：Whereas car emissions in developing countries more than doubled, industrialised countries dropped by half.

改：car emissions in developing countries 和后面的 industrialised countries 不一致。

正：Whereas car emissions in developing countries more than doubled, those in industrialised countries dropped by half.

译：发展中国家的汽车尾气的排放量超过以前的两倍，而工业国家的尾气减半。

问题 *12*：before 和 after 有什么替代词？

回答：before 的近义词有 prior to, ahead of, preceding，而 after 的近义词有 following, subsequent to。

问题 *13*：有时候图里出现 million，后面还有单位，如 units，数据读多了会觉得很烦，可以不可以省略？

回答：million 和 thousand 这些词肯定不能省略，但是单位在后面可以省略。试看下面《剑 9》的第二套考官范文的例子。不难看出，开始写了个单位 minutes 后，后面就没写，但是 billion 这个数字是不能省略的。

例：Local fixed line calls were the highest through the period, rising from 72 billion minutes in 1995 to just under 90 billion in 1998.

问题 *14*：可不可以用 that 去替换名词，从而加分？

回答：用对了就可以，但是根据我的经验，在小作文中能用到的机会不是很多，而且很多考生都用错。

例：The proportion of expenditure on food in Turkey was higher than that of Italy.

改：大家可以看到，在这个句子里，前面是 proportion of expenditure，和后面的 that of Italy 根本就不对称。

正：The proportion of expenditure on food in Turkey was higher than the figure for Italy.

或者：The proportion of expenditure on food in Turkey was higher than that in Italy.

问题 15：in 和 by 放在年代面前有什么区别，如 in 2006 和 by 2006 有什么区别？

回答：前者用一般过去时，后者用过去完成时。

例 1：The crime rate rose to 2% in 2006.

例 2：The crime rate had risen to 2% by 2006.

如果是预测值，in 和 by 区别不大。

例 3：The crime rate is projected to rise to 2% by/in 2050.

问题 16：小作文什么时候可以用到 when，where 引导的定语从句？

回答：when 一般修饰年代，而 where 一般修饰地点或者科目。

例 1：Chicken consumption rose to 200 grams in 2001, when it surpassed that of beef.

译：鸡肉消费量在 2001 年涨到 200 克，在那一年，它超过了牛肉的消费量。

例 2：The most severe land degradation was in Europe, where 23% of land was degraded.

译：最严重的土地退化发生在欧洲，在那里，23% 的土地退化了。

问题 17：小作文可不可以用 furthermore，meanwhile，in addition 这样的连接词？

回答：一般不怎么使用。即便使用，也要注意恰当性。大作文也应该减少使用这些词。

小作文常用的连接词有 also, similarly, in contrast, by contrast, however, on the other hand。

和大作文一样，连接词使用要恰当，不能机械。

4.6 图表作文常见错误汇总

4.6.1 普通图表作文

错误 1：millions 或者 thousands 在句子中出现时不能加复数，只有数字 + million or thousand 的说法。

错误 2：the number of 后面一般接可数名词的复数形式，the amount of，the quantity of 和 the volume of 类似，后面一般接不可数名词。

错误 3：图表作文中不可以出现 I 或者 we，雅思图表作文需要正式的书面语言，因此在语言使用方面要减少第一人称的使用，减少非正式的说法。

错误 4：引用数据时不需要使用定语从句，直接引用数据即可。

错误的例子：North America had a lower proportion of degraded land, which was only 5%.

正确的例子：North America had a lower proportion of degraded land, at only 5%.

错误 5：表示"上升"和"下降"的词（increase, drop 等）都是不及物动词，没有被动语态。也就是说 was increased 是错的。

错误 6：reduce 和 raise 这两个词小作文里用不到，因为是及物动词；arise 也不能替代 rise；

ascent/descent 不能用在小作文里。

错误 7：表示"占据"的时候，最好不要用 occupy，而是使用 account for/represent/constitute。

错误 8：outnumber 的主语一般是可数名词的复数形式，不能是不可数名词；而 overtake/surpass 的主语多为不可数名词，或者是 number/figure/amount/proportion 这样的词；exceed 表示超过某一个特定的数字或容量。

错误 9：对象词错误。对象词就是图里的数字所代表的东西。

错误 10：时态错误。图表作文里多用一般过去时，有时候可能使用一般现在时或者将来时。过去进行时不可能出现。

错误 11：描述动态图表时过分注重数据和小的波动，而忽视趋势。所谓趋势，就是一个区间内最主要的一个变化（例如，如果大部分时候是上升，就是上升趋势）。

错误 12：描述静态图表时过分侧重数据，没有将数据归类和归纳（具备类似特征的数据要放在一起）。

错误 13：很多考生使用奇怪的表示"上升"或者"下降"的替换词，而忽视词性的变换（应该使用名词或者分词去替换动词）。

错误 14：increase/rise/drop 这些词用作名词的时候，前面要用不定冠词 a 或 an，如 saw a drop。

错误 15：比较句中，比较对象不一致。

错误 16：doubled 是不及物动词，没有被动语态。

错误 17：rise 的过去时是 rose，而不是 rised。其过去分词是 risen，而不是 rose。

错误 18："percentage/proportion…accounted for"永远是错的，只有人或者物可以充当 accounted for 的名词。

错误 19：while 是连词，要连接两个句子。

错误 20：副词修饰动词，应该放在动词后面。如 increased slightly，但是不能说 slightly increased；slightly 也不能修饰名词，也就是说 a slightly increase 是错的，应该是 a slight increase。

错误 21：形容词不能修饰比较级，如 was slight higher than 是错的，应该是 was slightly higher than。

错误 22：remained 后面只能加形容词，也就是说 remain constantly 是错的，应该是 remain constant。maintain 不是 remain 的替换词，只能说 remained the most important means of transport，而不能是 maintained。

错误 23：reach 这个词后面直接可以跟数据，如 reached 32 million，不需要加 to。

错误 24：在动态图表里，一般是 rose + "数字" + -fold，而不是"rose five times"。

错误 25：没有 comparing with 的说法，只有 compared with 的说法。

错误 26：当表示"数字很低，几乎可以忽略"的意思时，应该用 minimal，而不是 minimum。

错误 27：表示年龄的时候，可以说 people aged between 20 and 40，不能把 aged 写成 age。

错误 28：图表作文总结段不能表达个人观点、进行推测和预测，只需要根据数据进行总结和分析。

错误 29：图表作文总结段不能出现数据，因为数据的表述已经在主体部分完成。

错误 30：图表作文最好不要出现 in addition, moreover, meanwhile 这些连接词。

4.6.2 流程图

错误 31：equipment 是不可数名词；facilities 是可数名词的复数形式。

错误 32：materials 是"材料"的意思，而 element 是"元素"的意思（不能用于流程图）。

错误 33：如果 A 步骤是在 B 步骤之前发生的，那么应该是 A happens, before B。

错误 34：流程图中不能使用祈使句。

4.6.3 地图

错误 35：cross 是动词，而 across 是介词（不能充当谓语）。

错误 36：expand 是"扩大"的意思，而 expend 是"花费"的意思。

错误 37：happen, take place 是"发生"的意思，都没有被动语态。

错误 38：地图题只能说西边和东边（western side 或者 eastern side），不能说左边和右边（left side 和 right side）。

4.7 流程图写作攻略

很多考生将流程图视作"洪水猛兽"。流程图以前每年出现四次左右，但是自 2014 年以来，流程图出现的概率大幅度提高。一般来说，流程图和普通图表的区别在于：

● 流程图基本上不会出现数据，文字信息占主要地位。

● 流程图以描述为主，比较的机会比较少。

● 流程图需要描述图中出现的所有信息，而普通图表则不需要描述每一个数据。

● 流程图的时态比较单一，主要是用一般现在时。

● 流程图的分段比较灵活，只要不同阶段之间的差距很明显，就可以另起一段。

流程图有两种：一种是工序图，一般是描述一个产品怎么制作的，服务怎么提供的。另一种是生物生长图，一般是描述一个生物是怎么成长的。

这两种图有一定的区别。

	工序图	生物生长图
谓语	被动语态为主	主动语态比较多
时间	一般不会出现	每个生物生长阶段都可能会描述时间
对比	有时候一道工序有几种加工的方法，需要对比	主要是不同阶段生物个体（如大小、行为）的对比

流程图的备考要注意四点：

注意 *1*： 常用的表达。

注意 *2*： 词语的转换和连接词的使用。

注意 *3*： 确定流程的第一步。

注意 *4*： 流程图不要使用祈使句。

注意 *1*： 常用的表达。

考生要注意掌握段落连接或者不同阶段之间的说法（sequence expression）。

表示首阶段的一些说法：

① The process starts from + 名词 or 动名词

② At the first/initial stage, + 句子

③ At the beginning of the cycle, + 句子

④ During the initial phase, + 句子

⑤ The beginning of the whole cycle is marked by + 名词 or 动名词

⑥ 名词 or 动名词 + is the first step in + 名词 or 动名词

表示次阶段的一些说法：

① The second stage is + 名词 or 动名词

② The next step in the process is + 名词 or 动名词

表示最后阶段的一些说法：

① 名词 or 动名词 + is the last step in the procedure.

② The final phase of the procedure is about + 名词 or 动名词

③ In the final phase, + 句子

④ Entering the final phase, + 句子

⑤ 名词 or 动名词 + is the final stage.

注意 *2*： 词语的转换和连接词的使用。

单词的转换主要体现在名词转换成动词。

流程图中经常会出现一些器具的名词，如 grinder，mixer 和 heater，考生需要改成动词使用，如 ground，mixed 和 heated。

例： The powders are delivered to the grinder, where they are ground into cement.

当然，很多时候，有些动词是可以用在很多流程图作文中，如 process（处理），deliver（发送），transport（运输），send（发送）和 transfer（转移）。很多考生怕自己写的动词太俗，从而追求变化，但是往往用错了替换词。*流程图考查的是考生叙述的能力，连接词的使用和步骤的清晰比较重要，动词不要太过纠结。*

常用的连接词和动词如下图所示。表示"传送""转化"和"使用"的动词一般都是用在工序图里，使用被动语态。

传送	deliver, send, transfer, transport
转化	convert into, transform into
使用	utilise, employ, use
扔掉或者丢弃	remove, throw away, dispose of
生产，产生，制造	produce, generate, create, make
连接词	afterwards, subsequently, then, in the next step, after that, next, finally

注意3：确定流程的第一步。

考生要注意流程图读图的顺序。很多流程图都是以一个循环的形式出现，考生经常不知道从什么地方开始叙述。

常用的办法是从描述比较简单的地方开始，以下是一个例子：

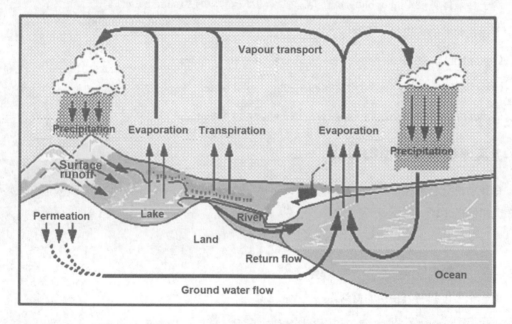

读图步骤：这个图表面上很复杂。最好的次序应该从降雨 (precipitation) 开始描述，直接说降雨到什么地方，然后说雨水怎么在地面上存在和运动，最后说水怎么重新回到天空。

如果先从水这一步骤开始描述，那么就非常复杂，毕竟水是从很多地方，用不同方式到达天空的。

注意4：流程图不要使用祈使句。

很多考生在流程图中喜欢写祈使句。万万不可，一定要写完整的句子。

看下面的例子。

错误的句子：Put these materials in the heater.

正确的句子：These materials are put in the heater.

流程图常问问题 1：经常写不够字数怎么办？

不管是普通图表还是流程图，如果字数不够，可以在结尾段总结的时候写得详细点。也可以在描述过程中加些文字信息，例如说这个过程比较复杂，或者用时比较长，或者工具比较复杂等。

流程图常问问题 2：为什么流程图的分词经常要用 "being done"，而不是普通图表里的 "doing"？

流程图很多时候涉及工具的使用，在某个东西的制作或者加工过程中，这些材料都是被处理，要用分词的被动语态 "being done"。大家可以看看下面两句话：

普通图表：The crime rate dropped to 2%, before rising to 3%.

流程图：The chocolate is heated, before being sent to the mould.

流程图常问问题 3：除了连接词之外，流程图中描述工序的时候，还有什么其他表达可以表示先后顺序？

可以使用分词结构和状语从句。试看下面的例子：

例子：液体黄油 (liquor butter) 在过滤之后，变成固体黄油 (solid butter)。

下面几句话的意思是一样的：

Liquor butter is filtered, before being converted into solid butter.

Once liquor butter is filtered, it is converted into solid butter.

Liquor butter is filtered, until it is converted into solid butter.

4.7.1 工序图写作要点和范文

很多考生在写流程图（工序图）的时候遇到的问题是：①信息太多，无从下手；②确定了信息后，不知道如何描述。

工序图的叙述流程可以遵循以下步骤：

步骤 1：确定材料。

每一个工序都有其使用的材料。

步骤 2：确定工具（假如图里给出工具的信息）。

每一个工序都有其使用的工具。

步骤 3：确定动词。

然后将这些信息写成一句话。

以《剑8》第三套的流程图为例。

步骤 1：确定材料是 limestone 和 clay。

步骤 2：确定工具是 crusher。

步骤 3：确定动词是 crush。

写成句子：Limestone and clay are crushed by the crusher into powder.

> ***The diagrams below show the stages and equipment used in the cement-making process, and how cement is used to produce concrete for building purposes.***
>
> ***Summarise the information by selecting and reporting the main features and make comparisons where relevant.***

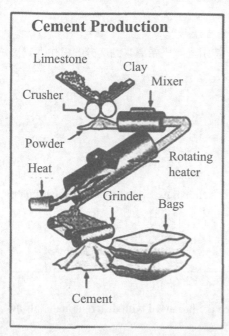

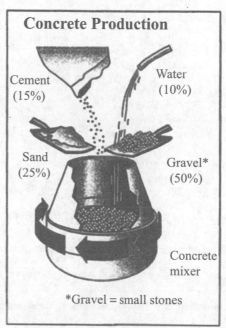

按照我们前面总结的流程图的三个步骤，我们可以一个个描述出来。

步骤 1 确定材料	步骤 2 确定工具	步骤 3 确定动词
确定材料是 limestone 和 clay	确定工具是 crusher	确定动词是 crush
句子：Limestone and clay are crushed by the crusher into powder.		
确定材料是 powder	确定工具是 mixer	确定动词是 deliver, mix
句子：Powder is delivered to the mixer, where it is mixed.		
确定材料是 mixture	确定工具是 rotating heater	确定动词是 send, heat, rotate
句子：The mixture is sent to the rotating heater, in which it is heated and rotated.		
确定材料是 powder	确定工具是 conveyor belt, grinder	确定动词是 place, grind
句子：Powder is placed on the conveyor belt.		
确定材料是 powder	确定工具是 grinder	确定动词是 ground

句子：Powder is ground by the grinder into cement.		
确定材料是 cement	确定工具是 bags	确定动词是 pack
句子：Cement is packed in bags.		
确定材料是 cement, water, sand, gravel	确定工具是 concrete mixer	确定动词是 rotate
句子：15% of cement, 10% of water, 25% of sand and 50% of gravel, four ingredients of concrete, are rotated in the concrete mixer.		

当然，这些句子有的是单句，需要变化一下，特别是对于希望拿到 7 分的考生尤其要注意句式的变换。

句式 1：使用分词结构。

句 1：Powder is placed on the conveyor belt.

句 2：Powder is ground by the grinder.

可以合成一句：Powder is placed on the conveyor belt, before being ground by the grinder.

句式 2：使用 once 或者 until 引导的状语从句。

例：Ingredients are rotated in the concrete mixer, until they are turned into concrete.

然后加入连接词，连接这些句子，就可以成为完整的文章。

The two diagrams show how cement and concrete are produced with different materials and facilities used.

<u>At the first stage</u>, limestone and clay are crushed by the crusher into powder. The powder is <u>then</u> delivered to the mixer, where it is mixed. The mixture is <u>subsequently</u> sent to the rotating heater, after which it is heated and rotated. <u>In the next step</u>, the rotated powder is placed on the conveyor belt, before being ground by the grinder into cement. This final product is packed in bags.

In the process of the concrete production, gravel accounts for 50% of materials, while cement, water and sand represent 15%, 10% and 25% respectively. These materials are placed in the concrete mixer, which rotates clockwise until concrete is produced.

To summarise, cement production consists of 4 stages, starting from crushing materials into powder and ending at bagging cement. In contrast, concrete production is simple, mixing four materials.

The chart shows how urban refuse is assorted for recycling.

Summarise the information by selecting and reporting the main features and make comparisons where relevant.

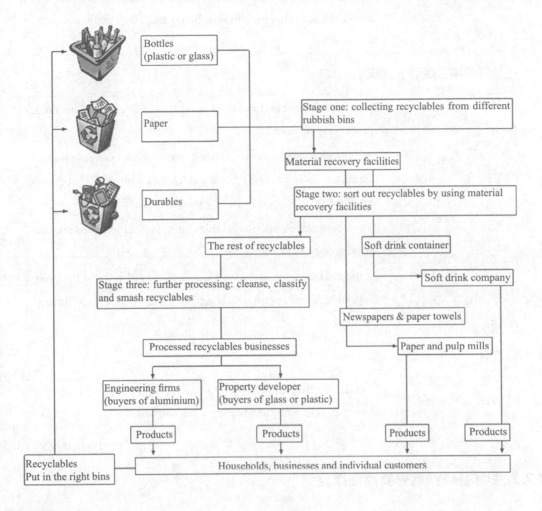

首段

改写题目	The diagram shows that the recycling of urban refuse consists of four stages.

主体部分第一段（第一和第二阶段）

第一阶段	The process starts from the collection of three different kinds of recyclables, namely bottles, paper and durables, from respective rubbish bins.
第二阶段	Following this stage, recyclables are delivered to material recovery facilities, where these recyclables are categorised and treated for different purposes.
	Newspapers and paper towels are transported to paper and pulp mills and transformed into products that can be used by end customers.

| | Another type of recyclables, soft drink containers, are processed in soft drink companies before being used by customers (e.g., households). |

主体部分第二段（第三和第四阶段）

	The rest of recyclables are cleansed, classified and smashed, constituting the third stage.
第三阶段	Once these procedures are finished, recyclables are subsequently distributed to engineering firms (which buy aluminium products) and property developers (who buy glass and plastic).
	These companies use recyclables to manufacture products for intended customers.
第四阶段	At the final stage, households are expected to dispose of the used, recyclable items appropriately and put them in the right bins as instructed.

总结段

| 总结趋势和主要特征 | Overall, the diagram shows how the recycling loop involves the classifying, cleansing and reusing of recyclables. |

(word count: 185 words)

4.7.2 生物成长图写作要点和范文

生物生长图的时态可以用一般现在时，有时候可以用将来时（表示以后可能生长的一种状态）。

大部分动词都是使用主动语态，如 grow, hatch, emerge, take place, occur, start, begin 等都是不及物动词，要用主动语态。

生物生长图经常涉及时间的叙述，要注意句式的变化：

It takes（放入时间）to...

This stage lasts for（放入时间）...

After a period of（放入时间），...

For（放入时间）...

During a（放入时间）period ...

生物生长图有时候要注意对比，对比主要体现在生物的变化，如长度、生活的地点、形态等。

下面我们首先分析一下《剑10》的一篇考官范文。

The diagrams below show the life cycle of a species of large fish called the salmon.

Summarise the information by selecting and reporting the main features and make comparisons where relevant.

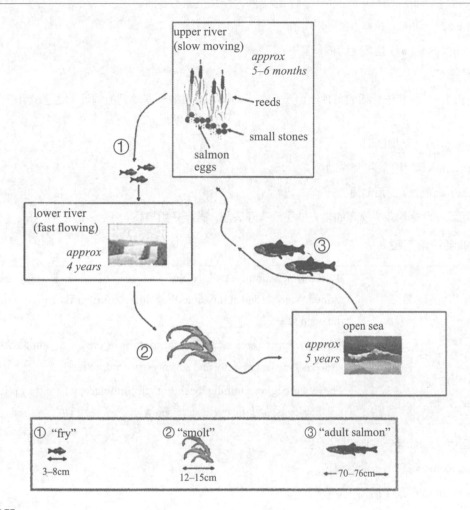

首段

句 1: 描述第一个图	Salmon begin life as eggs on a pebbly riverbed, hidden among reeds in the slow-moving upper reaches of a river.
句 2: 描述 ①	After five to six months the eggs hatch into "fry".
句 3: 描述第二个图	For approximately the next four years, these baby salmon will live in the lower, faster-flowing waters of their river.
句 4: 继续描述第二个图	During this time they measure between three and eight centimetres in length.

学习点 1: 流程图的难点之一是句子间的联系，生物进化图因为有时间，所以时间是一个连接句子的方式。

begin life... 生命开始

After five to six months... 5～6 个月之后

For approximately the next four years 差不多 4 年

学习点 2：流程图也可以使用代词，这点和大作文是差不多的。

these baby salmon 这些小鲑鱼

during this time 在这段时间内

they 它们

学习点 3：生物进化图的另外一个难点在于动词，这里的一些动词的词性发生了变化，很容易出错。

begin (life)，及物动词

hatch into（孵化），不及物动词

measure（测量），系动词

学习点 4：这篇范文有趣的地方就是没有开头段，直接开始描述。

主体部分第二段

句 1：描述②	By the time salmon reach twelve to fifteen centimetres, they are termed "smolt", and at this time they migrate further downriver into the open sea.
句 2：描述第三个图	After five years at sea, the salmon will have grown to adult size, which is between seventy and seventy-six centimetres.
句 3：描述③	They then begin swimming back to their birthplace, where they will lay their eggs, and the cycle starts anew.

学习点 1：看看一些连接的表达。

By the time 到了……的时候

At this time 在那个时候

After five years 在 5 年后

then 然后

学习点 2：学习一下词伙。

migrate downriver 向下游迁徙

open sea 大海

lay eggs 产卵

start anew 重新开始

总结段

句 1：总结阶段	The salmon passes through three distinct physical stages as it grows to maturity.

句 2：总结每阶段的特点	Each of these stages takes place in a very different aquatic location.
句 3：对比不同阶段的特点	It is noteworthy that the first two stages of this fish's life occur in a freshwater environment, while the third stage is lived in saltwater.

学习点 *1*：流程图的结尾都是总结整个过程有多少个阶段。

学习点 *2*：第二句和第三句说了一个地点，就是水环境的变化和不同；中间 take place 和 occur 进行了替换。

学习点 *3*：词伙。

distinct stages 不同的阶段

grow to maturity 成熟

aquatic location 水的位置

The diagram below shows the life cycle of the butterfly.

Summarise the information by selecting and reporting the main features and make comparisons where relevant.

The lifecycle of a butterfly

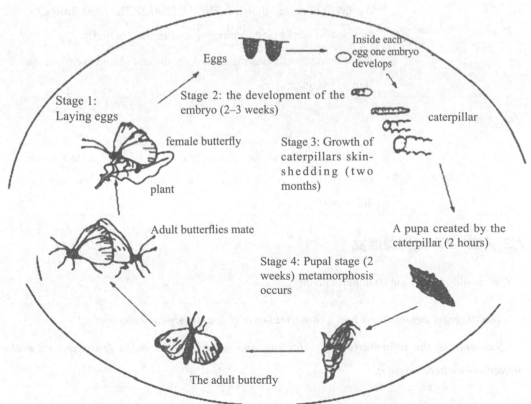

首段

改写题目	The diagram shows that the life cycle of a butterfly can be broadly divided into four stages.

主体部分第一段 (第一和第二阶段)

第一阶段	At the first stage, female butterflies lay eggs on plants, after mating with male butterflies.
第二阶段	It is followed by the second stage, which lasts for two to three weeks.
	At this stage, inside each egg is an embryo, which develops into a caterpillar eventually.

主体部分第二段 (第三和第四阶段)

第三阶段	The third stage is the longest, taking two months, during which time the caterpillar grows gradually until it is fully formed.
	This stage ends with a two-hour-long process in which the caterpillar creates a pupa.
第四阶段	At the final stage, known as the pupal stage, the pupa grows for around two weeks before emerging into an adult butterfly.
	Adult butterflies fly and mate, marking the end of one cycle and the start of the other.

总结段

总结趋势和主要特征	Overall, the lifecycle of a butterfly consists of four distinct stages and there are remarkable changes in the appearance of the insect in different stages.

4.7.3 《剑 12》流程图范文

You should spend about 20 minutes on this task.

> *The diagram below shows how geothermal energy is used produce electricity.*
>
> *Summarise the information by selecting and reporting the main features and make comparisons where relevant.*

Write at least 150 words.

Geothermal power plant

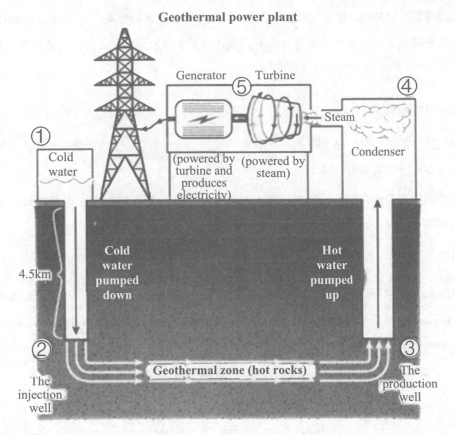

我写的范文（8分）

The flow chart shows the entire process of exploiting geothermal energy for electricity generation.

In the first stage, cold water stored in a container on the ground is pumped down through an injection well, which is 4.5 kilometers in length, to reach the geothermal zone. Here comes the second stage: the pumped water is heated as it flows through hot rocks, and subsequently pumped up, in the next phrase, by a production well to a condenser.

The other parts of the process are above ground. In the condensation stage, the heated water produces steam, which runs a turbine. It is the machine which can power a generator to create electricity, the end product of the whole procedure, and the power generated is to be transferred to the grid in the final stage.

Overall, a geothermal power plant operates by using water as a medium to convert geothermal energy into electricity, and the whole process involves five steps in total.

4.8 地图题（maps）的写作

地图题在最近两年的考试中频繁出现，体现了剑桥雅思考试中心出题灵活的特点。地图题和普通图表题里的动态图有两个相同之处：（1）两者都强调比较；（2）有可能出现不同年份。

和普通图表题不同的是，地图题没有数字，只是强调地点的描述。

地图题的写作和流程图一样，图上的所有信息都要包括，不能够忽略某个地点。当然，一些地点如果比较雷同，可以放在一起写。

按照地点的不同特征，我将地图题分成两种：第一种是普通地图题，第二种是建筑内部题。

两者的主要区别是：前者一般有指南针，后者没有，这就意味着在描述上语言有很多不同，包括方位词（east, west, north, south）的使用。

4.8.1 普通地图题

普通地图题的特点是一般这个地点比较大，比如一个城市、一个大公园、一个山村等。这种图中往往都会有一个指南针标志。

我将地图题又分成两种，一种是只有两个时间的，另一种是有两个以上时间的。前者用对比的方式去写比较好，而后者按照时间去描述比较方便。

两个时间

> *The two maps below show an island, before and after the construction of some tourist facilities.*
>
> *Summarise the information by selecting and reporting the main features, and make comparisons where relevant.*

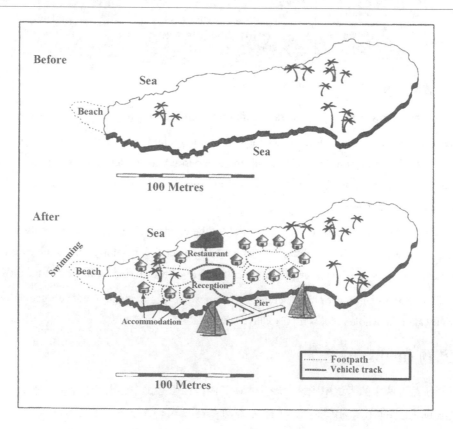

审题和完成的步骤：

第一步：观察图中有多少个时间。	这幅图中有两个时间，确定以对比为主。

第二步：选择第一个描述对象。一般按从左到右、从上到下、顺时针方向的顺序描述。	也就是描述第一幅图西边的 beach 和 trees。
第三步：对比下图对应地点的变化。	描述第二幅图西边的 beach，还有 accommodation，道路等。
第四步：选择第二个描述对象。	描述第一幅图东边的树。
第五步：对比下图对应地点的变化。	描述第二幅图东边的 huts。
第六步：描写两幅图中间的变化。	描述第二幅图中间的 restaurant，还有 pier。

在描述每个地点的时候，要注意两点：

● 每个地点的具体方位要说明一下。方位的描述有两种可能：（1）图上的地理位置；（2）相对于参照物的位置。例如，上面第二幅图中间的 reception，你既可以说它在岛的中间（in the centre of the island），这是它在图上的地理位置；也可以说它在两群房子中间（lying between two clusters of huts），这是这个 reception 相对于参照物 huts 的位置。

那么选择哪一种位置描述呢？我认为图上的地理位置优于参照物的位置，因为前者更加清晰和直接。但是，如果有些地点的位置不是简单的东南西北，也不是简单的中间或者东北角、西北角等，这个时候用参照物描述比较好。比如第二幅图中的 pier，地理位置就不好描述，这个时候说在参照物 reception 的南边更为方便。

有时候为了表达丰富，可以地理位置和参照物都描述。

● 选择动词，如 located, situated, sited, constructed, built, developed，诸如此类。

举例：

步骤 1：选择 beach 作为描述对象。

步骤 2：确定地理位置：① 图的西边；② 树的西边；以地理位置为主。

步骤 3：确定动词，如 located。

这样就写出了下面的句子：

A beach was located on the western end of the island.

描述对象　　动词　　　地理位置

下面我按照上面表格的描述次序，将每个地点描述一下。

开头段（主要是改写）

maps 改成 diagrams；

show 改成 illustrate；

增加一个 changes，突出改变；

题目中的 tourist facilities 改成 tourist attraction。

句子：The diagrams illustrate the changes to a small island, which has now developed into a tourist attraction.

主体部分第一段（描述岛屿西边的主要变化）

描述第一幅图的 beach	地理位置是西边	动词是 located
句子：A beach is located on the western end of the island.		
描述第一幅图的 trees	地理位置是西边	动词是 scattered
句子：Some trees are scattered in the western part of the island.		
对比第二幅图的 huts	地理位置是西边	动词是 built
句子：Some huts have been built in the western part of the island to accommodate tourists.		
对比第二幅图的 footpaths	地理位置是西边	动词是 connected
句子：These huts are connected by footpaths.		
对比第二幅图的 swimming area	地理位置是西边	动词是 designated
句子：An area has been designated for swimming off the beach.		

主体部分第二段（描述岛屿东边的主要变化）

描述第一幅图的树	地理位置是东边	动词是 scattered
句子：Trees are scattered in the eastern part of the island.		
对比第一幅图东边的 huts	参照物是东边的树木	动词是 constructed
句子：A circle of huts have also been constructed to the west of trees.		
描述第二幅图中间的 restaurant and reception	地理位置是中间	动词是 added
句子：A restaurant, as well as a reception building, has been added in the middle of the island.		
描述第二幅图下面的 pier	参照物是 reception	动词是 built
句子：A pier has been built to the south of the reception for docking boats.		

现在把这些句子放在一起看看：

A beach is located on the western end of the island. Some trees are scattered in the western part of the island. Some huts have been built in the western part of the island to accommodate tourists. These huts are connected by footpaths. An area has been designated for swimming off the beach.

Trees are scattered in the eastern part of the island. A circle of huts have also been constructed to the west of trees. A restaurant, as well as a reception building, has been added in the middle of the island. A pier has been built to the south of the reception for docking boats.

当然，这两段话有两个问题。

第一，是字数不够，如果只是写简单句为主，只有六句是不够的，要多写一句。

例如我们看到 restaurant, reception 和 pier 有路相连，那么可以说 All these facilities are linked by a road.

第二，这些句子内容比较零散，中间连接不是很密切，句子结构也比较单一。可以通过下列方法去增加句子的连接和变化。

- 加上一些强调变化的句子。

例如：

One remarkable change is...

Another significant change is that...

One main development is that...

A new addition is...

Comparing these two maps, we can see...

another development is...

那么第一段话，描述 beach 和 swimming area 的时候，可以说 Comparing two maps, we can see that an area has been designated for swimming off the beach on the western end of the island.

- 加上 where 引导的定语从句，解释某个地方的一些特点。

那么第一段话，描述房子的时候，可以和树木联系在一起，毕竟它们都在岛屿的西边。

可以说：Some huts have been built in the western part of the island, where there were only some trees, to accommodate tourists.

- 当出现单句的时候，可以尝试用 and 与其他句子连接。

如第一段的 footpaths，可以和上面这句话连接。

可以说：Some huts have been built in the western part of the island, where there were only some trees, to accommodate tourists, and these huts are connected by footpaths.

- there be 句型也可以广泛用在地图作文中，用于介绍一个新的地点。

如第二段的 huts。

可以说：There are also some huts which have been constructed next to trees in the eastern part of the island.

- while 可以用来连接两个对比的变化。

如第二段最后两句话，可以用 while 相连。

可以说：A restaurant, as well as a reception building, has been added in the middle of the island, while a pier has been built to the south of the reception for docking boats.

结尾段（总结）

最后，也是最重要的一个部分，就是写结尾。地图变迁题，主要是描述图里主要的变化。这两幅图的主要差距就是增加了很多的设施去满足游客的需要。

整篇范文如下：

The diagrams illustrate the changes to a small island, which has now developed into a tourist attraction.

Comparing two maps, we can see that an area has been designated for swimming off the beach on the western end of the island. Some huts have been built in the western part of the island, where there were only some trees, to accommodate tourists, and these huts are connected by footpaths.

There are also some huts which have been constructed next to trees in the eastern part of the island. A restaurant, as well as a reception building, has been added in the middle of the island, while a pier has been built to the south of the reception for docking boats. All these facilities are linked by a road.

In summary, the island has undergone many significant changes to cater for the needs of tourists, including a restaurant, huts and a pier, while the trees have been well preserved.

（字数：158）

多个时间

大家现在来看看地图题出现多个时间的情况。如果地图题出现多个时间，最好一个时间一个时间地写，每个时间里强调一下：（1）新的变化；（2）不变的东西。

> *Topic 2 : Chorleywood is a village near London. The map shows how the village developed.*
> *Prepare a report for a university lecturer describing the development of the village.*

按照我们前面总结的地图题三个步骤，我们可以一个个描述出来。

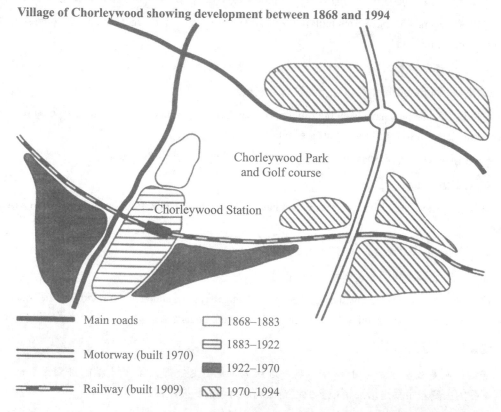

Village of Chorleywood showing development between 1868 and 1994

▬▬ Main roads	▭ 1868–1883
══ Motorway (built 1970)	▤ 1883–1922
▭▬▭ Railway (built 1909)	▦ 1922–1970
	▨ 1970–1994

这个地图题虽然只有一幅图，但是有四个时间，也就是事实上有四幅小图，每幅小图都要说清楚变化。

第一阶段：（1868 到 1883 年）主要有两条道路，白色的村庄，和中间的高尔夫球场

步骤 1	步骤 2	步骤 3
确定主路（main road）		
从左上方的道路开始看起	地理位置是从北到南	动词是 crossed
句子：A main road crossed the area from north to south.		

确定 village	参照物是 main road	动词是 located
句子：The village was located next to a main road.		
考虑到句子的变化，这两句话可以写成：The village was located next to a main road crossing the area from south to north.		
确定 park and golf course	参照物是 village	动词是 sited
句子：The park and golf course were sited to the east of the village.		
考虑到句子的变化，可以写成：There were a park and a golf course sited to the east of the village.		

第二阶段：（1883 到 1922 年）主要变化是增加了一条铁路和一个火车站，村庄也变大了，其他的不变

步骤 1	步骤 2	步骤 3
确定 village	参照物是 main road	动词是 expanded
句子：The village expanded alongside the main road to the south.		
确定 railway	地理位置是从西到东	动词是 built
句子：a railway was built from west to east.		
确定 railway station	参照物是 village	动词是 constructed
句子：The railway station was constructed in the village.		
为了句子变化，可以将两句话写成一句（通过 with 这个词连接）：		
A railway was built from west to east with the railway station in the village.		

第三阶段：（1922 到 1970 年）村庄继续变大，增加了一条新的主路

步骤 1	步骤 2	步骤 3
确定 village	参照物是 railway 地理位置是西南角	动词是继续扩大
句子：The development of the village continued next to the railway in the south-western corner of the area.		
确定 motorway	地理位置是东边	动词是 constructed
句子：A motorway was constructed on the eastern side of this area.		

第四阶段：（1970 到 1994 年）村庄继续变大

步骤 1	步骤 2	步骤 3
确定 village	参照物是 main road 和 railway 的交点以及 railway 和 the motorway 的交点	动词是 developed
句子：The village developed surrounding motorway intersections with the railway and one of the main roads.		

然后通过一些年代的信息，将这些句子连接起来，变成一篇文章（一般来说，一个时间写一个主体段，但是，因为最后两个时间的内容比较少，可以合为一段）：

The map illustrates the changes in an area called Chorleywood during the period from 1868 to 1994.

In 1883, the village was located next to a main road crossing the area from south to north. There were a park and a golf course to the east of the village.

During the period between 1883 and 1922, the village expanded along the main road to the south and in 1909, a railway was built from west to east with the railway station in the village.

The village continued the expansion next to the railway in the south-western corner of the area between 1922 and 1970, while a motorway was constructed on the eastern side of this area in 1970. During the next period, the village developed surrounding motorway intersections with the railway and one of the main roads.

Overall, it is clear that the major developments of the village took place around transport infrastructures.

（字数：153）

地图题常问问题 *1*：地图题使用什么时态？

地图题中如果出现了过去的时间，那么就使用一般过去时。

如果没有出现时间，或者出现的时间是 "present" 或者 "now" 的字眼，那么就用一般现在时。

有时候，地图题可能会出现预测的变化，那么这个时候可以用将来时，或者 "be predicted/projected/likely to" 这种表达。

这些时态的处理和动态图时态的处理是差不多的。

地图题常问问题 *2*：地图题一般会用哪些动词？

地图变迁题常用动词如下表所示：

词义	所用动词
位于	located, situated, sited 注：lie 也是个选择，但是没有被动语态
连接	link, connect（既可以用主动，也可以用被动）
某地点的面积变大	expand（一般用主动）
某地点的面积变小	shrink（一般用主动）
某地点被去掉	replaced, demolished, removed, displaced（一般用被动） vanish, disappear（一般用主动）
某地点转移	relocated（一般用被动）

地图题常问问题 *3*：地图题一般会用到哪些描述方位的词？

地图变迁题常用描述方位的词如下表所示：

常用表达	例句
east, west, south, north, southeast, southwest, northeast, northwest	• City A, some 120 km south-east of City B, is a big city. • The garden is in the northwest of the area. • The airport is a few miles to the south of the city.
...end, corner of ... 角落或者尽头 ...side of... 在……的一边 ...part of ……的部分	• The village at the north end of the forest expanded in the 1990s. • The park is less than five miles from the southwest corner of the city. • Residential neighbourhoods are primarily on the east and west sides of the town. • The park covers the southern part of the city.
located in/near... situated in/near/at... lie in/between... 位于，坐落于	• The building is located in the north-west corner of the district. • The library is situated near the war memorial. • The retail area lies between two main streets.
from the east to the west 自东向西 from the south to the north 自南向北	• The river flows from the east to the west.
alongside, along, near, next to, adjacent to 靠近，沿着	• Much of the park was located alongside the river. • The building is adjacent to the library. • The railway is located next to the bridge.
其余的表达：junction/intersection（交界处），in the proximity to...（在……附近）	

4.8.2 建筑内部题

建筑内部题一般是一个建筑的内部结构。这种题目中一般没有指南针，也就是意味着不能写东南西北。

写这种题目，可以关注下面的要点：

要点 *1*：这些图往往有一个 entrance（入口），你可以假设自己从 entrance 进去，然后开始描述屋内的房间和设施。当你描述一个地方之后，可以顺带说一下附近的地点（前后左右的房间等）。你可以想象自己在建筑物里面走，这个时候会用到一些动词。如：

穿过一个地方…… cross...

进入一个建筑 enter...walk into

右转 turn right

左转 turn left

图里经常会有过道，可以说：

沿着走廊走 walk through the corridor

沿着走廊往下走 walk down the corridor

沿着走廊往上走 walk up the corridor

沿着过道 along the corridor

在走廊的尽头 at the end of the corridor

走过走廊 cross the corridor

也可能会有楼梯和电梯，可以说：

上楼梯 walk up the stairs/go up the stairs

下楼梯 walk down the stairs/go down the stairs

到达楼梯底 reach the bottom of the stairs

坐电梯下去 take the lift down to...

坐电梯上去 take the lift up to...

要点 *2*：在描述建筑物里的房间的时候，描述地点的位置，可以用下面一些表达：

就在旁边 right next to...

就在右边 immediately on the right...

在左手边 on the left hand side

在右手边 on the right hand side

在远端 on the far side of

正对着 facing somebody

在楼的后面 at the back of the building

在楼的前面 at the front of the building

在第一层 on the ground floor

在第二层 on the first floor

在楼底下 below ground level

要点 *3*：建筑内部图在描述和分段上和地图变迁图差不多，如果是两个不同的时间，就强调变化；如果是三个不同的时间，就分开一个时间一个时间地写。在时态上：

- 如果图里出现过去的时间（也就是考试时间以前的年代，如 2014 年），就用一般过去时。

- 如果图上面写的是 now，或者是没有标明时间，就用一般现在时。

- 如果是强调过去到现在的变化，就用现在完成时。

- 如果图上的某些地点一直没变，可以用一般现在时。

- 如果图上出现了 future, proposed change, planned 这样的字眼，或者是出现了以后的时间，就用一般将来时。

大家用下面这个图练习一下：

> *The diagrams below are existing and proposed floor plans for the redevelopment of an art gallery.*

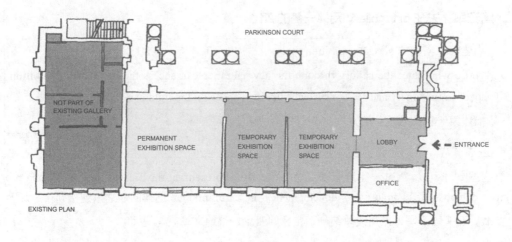

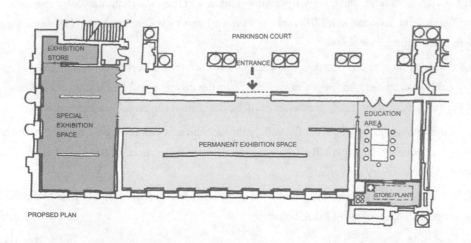

第一段：关注 entrance 附近地方的变化

描述第一幅图的 entrance，lobby 和 office
A visitor can enter the building from the entrance, and then walk into the lobby area. The office of the gallery is on the left hand side.
描述和第二幅图同一个位置的 education area, store
This section of the art gallery will be converted into an education area and a store.

第二段：关注 art gallery 中间的变化

描述第一幅图的中间部分
The central area of the art gallery is currently divided into three sections: a permanent exhibition space and two temporary exhibition spaces.
描述和第二幅图同一个位置的 exhibition space, 还有 entrance 的变化
The entrance will be moved to the Parkinson Court side of the building, and the entire central area will be designated for exhibitions.

第三段：关注 art gallery 另外一侧的变化

描述第二幅图的 special exhibition space
Those who enter the gallery through the new entrance can access the permanent exhibition space immediately and see the special exhibition space on the right hand side.
描述第一幅图的这个地方
This area is not part of the gallery at present.

这些句子可以通过一些连接词，如 currently, at present, at the present time, 或者 one proposed change, one possible change, a new development, in the future plan 这样的表达来连接句子。

然后开头段改写，结尾段总结一下主要的变化，整篇文章就写完了。

The two pictures show the potential changes to the layout of an art gallery.

Currently, a visitor can enter the gallery from the entrance, and then walk into the lobby area with the office of the gallery on the left hand side. This section of the art gallery will be converted into an education area and a store in the future floor plan.

The central arca of the art gallery is now divided into three sections: a permanent exhibition space and two temporary exhibition spaces. According to the new plan, the entrance will be moved to the Parkinson Court side of the building, and the entire central area will be designated for permanent exhibitions.

Because of this change, those who enter the gallery through the new entrance can access the permanent exhibition space immediately. They would also see the special exhibition space on the right hand side, and this area is not part of the gallery at present.

Overall, it is clear that the gallery will possibly dedicate more of its space to exhibitions in the future, and provide visitors with easy access to exhibition areas.

（字数：186）

第5章

书信写作攻略

雅思考试分为学术类和普通培训类(general training)。普通培训类的小作文不是图表，而是书信。

这个可以理解，毕竟参加这项考试的考生都是要移民的，而移民之后的生活和工作需要处理很多信件，例如和当地政府、税务局、雇主、邻居、商店等都有各种书信交流。

虽然两类考试的 Task 2（大作文）每次考试的题目都不同，但是差不多。最近几年，很多学术类大作文题目被用于普通类，两类考试在 Task 2 的区分已经越来越不明显了。

雅思考试中心自 2006 年起明确规定，考生在写书信的时候不需要写日期和地址。因此，雅思的信件主要分三个部分：称呼、主体部分和信末礼貌语及署名。

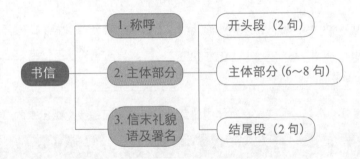

5.1 书信写作的评分标准

书信和图表作文的评分标准非常类似，除了第一部分 Task Achievement。我们可以再次看看这些评分标准。

标准 *1*：Task Achievement（写作任务完成情况）

标准 *2*：Coherence and Cohesion（连贯与衔接）

标准 *3*：Lexical Resources（词汇丰富程度）

标准 *4*：Grammatical Range and Accuracy（语法多样性及准确性）

书信写作的评分点和图表作文的评分点差不多，唯一的区别就是 Task Achievement 这一项有一定的差异。下面是我从雅思官方网站截取的 Task Achievement 的评分中英文对照细则，其他几个评分点请大家参考 3.1。

7分 Task 1 作文（图表作文）的特点（中英对照）

Task Achievement (TA)	写作任务完成情况
• covers the requirements of the task	• 写作内容涵盖写作任务的要求
• (General Training) presents a clear purpose, with the tone consistent and appropriate	• （普通培训类）清晰地呈现写作目的，行文语气一致且恰当
• clearly presents and highlights key features/ bullet points but could be more fully extended	• 能就主要内容 / 要点进行清晰的呈现与强调，但未能更为充分地展开

6分 Task 1 作文（图表作文）的特点（中英对照）

Task Achievement (TA)	写作任务完成情况
• addresses the requirements of the task	• 根据写作任务要求作文
• (General Training) presents a purpose that is generally clear; there may be inconsistencies in tone	• （普通培训类）写作目的基本清晰；行文语气有时未能保持前后一致
• presents and adequately highlights key features/ bullet points but details may be irrelevant, inappropriate or inaccurate	• 呈现并充分地强调了主要内容 / 要点，但有时含有不相关、不恰当或不准确的细节信息

根据这些评分标准，我们需要在写作中注意什么呢？下面是我总结出来的书信写作的要点。

评分标准	注意事项
Task Achievement	注意信件的 tone（语气） 信件有没有 clear purpose（说清楚目的） 信件有没有很好地对应题目的 bullet points（信件内容要点）
Coherence and Cohesion	连接词 描述信息是否有一定合理的顺序 分段恰当
Lexical Resources	用词注意信件的 style（也就是正式和非正式信件的用词区别） 单词使用的灵活
Grammatical Range and Accuracy	句子结构准确，富于变化 写没有错误的句子 时态准确

下面我们分析一下《剑10》的考官范文，看看范文是怎么诠释雅思评分标准的。

5.2 《剑 10》考官写的信件范文

题目

You are going to another country to study. You would like to do a part-time job while you are studying, so you want to ask a friend who lives there for some help.

Write a letter to this friend. In your letter

- *give details of your study plans*
- *explain why you want to get a part-time job*
- *suggest how your friend could help you find a job.*

题目大意

你要去其他国家学习。你想找一个兼职，因此要外国居住的朋友帮助你。

写信给你的朋友，在你的信里

- 写出你的学习计划
- 解释你为什么希望有这份工作
- 建议你朋友怎么帮助你找工作。

范文

Dear Sally,

My departure date for New Zealand is drawing near, and I am busy with preparations. I have enrolled at an institution called "ABC English" in Wellington, for a six-month Advanced course, full time. It is quite expensive but I am hopeful of improving my pronunciation, especially.

To assist in covering the costs of my study, I aim to find a part-time job. Not only are the co_____ high, but also I know that rental acco_____ [表明目的。] in the capita_____ 可以使用。 to say nothing of food and heating expenses! So I would very much like to arrange some temporary employment before I arr_____ [表明目的。]

> 感叹号，在非正式信件中可以使用。

I was wondering if you could ask around among your friends and colleagues to see if anyo_____ 缩写，在非正式信件中_____ner, gardener, or nanny for their children. I know you have a可以使用。 _____n Wellington which you could canvas for me, if you wouldn't mind. I'd be so grateful.

I look forward_____ 适合于非正式信件的结束语。 _____soon.

Best wishes,

Margot

范文大意

亲爱的萨莉，

去新西兰的出发日期越来越近，我正忙着筹备。我已经注册了"ABC 英语"学校的课程，在惠灵顿，这个高级课程为期 6 个月，是全日制课程。课程相当昂贵，但我特别希望改善我的发音。

为了支付学习费用，我的目标是找一份兼职工作。不仅是大学学费相当高，而且我也知道，在首都租房也不会便宜，更不用说食物和取暖费用！所以，我非常希望能够在出发前定下某一临时工作。

我在想，你是否可以问问你周围的朋友和同事，看是否有人想要请一个家庭清洁工、园丁，或者他们孩子的保姆。我知道你在惠灵顿有一个广泛的社会网络，如果你不介意的话，可以帮我安排一下。我会非常感激。

我期待很快见到你。

最美好的祝愿

玛戈特

范文分析

我在下表中罗列了一些书信的主要评分要点，并且解释了这封信如何符合评分标准。

评分标准	范文的执行情况
Task Achievement tone（语气）	这是一封写给朋友的非正式信件，所以这封信里出现了很多非正式信件的特点： ·有很多标点符号，如第二段用了感叹号。 ·出现了 wouldn't，I'd 这种缩写。 ·best wishes 是适合于朋友之间信件的结束语。
Task Achievement 信件有没有 clear purpose（清晰地说清楚目的）	信件分别在第二段和第三段的第一句话表明目的。 第二段的第一句话说 I aim to find a part-time job（我想打工）。 第三段的第一句话说 I am wondering if you could ask around...（我在想，你是否可以问问周围……）。
Task Achievement 信件有没有很好地对应题目的 bullet points（信件内容要点）	这封信件前三段，一段对应信件的一个 bullet point。 第一段关于学习计划。 第二段关于为什么自己要找工作的解释。 第三段关于请朋友帮忙。
Coherence and Cohesion 连接词	范文没有依赖那些比较明显的连接词，如第二段最后一句话的连词 so，而主要是依赖句子的意思连接。
Coherence and Cohesion 描述信息是否有一定合理的顺序	第一段的逻辑顺序是从原因到结果：去新西兰上课，改善发音。 第二段先说结果，然后解释原因：希望找工作，因为费用太高。 第三段也是先说结果，然后解释原因：希望朋友帮忙，因为有人脉。

Coherence and Cohesion 分段恰当	每段话长短差不多，都是 2~3 句话。
	每段话针对题目里的一个 bullet point。
Lexical Resources 用词注意信件的 style （也就是正式和非正式信件的用词区别）	这封信是非正式信件，用词可以比较随意，但是这封信中考官用了很多比较礼貌的表达，如 I am wondering if（第三段的第一句话）。这么做是因为在请求朋友帮忙，礼貌一点比较合适。
Lexical Resources 单词使用的灵活	这封信中使用了很多词伙： 如 part-time job 用 temporary arrangement 替换 date is drawing near 日期越来越近 improve pronunciation 改善发音 costs of my study 我的学习费用 college fees 大学费用 rental accommodation 租的房子 heating expenses 暖气费 a wide social network 广泛的社交网络
Grammatical Range and Accuracy 句子结构准确，富于变化	这封信的句子变化非常多，特别是第二段第二句话，用了 not only 引起的倒装句。 而第三段的 I know you have a wide social network in Wellington which you could canvas for me, if you wouldn't mind 用了宾语从句、定语从句和状语从句
Grammatical Range and Accuracy 时态准确	这封信是描述一件将来和现在发生的事情，所以使用的主要时态是将来时和现在时。

总的来说，考官范文执行了四个评分标准，内容充实，扣题，语言地道，句子连接紧凑，语气和用词合理，句子复杂、准确、变化，展示了很高的写作能力。

学生句子点评

我也让我的学生写了这篇文章，我从他们的作文里抽出一些常见的错误来分析一下。

学生的句子：Yes, please do not forget to tell me the contact person's name and email address.

错误的原因：请别人做事却用几乎命令的语气，不是很恰当。

提升的句子：I would be grateful if you could give me the contact details of the employer who would like to offer a job.

学生的句子：I am writing this letter to see if you can help me to find a part-time job in Sydney.

错误的原因：太过正式，这个句子更像是正式信件的开头语。

提升的句子：I am so delighted to tell you that I have got an offer from Sydney University and this means that we're gonna meet soon! But I do need you to do a favour if you don't mind.

学生的句子：I would like to get a part-time job during I am studying.

错误的原因：during 是介词，不能加句子。

提升的句子：I would like to get a part-time job when studying in Wellington.

学生的句子：I enrolled an oral English training class in Beijing and intend to improve my speaking English first.

错误的原因：时态错误，过去时表示的是过去发生的事情，应该用完成时态，表示结果。enrol 是不及物动词。

提升的句子：I have enrolled in an oral English class in Beijing and hopefully can improve my pronunciation.

5.3 信件完成的步骤

在考场上和练习中，学生在拿到一个书信题目后，可以通过下面的步骤在 20 分钟内完成写作。

步骤 1： 阅读题目	确定信件的类别（正式、半正式或非正式）。 确定语气（咨询、道歉、申请、投诉、请求、抱怨等）。 确定时态。
步骤 2： 编故事	确定一个合理的故事。 这个故事有内容，有相关的词伙最好。
步骤 3： 写开头	平时多积累信件的开头表达。 开门见山，说清楚来信的目的。
步骤 4： 写主体段落	主体段落要对应题目的三个小问题。 每个段落的句子要注意逻辑性，可以是演绎（deduction），也可以是归纳（induction）。
步骤 5： 写结尾和署名	平时多积累信件的结尾表达。

步骤 1：阅读题目

在这个过程主要是确定三个要素：

①类别（正式、半正式或非正式）。

提示：一般从收信人的身份来判断。

素未谋面的人一般是正式信件。

熟悉但是不算亲朋好友的人（如上司、老师等）一般是半正式信件。

亲朋好友一般是非正式信件。

②信件的目的（咨询、道歉、申请、投诉、请求、抱怨等）。

信件的目的决定了你的用词和语气。

例如写求职信，你不能说 I expect you to offer me this job.（我觉得你会给我这个工作），语气明显太强烈。

你可以说 I would be grateful if I can take on this responsibility.

询问信（语气客气，恳求；强调信息和帮助的重要性。）

求助信（语气客气，恳求；强调信息和帮助的重要性。）

意向或者申请信（语气客气，恳求；强调信息和帮助的重要性。）

建议信（语气客气；强调自己的建议有一定价值，但是只是建议，决定权在别人那里。）

友情信（语气客气，不要命令朋友做什么；随意，亲密，不要太正式。）

抱怨信（语气坚定，表明这是对方的问题和责任；语气委婉和礼貌，当希望对方做出补救措施或者赔偿的时候。）

③信件的时态。

信件写作和雅思的口语考试很相似，对时态的要求比较高，在过去、现在、将来三大时态中要做很好的选择。

一般信件的时态可以从题目中推敲出来。

例如，如果你是要申请一份工作，那么这份工作还没开始，很有可能在说到对这份工作的展望时，使用将来时。

如果你描述你以前的工作经历，那么要用过去时或者现在完成时。

如果你描述你现在的工作和情况，要用一般现在时。

步骤 2：确定你要写的事情和词伙。

信件和雅思口语的 Part 2 差不多，经常要你描述一个事件、一个物件等。

很多考生在考场上确定自己要描述的事件或者物件的过程耗时过长，耽误很多时间，从而影响整个考试。

我们在这里介绍的方法是"词伙逆袭法"，也就是根据你熟悉的词伙和话题来确定事件和物件。

例如，你最近学习了一个环境类话题的词伙，那么你完全可以转换一下，使其成为信件的内容。

例 1：信件要求你给你们公司准备一个演讲，那你可以说你准备了一个关于环保的演讲。

例 2：信件要求你写想在海外找工作，那你可以说希望做一个环境工程师。

例 3：信件要求你对城市的一个改建项目提意见，那你可以说这个项目会产生环境影响。

步骤 3：写开头段

开头段直接说明目的，很多考生最大的问题就是写很多背景，开头段太长，导致考官不知道这封信的目的是什么。

步骤4：写主体部分

主体部分是书信的重要评分部分，要注意下面四点：

① 一般来说，信件的题目会有三个 bullet points（要点）即三个小问题，大家一定要注意三个问题都要回答。

② 每个主体段落的中心句，也就是第一句话，要清晰明了，让考官知道这段话的主要内容。很多考生喜欢写很多背景，但是考官不知道你是否在回答题目，从而扣分。

③ 一定要分段。主体部分大概分2～3段，每段2～3句话。分段也是一个评分的标准，并且影响信件的可读性。

④ 注意时态和语气的准确性。这是信件写作的一个难点，一封信中往往需要考生在时态间进行有效和准确的转换。

用词要体现你对语气的正确判断：

① 咨询信、求职信、请求信和建议信一般来说语气要礼貌委婉。

② 抱怨信语气要坚定。

③ 友情信和邀请信语气可以轻松随和。

其他评分标准，如语法、用词、逻辑、句子结构等，都是和大作文差不多，在此不再赘述。

步骤5：写结尾和署名

结尾以简洁为主，有固定的常用语，可以记忆备考。

署名主要是由信件的 style 决定的。

我们下面通过几篇范文的讲解，分别阐述书信写作比较重要的一些环节。我的关注点主要还是在前三个评分标准，也就是 Task Achievement，Coherence and Cohesion，还有 Lexical Resources。而关于语法和句子结构，和大作文的评分标准差不多。

5.3.1 范文 1＋tone/style

> *You and your family are moving to another country, and you are looking for rented accommodation there.*
>
> *Write a letter to a property agent, in your letter*
>
> • *introduce yourself and your family*
>
> • *describe the type of accommodation that you hope to find*
>
> • *give your preference for the location of the accommodation.*

题目大意

你和你的家人都移居到另一个国家，你正在那里寻找出租房。

写一封信给一个房地产经纪人，在你的信里

- 介绍你自己和你的家人

- 描述你希望找到的住处类型

- 给出你偏爱的住宿的位置。

类别：求助信，正式信件

范文及点评

Dear Sir or Madam,

I am writing to ask for your help finding suitable accommodation in New Zealand.

My name is James Chen, and my permanent residency application has been approved by New Zealand Immigration. I am about to move to Auckland with my wife and two children in August.

I am interested in a three-bedroom house or apartment, preferably with heating available, because I have been told that the winter in Auckland can be chilly. I hope that my children can live in a warm and cozy place, which I believe can help them to adapt to the new environment.

We would meanwhile prefer a quiet neighbourhood where my children can attend good schools. It would also be appreciated, if the location is close to supermarkets and other amenities such as parks. We would possibly travel to work by public transport, so hopefully we have easy access to bus stops.

I am confident in your support in our house search, and I look forward to hearing from you.

Yours faithfully,

James Chen

考试中，这种称呼是直接给出来的，事实上也在提示你这是正式信件。

正式信件的开头。

不能缩写成 I'm 的形式，因为这是正式信件。

这样的表达能突出这是请求信。

正式信件的结尾。

正式信件的信末礼貌语。

学习要点

信件写作的一个难点是 tone 和 style 的选择。信件一般按照写信人和收信人的关系分成三种。

如果与收信人不认识，是**正式信件**。

如果与收信人认识，但是不属于特别亲的朋友，如上司、邻居，是**半正式信件**。

如果与收信人是亲戚或者朋友，是**非正式信件**。

下面这个表格是信件 style 的主要区分和注意要点。

	Formal（正式）	Semi-formal（半正式）	Informal（非正式）
称呼	Dear Sir or Madam	Dear Mr. ... Dear Ms. ... （一般写姓）	Dear...， （一般写名字）
收信人	一般是写给不认识的人，或者是写给一个机构或者公司	一般是写给认识但是可能并没有很多私交的人(如房东、邻居，甚至是同事)	一般是写给很熟悉的朋友或者家人
句子结构和标点符号	一般不能出现感叹号和问号，因为都是陈述句	类似于正式信件	很有可能出现感叹号和问号，有可能出现问句和感叹句
缩写	不能用缩写，如用 I am 而不是 I'm	类似于正式信件	可以缩写，如用 I don't 而不是 I do not
结尾	I await your prompt response	类似于正式信件	Give me a ring and let me know... Hope to see you soon.
信末礼貌语 （注：很多同学经常搞错 yours faithfully 和 yours sincerely）	Yours faithfully,（如果你不知道对方的名字） Yours sincerely,（如果你知道对方的名字）	Yours sincerely,	Best wishes, Lots of love, With love,

此外，考生还要注意用词的差异。你的用词需要随着信件的类型而改变。

在写请求信时，你的语气要客气，如这封信里就有很多客气的表达，如 ask for your help，还有 in your support。

在写抱怨信时，你的语气要坚决，如 I have decided that I would like you to...

在写友情信时，你的语气要比较放松，如 I am so happy that...

在写求职信时，你的语气要自信，如 I am confident that I am able to...

5.3.2 范文 2 ＋ 主旨 ／ 扣题 ／ 分段

> *Your neighbours have recently written to you to complain about the noise from your house/flat.*
>
> *Write a letter to your neighbours. In your letter*
>
> • *explain the reasons for the noise*
>
> • *apologise*
>
> • *describe what action you will take.*

题目大意

你的邻居最近写信给你，抱怨你的房子里传出的噪声。

写一封信给你的邻居。在你的信里

- 解释噪声的原因

- 表示歉意

- 描述一下你会采取什么措施去解决这个问题。

类别：道歉信，半正式信件

范文及点评

Dear James,

I was very shocked to get your letter saying that the noise from my flat has been spoiling your evenings and causing you problems. I am really, really sorry about that. I had no idea that you would suffer so much, so I hope you will accept my apologies.

As you know, I am trying to refit my kitchen in the evenings when I get in from work. Unfortunately it is all taking longer than expected and I have been having problems with getting things to fit properly. This has meant a lot of banging and hammering.

As the kitchen is nearly finished, I have decided to call in a professional builder who will finish off the work in a day or two. He'll work only during daytime hours, so you won't be disturbed in the evenings by the noise.

Sorry to have caused these problems,

Bill

(批注：信件一开头没有任何寒暄、问候，直接就说，我这封信是解决你所提到的噪声问题。)

(批注：回答题目的第二个要求：apologise。)

(批注：回答题目的第一个要求：explain the reasons for the noise。)

(批注：回答题目的第三个要求：describe what action you will take。)

(批注：结尾再一次点明自己写信的目的。)

学习要点

上面这篇书信的范文来自《剑5》。我们通过范文，可以比较清晰地了解考官在写书信的时候如何注意书信的主要目的，回答书信题目的三个要求。

G 类信件一般来说每个题目都有三个小要求。例如这个题目的三个小要求：

- explain the reasons for the noise

- apologise

- describe what action you will take.

在写信的过程中，考生有几点需要注意：

① 不能够忽视任何一个要求，每个都要回答。

② 回答这些要求的篇幅应该长度差不多（2～3句话），尽量不要相差太多。

③ 一般是按照题目的顺序回答，有些时候可以打乱（如这封信先回答第二个要求，然后才是第一个要求）。

④ 每个要求可以独立写一段，这样比较符合书信写作关于分段（paragraphing）的要求。

另外很重要的一点就是，信件一定要在第一段直接说清楚目的。

我们中国文化比较委婉，信件的开头会有大量的背景和问候。但是西方文化很直接，第一句话就说到整个信件主要的目的，特别是正式或者是半正式（formal or semi-formal）的信件。

5.3.3 范文 3 + 时态／人称

> *Write a letter to director of a night school about a problem in some part of a course you have taken. In your letter*
>
> • *give information about the course*
>
> • *describe problems with the course*
>
> • *suggest solutions.*

题目大意

关于你读的一门课程的问题给夜校主任写一封信。在你的信里

• 提供有关课程的信息

• 说明课程的问题

• 建议解决方案。

类别：抱怨信，正式信件

范文及点评

Dear Sir or Madam,

I am writing to you to express my dissatisfaction with one course of your school.
第二人称，指的是阅读信的人。

I enrolled in this training course two weeks ago to prepare for IELTS. The course, as suggested by the pamphlet of your school, aims to help students improve vocabulary and speak fluent English. The advertisement also claims that the course is taught by well-qualified teachers, who can help us acquire a foreign language
一般过去时，因为注册课程是过去发生的事情。

一般现在时，因为这个课程的目的一直没变。

一般现在时，因为这个课程的广告一直没变。

338

effectively within one month.

There is, however, a gap between these claims and the quality of the class. First of all, the class was oversized, and the teacher was not able to adapt class materials to suit the needs of different students. The teaching methods are another problem. The teacher required us to learn vocabulary by rote, and I have found that pronunciation remains a problem.

一般过去时，因为描述的是学生过去的上课体验，现在这个课程可能不是这样的。

因为我的发音问题现在还存在，这是现在的事情，所以用现在完成时。

I would like to suggest some changes to this course. Students of different levels should be assigned to different courses, so high-level groups can progress at a faster pace. It is also important to give us more opportunities to practise vocabulary rather than learning it by heart.

情态动词，因为这些事情还没发生，是对以后改变的一个建议。

I am looking forward to developments in the course.

Yours faithfully

学习要点

书信写作的人称和时态比大作文还有图表作文要复杂很多。这些作文在时态和人称上的区别见下表：

	人称（除了信件之外，很少用到第二人称 you）	时态
大作文	第一人称 (I, we) 和第三人称（在观点类题目中，第一人称经常用于表达自己看法的时候）（雅思作文和大学作业不同，大学作业一般不用第一人称，而雅思作文用第一人称很正常）	一般现在时 现在完成时 一般将来时 有时候，可能会用到一般过去时或者虚拟语气
图表作文	第三人称	一般过去时或者过去完成时 如果图里没有时间，一般现在时 如果图里有预测值，用将来时或者一般现在时
流程图	第三人称（工序图一般是被动语态）	一般现在时

地图	第三人称	一般过去时和过去完成时（如果是地图变迁题） 一般现在时（如果是地图描述题）
书信	三种人称都有可能用到	时态和大作文差不多，但是更为丰富，有可能用到现在进行时或者是现在完成进行时

然后，时态无疑是一个重点，也是难点。因为我们中文动词是没有时态区别的。英文的时态大概分成三种：过去、现在、将来。选用哪种时态取决于所描述的动作是发生在过去、现在还是将来。

我们用剑桥雅思的一个题目作为例子来看看时态的区别。

> ***You want to sell some of your furniture. You think a friend of yours might like to buy it from you.***
>
> ***Write a letter to your friend. In your letter***
>
> - ***explain why you are selling***
>
> - ***describe the furniture***
>
> - ***suggest a date when your friend can come and see the furniture.***

题目的"want to sell"说明这个题目的时态应该是现在时和将来时，因为这件家具还没卖出去。

我把这篇范文改编成了一个时态练习题，大家做一下选择，熟悉一下时态的区别。

Dear Jan,

As you know, we …1… to a new house soon and there are a few things that I …2… to take with me. The new house …3… a bit smaller so I have to sell some furniture and I am wondering If you …4…?

In particular I …5… my big dinning table. Do you remember it—the one in the living room? It …6… wooden legs and grey glass top and it's big enough for six people. There are six matching chairs to go with it.

I know you …7… this furniture so I …8… let you have it at a good price. I'd rather sell it to you than to a stranger!

Why don't you come around and take another look at them on Saturday? We …9… here all day, so maybe we …10… some lunch together?

1. A. will be moving　　　　B. have moved　　　　C. moved

2. A. will not be able　　　　B. was not able to　　　　C. am not able

3. A. will be　　　　B. was　　　　C. is

4. A. might be interested　　　　B. are interested　　　　C. will be interested

5. A. want to sell   B. wanted to sell   C. will want to sell

6. A. had   B has   C. will have

7. A. like   B liked   C. have liked

8. A. have   B will   C. could

9. A. are   B will be   C. were

10. A. can   B. could   C. will

答案和讲解

1. 选 A。soon 提示这件事情"很快"会发生，也就是还没发生，因此 B 的完成时、C 的过去时都不对。

2. 选 A，也可能选 C。说明我"现在"或者"以后"都不可能带着家具走。B 是错的，不能说过去，因为过去不能带走家具，未必说明现在不能带走。

3. 选 C。因为这所房子现在已经存在了，所以用现在时。B 表示过去有这么所房子，现在未必有了。A 是将来时，也不恰当，因为作者显然已经买到了新房子，现在是描述这个房子的特点。

4. 选 A。might 代表猜测。B 肯定不对，因为意味着作者已经感觉到对方喜欢了，现在写信米确认。

5. 选 A。如果选 B，意思就是过去想卖，现在不想卖了。C 也不恰当，因为 want to 本来就有现在还没卖以后要卖的意思，用 will 就多余了。

6. 选 B。描述一个现有物体的特点。

7. 选 A 或者 C。A 是一般现在时，表示收信人现在喜欢，而 C 是完成时态，表示一直喜欢。B 肯定不对，表示过去喜欢，那么现在应该是不喜欢了。

8. 选 B 或者 C。B 表示"肯定"会便宜卖给对方，而 C 表示"有可能"。

9. B。因为周日还没到来，用将来时只是表示以后的事情。A 肯定不对，因为一般现在时表示的是今天在家。C 严重错误，因为表示过去。

10. B。因为和别人吃午饭也要征得人家同意，带有不确定的语气显得更加尊重对方。can 感觉比较居高临下，而 will 也过分肯定。

5.3.4 范文 4 + 编故事的合理性

You are working for a company. You need to take some time off work and want to ask your manager about this.

Write a letter to your manager. In your letter

* *explain why you want to take time off work*

* *give details of the amount of time you need*

* *suggest how your work could be covered while you are away.*

题目大意

你为一个公司工作。你需要请假，希望你的经理批准。

写一封信给你的经理。在你的信里

- 解释你为什么要请假

- 说说你需要的假期时间

- 建议你的工作由谁去做。

类别：申请信，半正式信件

范文及点评

Dear Jennifer

开头段直接说清楚目的。

I am writing to request some unpaid leave next month.

My parents' 60th wedding anniversary is on March 21st, and they are planning to celebrate this signifi 主体部分第一段开始解释请假 th all their children and grandchildren. To do this 的原因（父母的结婚纪念日）, e big enough to 对应题目的第一个要求。 accommodate the whole family.

To participate in 对应题目的第二个要求，给 I would need to be away from work for four days, from 出请假的时间。 sday 23rd. My schedule for that week is relatively light, apart from two meetings with clients. Netta would be able to attend these in my place, a 这里回答了第三个要求，可以另起一段 ngs with both companies and knows the releva 考官可能考虑到再分段，整个信件每段 rgent work commitments at that time. 话就比较短，所以选择了合并段落。

I would be very grateful if you could allow me this time. These few days are very important to my parents and the wh 结尾。 nily, and it would be a way to thank them for all the support they have given me.

Best wishes

学习要点

上面这封信是《剑9》的一篇考官范文，我们除了利用这篇范文复习一下书信的要点，还可以想想为什么考官用"父母要过结婚纪念日"这个理由去请假。

G类信件有一个难点，就是你经常要去编故事，如道歉信，你要想一个理由去解释为什么自己没有做好某件事情。

又如申请信，你要想一个理由去解释为什么要申请。

或者求助信，你要想清楚，为什么你要对方帮助你。

如果你想的观点比较牵强，那么整个信件就没有说服力。正如我在课堂上说过的，雅思作文不只是语言的考试，还是思维和知识的考试。

这封信件的目的是请假，如果你说自己想去散心，或者是想去外地看球赛，这些理由都是没有说服力的。如果你说去其他公司面试，那基本上考官就觉得你是个白痴了，移民只会拉低外国人的平均智商。

但是如果你说庆祝自己父母的结婚纪念日，或者社区有什么宗教活动，或者妻子临产需要照顾，或者去海外出席孩子的毕业典礼，都比较有说服力，因为这些事情都比较特殊。

下面是各种信件编故事要注意的。

求助信	要突出这个事情对你的重要性。
例子：借朋友的行李箱。	
不合理的故事：不想买，朋友的资源不用白不用。	
合理的故事：商店没有那么大的。	
邀请信	要突出这件事情的重要性，还有你的诚意。
例子：邀请朋友参加旅行。	
不合理的故事：自己觉得闷，邀请一个工作很忙的同学去参加一个昂贵的旅行。	
合理的故事：这是一个很好的旅行，你朋友很喜欢。	
道歉信	要突出你的错误是情非得已。
例子：和上司道歉自己不能够出席会议。	
不合理的故事：和女朋友去郊游；除非你女朋友是王妃，否则写出这种理由是等着上司解雇的。	
合理的故事：父母生病、自己生病、朋友的婚礼等。	
抱怨信	要突出对方的问题是不可以忍受的，不符合行业标准。
例子：抱怨电脑店的服务不好。	
不合理的故事：商店没空调，人太多，换的零件不是最好的。	
合理的故事：不遵守合同，索取多余费用，问题没解决还造成了破坏。	
求职信	要突出你的实力，对公司的贡献，而不是公司对你有什么好处。
例子：申请去海外工作。	
不合理的故事：我可以开拓海外的关系圈，加强外语；我想去海外，因为我丈夫有外遇，我要离开这个伤心地。	
原因：公司请一个人是因为这个人有价值，而不是为这个人提供一个跳板。	
合理的故事：我的双语能力有助于公司拓展业务。	

5.3.5 范文 5 ＋ 段落的叙述逻辑和顺序

> *You have some problems in your work and write a letter to your friend for advice. In the letter*
>
> • *outline what you do in your job*
>
> • *explain the problems facing you*
>
> • *suggest what advice you want to take from your friend.*

题目大意

你的工作有一些问题，你写信给你朋友希望得到对方的建议。在你的信里

• 描述你的工作

• 解释你所面临的问题

• 说说你想从你的朋友那儿得到什么意见。

类别：友情求助信，非正式信件

范文及点评

Dear Alex,

I know you are overloaded with your work, but I do need your help and advice about one application I'm handling now!

开门见山，说明来意。

感叹号，可以用于朋友间的信件。

As you know, I just got promoted to a new position in this bank as a risk management manager. One of my major responsibilities is to check the financial statements of every business applicant to ensure that we lend money to companies which are able to repay loan.

对应题目的第一个小问题，介绍工作，扣题。

But the application from a trade company, which exports hair dryers and other electrical devices to other countries, has driven my crazy! I am impressed by the sales figures, the net profit and also the asset value of the company, but I wonder whether their flawless statements are trustworthy and, honestly, whether the company has cooked the books.

段落连接词，增强衔接性。

如果你是会计，熟悉会计的术语，不妨写一下会计的专业用语，显示你比较得心应手。

You have built a remarkable reputation in the industry for detecting companies which produce fake financial reports, so could you please check the financial statements

这些词伙，包括后面的 financial reports 等，都体现了用词的灵活性。

enclosed and give me some ideas how I figure out where figures are authentic or manufactured.

> 两个宾语从句，体现句子表达的复杂性。

Thank you so much for helping me with this, and you know how important it is not to let my boss down!

> 比较口语化的表达，突出这是朋友间的信。

Kind regards,

Sunny

学习要点

很多 G 类考生在写书信的时候缺乏逻辑思维，写的句子前言不搭后语。G 类信件主题部分大概写 3 段话，每段话对应题目的 3 个小问题，每个段落大概写 2～3 句话，有一定的逻辑顺序。

逻辑顺序有两种：

顺序 1：结论在前，解释在后。

段落的第一句话先说结论（或者总的看法、一件事情的概括），然后进行解释。

如信件主体部分的第二段说的是：

公司的会议表让我很抓狂（这个是一件事情的概括），然后具体解释会议表有什么特点和问题。

顺序 2：解释和铺垫在前，结论在后。

段落的第一句话可以写具体的东西（给出原因，或者是解释，或者是背景），然后进行归纳、总结，或者给出结果。

又如信件主体部分的第三段：

首先说朋友在审核会议表方面有很高的声誉（细节或者铺垫）。然后说朋友应该可以给自己建议可以做的事情（这是结果和总结）。

这种逻辑表达的顺序看上去很简单，但是很多考生如果平时不注意练习，往往就会忽视。特别是考场上时间一紧，可能就会写出很多没有逻辑关系的句子来。

5.4 信件的其他范例

范例 1：友情信＋音乐会

> *You bought a ticket for a music concert.*
>
> *You're unable to attend the concert. You want to offer the ticket to your friend. Write a letter to give him the ticket. In your letter*
>
> *• give detailed information about the concert*
>
> *• explain why you're unable to attend the concert*
>
> *• tell him how to get the ticket.*

Dear Tom,

How have you been these days? I am writing to ask if you are interested in attending a concert next weekend; I have a ticket for you.

I know that you are a real classical music lover and I believe that you would love to attend this orchestral concert. You have been busy with your business and you deserve a break! Many musicians of the orchestra have earned a reputation worldwide. I am sure the orchestral music can calm your nerves and you will feel refreshed and reinvigorated!

I waited in line for many hours to buy the ticket, but unfortunately, I will have to give up this opportunity due to a business trip arranged by the company at short notice. I hope you would not miss out on this opportunity, even though you have a tight schedule.

Please come to my office to pick up the ticket or you tell me your address, so I can post it to you.

Hope you enjoy the concert!

Regards

范例2：申请信＋大学课程申请

> *Write a letter to administration of a university because you are interested in one of their short courses. In your letter*
> - *give information about where you got the information*
> - *outline your education background and practice*
> - *explain why you chose this university and this course.*

Dear Sir or Madam,

I am writing to enquire about one course provided by your university. I wonder whether I can enroll on this course to increase my knowledge about food science, which is certain to help me deal with some problems in my job and further my career.

I am currently working for a restaurant and my employer has recently decided to integrate some western food options in our menu, but we have little knowledge about the impact of bacon, sausage and cheese on health. I then did some research online and discovered that your university had a two-week course which addresses this area of expertise.

I believe that I am qualified and well-prepared for attending this course. I completed a degree in Food Science in New Zealand and gained an insight into the nutritional value of different food ingredients and materials. Therefore, I am familiar with all the vocabulary and terminology of this subject and basics of nutrition.

Your university has achieved fame in industry for the expertise and academic research on health benefits of mixing different styles of cooking. I hope that I can gain this opportunity to deepen my understanding of how to design a menu for health-conscious customers.

Thanks for your time reading my application, and I would be grateful if you can send me more material about this course, such as the topics covered and the timetable.

Faithfully yours,

Lisa

范例3：友情信＋不能接朋友

> *Your friend is coming from abroad to holiday in your city. You can't go to the airport to pick him up. Write a letter to him. In your letter*
> - *mention the reason*
> - *suggest the alternative way to go to the hotel*
> - *talk about the plan to visit the city.*

Dear John,

I am so happy to hear that you are gonna come to our city for a business trip! I hope that you can stay here for a week so I can show you around and visit some famous attractions.

I am, unfortunately, unable to pick you up at the airport because I will leave town for an important business meeting tomorrow. I have asked my boss to find somebody else for this task but he turned down my application.

It is, however, easy for you to get to the hotel, and the airport has free shuttles, which will bring you to the city centre. The bus driver will tell you how to reach the destination.

I will be in town on April 25, which means that we have plenty of time to meet each other before your departure. We can take a ferry trip along ABC river to take in the view of the city, and also visit some of the largest botanical gardens, where you can will see a broad range of unique local plants.

Anyway, I cannot wait to see you and have a drink! Please tell me if you want me to do anything to help you make an enjoyable trip!

Best wishes

范例4：友情信＋很久不联系

> *A friend got a new job and you didn't contact with him for a long time. Write a letter to him. In your letter*
> - *express why you did not contact him*
> - *ask questions about his or her new job*
> - *and tell him when and where you will meet each other.*

Dear James,

It has been quite a long time since our dinner, well, I suppose, in the last year. I have just heard from Jamie that you are working for Microsoft now. I am so happy for you so I am writing to say congratulations!

I meanwhile want to say sorry for not having contacted you since your last phone call, because I was totally overwhelmed by the heavy workload. As you know, I have always been working overtime since last year and the situation has become even worse after my company signed a new contract with the government to build public sports facilities.

Well, once again, I just want to say I am thrilled by your new job, which I know is one of your career objectives. I am so glad that you have finally passed the interview. I remember that you are seeking a position of marketing manager. So, it that the position you have filled?

Anyway, we might have some coffee together and do some catching up. If you don't have any other plan, why don't we meet at Cafe Flora this Saturday? I will be available for a whole day so just call me back to let me know whenever it is convenient to you!

Yours,

Ken

范例 5：申请信＋退课

> *You have a full-time job and an evening course, but for some reason you cannot continue the evening course. Write a letter to the course coordinator. In your letter*
>
> *• explain reasons*
>
> *• specify when you want to resume the course*
>
> *• inquire about whether to pay more.*

Dear Mr. Smith,

I am a student currently finishing an evening course in your school, and I am writing to inquire if it is possible that I can withdraw from the current class.

I am working full time at Telecom Telecommunications Company. One of my colleagues is now having two months maternity leave, and the company cannot find any replacement, thereby requiring me to work overtime every day to complete this colleague's daily tasks.

In addition to my job, my experience in the Spanish language study is another problem. As I am a new learner, I have met difficulty in keeping pace with the class. I consider it better for me to do some revision first, before moving to the further stage.

If possible, I would like your school to grant me a four-week break. I am expecting to continue my class, once the break is finished. I also hope that this decision would not lead to any extra payment, since I have been working hard to feed my two children. To save you the trouble of replying, I prefer to telephone you if you permit.

Thank you for considering my request.

Yours sincerely

范例 6：道歉信＋开会改时间

> *You had a meeting, but cancelled it for some reasons. You are writing to your business partner. In your letter*
>
> - *explain reasons*
>
> - *suggest date or venue of a new meeting*
>
> - *apologise for your absence.*

Dear Mr Gavin Levis,

I am writing to you in some embarrassment and with many apologies for my failure to attend the meeting we arranged on Feb 25th, 2004. If there was any inconvenience my absence may have caused you, please forgive me. I trust you will understand my reasons.

First, two machines of the factory I am running failed to operate two days before our meeting, so I had to coordinate technicians to fix machines so as to avoid downtime. Both machines are fully repaired now and the manufacture is back to normal.

Second, one of my cousins was caught up in a traffic accident. Although he was recovering fast, I had to look after him, since his parents were on a business trip far from home.

I wonder if it is possible we can arrange a new meeting in not too distant future. If it is convenient, Hilton Hotel at 7 pm on Feb 27th, 2004 is a favourable choice for me. If it does not suit your schedule, please notify so we can make alternative arrangements.

I look forward to your confirmation and apologise again for cancelling the appointment at short notice.

Yours sincerely

范例 7：申请信＋课程

> *Your company is organising a language study program, and all participants should go overseas to receive training. Write a letter to apply for participation, in your letter*
>
> - *describe your work in your company*
>
> - *explain how it will help your work*
>
> - *justify your application.*

Dear Mr. Richard Bean,

I have heard that the company is organising a language training program, and you are the chief program administrator. I wonder whether there are still some places available in his program.

I am currently working in the marketing department as a manager assistant. One of my tasks in this year is to explore the possibility of exporting products to countries such as Canada, Australia, and New Zealand, most of which are English-speaking. As the chance of introducing our products to foreign customers is escalating, I feel compelled to improve my ability to speak English more fluently.

Our department head agrees on my application, since a good command of this language can improve efficiency and reduce misunderstandings when I communicate with foreign clients. He believes that this is exactly the overriding objective of the whole programme, to prepare staff of the company for the global market.

I understand that the program will last for two months from July to August, but I am convinced that my colleagues are capable enough of coping with my work over that period, as the busiest season normally starts from September. Please take my request into consideration, and I am looking forward to your favourable reply at an early date.

Sincerely yours,

Joanna Hopkins

范例 8：抱怨信＋产品质量

> *You bought a CD player from a shop, but found it doesn't work. You are writing to the manufacturer for compensation. In your letter*
> * *describe the problems with the CD player*
> * *explain the way the shop assistants treated you*
> * *suggest solutions to this problem.*

To whom it may concern,

I want to inform you of my dissatisfaction with a CD player (RHE 340) produced by your company. I purchased this item on January 12 at the Novel Store in New Market for £ 750 dollars.

The CD player is faulty and has the following problems: First, it fails to read songs sometimes. Second, I saw several scratches on the CD player, when I first unfolded the package. My friends have asked me whether it is a used CD player I purchased in a flea market.

I brought it back to the retail shop one week later, but the shop attendant refused to either fix or replace it, saying that it is the responsibility of the manufacturer. I have no choice but forward this issue to your company, since I believe that it is covered by a two-year-long warranty.

Unless you replace this CD player with a new one or refund the purchase price in full, I will be forced to contact local newspapers or take legal action. Your earliest response would be highly appreciated.

Yours truly.

范例 9：抱怨信＋产品质量

> *You wanted to have your computer fixed by the computer shop you bought it from, but the shop refused to repair it. Write a letter to the manager of a computer shop. In your letter.*
>
> • *describe the problem with your computer*
>
> • *explain why you are not satisfied with the service*
>
> • *explain what you want the shop to do.*

To whom it may concern,

I am writing to notify you of a claim for damaged goods against your shop. Besides, I am disappointed concerning your attendants' rude and brusque manner when dealing with clients' request. It is hurting your business.

I purchased a HP computer in your computer shop early last week. It worked well in the first week, but later displayed some obvious problems. First, on the screen, some dark dots appeared, which have seriously blurred the screen. Second, it was difficult to reboot the computer from time to time, and I am not sure whether it was due to the CPU or any other part.

I thought that your shop would at least manage to check the computer and give me some suggestions, as the computer is under one-year-long warranty. However, much to my astonishment, shop attendants insisted that they were not responsible, and the only suggestion they generously left me is to refer this problem to the manufacturer directly. This situation is causing me considerable anxiety.

Unless you take prompt action to fix the computer or refund the purchase price in full, I will be forced to take legal action. I hope we can work something out to our mutual benefit.

Your earliest response will be appreciated.

Yours faithfully

范例 10：抱怨信＋服务质量

> *You booked a holiday with a travel agency but the tour did not live up to your expectations. Write a letter to the agency. In your letter*
>
> • *explain what you expected on your holiday*
>
> • *describe the problem*
>
> • *explain why you want the travel agency to do.*

Dear Mr. Jackson,

I am writing this letter to complain about the service provided by one of your employees, Jenny Chang. I booked a holiday in Sydney for a total cost of $ 2,000, but the whole trip turned out to be a disappointing and devastating experience.

On February 13, 2006 I talked to Mrs. Jenny, Chang and reminded her of some special requirements I had, including a double room in a four-star hotel, ten main places of interest and so forth. Your tour operator confirmed that these would be surely arranged.

Unfortunately, these requirements were not met. The four-star hotel is in fact a three-star hotel, and the room service was below the average. The so-called double room was cramped and caused considerable discomfort. The guide took us to six places of interest (instead of ten, as suggested in the contract) and, some famous tourism sites were not on our itinerary.

Since you undertook to book a holiday in accordance with my requirements and your tour operator assured me that all my requirements would be met, I must hold you responsible for my disappointment. Unless you offer reasonable compensation or take any action to protect your reputation, I will have to turn to the legal consulting service provided by the city council.

Yours sincerely

5.5 书信的常用语

5.5.1 投诉信 (Letter of Complaint)

信头

I am writing to complain about a serious defect found in the computer I bought from you.

我写信来投诉关于我从你们那里购买的电脑的一个严重缺陷。

I am writing to notify you of a claim for damaged goods against your company.

我写信是对贵公司损坏的产品提出索赔。

I am writing to request you to take corrective actions concerning...

我写信请求你对……采取弥补的措施。

I am writing to express my concern/dissatisfaction about...

我写信来表达我对……一事的关注/不满。

I would like to draw your attention to...

我希望可以引起你对……一事的注意。

It has come to my attention that...

……这件事情已经引起了我的注意。

A very serious problem has arisen in connection with a language course you provided and operated.

你方提供并运营的课程已经出现一个非常严重的问题。

I am writing to request a full refund of the course fee I have paid.

我写信请求退还我所支付的全额课程费用。

Over the last few weeks I have become increasingly concerned about my neighbour's erratic habit, burning rubbish in his garden.

在过去的几周里，我已经逐步关注到我邻居的古怪行为，他在花园里烧垃圾。

I sincerely regret having to write this letter and have been delaying it in the hope that things would improve.

我由衷地抱歉需要写这一封信，我一直拖延写此信，木是寄希望于情况可能有所改观。

I am writing to request a refund of the 300 dollars I paid for the CD player.

我写信请求将我为 CD 机支付的 300 美元退还给我。

I am writing to ask you to replace the CD player I bought from your shop with another in good working order.

我写信来要求退换在你店购买的 CD 机。

I thought I should draw your attention to the situation since…

我觉得我应该引起你对这件事的注意，因为……

The devastating effect could be multiplied if this problem cannot be solved immediately.

如果这个问题不能够立即得到解决，它的影响会更坏。

I am certain that this situation is causing us considerable anxiety.

我可以肯定这种情况正在造成我们极大的不安。

I would be grateful if you could manage to help me out of the problem.

我会很感激您，如果您可以帮助我处理这个问题。

信末

Unless you take prompt action to correct the car's defects or refund the purchase price in full, I will be forced to take legal action.

除非你立即采取行动去修理汽车的毛病，或者按购买价全额退款，否则我将被迫采取法律行动。

I believe this is the only way to get this matter settled.

我相信这是唯一解决这个问题的方式。

Please make the adjustment to my bill.

请调整我的账单。

It is too bad this unfortunate accident occurred. Otherwise, I was very pleased with your service.

这种不幸事故的发生实在是太令人遗憾了。除此之外，你们的服务本来还是很令我满意的。

I will have to refer this matter to my attorney.

我将不得不把此事移交给我的律师处理。

I am glad to see what you can do to rectify this situation.

我会拭目以待，看看您可以做什么来扭转这个局面。

I urge you to reconsider your consideration.

我促请您重新考虑您的决定。

I would be grateful if you would ensure that the same thing does not happen again.

如果你保证同样的事情不再发生，我会很感激。

If you could find time to let us know, it would set our minds at rest.

如果你能抽出时间通知我们，我们就放心了。

I am reluctant to take the matter up elsewhere and hope that you will be able to let me have some explanation of the incident.

我不愿意再将此事麻烦他人，而希望你可以就这个事件给我一些解释。

A time for further discussion on this issue can be arranged either by telephoning me at 1345 6789 or writing to me via the address…

可以给我打电话（1345 6789）或者写信（地址……）来安排进一步商讨这个问题的时间。

I hope we can work something out to our mutual benefit.

我希望我们可以找出符合双方利益的方案。

Your agreement to the suggested course of action will be appreciated.

如果您认同所提议的措施，我将不胜感激。

Your comments will be appreciated.

如果您能给出看法，我将不胜感激。

I would like to discuss this matter with you further. Please contact me at 021 047 564. I look forward to resolving this matter with you.

我希望进一步和你讨论这一问题。请电话联系我（021 047 564）。我期待和你一起处理这个问题。

I trust this matter can be resolved quickly and look forward to your early reply.

我相信这个问题可以很快得到解决，期待您尽早答复。

Please let me know what you propose in relation to this issue as soon as possible.

请尽快让我知道你对于此事的提议。

I am sorry to write to you in this manner and I hope that you will not be offended.

我很抱歉用这种方式给您写信，希望您不会觉得唐突。

If this matter is not put right soon, I fear it could have serious consequences.

如果这个问题不能很快得到妥善处理，我担心会有严重的后果。

I await your reply and trust that it will contain an explanation that some mistake has been made by your company.

我等待您的答复，我相信您的答复会包含一个关于你们公司所犯错误的解释。

I would like to stress that I will not tolerate a situation such as this.

我想强调的一点是，我不会容忍类似这种情形。

I trust that you will be able to correct these matters without delay and that no further action will be necessary on my part.

我相信您可以毫不拖延地善理此事，而我不需要采取任何进一步的行动。

I understand that my rights are covered by laws and am looking to your company for a return of the price paid within 14 days.

我知道我的权益受到法律保护，我等待你们公司在 14 日内全价退款。

I would be glad of a reply without further delay, or I may have to consider legal action.

我很乐意立即接到您的答复；否则的话，我或许不得不考虑采取法律行动。

I am wondering if it would be possible for us to meet and discuss the situation.

我想知道我们是否可能见面，商讨现在的情形。

I hope we can meet and get it sorted out very soon.

我希望我们可以见面并尽快处理此事。

I trust that we can resolve this matter quickly and amicably.

我相信我们可以迅速、不伤和气地解决这一问题。

If I do not hear from you within the next seven days, I will have no option but to go to the city council to have my complaint heard.

如果我在未来的七天之内没有收到你的答复，我别无他选，而只能去市议会投诉。

I am sure you will understand that this problem is causing me considerable inconvenience and expense, and I am anxious to have it settled as soon as possible.

我肯定您会理解，这个问题正在给我造成极大的不便和损失，我急切想要尽快解决这个问题。

I look forward to receiving a replacement as soon as possible.

我期待尽快收到换货。

I think that 300 dollars would be a reasonable sum of compensation and I look forward to receiving your cheque.

我觉得 300 元是比较合理的赔偿额度，我期待收到您的支票。

If it happens again I will commence legal action without further notice.

如果这个事情再次发生的话，我会采取法律行动，而再不另行通知。

5.5.2 咨询信 (Inquiry Letter)

I am writing to enquire whether I may become a member of your club.

我写信是为了咨询是否可以加入你们俱乐部。

I would be grateful if you could let me know your annual fee charges and any other information which would be useful.

如果您可以告诉我你们的年费并提供其他任何有用的信息，我会很感激。

Please let me know as soon as possible how you propose to settle this matter.

请尽快让我知道您对解决此事的建议。

You are welcome to call in or to telephone me on 021 56789.

欢迎您来访，或者给我打电话 (021 56789)。

Please contact me on 021 567894 if you would like to talk about it further.

如果您愿意就此事进一步商讨，请联系我 (021 567894)。

Thank you for your attention.

感谢您的关注。

Please let me know as soon as possible whether or not you will accept this offer.

请尽快让我知道您是否可以接受这个条件。

Although at this time of year you will have more work to deal with than usual, I would appreciate a reply in a not too distant future.

虽然一年当中这个时候您要处理比平时更多的工作，我期待不久的将来会得到您的答复。

5.5.3 求助信 (Request Letter)

I would like to make an appointment to speak with you about my wallet I lost on the flight AUS 123.

我想定个时间和您说一下我在 AUS 123 航班上丢失的钱包的事。

I would like to arrange an appointment for next Friday (15 October) at four fifteen.

我想约下星期五 (10 月 15 日) 的 4 点 15 分会面。

I would be grateful if you could give any assistance.

我会感激您所提供的任何帮助。

I would be most grateful if you can give me instructions.

如果您可以给我提供指导，我会非常感激。

I would be very grateful for any advice you can offer.

对于任何您可以提供的建议，我都是非常感激的。

I do hope you will be able to send me a favourable reply and I look forward to hearing from you in due course.

我真的希望您可以给我一个理想的答复，我期待适当的时候得到您的答复。

I would be most grateful if you would intervene in this matter.

如果您能够干预此事，我会非常感激。

I hope you will consider my request favourably.

我希望您能够很好地考虑我的请求。

5.5.4 投诉信 (Letter of Apology)

I just wanted to write you a quick note to apologise for not being able to keep our appointment tomorrow.

我只想给您写一封快信，为我明天不能够赴约而道歉。

In deference to your valuable time, I would like to get straight to the point and admit that I was wrong.

为了尊重您宝贵的时间，我愿意直接承认我的过错。

I just really hope that you will be able to accept my apology.

我真的希望您可以接受我的道歉。

Please let me have your views about this matter as soon as possible.

请尽快让我知道您对这一问题的看法。

Please accept my apologies for...

请接受我对于……一事的歉意。

Please accept my sincere apology for missing the interview scheduled for …

由于错过了原定于……的面试，请接受我诚恳的道歉。

I would appreciate any consideration you can give me in rescheduling our meeting.

我会非常欣赏你对于重新安排我们会面所作的任何考虑。

Thank you for your anticipated patience in this matter.

感谢你在此事上所有的耐心。

Please accept my apology for the delay and thank for your understanding.

请接受我关于日期推迟的道歉，感谢你的理解。

I will do everything in my power to ensure that this type of error does not occur again.

我将会尽我所能确保此类错误不再出现。

Although I make every attempt to insure that..., this unfortunate incident can occasionally occur.

虽然我尽力确保……，但是这种不幸的事情偶尔还是可能发生。

5.5.5 建议信／提供信息信 (Letter to Provide Information or Advice)

If I can be of any assistance in any way, please do not hesitate to call on me.

如果我有任何可以协助的地方，请直接联系我。

I am available at Flat 304, Green Revenue, St Eden if you require any further information.

如果您需要任何进一步的信息，可以到 Flat 304, Green Revenue, St Eden 找我。

I am happy to supply any further information you may require and I look forward to hearing from you shortly.

我很乐意提供任何您或许需要的信息，而我也期待很快收到你的答复。

Please contact me if I can be of any assistance.

如果有需要我帮助的地方，请联系我。

If you need any further information, please contact me via email abcd@hotmail.com.

如果你需要任何进一步的信息，请通过电子邮件 abcd@hotmail.com 来联系我。

5.5.6 感谢信 (Letter of Thanks)

I just wanted to send a note to say how much I appreciate the help you have given me.

我只想发信告诉您，我是多么欣赏您所给我提供的帮助。

I am writing to thank you for permitting us to use your resources.

我写信是为了感谢您允许我使用您的资源。

With very best wishes and thanks.

带着最好的祝愿和谢意。

I appreciate the support you have provided and your assistance has been invaluable to me.

我欣赏你所提供的支持，你的协助对我来说是无价的。

5.5.7 邀请信 (Invitation Letter)

Perhaps you could give us a call or write to us to let us know what time you expect to arrive.

或许您可以给我打一个电话，或者写信给我，让我们知道您大概什么时候会到达这里。

I thank you in anticipation of your arrival.

我感谢和期待您的光临。

I am so pleased that you are planning to drop by.

得知你将降临寒舍，我很高兴。

I would like to offer you...

我愿意为您提供……

I would like to invite you to dinner and be our guest.

我很乐意邀请您来作客，和我们共进晚餐。

I would like to invite you to join us and attend this meeting.

我很乐意邀请您和我们一起出席这一会议。

I am glad to invite you to participate in my graduation ceremony.

我很乐意邀请您参加我的毕业典礼。

I am honoured to invite you to our wedding, as I understand that you only come to visit on special occasions.

能够邀请您出席我们的婚礼，我倍感荣耀，因为我知道您只出席特殊的场合。

5.5.8 求职信 (Letter of Application)

Further to your advertisement in yesterday's *Washington Herald* for a senior PA, I would very much like to be considered for this vacancy.

就你们昨天在《华盛顿先驱报》上关于招聘私人助理的广告，我希望自己可以被考虑去填补这个空缺。

I am writing with regard to your vacancy for a language tutor.

我写信是关于应聘你们语言辅导教师一职的空缺。

I was most interested to read your advertisement for a bookkeeper and feel I could be just the person for your vacancy.

我对于你们簿记员一职的广告很感兴趣，也觉得我会是适合这个空缺的不二人选。

I write to enquire if you have an opening for a sales representative.

我写信是想咨询是否您在销售代表一职上有空余的职位。

I do hope to hear from you soon.

我真的希望可以很快得到您的回音。

I do hope that I will be successful, and that I may hear from you in the near future.

我真的希望我能成功，我也希望我可以在近期得到您的答复。

I do hope that I may be considered for the job and that you may invite me for an interview in the near future.

我真的希望我可以被考虑做这份工作，也希望您或许可以让我近期参加面试。

附　录

附录1　本书词伙一览表

A

a better quality of life	更好的生活质量
a bricks and mortar college	实体的学院
a budget surplus	预算盈余
a conservative attitude towards...	对……的保守态度
a correctional method	矫正方法
a firm grounding	坚实的基础
a fulfilling career	有成就的事业
a global language	全球性的语言
a good command	良好的掌控力
a good job prospect	良好的工作前景
a long prison term	长期监禁
a moral compass	道德指南针
a peaceful, closely-knit society	一个和平的、团结的社会
a positive light	正面的角度
a rural-to-urban shift	从农村向城市的转变
a sense of security	安全感
a socially responsible way	对社会负责的方式
a universal language	通用语言
a well-educated workforce	受过良好教育的劳动力
a world of knowledge	知识的世界
abnormal weather	异常天气
abolition of tuition	免除学费
absorb information	汲取信息
academic courses	基础理论课程
academic groups	学术团体
academic subjects	基础理论科目
access to education	受教育
accommodate a large population	容纳大量人口
achieve potential	发挥潜力
achieve success	取得成功
achieve the goal of income redistribution	实现收入再分配的目标
acquire a second language	习得第二语言
acquire foreign languages	习得外语

acquire mathematical skills	学到数学技能
acquire some skills	学到一些技能
across borders	跨越国界
address some of their needs	满足他们的一些需求
adopt a healthy lifestyle	采取健康的生活方式
adopt cutting-edge technology	采用尖端技术
advent of the Internet	互联网的出现
advertisements aimed at children	针对儿童的广告
advertising campaigns directed at children	针对儿童的广告宣传
afford educational expenses	负担得起教育费用
afford home ownership	买得起房
air companies	航空公司
air tickets	机票
alleviate the food shortage	缓解粮食短缺
ambitions to achieve	有待实现的抱负
an ageing population	正在老龄化的人口
an ever-changing world	不断变化的世界
architectural styles	建筑风格
at an astounding rate	以惊人的速度
at low prices	价格低廉
attend lectures	听讲座
audio-visual information	视听信息
aviation sector	航空部门

B

behaviour norms	行为规范
behavioural problems	行为问题
bombarded with advertisements	广告轰炸
boost their confidence	增强他们的信心
break the cycle of poverty	打破贫困循环
bridging the gap	缩小差距
bring enjoyment	带来快乐
broaden people's minds	开拓人们的思路
broadening their horizons	拓宽他们的视野
build close relationships	建立亲密关系
build expertise	储备专业知识
build up a network of contacts	建立人脉
building a prosperous society	建设一个繁荣的社会
business etiquette	商务礼仪
business owners	企业主
business world	商业世界
buying power	购买力

361

C

career achievement	职业成就
career development	职业发展
career path	职业道路
challenge domestic manufacturers' dominance	挑战国内厂商的主导地位
city dwellers	城市居民
cleaning their bedrooms	打扫卧室
collect information	收集信息
commit crimes	犯罪
commit serious offence	犯严重罪行
competitively priced	定价有竞争力
complete a degree	完成学业
complete a university degree	完成大学学业
complete work	完成工作
completing all courses	学完所有课程
considerable number of	相当数量的
consumer goods	消费品
contract heart diseases	患上心脏病
contribute extraordinarily to	贡献非凡
contribute positively to	做出积极的贡献
cooking styles	烹饪方式
cope with all financial matters	处理所有财务
cope with challenges	应对挑战
cope with demands	应付需求
core subjects	核心科目
cost of living	生活费用
cost of production	生产成本
create a closely-knit community	创建一个团结的社区
criminal record	犯罪记录
cultural diversity	文化多样性
cut prices	降价

D

damages to health	损害健康
delay retirement	延迟退休
demographic change	人口变化
densely populated	人口稠密
desk jobs	科室工作
deter crime	震慑犯罪
deterrent effect	威慑作用
develop a strong working relationship	发展良好的工作关系
develop and maintain healthy habits	养成和保持健康的习惯

develop good behaviour patterns	养成良好的行为模式
develop some life skills	培养一些生活技能
devote their time to	花时间去
dietary habits	饮食习惯
digesting information	消化信息
disadvantaged children	弱势儿童
discover business opportunities	发现商机
discover the value	发现价值
discover their talents	发掘他们的才能
disobey rules	违反规则
disposable income	可支配收入
dispose of household waste	处理家庭废品
disseminate information	传播信息
disseminate knowledge	传播知识
distinguish right from wrong	区分正误
do a wide range of activities	参与多种活动
dominant language	优势语言
draw upon the expertise of...	借鉴……的专业知识

E

earn a fortune	赚大钱
earn a living	谋生
earn higher salaries	赚取更高的薪水
earn more money	赚更多的钱
earn profits	赚取利润
ease the pressure	缓解压力
economically tough times	经济困难时期
educational opportunities	教育机会
educational programmes	教育规划
educational value	教育价值
electronic products	电子产品
emotional needs	情感需求
emotional tie	感情纽带
empirical knowledge	经验知识
employment opportunities	就业机会
end up in landfill sites	最终到了垃圾填埋场
endanger some minority languages	危及一些少数民族语言
endanger their health	危及他们的健康
energy consumption	能源消耗
enforce some laws	执行一些法律
engage their interest	激发他们的兴趣

English-speaking countries	说英语的国家
enter the university	进入大学
enter the workforce	进入劳动力市场
environmental awareness	环境意识
environmental destruction	环境破坏
environmental groups	环保组织
environmental protection	环境保护
essential services	基本服务
evade taxes	逃税
excessive consumption	过度消费
exempt from tuition	免学费
exercise creative potential	发挥创造潜能
exotic locations	有异国情调的地方
experiencing different cultures	体验不同的文化
extension of life expectancy	延长寿命

F

fake products	假冒产品
family life	家庭生活
family meals	家常便饭
family relationships	家庭关系
fashionable clothes	时尚服装
fast food advertisements	快餐广告
fast food chains	快餐连锁店
fast pace of life	快节奏的生活
fight crime	打击犯罪
financial analysts	金融分析师
financial statements	财务报表
financial support	金融支持
find decent jobs	找到体面的工作
find employment	找到工作
find enjoyment	找到乐趣
first-time offenders	首次违规者
follow social rules	遵循社会规则
foster innovations	培育创新
free education	免费教育
frequent fast-food restaurants	频繁光顾快餐店
fried chicken	炸鸡
from deprived backgrounds	出身贫寒

G

gain a full understanding	得到充分的理解

gain a sense of accomplishment	获得成就感
get away from everyday lives	远离日常生活
get distracted	分心
global community	全球社区
global setting	全球环境
go bankrupt	破产
go to the gym	去健身房
go to university	上大学
good sanitation	良好的公共卫生
government spending	政府支出

H

habitual offenders	惯犯
harsh penalty	严厉处罚
have a destructive effect	有破坏性的影响
haves and have-nots	有产者和无产者
health care costs	医疗费用
healthy eating	健康饮食
healthy lifestyle	健康的生活方式
high in fat, sugar	高脂肪，高糖
high income earners	高收入者
high income group	高收入群体
high income tax rates	高所得税率
higher education	高等教育
higher participation rates	较高的参与率
higher socioeconomic status	较高的社会经济地位
historical events	历史事件
household appliances	家用电器

I

impart their knowledge and skills	传授他们的知识和技能
imparting some important virtues	传授一些重要的美德
impose a burden on	给……强加一个负担
imposing rules	强加规则
imposing sentences	判处刑罚
improve critical thinking skills	提高批判性思维能力
improve employability	提高就业能力
improve living standards	提高生活水平
improve mutual understanding	增进相互了解
improve productivity	提高生产率

improve research skills and collect information	提高研究技能并收集信息
improve their academic performance	提高他们的学习成绩
improve their problem-solving abilities	提高他们解决问题的能力
improving job prospects	改善就业前景
improving social skills	提高社会技能
in a globalised world	在全球化的世界中
in a socially acceptable way	以社会接受的方式
in adult life	在成人生活中
in economic terms	在经济方面
in large portions	大部分情况下
in the real life	在现实生活中
in the real world	在现实世界中
income disparity	收入差距
increase earnings	增加收益
increase knowledge	增加知识
increase the artistic appeal	增加艺术感染力
increase their income	增加他们的收入
increase their practical experience	增加他们的实践经验
increasing screen time	增加看电视的时间
informative television	使人增长见闻的电视节目
innocent people	无辜的人
innovations they have advanced	他们的创新成果
interactive activities	互动活动
interactive communication tools	互动交流工具
interactive technology	互动技术
interfere with children's studies	干扰儿童学习
interfere with their studies	干扰他们的研究
international conferences	国际会议
international cooperation	国际合作
interpersonal skills	人际交往能力
introduce laws	颁布法律
irregular working hours	弹性工作时间

J

job insecurity	工作上的不安感
job opportunities	工作机会
job prospects	工作前景
job skills	工作技能

juvenile offenders	少年犯

K

keep pace with the changes	跟上变化的步伐
keep their voices down	（他们）小声说话
keep up to date with	跟上步伐，密切关注
key disciplines	重点学科

L

launch awareness campaigns	开展宣传活动
law-abiding citizens	守法公民
lawless society	没有法律约束的社会
lay off some employees	解雇一些员工
lead a hectic life	过着忙碌的生活
leading universities	一流大学
learn responsibility	学习承担责任
learn the latest technology	学习最新技术
learning costs	学习成本
legal responsibilities	法律责任
levying taxes	征税
life expectancy	预期寿命
lifeblood of the economy	经济命脉
lifestyle choices	生活方式的选择
lifestyles more sustainable	（使）生活方式更可持续
limit freedom and stifle creativity	限制自由和扼杀创造力
live an independent life	过独立的生活
live in harmony	生活在和谐中
live their lives	过他们的生活
live under enormous pressure	生活在巨大的压力下
lose employment	失业
lose freedom	失去自由
lose self-confidence	失去自信
lose their jobs	失去他们的工作
low income families	低收入家庭
low income group	低收入群体
low profit margin	低利润空间
low socio-economic status	低社会经济地位

M

maintain a good relationship with...	与……保持良好的关系
maintain day-to-day contact with...	与……保持日常联系

maintain order	维持秩序
make a positive difference to	制造正面差异
manage time	管理时间
managing finances	理财
manufacturing sector	制造业
many parts of the world	世界上的许多地方
mass production	大规模生产
means of food preparation	食品制备方法
medical needs	医疗需求
medical system	医疗系统
meet the growing demand	满足日益增长的需求
meet the requirements	符合要求
members of society	社会成员
mental health problems	心理健康问题
method of learning	学习方法
metro stations	地铁站
migrate to cities	迁移到城市
minor crimes	轻微的罪行
minority languages	少数民族语言
mitigate this problem	缓解这个问题
money is a great motivator	钱是一种强大的动力
moral principles	道德原则
mother tongue	母语
movement of population	人口流动

N

native language	母语
newest generation	最新一代
next generation	下一代
noise pollution	噪声污染
nutritional content	营养成分

O

obesity epidemic	肥胖症的流行
obey the law	遵守法律
of educational value	具有教育价值
online course	在线课程
opportunities for economic prosperity	经济繁荣的机会
organise events	举办活动
overcome difficulties	克服困难
overcome language barriers	克服语言障碍

overweight people	超重人群

P

parts of the world	世界各地
pay tax	纳税
permanent job	稳定的工作
personal resources to draw upon	利用个人资源
personal wealth	个人财富
personality traits	人格特质
poor employment prospects	就业前景不佳
poor eyesight	视力不好
poor grades	成绩差
poor living conditions	生活条件差
population shift	人口迁移
poses a threat to people's health	对人们的健康构成威胁
pour more money in	投入更多的钱
practical implications	实践意义
pre-prepared food	预先准备好的食物
present their information	展示他们的信息
prison sentence	徒刑
problem-solving abilities	解决问题的能力
promote brain	促进大脑（发育）
promote economy development	促进经济发展
pronc to poor health	容易出现健康状况不佳
public money	公共资金
public services	公共服务
public transport system	公共交通系统
pursue a degree	攻读学位
put their ideas into practice	把他们的想法付诸实践
put us in a good mood	让我们置身于好心情中

R

raising airfares	提高机票价格
raising environmental awareness	提高环保意识
raising funds	筹集资金
rapidly changing	快速变化
receive a good education	接受良好的教育
receive more funds	获得更多的资金
receive some practical training	接受一些实践训练
receiving a university education	接受大学教育
recycle disposable goods	回收利用物品

reduce diseases	减少疾病
reduce life expectancy	减少预期寿命
reduce our pressure	减轻我们的压力
reduce the environmental impact	减少对环境的影响
reduce the strain on	减轻对……的压力
reduce work efficiency	降低工作效率
reduced the cost	降低成本
reform offenders	改造罪犯
regulating our behaviour	规范我们的行为
rehabilitation programs	康复计划
reintegrating into society	重新融入社会
relax regulations	放宽规定
replay the video	重播视频
restrict our freedom	限制我们的自由
reverse this trend	扭转这一趋势
revitalise the local economy	振兴地方经济
rewarding experience	令人有所收获的经历
rite of passage	成人礼
run a small business	经营一个小企业
run out of money	钱用完
running cost	运行成本

S

safe community	安全社区
salt and calories	盐和热量
sample local food	品尝当地食物
satisfy their needs	满足他们的需求
sedentary lifestyle	久坐不动的生活方式
self-contained economy	自给自足的经济
senior workers	高级工人
sense of community	社区意识
sensitive to prices	对价格敏感
sentenced to prison	被判入狱
set up a business	开创业务
sharpen their skills	磨炼他们的技能
sharpening skills	磨炼技能
shattering their confidence	粉碎他们的信心
shortage of labour	劳动力短缺
shortage of land	土地短缺
show good manners	展现良好的风度
show self-restraint	展现自我克制力

sit in front of a screen	坐在屏幕前
slow pace of work	放缓工作步伐
social experience	社会经验
social lives	社会生活
social network	社交网络
social norms	社会规范
social progress	社会进步
social relationships	社会关系
social responsibilities	社会责任
social rules	社会规则
society cannot advance	社会不能进步
solve math problems	解决数学问题
sound financial planning	健全的财务规划
stifle children's creativity	扼杀孩子的创造力
strict discipline	严肃的纪律
strict upbringing	严格的教养
strong appetite	旺盛的食欲
suits students' needs	满足学生需要

T

take away their study time	占用他们的学习时间
take stock of their lives	盘点他们的生活
tangible benefits	实实在在的利益
tax penalty	税收处罚
tax revenue	税收
technological innovations	技术创新
technological progress	技术进步
the airline industry	航空业
the last years of life	生命的最后几年
the modern world	现代世界
theoretical knowledge	理论知识
threaten social stability	威胁社会稳定
throw-away culture	丢弃文化
tightening regulation on	收紧对……的管控
times of economic recession	经济衰退时期
to push forward the boundaries of knowledge	推进知识的界限
traditional cuisine	传统烹饪
traditional dishes	传统菜肴
traditional recipes	传统食谱
traffic accidents	交通事故
traffic congestion	交通拥堵

traffic regulations	交通规则
transport system	运输系统
travel all over the world	到全世界旅行
travel to and from work	通勤
travelling great distances	长途旅行
tropical countries	热带国家
turbulent business environment	动荡的商业环境

U

university accommodation	大学住宿
unnecessary journeys	不必要的旅程
unpredictable factors	不可预测的因素
upgrade their skills	提升他们的技能
upon ideas	在思想观念上
urban life	城市生活
use bad language	说脏话
using imagination	运用想象力

V

valuable asset	有价值的资产
varied career	多变的职业
via email	通过电子邮件
video games	视频游戏
violate laws	违反法律
violent electronic games	暴力电子游戏
visually attractive	视觉上有吸引力
vocational training	职业培训
voluntary services	志愿服务
volunteer work	志愿者工作

W

wasteful use of...	浪费……
watching videos	观看视频
ways of life	生活方式
widening gap	扩大的差距
widening income gap	扩大的收入差距
with up-to-date features	具有最新功能
work closely with...	与……紧密合作
working lives	工作生活
worrying trend	令人担忧的趋势

附录2 8.5分大作文范文

中国大陆考区 2012 年 12 月 6 日的考题

Nowadays, people always throw old things away and buy new things, whereas in the past, old things were repaired and used again. What factors cause this phenomenon? What effects does this phenomenon lead to?

考试后我回忆的范文

One of the most worrying trends in modern society appears to be toward discarding goods even though they are still usable. This trend, as it grows, has attracted attention, in view of the fact that previous generations used these goods for a length of time. What has driven this change and how this has impacted on us will be explored in this essay.

While technological advances in recent years have made many consumer goods more durable, these remarkable changes have failed to steer us toward a sustainable future. Mass production, along with the widespread application of machinery, has led to substantial reductions in prices of goods and created incentives for replacing goods with the newest counterparts. This is understandable considering that the cost of repair and maintenance has risen due to the dwindling number of specialists who can perform this task.

Another explanation for the disposable lifestyle is that people today gain a sense of self-esteem from purchasing and possessing material goods. In a world where materialism prevails, people are ashamed of keeping the same items (e.g., mobile phones, laptops and other gadgets) for long, because this will distinguish them from those financially better off, who can sustain extravagant shopping and have a new inventory of material possessions.

People might derive pleasure from this habit, but this has negative repercussions for the environment. Consumer goods, disposed of before they expire, end up in waste landfills, posing a threat to the ecosystem. This is particularly the case when waste is not managed well and the toxic substances contained in these goods contaminate water and degrade soil. Apart from this, the relentless consumption of goods can drive the demand for minerals and natural resources, which are required for the production of these products, so mining, drilling and other environmentally destructive activities will possibly go unimpeded, devouring the natural world on which our future generations depend.

To summarise, the overconsumption of goods arises from the fact that technology makes these goods available at lower prices and also from the fact that people perceive this as a status symbol. This should ring the alarming bell, because it distracts us from the sustainable use of natural resources and make the ecosystem approach the tipping point.

下面我简单分析一下大作文。

1. 本文的背景句是《顾家北手把手教你雅思写作》中的一个背景句，至少用了一个词伙(worrying

trend）。

2. 灵活使用我们教过的三大从句和复杂句，而不需要用什么感叹句和反问句。

3. 文章采用的是主体部分三段的方式，每段一个中心句。

4. 文章的论述方式是 ABC，注意逻辑和拓展。

5. 文章没有模板，只用了两个传统的连接词 another explanation 和 apart from this。

6. 整个文章没有任何语法错误，符合我在本书中提到的核心的思想：你要减少语法错误，分数才能大幅度提升！这个理念和传统观念完全不同。传统观念只关注所谓的"高分"句子，但是不注意基本语法的准确性。

7. 文章没有使用任何大词，但是大量使用我们上课说过的、本书里出现过的、BBC 上出现过的词伙。这些词伙我已经标注出来。

8. 至于为什么没有考到 9 分？我觉得一个原因是太长，整篇文章 360 字，特别是开头段，没必要那么长。其次就是有一些词使用不够恰当，如 a new inventory of material possessions。

9. 整篇文章不断出现关键词，中心句也非常注意对应题目。

5

附录 3　8.5分图表作文范文

The tables show results of surveys about how people in a city felt about different aspects of their lives in 1980 and 2010.

	Good (%)	Neither good nor bad (%)	Bad (%)
Education	81	10	9
Living environment	65	10	25
Medical services	63	8	29
Shops	71	9	20
Employment opportunities	63	21	16
Public transport	53	25	12

	Good (%)	Neither good nor bad (%)	Bad (%)
Education	72	11	17
Living environment	82	10	8
Medical services	73	15	12
Shops	62	20	18
Employment opportunities	72	18	10
Public transport	38	34	28

The tables illustrate the changes in the extent to which residents of a city were satisfied with their lives.

The improvement of the living environment received the highest recognition (82%) in 2010, compared with 65% two decades earlier. There was also an increase in the level of satisfaction with medical services, rising from 63% to 73%. Likewise, the proportion of people who were happy with access to employment opportunities saw a rise of 9% to 72%.

文字信息, 注重最高值。

句式变化, also 增加句子连接。

分词改变句子结构。

注意对象词的准确, 人的百分比。

In contrast, only 72% of people were satisfied with education in 2010, although education received the highest rating in 1980. The proportion of respondents who either agree or disagreed with the access to education remained

连接词增加段落的连接。

替换表达。

roughly unchanged, at 10%. There was also a drop in the figure for shopping and public transport. Only one third of residents were satisfied with public transport, while the proportion of who had a low opinion of this more than doubled to 28%.

替换表达。

To summarise, there were considerable improvements to living environment, medical service and employment opportunities in this city, but the figures for other aspects of life saw a decline in 2010, by which time public transport had become the main problem.

所有满意度提高方面的总结。

所有满意度下降方面的总结。

考试日期	2013/05/16				
考点名称	深圳 深圳赛格人才培训中心　　[详细地址]				
考试类型	学术类				
注册号 (用于雅思报名注册过程)					
IELTS考号 (用于参加雅思考试以及考后服务)					
考试成绩	总成绩	听力	阅读	写作	口语
	8	7.5	8.5	8.5	7.5

重要提示：考试成绩以您最终收到的成绩单为准，本网站信息仅供参考。您的成绩单将在笔试后第10个工作日以EMS快递寄送给您，请随时关注物流跟踪信息。

附录4　8分书信作文范文

我在2015年的10月24日参加了一次G类考试。这是我参加过的唯一一次G类考试。考试完后，我回忆了自己考场上写的G类信件。备考G类的同学可以看一下，看看我的文章是怎么符合四个雅思评分标准的。

You have lived in an apartment for a year and the landlord wants to increase the rent. You are not happy about that.

Write a letter to the landlord, in the letter

- *identify yourself*

- *explain why you think the rent should not be increased*

- *say what you will do if the rent increases.*

范文

Dear Mr Smith,

I am writing with regard to your proposed change to the rent, and I am the tenant living in the flat you own at Albert Street. We signed a 2-year-long lease one year ago, so I have to argue that your arrangement is neither legal nor morally acceptable.

开门见山。

回答第一个小问题。

说明来意。

When I first approached you one year ago, I made it clear that I wanted to rent accommodation in a quiet, suburban area without being disturbed by any form of noise. You suggested that the apartment was situated at a side street, and without any time to verify your statement, I signed the agreement, but I later discovered that I have to bear the unacceptable level of noise created by pubs and clubs nearby. You did not give any explanation, leaving me no option but adapting to this unbearably noisy environment.

复杂句，前面是状语从句，这里是宾语从句。

出现一些关于建筑和城市的词伙。

给出第一个原因为什么不应该加租，对应题目第二个问题。

In addition to this problem, I have also found that the apartment building does not have central heating, which is not consistent with the description of the advertisement you placed in the newspaper. You also mentioned that the

段落的连接。

并列的观点用 also 连接。

flat was well-furnished, but the wallpaper of the bedroom peeled from the wall shortly after I moved in. you promised to redecorate the room, but have failed to meet this promise.

关于房屋的词伙。

关于房屋的词伙。

While I have been tolerant of all these problems, you are now proposing to increase rent. I strongly advise you to rethink your decision; otherwise, I have to turn to the legal service of the city council or consult my lawyer about your repeated attempt to breach the contract. Please inform me of your position on this matter within three days.

回答第三个问题。

Yours sincerely,

Ken

Thank you for your Enquiry on Results.

The British Council's Senior Examiners have re-marked your IELTS Writing and Speaking tests in confidence as a result of your enquiry.

Your Writing and Speaking tests were re-assessed. The band-score awarded for your Writing test has increased from band 7.5 to band 8.0, and the band-score awarded for your Speaking test has increased from band 7.0 to band 7.5.

You did not request for your Listening or Reading test to be re-marked. The band-scores awarded for these tests are therefore unchanged.

Your overall band score remains at band 8.0.

Your test centre will issue you with a new Test Report Form showing the following band-scores. The Enquiry on Results fee will be refunded shortly by your test centre.

Listening	8.5	
Reading	8.0	
Writing	8.0	OVERALL BAND SCORE: 8.0
Speaking	7.5	

Please note that the above decision is final.

The British Council would like to thank you for your custom.

Yours sincerely

IELTS EOR Team
British Council

附录5　读者9分反馈

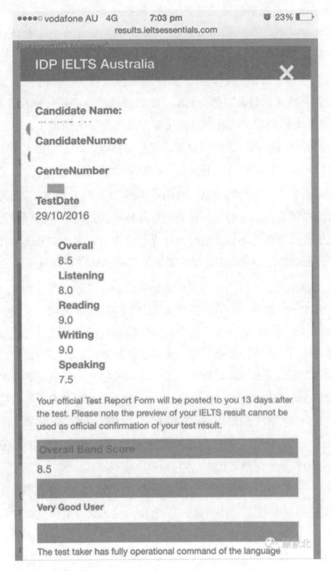

这个写作9分我自己看着也觉得不可思议，好多同学让我介绍经验，我就写在给顾爸爸的反馈里吧。有人说我在国内考肯定考不出9分，其实，就算让我在澳洲再考一次，我也不见得还能考出9分啊。所以大家全当我这个9是一种鼓励吧。还有啊，顾爸爸在雅思写作界的男神地位是永远不可撼动的好嘛，我修炼成鲤鱼精也仰望着他，分数只能说明我跟对了人，走对了路，努力了；考官那天可能中彩票或者求婚成功了。我废话真多，我现在掏心掏肺地分享一下心得（只说写作和口语）。

作文：

① 学习资料：《剑桥雅思真题集8–10》《顾家北手把手教你雅思写作》。没了……（说实话，《剑10》后面的范文已经超越我的理解能力了，不如看顾爸爸的范文。）

② 上过的课：老顾的精品班、预测班、精批班（精品班让我系统地学习了雅思作文要怎么写，

包括都有哪些题目类型，哪种类型应该怎么回答，整篇文章架构怎么搭建，如何拓展思路；预测班主要是练各种难题，积累素材；精批班顾名思义就是去接受精准的批评，简称"精批"。）

没上老顾的课之前我看了看真题就去考是 6 分（我不是英语专业，不能给英语专业的丢脸）。上了老顾的课之后第一次考就是 7.5 分，然后跌跌撞撞地竟然拿了 9 分，我自己也是一脸茫然状。我现在把我明白的一些道理和做法说一下：

逻辑：我觉得其实逻辑思维能力（包括扣题）是决定雅思作文分数的一个很关键的点。老顾经常在微博上推送作文题和思路，我每次都先看题，然后自己动脑筋想一遍自己的观点（包括自己可以举什么例子），再对比老顾的观点，看看差异在哪，自己是不是想错了，想歪了，老顾有什么更好的观点。大家不要小看这个过程，即使你没时间练习写整篇文章，但是这个锻炼逻辑思维能力的过程会让你在考场上短时间内想到观点，节省更多的时间让你下笔。

内容：雅思作文要有内容，不能写空话、套话。这是我从老顾这里学到的最精髓的东西。在保证语法正确、逻辑合理的情况下，内容才是帮我们提高分数的东西。老顾经常强调解释、举例还有具体化之类的拓展方法，大家在练习作文的时候要逼自己去用。然后你要去对比自己写的和老顾写的差距在哪，你是不是在车轱辘话来回说，是不是真的在举例子，还是只在说空话。

语法：老顾经常强调作文上 6 分的前提就是语法要正确。是的，而且想拿高分语法更是重要，因为你要保证语法不被扣分，你在其他几项评分标准上下的功夫才值当。我没法在语法方面给太多经验，因为我自己其实不太会分析各种句子成分，但是我会去模仿，简单地说就是考官范文和老顾怎么写句子，我就模仿着写。老顾精品班几乎每天都推送翻译练习，我得空都会看，有时候留言会被老顾一下子找到语法错误。但这些就是积累，是你从 6 分到 7 分甚至更高分的基础。我曾经在考到 7 分之后还写出过 Somebody is easy to do something 这种错误的句子。所以很多东西你一定要落实在纸面上，要写出来，光看是不能看出自己的错误的。还有，我曾经愁眉苦脸地唠叨考不到 7 分的时候，被好朋友训了一通，她就问我：顾家北的 10 大句型你现在能背出几个？可能是从那一刻开始我才脚踏实地了，然后事实证明，把 10 大句型背下来我就上 7 分了。

词汇和表达：作为一个外国人写英文，如果你能保证上面 3 项都做对了，那么词汇是给你提分到 7 的关键。我觉得能把"手把手"系列里的好词，老顾上课给大家的范文里的词汇都学会，已经足够你去考 7 分以上了。老顾经常会推送 Simon 的范文，同时加上他自己用词的对比，可能很多同学没有关注过老顾这个做法，其实这就是在教大家如何在写作的时候灵活地替换不同词汇和表达。很可惜这一点上没有捷径，除非你记性特好、天分特高，否则只能靠积累。想考 7 分以上的同学特别要注意这一点。另外，表达也很关键，说白了就是一句话，外国人怎么地道地表达，用什么当主语、谓语、宾语，甚至用什么介词和副词，我们表达一件事情的时候习惯用冗长的形容词、名词，而外国人有时候喜欢用动词和副词，这些真的需要自己去钻研和积累。所以多看老顾和考官的范文很重要，除了学词汇，更要学表达。如果说语法和词汇是上 7 分的关键，那么去模仿地道的表达我觉得是雅思作文上 8 分的关键。

说了那么多，其实还有一个关键的事情我没有说，那就是：老顾有那么多范文，推送了那么多 Simon 的东西，你有用心去复盘，去模仿了嘛？写完之后是不是就完了？你有去对比，去找差距吗？你知道为什么同一个表达老顾用一个词而你用另外一个词吗？我会把上课练过的作文再挑难的出来写段落，跟老顾的对比，把老顾和考官的范文一句话一句话掰开揉碎了分析，遇到不确定的词就去查朗文字典，下次再写类似的东西，就记得用上，然后再对比，再找差距。相信我，每次都能学到新东西，感觉永远也学不完。

作文就这样了，不知道能不能帮到大家，其实说白了就是：练。

口语：口语真没什么可说的，还是练……想拿高分，把 Part 2 题目都过一遍，每一个题目心里都起码有个 idea，如果自己抽到的话打算说什么。除非你超级自信而且底子好，否则 Part 2 提前准备 idea 太重要了，让一个外国人就一个奇怪的 Part 2 话题说 2 分钟也不见得可以拿 7 分。Part 3 就按照老顾写主体段的方法拓展，多给解释，多给例子，考官喜欢这种。口语里面语法是评分项，所以要注意尽量慢一点说，给自己思考的时间。然后要多用作文里学到的好表达。用上 5～6 个词伙上 7 分是很容易的。很多同学口语提高不了还是开口练得少。

可能有人会觉得在澳洲的话，有语言环境所以口语容易提高，其实……（你懂的），在国外跟外国人交流和雅思考试其实是两码事儿，你生活里口语再烂，随便吐几个词老外也能明白你要说什么。考试的时候就不是了，你得说的既流利又有内容，还得符合逻辑。同样，你口语得分再高，到了生活中可能还是会有不知道怎么表达憋到死的尴尬。所以，对于口语考试而言，想拿高分，提前准备是很重要的。

就这么结束了吧，因为我实在不知道还能帮到大家什么。就像老顾说的，考雅思只是开始，这只是你提高语言能力的过程。大家再有什么问题，我再看，然后再量力而为地回答吧。

图书在版编目（ＣＩＰ）数据

顾家北手把手教你雅思写作：5.0版 / 顾家北编著. —北京：中国人民大学出版社，2017.9
ISBN 978-7-300-25007-6

Ⅰ.①顾…　Ⅱ.①顾…　Ⅲ.①IELTS-写作-自学参考资料　Ⅳ.①H315

中国版本图书馆CIP数据核字（2017）第228652号

顾家北手把手教你雅思写作（5.0版）

顾家北　编著

Gujiabei Shoubashou Jiaoni Yasi Xiezuo (5.0 Ban)

出版发行	中国人民大学出版社
社　　址	北京中关村大街31号　　　　　**邮政编码**　100080
电　　话	010-62511242（总编室）　　　010-62511770（质管部）
	010-82501766（邮购部）　　　010-62514148（门市部）
	010-62515195（发行公司）　　010-62515275（盗版举报）
网　　址	http://www.crup.com.cn
	http://www.1kao.com.cn（中国1考网）
经　　销	新华书店
印　　刷	北京玺诚印务有限公司
规　　格	185mm×260mm　16开本　　　**版　次**　2012年8月第1版
印　　张	24.75　　　　　　　　　　　　**印　次**　2017年9月第5版
	2018年4月第12次印刷
字　　数	567 000　　　　　　　　　　　**定　价**　58.00元